Irish Popular Culture
1650–1850

Edited by
James S. Donnelly, Jr.
and
Kerby A. Miller

IRISH ACADEMIC PRESS

First published in 1998 by
IRISH ACADEMIC PRESS
44 Northumberland Road, Dublin 4, Ireland
and in North America by
IRISH ACADEMIC PRESS
c/o ISBS, 5804 NE Hassalo Street, Portland, OR 97213.

A catalogue record for this title
is available from the British Library.

ISBN 0-7165-2551-8

This book was set in 11 on 13 point Ehrhardt
by Woodcote Typesetters

Printed byColour Books Ltd

Contents

Acknowledgments

Our first debt is to the contributors. Other pressing duties and responsibilities have kept the editors of this volume from bringing the important essays of our contributors into print with the dispatch that they deserved. We hope that their extraordinary patience with us eventually receives its just reward, if not in this life, then in the next. Besides paying tribute to their patience, we also wish to acknowledge their responsiveness to our suggestions for revision. We caused them far more trouble than they ever caused us, and we trust that the appearance of this volume will raise our credit at least a little in their eyes.

Together, the editors and contributors wish to acknowledge the indispensable assistance which we have received from the numerous libraries and archives in which our researches have been conducted. In particular, we are extremely grateful to the directors and curatorial staffs of the National Archives and the National Library of Ireland in Dublin for making their rich resources so readily available to us. We also owe a special debt of gratitude to Professor Séamas Ó Catháin, Head of the Department of Irish Folklore in University College, Dublin, and to his always helpful staff. We wish to acknowledge the kindness of the Huntington Library in San Merino, California, in giving access to, and permission to quote extensively from, the Andrew Johnston papers. And we wish to express our deep thanks to Cork University Press and Field Day Publications for their permission to republish here in a modestly revised form the essay by Kevin Whelan which appeared originally in his book *The tree of liberty*.

Lastly, we wish to take special note of the tragic and untimely death of one of our contributors, J.R.R. Adams. His passing is a severe loss to Irish historical studies and to the scholarly examination of Irish popular culture.

James S. Donnelly, Jr.
Kerby A. Miller

Abbreviations

For abbreviations used in the notes of this book, kindly consult "Rules for contributors to Irish Historical Studies" in *Irish Historical Studies*, supplement I (January 1968).

Notes on Editors and Contributors

The late J.R.R. ADAMS was Librarian and Archivist at the Ulster Folk and Transport Museum at Cultra, Co. Down.

SEAN J. CONNOLLY is Professor of Irish History at Queen's University, Belfast.

JAMES S. DONNELLY, JR., is Chair and Professor of History at the University of Wisconsin–Madison.

RAYMOND GILLESPIE teaches modern history and local history at St Patrick's College, Maynooth.

ELIZABETH MALCOLM is Senior Research Fellow in the Institute of Irish Studies at the University of Liverpool.

KERBY A. MILLER is Professor of History at the University of Missouri–Columbia.

NIALL Ó CIOSÁIN lectures in Irish history at University College, Galway.

GEARÓID Ó CRUALAOICH is a lecturer in the Department of History at University College, Cork.

DIARMUID Ó GIOLLÁIN is a lecturer in the Department of History at University College, Cork.

GARY OWENS is Professor of History at Huron College of the University of Western Ontario.

KEVIN WHELAN, formerly Burns Library Visiting Scholar in Irish Studies at Boston College, was most recently a visiting professor history at the University of Notre Dame.

Introduction

In the last thirty or forty years Irish society has changed so radically that today we are apt to associate the island's 'traditional' popular culture with that of Eamon de Valera's Ireland, with the customs and values that became dominant during the long post-famine era, that were apparently ossified in de Valera's 1937 constitution, and that collapsed under the impact of massive economic and social changes—and under the weight of their own contradictions—beginning in the 1960s.

In fact, of course, the cultural patterns of de Valera's Ireland were by no means 'traditional', but in most respects were markedly different from those which had prevailed during the two centuries prior to the great famine. By the mid-twentieth century, for example, English, not Irish, was the language of the overwhelming majority of Ireland's Catholics, and the old Hiberno-Norman, Lowland Scots, and other dialects once prevalent in parts of Leinster and Ulster especially, had virtually disappeared. Meanwhile, the once-important cultural distinctions between Irish Catholics of Gaelic and Norman descent, and even between Anglican and Presbyterian settlers, had largely been eradicated. Likewise, religious practices and beliefs in de Valera's Ireland had been confined almost entirely to institutional churches whose clergy had nearly banished the boisterous patterns, pilgrimages, wakes, maypoles, and other celebrations and symbols that had characterised popular devotion in the pre-famine period. Primary education and the ability to read and write had become universal, but ironically the former was more closely supervised by the clergy and the later perhaps more effectively censored by the state than one or two hundred years earlier. Drinking patterns were now also largely enclosed in tightly-controlled, indoor spaces, and (except during Northern Ireland's 'marching seasons') the violence of the old fairs, faction-, and party fights had been channelled into supervised recreation under the auspices of the G.A.A. and similar organisations.

Perhaps most important, Ireland's class structure had changed dramatically, with crucial consequences for the island's political culture. In the countryside at least, the economic power and the cultural hegemony of the Protestant upper class had vanished, while famine mortality and massive emigration had decimated the ranks of the predominantly Irish-speaking cottiers and labourers who had often resisted—sometimes violently—the processes of socio-economic and cultural change. By the early twentieth century a bourgeoisie—composed of strong farmers, shopkeepers, and their clerical and legal allies (and of wealthy businessmen in Dublin and in Protestant Ulster)—had emerged triumphant, culturally as well as socially, and it is arguable that in both southern and northern Ireland the range of political options and of popular political action had become more constricted, at least since the post-Penal Law era when Volunteers, Whiteboys, Orangemen, and the massive forces mobilised by the United Irishmen and later by Daniel O'Connell had competed for allegiance and influence.

Thus the popular and political culture of de Valera's Ireland were the products of at least two hundred years of radical changes—of alterations dramatically and horribly accelerated by the great famine but which had been occurring at least since 1650. The collective purpose of this volume is to describe some of the cultural forms and relationships that prevailed in early modern Ireland, to analyze how and why crucial cultural changes occurred, and to demonstrate the consequences of those changes. In the broadest sense these developments reflected the general European processes of 'modernisation' associated with the expansion and transformations of capitalism, of centralised legal and religious administrations, of education and literacy, and, perhaps especially, of the growing hegemony of the bourgeoisie. However, in Ireland these overall trends were affected by the experiences of conquest, colonisation, and confiscation that created parallel but (in terms of power relationships) unequal social and cultural systems, each of which in turn was characterised by regional, class, and cultural distinctions and conflicts.

It is the dialectical relationships both between and within these unequal systems that make the history of cultural change in early modern Ireland so complex and fascinating. And it is these interactions that the authors of the following essays describe and analyse from a variety of different perspectives and from a range of disciplines, for our volume presents the research of anthropologists and folklorists as well as social and cultural historians. 'Popular culture', of course, is so pervasive and broadly defined that we cannot pretend that the essays in this volume are inclusive in their coverage of all the important topics and issues of Irish cultural history. Nor, for the most part, have we or our contributors always endeavoured to compare developments in Ireland with those in Britain or in continental Europe. Nevertheless, we hope that this volume will make a significant contribution to the understanding of cultural change in early modern Ireland, and that it will provide both examples of current work on this topic and a stimulus to further research.

The observant reader of this volume will discover numerous echoes of Peter Burke's important study, *Popular culture in early modern Europe*, which, although first published almost two decades ago, still exercises a powerful influence over the ways in which scholars think about and do research in this field. For example, one of Burke's central ideas concerns the participation of political and social élites in most forms of popular culture, at least until the late eighteenth century. According to Burke, until 1750—and in some parts of Europe later still—élite groups embraced or tolerated the cultural forms of expression of the popular classes, even those forms which challenged élite domination and popular subordination, as encapsulated in notions of 'the world turned upside down'. Thus between 1750 and 1850 it was the withdrawal of those élites from active involvement in popular culture that led, as some would say, to its decline and eventual destruction, or as others would contend, to its disorganisation and reorganisation.

Until fairly recently, students of Irish popular culture drew a different picture. For example, Daniel Corkery was so impressed by the brutal consequences of Irish colonisation that in his famous book of 1924, *The hidden Ireland*, he portrayed a culture that was radically and uniquely polarised. And despite Louis Cullen's devastating criticisms in 1968 of Corkery's central assumptions, there is still a tendency to assume that Protestant-landlord domination, fully established by the 1660s, produced a sharp differentiation between the cultural worlds of the rulers and the ruled. However, in this volume's lead-off essay Sean Connolly marshalls considerable evidence for a picture of élite-popular cultural relationships in Ireland that is much closer to the general pattern for *ancien régime* Europe, as outlined by Burke, albeit with certain significant modifications. According to Connolly, elements of both change and stasis helped to bridge the gap between the cultural worlds of rulers and ruled in the century after 1660. On the one hand, substantial changes in Irish peasant life between 1600 and the Restoration meant that many Irish peasants of the late seventeenth century were not so alien to the Irish landed and political élite as they would have been at its beginning. On the other hand, the lesser provincial gentry in Ireland, probably dominant numerically, were (like their counterparts elsewhere) culturally 'rough' and relatively unsophisticated, enmeshed in rural life in ways that often brought them into close contact and cultural commerce with their social subordinates.

To be sure, Connolly recognises the persistence in the years 1675–1750 of longstanding cultural prejudices and acute political insecurities among the Anglo-Irish élite. And he also acknowledges the prevalence of numerous differences *within* both élite and popular cultures as well as between them in the same period. His is indeed a subtle interpretation of the special complexities of the Irish cultural landscape. In spite of these admitted complexities, however, Connolly emphasises the many important linkages between élite and popular culture in Ireland, and he provides arresting examples of these linkages by examining the cases of the theatre, musical performances, hurling, and other sports. He points out that the cultural interaction between the élite and the popular classes was a two-way traffic, as he demonstrates by reference to the matters of diet and dress. Bridging and linking élite and popular cultures were a variety of intermediaries, of whom the most important were the Catholic clergy. But many members of the Anglo-Irish élite themselves appreciated the usefulness of bridging social gaps by promoting or lending support to a range of public and private festivals or celebrations which fused, even if only temporarily, the cultural worlds of rulers and ruled. Yet if the linkages between the two were numerous and important in the late seventeenth and most of the eighteenth centuries, the tumultuous events of the 1790s, with their bitter sectarian and political confrontations culminating in violent revolution and brutal repression, broke many of the old cultural interconnections, and in the next half-century the process of élite withdrawal from, and vigorous assaults upon, most forms of traditional popular culture became thoroughgoing and inexorable.

Pursuing some of the very same questions as Connolly, Kevin Whelan takes a different but equally fruitful angle of approach in his contribution to this volume. Shifting the main focus away from the Protestant gentry, Whelan's essay attempts to recover the *mentalités* of Catholic middlemen and large farmers, the former primarily the descendants of the old Catholic landowning families dispossessed by the confiscations of the seventeenth century and before. Among the most important points made by Whelan is that which concerns the striking differences in values and behaviour between the two Catholic groups—one downwardly mobile, the other upwardly mobile—that coalesced in the course of the eighteenth century to form what he calls 'the Irish big-farm class'. On the one hand, there were the farming families descended from the dispossessed Catholic gentry, who, according to Whelan, were more numerous and more influential than many historians have previously recognised. If the estates of Catholic 'converts' are included in the calculations, then 'the figure for "Catholic" ownership of land reaches about 20 percent' in the third quarter of the eighteenth century, rather than only about 5 percent, as usually supposed. For at least part of the land they held, these surviving Catholic landowners were middlemen, the head-tenants of some (usually Protestant) proprietor. As Whelan explains in rich detail, these Catholic middlemen as a group were associated with social and cultural conservatism or continuity. This meant, among other things, that they were still the focus of respect, deference, and allegiance from their Catholic social inferiors and remained in cultural control of Catholic communities. Helping them to maintain such control was the exercise of their functions as dispensers of patronage, hospitality, and philanthropy. In general, Catholic middlemen of this type were deeply immersed in popular culture up until the 1770s. They enthusiastically promoted cock-fighting, horse-racing, hunting, and hurling. Many of them continued to display lavish hospitality in the provision of food and drink. In addition, members of the group acted as cultural brokers, moving between the traditional and more modern spheres of life, between the local community and the wider world beyond it. Lastly, they were bulwarks of the resurgent Catholic church, furnishing senior clergy, convent superiors, chapel sites, and money for a variety of ecclesiastical enterprises.

In contrast to the downwardly mobile Catholic middlemen who engaged in a culturally determined prodigality that often seemed at odds with their declining material resources, there stood on the other hand those farm families who took advantage of the eighteenth-century economic expansion to rise out of small-farm ranks and ascended into the big-farm class. Members of this second group, as Whelan shows, embraced frugality and hard work as the supreme values, and when they prospered, as they did in increasing numbers during the century before the great famine, they habitually concealed their growing wealth. Unlike the Catholic middlemen, they engaged in remarkably little conspicuous consumption. Their housing, for instance, could be deceptively mean-looking and thus usually fooled English or foreign travellers. In negotiating for lucrative leases and in arranging advantageous marriages for their children, such Catholic big-farm families exercised high degrees of discipline, calculation, and foresight. The dedicated practice of such virtues was an essential ingredient in the gradual rise of this growing class of large Catholic tenant farmers to an eventual position of social and political dominance.

Whelan does not neglect the important political and sectarian aspects of the social and cultural phenomena with which he is primarily concerned. Irish Protestants found much fault with both the upwardly and downwardly mobile segments of the Irish big-farm class. Through its addiction to frugality and hard work the rising segment, by offering to pay higher rents, often outbid Protestants for lucrative leases or threatened to do so. In addition to their resentment over this behaviour, Protestants had long complained loudly about the social pretensions of the middlemen derived from old Catholic gentry families, a group known to be hostile to the descendants of the Cromwellian settlers and often alienated from the Protestant-dominated state and its laws. The survival of this element of the Catholic social élite had discomforted the more extreme Protestants even before the 1790s, and when many such Catholics sided with reform or (much worse) revolution during that tumultuous decade, Protestant antipathy intensified and widened. Whelan draws our attention to the way in which Protestant opponents of the Defenders and United Irishmen were obsessed in their rhetoric with the perceived desire of dispossessed Catholics for the recovery of their ancient estates. Besides having these political motives for rooting out alienated and presumably revanchist Catholic middlemen, the Protestant landed élite also had increasingly strong economic reasons to extinguish the Irish middleman system in general. Ironically, as Whelan points out, their assault on the middleman system actually hit the Protestant sub-gentry hardest and thus had the general effect of strengthening the position of the Catholic tenant farmers.

The shifting balance at the top of Irish Catholic society in the late eighteenth century was also reflected in the pronounced withdrawal of Catholic middlemen from popular culture. Partly responsible for this withdrawal was the improving status of well-to-do Catholics as the penal laws were gradually dismantled. But this development could not explain why a similar withdrawal was occurring at roughly the same time among the Protestant gentry and sub-gentry. Whelan identifies a highly significant factor to which both groups were no doubt responding, namely, the rapid progress of social stratification and growing class conflict.

As hostilities increased on both sides of the economic divide separating the subaltern population from the landed élites, Catholic and Protestant, what the élites had once patronised and participated in came to be increasingly seen by them as unrespectable and even dangerous.

In the end, though they would agree on much else, Whelan sees less reason than Connolly to characterise eighteenth-century Ireland as an *ancien régime* society. For Whelan the main difficulty with this interpretation is the unusual role played in Irish social competition by the Catholic big-farm class, 'the ultimate winners', whose 'resistance and stability derived substantially from their self-image as an old landowning class, displaced in the seventeenth-century upheavals'. Thinking of themselves in this way, the Irish big-farm class acquired and preserved 'a character different from that of other European societies' and at the same time 'created an ambiguous position for the Irish gentry' of that era. This viewpoint prompts Whelan to prefer a colonial context over an *ancien régime* model for helping us to understand the social and political dynamics of eighteenth-century Ireland.

While both Connolly and Whelan are sensitive to the important ways in which religious affiliations affected relationships between rulers and ruled or between élites and subalterns, they are not directly concerned with religious life itself. This is the central focus of Raymond Gillespie's essay, which examines both the nature of religious belief in early modern Ireland and its relevance to the realities of everyday life. Gillespie rejects the perspective of those scholars who see power relationships as crucial to Irish religious life in this period. While admitting that reform-minded bishops and priests undertook campaigns to impose religious orthodoxy on the laity, he points out that these campaigns suffered from serious weaknesses (above all, a shortage of well-trained clerical personnel) and long failed to achieve many of their primary goals. Elsewhere in Europe religious reformers might enjoy the assistance of the state or the backing of the Inquisition in advancing their agendas of reconstruction, but in Ireland Catholic agents of religious change lacked such strong institutional support.

Instead of viewing power relationships as central, Gillespie sees religious ideas in early modern Ireland as 'the outcome of a dialogue between the doctrinal positions offered as coherent intellectual systems by the various churches on the one hand, and the religious needs of the inhabitants . . . on the other'. Moreover, he argues that the dividing lines between the élite and the popular versions of religion were often quite blurred. This was primarily because the two religious cultures shared a common set of assumptions that defied social and confessional boundaries, especially the assumption that God and the devil were constantly intervening in the natural world. In fact, for Gillespie the cardinal experiences of 'all popular religion' were these recurrent manifestations of 'the holy and its opposite in the natural world'.

Since good and evil supernatural forces were so widely seen to be almost constantly at work right here on earth, determining whether people and animals lived or died, remained healthy or fell seriously ill, prospered or met misfortune, it is scarcely surprising that the overriding question or preoccupation became how to gain access to the holy so as to ward off or repel evil and the diabolic. Among Catholics, of course, priests and especially those belonging to religious orders had long been viewed as active channels to the holy, and in early modern Ireland clergymen who had acquired reputations as exorcists or miracle workers were capable of attracting large followings. In addition, the secular and the regular clergy both vigorously promoted the long-established cults of the saints as dependable channels to the holy. But as Gillespie makes clear, the clergy were far from exercising a monopoly over this route to the sacred. Many saints' relics or reputed relics were in lay hands, diffused in local communities, and the clergy also had little control over the extremely widespread and socially inclusive cult of holy wells—those thousands of miraculous sacred springs dedicated to particular saints and found in both urban and rural settings all around the country. Even the rosary was frequently transformed by members of the laity from its original use as an aid to prayer into a sacred object capable of repelling evil in the same manner as saints' relics and the healing waters of holy wells. As Gillespie observes, this widespread diffusion of the sacred in the physical space of local communities was highly important in sustaining popular notions of the interpenetration of the natural and supernatural worlds.

Official Protestantism had a different view about access to the holy in early modern Ireland. Whereas Catholics generally believed that the sacred was manifested 'in particular places, at particular times', the official Protestant position was that access was readily available through the bible and through prayer and meditation. Thus neither the place nor the time of seeking the holy was crucial or even important. But just as among Catholics, so too with ordinary Protestants, there was, Gillespie maintains, a dialogue between officially sanctioned doctrinal positions and the people's religious needs. The result was that in their urgent desire for access to the holy many Protestants participated in exorcisms, miraculous healing, and the cult of holy wells. Thus among both Protestants and Catholics the efforts of the official churches to discipline popular religion encountered serious resistance. The Tridentine reform program, centered on the parish church and focused on the sacraments, and with the parish priest in control of religious ritual, was still far from accomplishment in 1750. And a similar detachment from official orthodoxy was apparent among many Protestants.

Just as reform-minded officials of the Catholic church in early modern Ireland wanted to bring religion indoors, within the walls of the parish church, in order to shape it in accordance with the Tridentine program, so too the Protestant-dominated state eventually sought to bring drink consumption indoors, within the walls of the public house, in order to tame it in the interests of political and social stability. It is the complicated story of this latter development that Elizabeth

Malcolm, the premier historian of Irish temperance, tells with new insights based on fresh research. We are accustomed to thinking about the pub as a principal centre of Irish popular culture in the post-famine period and especially during its heyday between about 1850 and 1950. While Malcolm reviews the roles and functions of pubs and publicans in this relatively recent period (pointing out along the way that these important subjects still await full-scale historical treatment), she is really concerned with the rise of the pub in what she considers 'two particularly critical periods', that is, the years 1600–70 and 1780–1860.

In taking this approach, she modifies significantly the interpretation offered by Peter Burke, who identified the pub or tavern along with the church and the marketplace as the three main public settings for popular culture. Taking a cue from recent studies of popular culture (including drink places) in England, Malcolm warns against excessive emphasis on the late eighteenth and early nineteenth centuries 'as a critical period of cultural transformation' from 'traditional' to 'modern' forms of thought and conduct. Through its adaptability the pub, at least, was capable of surviving as a centre of popular recreation throughout the early modern period and into that of commercialised popular culture in the nineteenth and twentieth centuries. Also in contrast to Burke, Malcolm stresses that pubs, unlike the home, the church, or the marketplace, were subjected to increasingly vigorous control in Ireland by the government and its local agents. If it was government regulation that 'largely created the pub as we know it today', Malcolm asks, can the pub still be viewed as an authentically popular institution, or did the regulatory actions of a long succession of governments eventually result in the suppression of 'genuine popular culture'?

What was especially significant about the first critical period (the years 1600–70) identified by Malcolm was that for the first time the government attempted to create an 'indoor, public, supervised space' in which drinking and other recreational activities associated with it could be confined and controlled. What primarily motivated these efforts were fears of political revolution or rebellion in response to the punishing process of conquest, confiscation, and colonisation from England and Scotland. In the wake of English and Scottish settlement during the seventeenth century unlicensed alehouses had increased sharply in number. The government was partly concerned about the resulting loss of revenue, but an even greater spur to action was the use of these alehouses by Irish rebels. Malcolm concedes that even by the late seventeenth century much of the consumption of drink, especially in rural and heavily Gaelicised areas, still occurred either outdoors or at home, and that the local magistrates charged with enforcing the laws regulating alehouses and other drinkshops were frequently inefficient or dishonest. In spite of these glaring shortcomings, she argues, the regulatory regime erected by the government in the period 1600–70 constituted 'an important step on the road to the disciplining of the Irish pub as a popular cultural venue'.

But it was in the second 'critical' period from about 1780 to 1860 that another battery of regulations, this time affecting the whole of the Irish drink industry, was carried into law. The main target of this new regulatory regime was not the alehouse, as in the seventeenth century, but rather the public houses and shebeens retailing spirits and above all whiskey, many of them illegally. The cheapness of whiskey led to a boom in consumption and a shift away from beer and ale. Excessive consumption of spirits was invariably singled out as the primary cause of the fighting and violence now associated on a grand scale with the staple events of Irish popular culture: fairs, patterns, and wakes. In the eyes of the authorities, both secular and clerical, the links between whiskey consumption and the violence of faction-fighting and agrarian secret societies were incontrovertible. Partly from their determination to check and (if possible) extinguish these 'abuses' there arose a far-reaching attack on Irish popular culture which had as one of its primary aims the establishment of thoroughgoing control over the drink trade and public consumption of drink.

Whereas the earlier regulatory regime had been undermined in practice by lax enforcement, the new one was much more vigorously enforced by the Irish constabulary, which beginning in the 1830s acquired increasingly wide authority to close unlicensed premises and to ensure that licensed houses engaged in no illegal selling. Of equal importance was the contemporaneous campaign by government, magistrates, and police to discourage the sale of drink at such large outdoor gatherings as fairs, patterns, and race-meetings, and to force drink consumption into the now minutely regulated pubs. As Malcolm observes, the assault on popular culture that led to the extinction of many popular festivals by 1850 (or even earlier) also elevated the pub to a new pinnacle of importance as 'the principal Irish recreational venue'. But as Malcolm also demonstrates, the disciplined customers of Irish pubs no longer enjoyed the kind of freedom that had prevailed in regard to drink consumption at outdoor festivals until the 1830s.

If the Protestant rulers of early modern Ireland saw taverns and pubs as hothouses of sedition that must be brought under control, they also projected causal links between political and agrarian rebellion on the one hand and the widely circulating literature of criminality on the other. In his contribution to our volume Niall Ó Ciosáin brings under his microscope the chief Irish example of this literary genre, J. Cosgrave's *A history of the most notorious Irish tories, highwaymen, and rapparees*, often given the short title *Irish rogues* and reprinted many times after its first publication in the mid-eighteenth century. The general class of literature of which this work constitutes a prime example—the so-called chapbooks circulated by travelling pedlars in countryside and town across western Europe—has attracted substantial attention from social historians in recent years because the chapbooks seem to offer an important window on rural popular culture. While agreeing wholeheartedly that this attention is thoroughly deserved, Ó Ciosáin warns against the frequent assumption that chapbooks of the period 1600–1750 were directed at the peasantry when in fact they were often targeted at an urban bourgeois readership. He also cautions against the tendency of earlier studies to adopt a taxonomic approach, classifying such materials as 'religious', 'secular', 'escapist', or 'realist', and drawing conclusions about popular culture accordingly, because most readers had books in their hands only rarely and may have concentrated their attention on just one book for months at a time.

Instead of stressing the production of this chapbook literature, Ó Ciosáin emphasises the importance of trying to assess its consumption or reception. He maintains that 'the ways in which the texts were adapted from their sources for a popular audience can . . . offer a guide to reading practices'. The particular research strategy which he adopts is to follow *Irish rogues* through its 'various formats of production and manners of reception'. As a necessary prologue to this detailed examination, Ó Ciosáin discusses the literary conventions and strands of influence that shaped the construction of the literature of criminality or criminal biography. Among the most significant of these influences were (1) that widespread genre of official or élite writings which represented such marginal or outcast groups as the poor or beggars as belonging to counter-cultures with their own rules of behaviour; (2) the picaresque novel, which both continued and extended this first genre by emphasising the marginal or criminal and by constructing its narrative around a single rogue; and (3) the 'specifically criminal literature', which purported to provide accounts of the lives of notorious or famous condemned criminals and of their trials or last speeches before their execution. Since these strands constituted the literary framework from which *Irish rogues* was derived, Ó Ciosáin's essay illustrates again the difficulty of drawing sharp distinctions between élite and popular culture, for to judge from these three related types of literature, the two cultures or audiences had a common interest in the same or very similar content.

Ó Ciosáin's comparison of *Irish rogues* with its mainly English sources is also highly revealing, though in different ways. It turns out that Cosgrave, the Irish author/compiler of *Irish rogues*, cribbed much of his material from two well-known early eighteenth-century English collections of criminal biography—those by Alexander Smith and Charles Johnson. But in contrast to these expensive tomes directed at a middling or upper-class English audience, *Irish rogues* appeared as a cheap chapbook, with mostly rural characters, and was aimed (initially at least) at an audience of well-to-do tenant farmers, of the kind belonging to the nascent Irish big-farm class described by Kevin Whelan. Another distinguishing feature of *Irish rogues*, marking it off from its English prototypes, is a general avoidance in the collection of outright condemnation. As Ó Ciosáin declares, 'this is fundamentally a collection of heroes'. From its English sources, which included accounts of heroes, brutes, and buffoons, *Irish rogues* took only heroes and buffoons, leaving out brutes altogether and no doubt deliberately. In his account or 'life' of Redmond O'Hanlon, the longest of the lives in *Irish rogues*, Cosgrave constructed an Irish bandit-hero of the classical type, a figure apparently very different from the historical reality. As represented by Cosgrave, O'Hanlon was 'the son of a reputable Irish gentleman who had a considerable estate', of which he was dispossessed by English invaders.

In fact, as Ó Ciosáin emphasises, in many of the criminal lives presented in *Irish rogues* the social condition of dispossession is advanced as an explanation of why the hero turned to crime. The elevated social status of these heroes, who are frequently presented as dispossessed gentlemen, combined with their portrayal as leaders of rival power structures, helped to legitimise these 'criminals' as challengers to the Protestant-dominated state and its authority. Ó Ciosáin appropriately links this literary representation, and especially the recurrent motif of dispossession, to the historical experience of the defeated and despoiled Catholic gentry of the seventeenth and eighteenth centuries. This assessment prompts Ó Ciosáin to speculate that the earliest appeal of *Irish rogues* 'was probably to surviving members of Catholic gentry families who had lost their land'. But there is strong evidence that the little book had descended the social scale in its readership by the late eighteenth and early nineteenth centuries. This significant shift in audience, Ó Ciosáin argues, 'indicates a generalisation of the feeling of dispossession among the population at large (or at least among tenants)'. Working from very different sources, Ó Ciosáin and Whelan thus arrive at much the same conclusion about the critical role of dispossession in Catholic cultural and political consciousness.

If chapbooks like *Irish rogues* slipped well down the social scale in the two or three decades before and after 1800, this broadening of the effective audience was undoubtedly tied closely to the striking extension of popular education in the late eighteenth and early nineteenth centuries. This development, which greatly facilitated Catholic political mobilisation in this period, is one of the primary concerns of the late J.R.R. Adams's essay on hedge schools and schoolmasters along with the changing character of the books in use. It was indicative of the intense popular demand for education in the three Rs by the early nineteenth century that so many Catholic parents were prepared to entrust their children to schools connected with one or another of the various Protestant education societies, whose mass extension Adams charts. Most of these societies were strongly or at least moderately proselytizing in their ambitions, with the significant exception of the Kildare Place Society, and even that body eventually came to be regarded with hostility or suspicion by many Catholic priests.

In discussing the wide variety of printed aids to literacy available in the hedge schools of Ireland, Adams attributes far-reaching importance to the underappreciated publishing triumph of the Kildare Place Society. In the 1810s and 1820s this body sponsored the publication of a library of some eighty small books (on religion, natural history, fiction, and especially travel) which it distributed to its own schools and those of other societies. Sales of its books at cheap rates outside the schools also took place, with the general result that by 1831 almost 1.5 million volumes had passed into circulation. 'The effect of these books', according to Adams, 'was enormous', mainly because they constituted effective rivals at competitive prices to the traditional chapbook fare. Educational reformers had hopes that the good coin of these many new books would drive out what they considered the bad coin of the chapmen's stock, but the new seems to have supplemented rather than replaced the old.

On the whole, Adams takes a fairly positive view of the cheap chapbook literature about which he wrote extensively in his earlier study *The printed word and the common man* (1987), and which he briefly surveys in his essay here. His consideration of the medieval romances and neo-chivalric novels that formed such a large part of the chapbook fare prompts the conclusion that these interesting and imaginative stories 'would have been of real use in the teaching of literacy, probably of more use . . . than the dry-as-dust material that succeeded them when the national system of education became entrenched'. About even the numerous little books of criminal biography and the many tales of 'apparitions, witches, and fairies' Adams concludes that 'there is no reason why a diet of such works should not have provided a reasonably good standard of literacy along with enjoyment, given a capable schoolmaster. . .'.

Despite the impressive strength of the popular demand in this period for basic education in the three Rs, schoolmastering was a distinctly ill-paid profession with many poorly trained teachers. Though Adams emphasises that there were gradations in quality, he leaves the impression that the incompetent and the barely competent may have considerably outnumbered those who were quite adequate or even excellent teachers. Part of the problem was that the supply of fee-paying pupils, at least outside the towns, was subject to sharp seasonal variations (strongest in summer, weakest in winter, but with low attendance in spring and harvest as well), and thus equally variable was the schoolmaster's income from fees. A significant part of his support came in kind, either in lieu of fees or as a supplement to them, but this was probably not an asset so much as a sign of difficulty. As Adams observes, many schoolmasters were compelled by their meagre income to eke out a precarious existence by resorting to other supplementary jobs as parish letter-writers, surveyors, and even labourers. And if the quality of the teachers varied greatly and tended strongly toward the negative side of the spectrum, much the same might be said of the physical fabric and internal conditions of the hedge schools themselves, a subject which Adams also addresses in his essay.

Against these admittedly serious deficiencies Adams sets their relative assets in comparison with the successor national schools. Besides the attention-fixing reading material which he evaluates so favorably as an aid to literacy, Adams stresses the non-denominational character of most hedge schools. Although there invariably was catechetical instruction, it was the common practice to teach students the catechism appropriate to their own religious persuasion. This situation, Adams concludes, 'was a far cry from the ultimately segregated classes and dull readers of the national schools which began to supplant [the hedge schools] in the 1830s'.

The extinguishing of the hedge schools by the so-called national system of primary education may be considered part of the modernising or 'civilising' process, and so too can the vigorous assault of the Irish middle and upper classes, allied now with the reforming bishops and clergy of the Catholic church, on the 'merry wake' and the pattern—two of the most important institutions of traditional popular culture. Basing his examination of the first of these institutions on rich ethnographic data drawn from parts of counties Cork and Galway, Gearóid Ó Crualaoich finds that the merry wake and its associated beliefs and rituals were still very much a widespread social reality in the years 1700–1850. Part of his fascination with the traditional wake stems from its role as 'a central social mechanism for the articulation of resistance' by Irish peasants to 'new forms of civil and clerical control' from the seventeenth to the nineteenth centuries.

It is a necessary part of Ó Crualaoich's demonstration of the symbolic meaning and social function of the merry wake to identify and explain the principal targets of clerical censures and criticisms in relation to it. These ecclesiastical denunciations, extending in Ireland over no less than three centuries, were essentially directed at two aspects of rural Irish mortuary ritual—(1) the merriment (music, dance, games, etc.) and license (profanity, heavy drinking, expressions of sexuality), and (2) ritual public mourning, especially the practice of keening. The ecclesiastical authorities disapproved of these key features of the traditional Irish wake and funeral ultimately because they recognised or suspected that what was involved here was the expression of a religious sensibility that derived 'as much from a Celtic or pagan cosmological tradition as from a Christian one'. To put the point another way, there was a generalised ambiguity among the Irish rural masses (and indeed among peasants elsewhere in Christian Europe) about the meaning of death and the afterworld; on these critical matters there were at least two rival sets of conceptions, only one of which was Christian.

For Ó Crualaoich the dramatically protracted resistance of the Irish peasantry to ecclesiastical condemnations of the merry wake is highly suggestive and deeply revealing. Most obviously, it shows the sturdiness and resilience of traditional popular culture in spite of vigorous clerical assault. And it also suggests how much significance must have been attached by the Irish rural population to their non-Christian conceptions of the symbolic meaning and social function of the merry wake. Ó Crualaoich argues that the merry wake is an example of that structural principle of traditional cosmology in Ireland in accordance with which community life was centered on occasional sacred assemblies whose main functions, according to Liam de Paor, were 'to renew social order as well as to acknowledge and venerate supernatural forces'. The social function of the merry wake, then, was to allow the community to heal itself and to reestablish social order 'in the face of the disruptive power of death'. The so-called 'borekeen', locally designated as the presiding genius behind the games and pranks at the wake gathering, was 'the agent of that socially cathartic chaos out of which a renewed social order' could emerge. By this means the community proclaimed and manifested its social solidarity and continuity.

Contrasting with this social function of the merry wake was its sacred purpose or symbolic meaning, which was concerned with the successful incorporation of the deceased individual into the afterlife, with its dangers for the dead as well as the living. Here the critical performer was the keening woman (bean chaointe), who was, as Ó Crualaoich puts it, 'the agent of the transition to the next life of the individual . . . whose passing is ritually mourned all the way to the grave in the highly charged performance of the female practitioners of the caoin'. Ó Crualaoich's understanding of the incorporation process in the Irish mortuary tradition leads him to offer an important criticism and revision of earlier interpretations of the merry wake by Seán Ó Súilleabháin, Reidar Christiansen, and Sean Connolly. It is, he states, a fair summary of their views to say that 'the merry wake existed to assuage the anger of the deceased individual, to heal the social wound of death, and to manifest the continuing vitality of social life in the face of sudden rupture'. The problem with this interpretation, Ó Crualaoich argues, is that the merriment and license associated with the traditional wake were either absent or quite subdued in the case of untimely deaths, such as those of children or healthy adults dying by accident or catastrophic misfortune, when it might have been predicted that in such cases the anger, social wounding, and sudden rupture would be greatest. In fact, merriment and license were at their most exuberant in cases of timely death—the demise of people who had lived to the proverbial 'ripe old age', and whose departure from this world should have prompted the least anger, social wounding, and rupture of family and community. Ó Crualaoich justifies this distinction between timely and untimely death by relating the two kinds of demise to 'two separate cosmological mechanisms or agencies of death, the one ancestral or Celtic, the other Christian'. Thus, for example, the accidental or unexpected sudden death of a child, a healthy adult, or a mother in childbirth would have been attributed by many Irish peasants before 1850 to the malevolence of the fairies or some other diabolic force. In such cases the emphasis in the traditional wake and funeral shifted away from the 'borekeen' and his orchestration of wake games and toward the performance of the keening women, who were primarily responsible for 'effecting the transition of the deceased to the afterlife and ensuring his or her incorporation with the family ancestors'.

Ó Crualaoich makes effective use of his understanding of the different funereal behaviours appropriate to timely and untimely death in order to explain the fights that commonly occurred at the funerals of women who had died in childbirth.

These physical conflicts pitted the family of the deceased woman, whose death was generally attributed to fairy abduction, and her husband's family, 'with each side seeking to bury the body in their own ancestral graveyard with their own ancestors'. What was at issue in these fights were differing conceptions about the deceased woman's prior incorporation into her husband's family and about her threatened potential for incorporation into the proper group of ancestors in the afterlife. In teasing out these fresh insights from his rich ethnographic material, Ó Crualaoich gives us a deepened appreciation of the symbolic meaning and social function of the merry wake, and he also provides abundant confirmation for his argument that both pagan or Celtic and Christian cosmologies had firmly lodged themselves in Irish peasant minds.

Another central fixture of traditional popular culture which came under assault from the ecclesiastical authorities (and in this case, from secular officials too) in the late eighteenth and early nineteenth centuries was the pattern, that remarkable combination of religious devotions and profane amusements whose heyday, decline, and renewal Diarmuid Ó Giolláin discusses in his contribution to this volume. It could be argued that the pattern was not as resilient in the face of assault as the merry wake, and that this difference is largely attributable to the rigour of the state's attack on the recreational side of the pattern in the early nineteenth century, as discussed by Elizabeth Malcolm in her essay on the rise of the pub. But after having been shorn of all or most of its recreational features, the pattern, as Ó Giolláin shows, experienced a revival in the early twentieth century.

In fact, Ó Giolláin begins his study with a detailed account of one such revived pattern at St Gobnait's well in the parish of Dunquin in Kerry, partly in order to make the point that the devotional aspects of this pattern and others elsewhere have not changed greatly over time, even though the recreational side, once so exuberant, was not resuscitated after church and state had succeeded in suppressing it. Drawing on the direct observations of travellers, antiquarians, and other commentators, Ó Giolláin shows how both religious and recreational behaviour at traditional patterns commonly was carried to extremes by many of the participants. The religious rituals were rigorously penitential and must have severely tested the physical endurance of the pilgrims (or at least the serious ones)— whether in the number of prayers recited and repeated, in the number of circumambulations around holy wells or other sacred objects, sometimes barefoot or on bare knees, or in the long distances often travelled to the place of pilgrimage. The vigorous penitentialism of the religious devotions was paralleled by the boisterous and frequently riotous character of the recreational behaviour at patterns. Dutiful penitents transformed themselves into revelers, with lusty feasting, heavy drinking, energetic or even wild singing and dancing, and a great deal of fighting, much of it orchestrated by rival organised factions. If anything, the sources used by Ó Giolláin understate the violence associated with patterns by the early nineteenth century.

In illuminating the meaning and function of the pattern during its prime, Giolláin brings to bear a variety of concepts and perspectives. He points out that pilgrimage to a sacred site, which was at the heart of the religious side of the pattern, brought the faithful into direct contact with the holy, thus making possible 'the avoidance of the clerical intermediary and official church liturgy in a sort of democratisation of the sacred'. Giving added weight to this point, he reminds us of the radical dispersal of the holy throughout the physical space of Irish local communities: the 30,000 to 40,000 forts or raths regarded as abodes of the fairies; the more than 3,000 holy wells; and the hundreds of ruined churches and ancient burial sites. Such democratisation of the sacred was the very antithesis of the restructured Catholic church envisioned by the post-Tridentine reformers.

Ó Giolláin also helps us to gain a clearer understanding of a variety of religious phenomena related to the pattern by deploying the concept of sacralisation—the ritual process by which places or things are made or kept holy. Thus, for example, the circuits or circumambulations which pilgrims made around any holy well delimited the boundaries of the sacred site, marked it off from profane space, and by their complexity defended the holy from the uninitiated while giving access to the supernatural to initiates. Following the lead of anthropologist Victor Turner, Ó Giolláin urges us to consider the pattern pilgrimage as an especially 'liminal occasion', with the Turnerian term 'liminality' meaning 'any condition which is outside of, or on the margins of, ordinary life, a condition which is potentially sacred'. In going on pilgrimage, devotees take leave of their everyday selves, liberate themselves from the mundane structures or networks in which they are usually enmeshed, and seek a peripheral sacred place which is outside of ordinary time. Once arrived at this holy site, marginal to normal life, they engage in rituals of humiliation and penitential ordeals and strip away marks of special status, thus helping to produce what Turner called 'communitas or social anti-structure', a condition conducive to the creation of a new self in the midst of an egalitarian communion with others. Moving to the recreational side of the pattern, Ó Giolláin links this Turnerian vision of communitas to the ideas of Mikhail Bakhtin, particularly to his notion that the festive forms of expression stress what Bakhtin calls 'the material bodily principle', in accordance with which feasting, drinking, and sexual license encourage, in Ó Giolláin's words, 'the regeneration of the mass human body' and 'the triumph of material abundance'.

Increasingly after 1750, reform-minded Catholic bishops, followed after a considerable lag by most of the parish priests and curates, worked with determination to suppress patterns altogether or at least to purge them of their numerous 'abuses'. Moral reformers among the clergy regarded many recreational features of the pattern as scandalous abominations, while reformers of religion considered many pattern rituals as remnants of paganism and opposed what Ó Giolláin calls the democratisation of the sacred which pattern devotions represented. In contrast to Elizabeth Malcolm, who sees the state and its agents, especially the police, as having played the critical role in the demise of such popular festivals as the pattern, Ó Giolláin seems to attribute greater significance to the opposition of the Catholic church. He does so at least partly because he views the decline of traditional Irish culture, of which the pattern was an integral part, 'as an inevitable consequence of modernity', and because in his judgment the Catholic church has been 'in many ways . . . paradigmatic of the Irish experience of modernity'.

The physical violence associated with faction-fighting at patterns was only one of the major kinds of disorder with which the authorities contended in the half-century before the great famine. Another was deep-seated sectarian violence, which was by no means confined to the north of Ireland, as Kerby Miller emphasises in his recreation of 'the lost world' of an obscure Protestant middle-man named Andrew Johnston. Basing his judgment on familiarity with the thousands of Irish petitions to the British Colonial Office, Miller concludes that 'a desire to escape from violence was second only to the goal of economic independence in explaining why an estimated 500,000 Irish Protestants . . . emigrated during the pre-famine decades (1815–44)', seriously depleting the relatively small Protestant communities in counties outside the north of Ireland.

Among the groups critically affected by this drain were Protestant middlemen. In his essay earlier in our volume Kevin Whelan takes note of the attack mounted against the Irish middleman system by reform-minded landowners beginning in the late eighteenth century. He makes the important point that the gradual elimination of the middleman system ultimately redounded to the advantage of the Irish big-farm class and weakened the Anglo-Irish landed élite. While agreeing with this assessment, Miller stresses the crippling impact of the heavy attrition among Protestant middlemen on the rest of Protestant society in southern Ireland. As he remarks, not only were Protestant middlemen 'pillars of Protestant ascendancy, but also—in their roles as sublettors, investors, employ-ers, and magistrates—they served as vital mainstays for the humbler ranks of Protestant small farmers, shopkeepers, artisans, and labourers'. Members of these subaltern groups quickly lost their footing in the wake of the overthrow and emigration of the once-powerful Protestant middlemen.

In his microhistory Miller draws on local newspapers and on an unusually rich collection of letters from the older members of the Johnston family to their emigrant children and nephews in order to show how and why this particular Protestant middleman was crushed and to assess the wider meaning of these events. At the centre of the story stands a violent sectarian affray in September 1837 on the bridge of Ballymahon, Co. Longford, in which Thomas Ferrall, a young Catholic seminarian, was fatally stabbed, allegedly by John Johnston, one of the twelve children of the Protestant middleman Andrew Johnston. Though both father and son were indicted first for murder and then for manslaughter, they were each acquitted at the summer assizes of Longford in July 1838. In between Ferrall's death and the trial an unsuccessful attempt was made to kill Andrew Johnston in apparent retaliation. It was a near-miss, and soon after the trial ended in the double acquittal, Johnston and his whole family cleared out of Ballymahon and County Longford for good.

Miller's inspection of the coverage given to the affray, the coroner's inquest, the attempt on Andrew Johnston's life, and the trial by the three provincial newspapers serving County Longford (one O'Connellite and two Tory journals) shows how an overwhelmingly sectarian set of interpretations was placed on these events. The Catholic side saw only Protestant bigotry where the Protestant side saw only 'popish persecution'. These mirror images of sectarian malevolence in relation to the Ballymahon district become still more understandable when Miller locates them within the wider context of County Longford as a whole. From this contextualisation Longford emerges as a county having a bitter sectarian legacy stemming from the United Irish rising of 1798 and its brutal suppression, along with a depressing history between the union and the famine of recurrent outbreaks of organised agrarian and sectarian violence. Whiteboyism and Ribbonism were both remarkably energetic and widespread in the county. As if this were not already an explosive mix, the politics of Longford in the late 1820s and the 1830s pitted a newly emergent phalanx of middle-class Catholic laymen and priests against a beleaguered battery of Anglican clergymen, Protestant landlords, and Orangemen, with the two warring camps clashing repeatedly in the parliamentary elections of these years, and with the Liberal Catholics finally scoring an unprecedented double victory in the elections of 1837.

But if a knowledge of this wider political, agrarian, and sectarian context is necessary for a proper understanding of the fatal Ballymahon affray of September 1837 and the public reactions to it, Miller argues that the hostile general climate cannot satisfactorily explain the common Protestant perception that Andrew Johnston and his family had been specifically targeted by Catholics for persecution. This question brings Miller to a consideration of Johnston's economic interests (intermediate landlord of some 800 acres, lessor of local mills, and toll collector at local fairs and markets) and of how these interests were antagonistically regarded by local Catholics of different social levels. Miller contends that what united Catholics of all classes behind a rising Catholic bourgeois leadership was above all Johnston's control of the tolls and customs. He also shows how various local middle-class Catholics reaped material benefits from the downfall of the Johnstons, noting that 'for such men patriotism in the service of Catholic Ireland could be more than spiritually rewarding'.

But there was more to Andrew Johnston's downfall than sectarian conflict or agitation by local Catholics. His financial condition had been deteriorating sharply well before the events of 1837–8. Out of the dwindling profits of his own lands and those of the subtenants after 1815, he found it exceedingly difficult to meet his obligations to the head landlords, the Shuldhams. Johnston's position greatly worsened after 1832, when the death of one Shuldham brother led to the succession of another who adopted what Miller calls 'a much more instrumental and exploitive attitude towards his estate and its tenants'. Preferring to let his lands directly to the occupying tenants, the new proprietor showed no disposition to renew old leases to struggling Protestant middlemen like Johnston. Even though Shuldham did not terminate Johnston's various tenancies until just after the Ballymahon affray and the coroner's inquest, the writing was already on the wall for the Johnstons before then, as they themselves painfully recognised.

Miller exhibits considerable sympathy for the many Andrew Johnstons of early nineteenth-century Ireland. He views them as trapped anachronisms, caught between the upper millstone of 'a Protestant landlord class which preached traditional Toryism yet generally practised free-market liberalism', and the nether millstone of 'an aspiring Catholic bourgeoisie which waved the banner of anti-monopoly capitalism but used it to cloak sectarian warfare against their Protestant competitors'. In the final analysis, however, Miller displays even greater sympathy for the lower-class co-religionists of both the Protestant landed élite and the Catholic bourgeoisie. What united these two élites in the pre-famine decades, Miller argues, was their mutual commitment to a common economic agenda under which they 'sought to rationalise Irish agriculture, increase profits, and impose a free-market ethos on their poorer co-religionists'. Both élites, according to Miller, needed to deflect internal discontent from below and adopted the same tactic of using 'political and religious symbols to marshall their co-religionists into all-class alliances and crusades for sectarian advantage'. Weighed down by all the economic adversities of the three decades before the famine, Catholic and Protestant subalterns confronted the cruel choice of either 'supporting their own socio-economic exploiters or sailing to North America'. Like all good microhistory, this example of the genre thus illuminates much larger themes.

Among the all-class Catholic crusades led by the Catholic bourgeoisie in the early nineteenth century, the greatest was of course the series of so-called 'monster meetings' in 1843–5 which aimed at the repeal of the act of union of 1800. Whether the middle-class Catholic leaders of this campaign used it to deflect lower-class Catholic resentment against themselves, as Miller suggests, they certainly did employ political and religious symbols as a means of marshalling their co-religionists behind the banner of repeal. Indeed, it is the central purpose of Gary Owens's concluding essay in this volume to dissect the meanings of the symbolic language exhibited at the monster meetings—not the speeches but, as he puts it, the 'nationalism without words'.

Owens offers us a highly iconoclastic analysis and an entirely new way of looking at an extremely important set of events with which we thought ourselves quite familiar. As he remarks fairly enough, 'the popular image of monster

meetings'—and the image lodged in the history books—'has remained essentially unchanged' for a hundred and fifty years: 'it is one of immense crowds
sprawled thickly over many acres and listening intently to the inspirational
oratory of the Liberator', Daniel O'Connell. In contesting and revising this
image, Owens demonstrates first of all that repealers and repeal organs greatly
exaggerated the size of the crowds. But he also observes that even if nationalist
calculations were lowered by as much as 75 percent, it would still mean that the
monster meetings of 1843 had attracted about 'one quarter of the total population
of the three southern provinces'—a feat of political mobilisation unparalleled in
the British Isles. A second problem with the traditional image of the monster
meetings is that many of those who went to them did not remain long enough to
hear O'Connell's speeches, and of those who did stay, many others paid scant
attention to the orations. If, as one historian has remarked, the monster meetings
were political hedge schools, then, as Owens puts it, 'truancy and student apathy
were rampant'.

As a substitute for the discredited traditional image, Owens proposes that we
think about the monster meetings as 'collective ceremonies' or secular rituals in
which most of those in attendance actively participated in one way or another.
The monster meetings yoked together three standard features of current Irish
political culture—processions, outdoor oratory, and formal public banquets. Of
these features, Owens concentrates his attention on the first, partly because 'the
largest and most popular of the three events was unquestionably the procession',
and partly because it was primarily the procession which exhibited a host of
political messages through the creative and dramatic use of symbolic language
and ritual.

Owens subjects the great processions of the monster meetings to minute
analysis. He certainly does not ignore the entertainment aspect of the processions—the tableaux, the floats, the bands, the flags and bunting—the various
elements which, when brought together, turned these processions into spectacular displays. But what interests him more are the ways in which the processions
gave visual expression to romantic allegory and dramatic vignettes conveying a
variety of uncomplicated political messages. In such cases the procession func-
tioned as a stage (or a series of stages), and the 'directors' frequently organised
the performances around O'Connell, who was not just the center of attraction
but also the symbolic head and unifier of the social and political entities which
the procession represented, either in reality or in imagination. Proclaiming still
other political messages were the triumphal arches and banners to be found in
luxuriant supply at all of these mass gatherings.

While most of the political messages conveyed by banners, dramatic performances, and other processional devices were transparent in their meanings, Owens
also discusses other devices and forms of ritual whose messages were intentionally
opaque or ambivalent, at least to the uninitiated or cultural outsiders. This kind

of concealment or ambiguity helped to make possible symbolic subversion which the authorities were unlikely to punish. The evergreen plants so popular among Irish Catholic processionists provide a case in point. As Owens remarks, 'When thousands of marchers paraded with green boughs, bushes, and whole trees, they were symbolically brandishing nationalist emblems'. As social scientists have noted in their studies of peasant cultures in general, such behaviour involving tricks and ruses has been and still is a standard ideological weapon of the weak in resisting the domination of the strong. It was not without political significance in the Irish case that most of the greenery used in processions had to be plundered from landlord plantations and thus became, as Owens says, 'spoils of symbolic battle' and 'victory trophies'.

Drawing on the recent work of scholars dealing with public spectacles in other countries, Owens discusses additional ways of reading the meanings of these processions. Meaning was invested in the structure of parades. The order of march frequently recapitulated the social and political structure of the community, thus enabling the procession to function as a representation of the community to itself as well as to outsiders. Owens stresses O'Connell's position at 'the symbolic centre of every procession', thus allowing him to fuse symbolically the various elements of the community which had previously been divided, and thus turning the procession into 'a visual metaphor' for the Liberator's capacity to create an all-class alliance, at least among Catholics, in the interest of repeal. And if processions could be read as social and political texts from their very organisation, they could also be read as claims to territory from their routes of march. Historians have invariably noted how the organisers of the monster meetings took pains to hold them at sites with strong historical significance—sites which evoked a glorious Irish past or perhaps, like Mullaghmast in County Kildare, the memory of English treachery. More than one Dublin procession took in along its route the old Parliament House in College Green, thus visually proclaiming to the marchers that its restoration was their coveted goal.

What made the monster meetings of 1843–5 a kind of hedge school for at least the Catholic portion of the nation was above all the active participation of such a large segment of the population. As Owens demonstrates, this participation was focused on the great processions with their rich repertoires of symbolic forms and rituals. Thus, from a new awareness of the modalities of political communication which Owens uncovers, historians should glean a much deeper understanding of the grand political mobilisation that they have long associated with the monster meetings. And it is fitting to conclude this volume with an essay focusing on Daniel O'Connell, for his death in 1847, during the depth of the great famine, is a familiar symbol of the demise of 'traditional' Irish society and culture, although O'Connell himself, especially through his political mobilisations, was a powerful agent for cultural change.

'Ag Déanamh *Commanding*'[*]:
Elite Responses to Popular Culture, 1660–1850

SEAN CONNOLLY

Daniel Corkery's *The hidden Ireland*, first published in 1924, set out what was to become a widely accepted and enduring image of the relationship between élite and popular culture in eighteenth- and early nineteenth-century Ireland. Writing in the aftermath of the war of independence, and at a time when the land war of the 1880s was still within living memory, Corkery presented a picture of unique cultural polarisation. Traditional Gaelic Ireland had been characterised by a perfect cultural unity between lord and peasant, 'a phenomenon not known anywhere else in Europe'. The Tudor and Stuart conquest, however, had shattered this unity forever. In its place were now two wholly separate Irelands. On one side there were the peasantry, 'grubbing their bit of rock-strewn land', whose world was preserved in a materially impoverished but productive Gaelic literary tradition, characterised by the three themes of 'nationality, religion, rebellion'. On the other there was the Protestant, anglicised Ireland recorded in the conventional historical sources: 'the wine-flushed revelry of the alien gentry, the hunting, the dancing, the drinking, the gambling, the duelling', and the proceedings of the Dublin parliament, 'that noisy side-show, so bizarre in its lineaments and so tragicomic in its fate'. Contact between the two worlds was non-existent. The new landed élite 'differed from the people in race, language, religion, and culture; while the landscape they looked upon was indeed but rocks and stones and trees'.[1]

Corkery's overall presentation of eighteenth-century Irish society has long been superseded. L.M. Cullen's detailed critique, published in 1968, pointed up the central weaknesses. Corkery's simple juxtaposition of landlord and peasant overlooked the complexity of Ireland's rural structure, with its multi-tiered hierarchy of labourers, cottiers, tenant farmers, graziers, and middlemen. His picture of unrelieved poverty ignored a great deal of contrary evidence, even in his own Gaelic literary sources. He also failed to recognise the extent to which what he took to be expressions of a general alienation from the political and social establishment were in fact the laments of a particular social group, the professional poets, for a vanished social order in which they had enjoyed a privileged position.[2] Over

---

[*] 'Ag déanamh' is the Irish verb for 'doing'. For the context, see below, p. 27.

the past two decades a new image of eighteenth-century Ireland, as a complex
society experiencing rapid economic expansion, has come to be generally accepted.[3] Yet the implications of this rethinking have yet to be extended to the
cultural issues that were Corkery's main concern. A handful of specialist studies
have drawn attention to findings that sit uneasily with the assumption of wholly
separate and mutually antagonistic cultural worlds.[4] Yet there has so far been no
attempt to develop an alternative overall framework. And it was still possible for
a recent survey of the impact of the French revolution to take as its starting point
the assumption that 'Ireland's colonial experience meant that cultural differentiation between classes took extreme forms', of a kind not found in other
European societies of the same period.[5]

The aim of this essay is to offer an overview of the interaction of élite and
popular cultures in the two centuries between the Restoration and the famine. If
Ireland in this period can no longer be conceived in terms of the simple duality
of anglicised landlord and Gaelic peasant, what alternative can be substituted for
Corkery's model of two wholly separate and antagonistic cultures? In particular,
is it possible to analyse the relationship between élite and popular culture in terms
similar to those that have been developed by Peter Burke and others for pre-
industrialised Europe as a whole?[6] Or is it still necessary to see the ethnic,
religious, and political conflicts created by Ireland's particular history of conquest and colonisation as creating a radically different relationship between the
cultural worlds of rulers and ruled?

I

The first point to be made regarding Corkery's image of a popular, Gaelic culture
uniquely estranged from that of the ruling élite is that it depends on a wholly
unrealistic contrast between Ireland and other parts of *ancien régime* Europe. To
take only the most obvious example, Ireland was not by any means the only early
modern society in which the language of the ruling élite differed from that of the
common people. In parts of Italy, for example, the educated and powerful spoke
French, in Bohemia German, in Norway Danish, and in Finland Swedish. In
Russia the aristocracy, from the second half of the eighteenth century, took up
French as a positive badge of status, differentiating them from a Russian- or
Ukrainian-speaking peasantry, and a German-, Swedish-, or Yiddish-speaking
mercantile class. Closer to home there were Wales and highland Scotland, where
an increasingly anglicised gentry presided over populations still predominantly
Gaelic- and Welsh-speaking. Even in ostensibly monolingual France almost half
the population of the late eighteenth century still spoke a local dialect rather than
the standardised language of the élite, and one person in four understood nothing
else.[7] It is also important to remember that attitudes to popular culture every-

where in early modern Europe were to some degree censorious. Fear of the 'many-headed monster', and contempt for popular idleness, debauchery, and irrationality were commonplaces of élite discourse.[8]

In seventeenth-century Ireland these general attitudes were reinforced by political and ethnic antagonisms. By this time, it is true, Gaelic Ireland had already been largely demilitarised, and its political structures were being rapidly undermined by confiscation, legal redefinition, and cultural assimilation. Yet New English and Old English observers alike continued to see the traditional Irish pattern of landownership, with its emphasis on personal rule and its sanctioning of unlimited demands on tenants and dependants, as a major potential threat. For the New English, cultural antagonism was reinforced by religious divisions. The result was a stereotype of the Irish lower classes as irredeemably barbarous: cruel, untrustworthy, and wholly lacking in the civic virtues, in thrall to a superstitious religion, and drawn by their idleness to a wasteful and unproductive pastoralism, with all the squalor and poverty which such a way of life entailed.[9]

Even at the beginning of the seventeenth century, however, there are indications that this negative and dismissive stereotype did not wholly sum up the realities of cultural coexistence. The Old English were always ready to shore up their own threatened political position by contrasting their English ancestry and continued political loyalty with the culturally and politically alien world of Gaelic Ireland. But they nevertheless intermarried freely with Gaelic families, and there were frequent complaints of the spread of Irish language and manners even among the merchants and government officials of the Old English towns.[10] Nor did the New English necessarily keep their distance to the extent that some contemporary writings would suggest. Robert Boyle, earl of Cork (1566–1643), normally seen as the epitome of this class, maintained friendly relations with Gaelic families, had his own sons instructed in the Irish language, and included an Irish harp among the furnishings of his house at Lismore.[11] The extent to which such contacts should modify the image of cultural and ethnic apartheid derived from more polemical writings remains the subject of debate.[12] What is clear is that by the end of the seventeenth century there had been a major change. By this time, even the least sympathetic observers had begun to accept that the culture of the Irish lower classes no longer represented a credible social or political threat.

There were three main reasons for this. The first was what amounted to a transformation in the character of popular culture itself. The middle decades of the seventeenth century saw a revolution not just in Irish politics and the structure of landownership but in the customs and lifestyle of the common people. Perhaps the most obvious changes were in language and physical appearance. Although the lower classes remained overwhelmingly Irish-speaking, a growing proportion knew at least some English, and observers were also cheered by the apparent evidence of linguistic fossilisation provided by the spread of

English loan words in Irish.[13] The traditional dress and hair-style—mantle and glib—referred to repeatedly in early seventeenth-century accounts had largely disappeared by the 1660s, if not before. Sir Henry Piers, writing in 1682, observed that in Westmeath and the adjoining counties the people 'are in our days become more polite and civil than in former ages and seem very forward to accommodate themselves to the English modes, particularly in their habit, language, and surnames'.[14] From the opposite ideological perspective the anonymous author of the Gaelic poem *Páirlimint Cloinne Tomáis*, writing as early as the reign of James I, viciously satirised the first stumbling attempts of the 'churl' to speak in English. A sequel written in the early 1660s took the spread of English among the lower classes for granted. Instead, it concentrated its fire on other manifestations of rising social aspirations, such as the abandonment of the traditional dress of trews and mantle.[15]

Meanwhile, there were deeper changes in economy and social organisation. The spread of consumer goods, notably tobacco, reflected the extension, even among the rural lower classes, of a commercialised, monetary economy.[16] Agriculture was still predominantly pastoral, but the shifting, impermanent settlements and itinerant herdsmen noted by Tudor observers had almost wholly given way to a more settled pattern of farming.[17] Between the 1590s and the 1640s Irish Catholicism was also substantially reshaped. A better trained and more effectively supervised clergy, operating within a newly tightened diocesan and parochial framework, began the task of promoting a more regular pattern of popular religious practice, purged of its most glaringly folkloric elements.[18] Agrarian and religious change may both have contributed to another significant transformation: the process whereby the casual acceptance of concubinage, illegitimacy, and divorce, commented on by Tudor and early Stuart observers, gave way to tighter family structures and a more restrictive sexual discipline.[19] In all these ways the Irish peasant of the later seventeenth century was far less a self-evidently alien being than his counterpart of even sixty years before.

These cultural changes in part reflected and in part permitted the more complete integration of the Catholic lower classes into the economic structures of Anglo-Ireland. As late as the 1650s it had been possible for Cromwellian policy makers to contemplate the wholesale expulsion of the Catholic population from three-quarters of the country and their replacement by English settlers. This project of mass transportation, as is well known, collapsed when the Protestant gentry took alarm at the prospect of losing their tenants and labourers.[20] On the other hand, the 1640s and 1650s did see widespread expulsions of Catholics from the towns. For a time urban Ireland became an archipelago of more or less undiluted Englishness and Protestantism. But even this purification did not last. In 1679, during the emergency created by allegations of a popish plot, the earl of Orrery demanded that government expel the large numbers of Catholics living in urban centres. He was told that this was impractical. The Catholics of whose presence he complained had been introduced into the towns by the Protestant inhabitants: 'they know not well how to live without them; they wanted servants, they wanted tenants, and they wanted tradesmen'. These servants, tenants, and tradesmen could not now be removed 'without laying waste upon the matter most of our towns and lands which are mostly inhabited and tenanted by them'.[21] If cultural change was making it more difficult to see the Catholic lower classes as the equivalent of the native populations of North America and other overseas colonies, economic development was making it impractical to think of treating them as such. By now, for better or for worse, they provided the labour on which the prosperity of the greater part of the kingdom depended.

Finally, and most important, the decline in hostility to the culture of the Irish lower classes was a direct result of increased political security. The wars of 1641–53 had completed the military and political subjugation of Ireland. The last remnants of the Gaelic social order had been destroyed, and central government control extended to even the most remote corners. Sir Richard Cox, writing from County Cork around 1685, spelt out the implications of the changes that had taken place:

> This county, and indeed all Ireland, is quite another thing than it was in Camden's time or even before the last rebellion. It is now very well inhabited by English and improved daily after the English fashion. All the inhabitants are answerable to the laws, which are the same as in England, except some few alterations by act of parliament here. There remains no considerable fastness to hide tories or shelter rebels, nor is there any part of the world more free from fear and disturbance than this kingdom. Tanistry, gavelkind, the brehon law, coshering, coin and livery, and all other old barbarous customs and unreasonable exactions are obsolete or abolished, and the English habit, language, and manners altogether used except by the poorer sort.[22]

This is not to suggest that Protestant Ireland felt wholly secure. The disaffection of the Catholic masses was generally taken for granted. What had disappeared was rather the sense of Gaelic Ireland as a rival power structure, whose resources could be mobilised for a renewed war against English government and its Irish supporters. Instead, there was a general tendency to see the Catholic lower classes as demoralised, lacking alike in weapons, organisation, and leadership. Anxieties, when they arose, focused on the possibility of a foreign invasion or (a real issue in the reign of the frighteningly ambiguous Charles II) of betrayal from within. Once order had been restored after the Williamite war, the civil and military authorities were, if anything, even more confident in their assertions that the Protestant population, organised in the militia, in firm control of all fortifications, and enjoying a monopoly of both weapons and military training, could be counted on to contain any purely internal disturbances.[23]

It would be misleading to suggest that long-standing cultural prejudices and political insecurities disappeared overnight. The survival of traditional stereo-types is evident, for example, in Sir Francis Brewster's description in 1698 of what he claimed was still a substantial class of old Irish gentry. Too proud to engage in profitable trade, they spent their time smoking by their firesides or— a detail that could have come out of any polemic of the previous two centuries— 'if the weather be warm, sleep or louse themselves under the hedges'. Those among them who retained any land 'live after a careless and prodigal way, pleasing themselves with a great company of followers, servants, and tenants'.[24] As late as 1707 an act of the Irish parliament provided for the transportation of 'all loose, idle vagrants and such as pretend to be Irish gentlemen and will not betake themselves to any honest trade or livelihood, but wander about demanding victuals and coshering from house to house amongst their fosterers, followers, and others'.[25] In 1697 Bishop Dopping of Meath dropped proposals which he had earlier made for sending Irish-speaking missionaries to work among the Catholic population on the grounds that 'this would too much encourage the Irish to continue their own language, which some statutes of force in that kingdom labour to prevent'. The same argument was used in 1711–12 to help sink John Richardson's scheme for a missionary drive among the Catholic lower classes.[26] Jonathan Swift, writing in the late 1730s, conceded that some knowledge of Irish might be of practical value to gentlemen living in the country. At the same time he warned of the danger of cultural pollution: 'I do not remember to have heard of any one man that spoke Irish who had not the accent upon his tongue, easily discernible to any English ear'.[27]

Inherited prejudices were also evident in the difficulty that Irish Protestants experienced in finding a satisfactory vocabulary of national identity. In the late seventeenth and early eighteenth centuries they had used the term 'Irish' as synonymous with Catholic, while referring to themselves as 'English'. From the 1720s onwards this latter usage was increasingly abandoned. Yet the term 'Irish' continued to have strong negative associations. Pole Cosby, son of a Queen's County landowner, visiting the Irish monastery at Prague in 1723, found the establishment 'but ordinary and Irish all over, very dirty'.[28] As late as 1738 the Rev. Samuel Madden, a member of the Dublin Society and by most criteria a 'patriot', was still anxious to argue that 'the children of those Englishmen who have planted in our colonies in America [may] be as justly reckoned Indians and savages as such families who are settled here can be considered and treated as mere Irishmen and aliens'.[29] Even in the late eighteenth-century heyday of Protestant patriotism, in fact, writers were prepared to employ an astonishing range of circumlocutions in order to avoid the terms 'Ireland' and 'Irish'.[30]

Yet, despite these continued reservations, the early and mid-eighteenth cen-tury saw the emergence among educated Protestants of a new attitude to the Gaelic portion of their cultural inheritance. Episodes from medieval Irish history, involving a more sympathetic treatment of pre-Norman Ireland than had previously been attempted, appeared on the Dublin stage in Shadwell's *Rotherick O'Connor* (1720) and Phillips's *Hibernia freed* (1722), about the defeat of the Vikings.[31] A translation of Geoffrey Keating's history appeared in 1723; a Dublin newspaper reported the 'esteem and favour' shown to the author Darby O'Connor when he presented a copy of his work to the prince of Wales.[32] Original historical work by English and Irish Protestant authors, in the 1720s and later, revealed a new willingness to concede that pre-Norman Ireland had had its own literature and a highly developed civilisation.[33] A collection of Carolan's tunes was published in 1721, and there were occasional further compilations.[34] An Irish Language Society was established in Dublin in 1752.[35]

Neither the importance nor the coherence of these different endeavours should be overestimated. In some cases what was involved was little more than a mild interest in local curiosities. More serious concern, where it existed, remained very much a minority taste among educated Protestants. In the last decades of the eighteenth century, on the other hand, there was a dramatic and much more widely spread growth of interest in all these areas of the Gaelic cultural tradition. James MacPherson's claims to have demonstrated, through the Ossian poems of 1760–3, that it was Scotland rather than Ireland that had been the true centre of pre-Christian Celtic civilisation created widespread outrage. A range of writers, Catholic and Protestant, came forward to denounce MacPherson's scholarship and reassert the cultural primacy of ancient Ireland.[36] In the decades that followed, authors like Charles Vallancey made progressively more extravagant claims for the glories of the Gaelic past. Charlotte Brooke's well-received *Reliques of Irish poetry* (1789) made a selection of early texts, suitably adapted to contemporary tastes, available to a general readership. The Royal Irish Academy, established in 1785, provided a prestigious new centre for discussion and publication.[37] The same period saw an unprecedented interest in traditional musical forms, culminating in the Belfast harp festival of 1792 and the publication in 1797 and 1809 of the first two volumes of Edward Bunting's major collection.[38]

This first Celtic revival can be seen as part of the 'discovery of the people' that took place everywhere in Western Europe in the later eighteenth century, reflecting a general revolt against what was coming to be seen as an excess of artifice and rationality.[39] But in Ireland, as in other areas, the new interest in history, popular culture, and antiquities also had a political dimension. Enthusiasm for the writings of Charlotte Brooke and others was closely linked to the surge of patriot sentiment that produced the Volunteer movement, the free-trade agitation, and the 'constitution of 1782'. Henry Flood, a leading patriot spokesman, bequeathed a fund to establish a chair of Irish in Trinity College, Dublin. The first president of the Royal Irish Academy was the 'Volunteer' earl of Charlemont.[40] The political self-confidence that lay behind this exhilarating mix of patriotism, scholarly discovery, and popularisation did not survive the horrific events of the 1790s. Yet even in the transformed environment of post-union

Ireland the appropriation of a version of Irish culture did not entirely lose either
its appeal or its political relevance. Several recent studies have analysed the
process by which a succession of Protestant intellectuals, from Davis and Ferguson in the 1830s and 1840s to Yeats in the early twentieth century, sought to
find in an engagement with Irish history and tradition a strategy whereby their
class could reaffirm its threatened position as the natural leaders of Irish society.[41]
Such projects, equally alien to an anglicised and bourgeois Catholic democracy
and to the hard-bitten pragmatism of mainstream Irish toryism, had little
practical effect. Yet, seen in a longer perspective, they represent the final stage in
a complex, shifting relationship, quite different from the simple dualities of *The
hidden Ireland*, between the Protestant élite and the popular culture of the society
in which they lived.

II

So far we have been concerned with fairly well charted developments in the world
of texts and ideas. But what about the lived culture of custom, recreation, and
sociability? To shift the discussion of relationships between different cultural
groups to this level is not just to move from the familiar to the largely unknown.
It is also to enter an area where the terms we have so far been using begin to reveal
their limitations. The notion of élite and popular cultures is never more than a
theoretical construct. The most influential recent study, aspiring to deal with
Europe as a whole, proceeds only on the basis of a whole series of heroic
assumptions regarding the possibility of generalisation across distinctions of
urban and rural, Catholic and Protestant, male and female, and across regional
and political frontiers.[42] Even within the more limited geographical confines of
Ireland it quickly becomes equally clear that neither élite nor popular culture can
be seen as uniform or wholly self-contained.

   As a broad political generalisation, the members of the Irish political élite can
be identified as a Protestant landed class of New English origin. Three-quarters
of the peers active in the Irish parliament between 1692 and 1727 were from
families established in Ireland since the Reformation; around the same proportion of the men who sat in the house of commons under George II were
descendants of Tudor, Stuart, or Cromwellian settlers.[43] Yet this leaves a substantial minority within the governing élite whose families were of Old English or,
less frequently, Gaelic origin. Then there were the surviving Catholic aristocracy
and gentry, still holding one-seventh of the profitable land at the start of the
eighteenth century.[44] Protestant polemicists like Brewster, and even the statutes of
Queen Anne's parliament, might have liked to keep up the stereotype of a lazy,
lousy chieftainry. But the reality was that the Catholic aristocracy and gentry were
part of the ruling class, even if not permitted to share in its power. Adherence to

Catholicism might exclude a peer or landowner from parliament and local office; it did not make him less a gentleman. This much was recognised in the willingness of the authorities to grant licenses to carry arms to those whose status was such that it would have been considered a disgrace to see them appear without their swords,[45] as well as in the ease with which members of this group were fully assimilated into the ruling élite once they had conformed to the established church.

These national and religious distinctions were undoubtedly reflected in the attitude of different sections of the élite to the culture of their social inferiors. The Cotters of County Cork and the O'Connors of County Roscommon are two examples of landowning families of native Irish origin who had adjusted their own lifestyles to the standards of a changing world, yet continued to act as patrons to Gaelic poets and men of learning. In other cases, as with the O'Connells of County Kerry, contact with the Gaelic cultural world was kept up by the women of the family for some decades after it had been abandoned by the men.[46] Gaelic, of course, did not mean popular. The literary tradition which these survivors from the old élite supported was in fact aristocratic, exclusivist, and—particularly in its years of decline—fiercely anti-egalitarian. Yet individuals from this background could also respond to aspects of popular culture for which even the most paternalistically inclined members of the newer propertied class could have little sympathy. Thus Roderick O'Flaherty, contributing to William Molyneux's projected survey of Ireland in the mid-1680s, recounted in total seriousness a tale of the vengeance wreaked by a local saint on two seamen who had omitted to make the customary obeisance as they sailed past his shrine. Another contribution to the same venture, by John Keogh, a Church of Ireland clergyman of Irish descent, showed a remarkable willingness to give serious consideration to the proposition that illness in cattle could be caused by darts fired at them by fairies whom the owner had somehow offended.[47]

To differences of ethnic origin must be added differences in wealth and status. Accounts from the early and mid-eighteenth century regularly commented on the rough and ready manners of the Irish lesser gentry, noting in particular their addiction to duelling and drinking, unsophisticated cuisine, and squalid houses.[48] It is of course necessary in the case of English observers to allow for a degree of metropolitan superiority mixed with national prejudice. Yet it stands to reason that there would in fact have been significant differences between the world of the great landed families and that of the lesser provincial gentry. The resident landowners of County Donegal, it was noted in 1701, included 'no very topping noblemen or gentlemen', but only 'conformable plain men [who] are easily obliged, a dish of good meat and moderate drink being all they expect'.[49] A further distinction, combining variations in income and differences of personal circumstance, was between those whose connections were wholly Irish and those (one recent account suggests that they should be regarded as the true 'Anglo-Irish'[50]) who had property or family connections in both Ireland and England.

Our difficulties do not end with the landowning class. First, there is the familiar problem of defining the position of the numerous middlemen, both Catholic and Protestant, whose leasehold interests and command over large bodies of subtenants allowed them a lifestyle difficult to distinguish from that of the landowning gentry.[51] Secondly, there are the professional and commercial middle classes, quite clearly bearers of élite rather than popular culture, yet inhabiting a world wholly different from that of the aristocracy and gentry. Within this group, moreover, we encounter yet further differences. The urban middle classes of the three southern provinces included both Catholic (mainly Old English) and Protestant (mainly New English) families. In Ulster there was the distinction, quite possibly more important still, between a Presbyterian urban élite of Scottish origin and a smaller but politically privileged Anglican middle class of mainly English descent.

If the culture of the élite was fractured by differences of economic status and ethnic origin, so too was that of 'the people'. By the beginning of the century about one-quarter of the population consisted of British immigrants or their descendants. English and Scottish popular cultures were well established, in varying degrees of relative strength, across the greater part of Ulster and were dominant in its eastern counties. An English cultural inheritance was also strong in the towns of the other three provinces. Even among the Catholics who made up a majority of the working population everywhere outside Ulster, there were important distinctions. The popular culture of the eastern counties, with their commercialised agriculture, well-developed urban centres, and rapidly expanding consumer market, must inevitably have differed from that of the poorer, subsistence-oriented west. Already by the 1770s, for example, there was a marked difference between Leinster, where fewer than 20 percent of those born in that decade were later recorded as being able to speak Irish, and Munster and Connacht, where the proportion was 80 percent or more.[52] Within each region, too, there was the emerging contrast between the tenant-farmer class and a rural poor consisting of smallholders, cottiers, and labourers.[53]

Once all this has been said, the distinction between élite and popular remains a valuable analytical tool. On the one hand, it is possible to distinguish an élite culture defined by transmission through the printed word, its access to the worlds of law and high politics, and its observance of a particular code of politeness and behaviour. On the other, there is the culture of the common people: not necessarily illiterate, but primarily dependent on the spoken word, governed by custom and ritual, localistic, community-minded, and conservative. Within these two broad categories there existed a range of subgroups; and the character of any interaction between the two depended crucially on who precisely was involved. Much also depended on the specific context. In Ulster and in the towns of the south, where English cultural influences were strong, interaction between high and low could be built around occasions familiar to both, such as the May pole and the cock-fight.[54] In rural areas outside Ulster more adaptation was required on both sides. In the larger urban centres, particularly Dublin, interaction took place partly within the framework of a highly organised body of civic ritual, and entertainment for all classes was more commercial in character. In the country-side, by contrast, participation in a shared culture tended to be less formal and more personalised. None of these variations, however, detracts from the central point. In post-Restoration Ireland, as elsewhere in pre-industrialised Europe, the worlds of élite and popular culture were linked by the bridges of shared interest, patronage, and emulation of social superiors.

III

Two specific examples may help to illustrate the very different forms that this process could assume. The theatre of the seventeenth and eighteenth centuries would normally be taken as a central institution of élite culture. And the Dublin theatre of this period did in fact depend heavily for its existence and growth on the patronage of the viceregal court, aristocracy, and gentry. Yet there was also, from an early stage, a significant popular audience for its productions. John Dunton, visiting Dublin in 1698, noted that the theatre 'is free to all classes and gives entertainment as well to the broom man as the genteel peer'.[55] An anony-mous account, written half a century later, offered a more specific description of the social gradations which by that time existed within a typical audience:

> In our playhouse in Dublin, besides an upper gallery for abigails, serving men, journeymen, and apprentices, we have three other different and distinct classes. The first is called the boxes, where there is one peculiar to the lord lieutenant, and the rest for persons of quality and for ladies and gentlemen of the highest rank, unless some fools who have more money than wit or perhaps more impudence than both, crowd in among them. The second is called the pit, where sit the judges, wits, and censurers, or rather the censurers without either wit or judgement. . . . In common with these sit the squires, sharpers, beaus, and bulliers, and here and there an extravagant male 'cit[izen]'. The third is distinguished by the title of the middle gallery, where the citizens' wives and daughters, etc., commonly take their places.[56]

Stratification was maintained partly by means of the admission prices usually charged: 5s. 5d. for a box, 3s. 3d. for the pits, 2s. 2d. for the gallery, and two pence for the upper gallery.

These social differences presented obvious problems for the dramatist. Charles Shadwell, writing in the early years of George I, commented wryly on the range of tastes that had somehow to be satisfied:

Ladies will smile, if scenes are modest writ,

Whilst your double entendres please the pit.
There's not a vizard sweating in the gallery,
But likes a smart intrigue, a rake, and raillery;
And were we to consult our friends above,
A pert and witty footman 'tis they love;
And now and then such language as their own,
A 'Damn the dog', 'You lie', and 'Knock him down'.
Consider then how hard it is to show
Things that will do above and please below.

Elsewhere he noted how the same scene could be received in wholly different ways by various sections of the audience: 'Our friends two storeys high/Do always laugh when other people cry,/And murdering scenes to them are comedy'.[57] Yet there was no simple opposition between genteel and plebeian taste. Complaints in 1755 of the 'dreadful irregularities' that arose from 'young gentlemen' coming drunk into the theatre, as well as the high cost of admission to the notoriously rowdy pit, suggest that a preference for boisterous audience participation over silent appreciation of the finer points of dramatic performance was in many cases part of the shared experience of gentleman and commoner.[58] All this, of course, was in Dublin, with its largely anglicised population and its substantial Protestant working class. There is no reason to believe that the journeymen and apprentices crowded into the upper gallery were drawn exclusively from that class; but in the absence of hard evidence one way or the other, it remains a possibility.

A second example provides more clear-cut evidence of interaction across divisions, not just of social class, but of religion, ethnicity, and language. This concerns the game of hurling. In the eighteenth century the sport took two main forms. The first, known throughout most of Ireland, was a winter game played with a narrow stick and a wooden ball. It was a community sport, played for the benefit of participants rather than spectators, and it had an exclusively lower-class following (although it was to be taken up in the nineteenth century, under the name 'hurley', by students at Trinity College, Dublin). The second form of hurling, found mainly in the province of Leinster and adjoining counties, was a summer game played with a broad stick and a horsehair ball. This was more commonly a spectator sport, in which highly skilled performers competed before an audience.[59] As such, it enjoyed substantial upper-class patronage as well as the support of popular audiences. A hurling match advertised in County Galway in 1746 was to be preceded by a buck hunt and followed by 'a ball at night for the entertainment of the ladies', while the venue originally announced was subsequently changed 'for the better accommodation of the ladies and gentlemen, and the benefit of a good road for carriages'.[60] In 1755 a match between the gentlemen of counties Kildare and Dublin was watched by the lord lieutenant as well as 'a most brilliant appearance of nobility and gentry'. As late as 1792 the countess of Westmorland, wife of another lord lieutenant, along with 'several of the nobility and gentry', attended a hurling match in the Phoenix Park, although on this occasion the match had to be abandoned when some of the 'vast concourse of spectators' invaded the ground.[61] It was only this patronage from members of the élite that made possible the very substantial stakes—up to 100 guineas in some cases—noted in newspaper reports of hurling matches in the mid and late eighteenth century.[62]

Gentry patronage was not confined to spectatorship. References to matches between the 'gentlemen' of different counties are possibly not to be taken at face value. But it is clear from other evidence that country gentlemen did in fact commonly take part in hurling contests. Dudley Cosby of Queen's County, who died in 1729, was famed for his athletic feats, his stamina in hunting, his skill at rope dancing and tennis, and for having been 'a most extraordinary fine hurler'.[63] In County Kilkenny John Cuffe, Baron Desart (1730–67), was remembered long after his death under the nickname 'Sean a' Chaipín' [Jack of the Cap] for the same accomplishment. A song in his honour provides intriguing glimpses, through the incorporation into the Irish text of key terms in English, of the interaction between cultural worlds that lay behind the sporting activities of this member of the social and political élite:

Tagann osna im chroí is deora im leacain,
Nuair ná feicim thú id jaicéad uaine is id chaipín dearg
Ag déanamh *commanding* ar na hiománaithe maithe.
Tá do chamán ar fiaradh fád leaba,
Is tá do liathróid á bualadh ag buachaillí an bhaile,
Is go mbuailfeá poc *ball* ann chomh hard leis an nglealagh.

[There is an ache in my heart, and tears on my cheeks, when I do not see you in your green jacket and red cap, commanding the fine hurlers. Your hurling stick is warping beneath your bed, and your ball is being knocked about by the boys of the townland, where you used to hit a ball as high as the moon.][64]

What was true of hurling was also true of a range of other sports. Prize-fighting, for example, attracted both popular and genteel spectators. A newspaper report of a match fought on the strand near Dublin in 1731 noted disturbances among 'the mob' in which 'several gentlemen' narrowly escaped injury. Horse-racing was another shared amusement. Lady Kildare in 1759 observed 'post-chaises in number' gathered to attend Easter races near Maynooth, while at the same time complaining that all the estate workmen had taken themselves off for the same purpose.[65] Even faction-fighting, the ritualised aggression of the countryside, could involve members of at least the lesser gentry. A Church of Ireland clergyman, writing in 1713 to the Sligo landowner Kean O'Hara, listed three mutual acquaintances as having taken part in a recent brawl between rival groups.[66]

Patronage was also extended to local festivals. Once again, the manner varied with local circumstances. The Protestant holland weavers round Lurgan, Co. Armagh, were able to celebrate May Day in 1737 by a semi-military display, marching in a body of some 300 men, each attired in a uniform of shirt and black trousers, 'cockades in their hats, and basket hilt swords drawn in one hand and Irish cambric handkerchiefs in the other', to the houses of local gentlemen. At Killala in County Mayo, five years earlier, the wife of the Church of Ireland bishop had presided over the less formalised festivities of what must have been a predominantly Catholic population. In the morning she rode in her coach to the strand, accompanied by other members of the household, to watch a series of horse-races. '. . . In the afternoon chairs were placed before the house, where we all took our places in great state; . . . then dancing, singing, grinning [by old women, for prizes of tobacco], accompanied with an excellent bagpipe, the whole concluded with a ball, bonfire, and illuminations.' William Farrell, born in Carlow town in 1772, remembered the factions that in his youth had organised rival May Day celebrations: 'every gentleman they had influence on, they went to him for a maypole and were never refused'.[67]

Nor was it only amusements that were patronised in this way. Musical and other performers also found audiences among the gentry as well as the common people. The household of the same bishop of Killala lamented the departure of the fiddler who had been staying with them, which had put an end to their dancing. But they awaited the arrival of 'a famous piper and hautboy', after which 'we shall foot it again most furiously'.[68] The patronage that the harpist and composer Turlough O'Carolan received from a range of landed families, Protestant as well as Catholic and English as well as Gaelic in origin, is well known.[69] Patrick Delany, Church of Ireland dean of Down, who helped to arrange for the publication of Carolan's tunes in 1748, maintained a harper in his house in County Down.[70] In the same way Arthur O'Neill, making his first tour as an itinerant musician in County Antrim in 1760, was received both by his namesakes, the O'Neills of Shane's Castle, and by the much more recently established Boyds of Ballycastle.[71] A visitor to the home of the County Monaghan peer Lord Dartry in 1773 heard the 'family bard' deliver an ode at the birthday celebrations for Dartry's eldest son.[72]

This is not to suggest that peer and peasant attended identical performances, either of music or of verse. Arthur O'Neill was proud of his status as a 'gentleman harper'. It was important to him, for example, that in the houses of the gentlemen he visited, 'the different gratuities I generally received were handed me in a private manner'. A Dr McDonnell of Belfast, in whose childhood home O'Neill had lived for two years as a teacher of music, confirmed much later that throughout his stay 'he was treated as a poor gentleman and had a servant'. There is also

O'Neill's approving account of the reply made by another harper, Ned MacAleer, to a lady who had required him to play a specimen of his music in her hall and then expressed disappointment at the result: 'Madam, as you were pleased to let me play in the hall, I played you tailor's and servants' music, which would otherwise be different'.[73] All this implies that different audiences were seen as meriting different levels of skill and sophistication, whether from the same performer or from individuals of differing levels of accomplishment. In addition, of course, the middle and upper classes had a second musical culture, imported from England and continental Europe, which was not accessible to the rest of the population. But the point remains that there was no absolute separation: members of the social and political élite, while maintaining their own largely exclusive tradition, were also prepared to patronise performers who either themselves played for popular audiences or employed the same instruments and idiom as those who did.

Cultural interaction, it should be emphasised, was not a one-way process. The dissemination among lower social groups of elements derived from the customs, manners, and values of the upper classes is more difficult to document than the incorporation into élite culture of popular elements. But it is clear that such downward penetration occurred. A visitor to County Down in 1745 lamented the influence of the spirit of emulation:

> I am very sorry to find here and everywhere people out of character, and that wine and tea should enter where they have no pretence to be, and usurp the rural food of syllabub, etc. But the dairymaids wear large hoops and velvet hoods instead of the round, tight petticoat and straw hat, and there is as much foppery introduced in the food as in the dress—the pure simplicity of the country is quite lost.[74]

Forty years later, a visitor to the Rosses, off the coast of Donegal, noted that the young men had abandoned the home-made clothing common until a short time before, and appeared 'fashionably dressed on Sundays in satin waistcoat and breeches, with white silk stockings, silver buckles, and ruffled shirts'.[75]

Nor was emulation confined to diet and clothing. Arthur Young noted in 1780 that the dances of the common people included not only the Irish jig but also 'minuets and country dances . . . , and I even heard some talk of cotilions coming in'.[76] At a later stage quadrilles, brought back from France by soldiers returning from the revolutionary and Napoleonic wars, were adapted to popular tastes by means of the adoption of faster rhythms and jig and reel steps, in which modified form they were to become the most popular dance in the Irish countryside for most of the nineteenth century.[77] A similar penetration took place in the case of music. Arthur O'Neill complained around 1810 that harpists increasingly performed the tunes of English composers like Charles Dibdin, so that 'the national tunes and airs' were now kept alive only by 'a few gentlemen in the different provinces I have travelled through'.[78]

To complete this brief survey of the interaction of high and low culture, it is necessary to note the existence of certain groups, themselves located in a frontier zone between the two worlds, whose members were well placed to act as bridges between them. To a limited extent, as already noted, landowning families of Gaelic descent were intermediaries of this kind.[79] On probably a wider scale there were the middlemen, depicted in one recent account as playing a key role in bridging the social gulf between landowners and a tenantry made up overwhelmingly of small occupiers.[80] Thirdly, there were what might be termed the Gaelic intelligentsia, following the closely related professions of scribe, poet, and schoolteacher. Again, it would be wholly wrong to equate the Gaelic and the popular. The Gaelic literati of the eighteenth century were custodians of a manuscript-based culture that they regarded as wholly distinct from the despised oral traditions of the lower classes.[81] Nor can contemporary accounts of a peasantry possessed, through the 'hedge schools', of an intimate familiarity with the Latin and Greek classics be taken at face value.[82] At the same time the teacher, literate, bilingual, geographically mobile, was a key figure, permitting the transmission down the social scale of a variety of elements—fragments of the high culture of the vanished Gaelic order, snatches of classical erudition, borrowings from the oral and printed culture of anglophone Ireland—in ways that are only now beginning to be unravelled.[83]

Most important of all, as intermediaries between élite and popular culture, there were the Catholic clergy. The Catholic church of the eighteenth century retained some pockets of aristocratic privilege. Between 1711 and 1791, for example, members of the prestigious Butler family provided three successive archbishops of Cashel as well as a bishop of Cork. By this time, however, the great majority of both higher and lower clergy were drawn from more humble backgrounds: sons of farmers, artisans, and traders. The gradual but increasing progress of ecclesiastical reform had ensured that even the least well qualified of the parochial clergy were literate and possessed of some degree of both theological and classical training. At the same time they had not entirely lost contact with the world from which they had been drawn. Edmund O'Doran, bishop of Down and Connor, seemed to an Englishwoman who met him in 1758 'the quintessence of an Irish brogueneer'. There is even a suggestion, based on his letters, that he was more at home in Irish than in English.[84] Nor had a clerical training divorced these men entirely from the beliefs and rituals of popular religion. Bishop Nicholas Sweetman of Ferns found it necessary in 1771 to forbid his clergy 'to read exorcisms or gospels over the already too ignorant, and by such ecclesiastics, too much deluded people, or act the fairy doctor in any shape', a prohibition that included 'all those who bless water to sprinkle sick persons, cattle, [and] fields with'.[85] In other cases priests continued up to the end of the eighteenth century or later to lend the sanction of their presence to the annual ceremonies performed at holy wells, or to such customs as the lighting of the mid-summer bonfire on St John's eve (23 June).[86] The parish clergy also took an active part in the social lives of their congregations. In particular, they presided as honoured guests at the celebrations that followed weddings and christenings, and dined regularly in private houses after the 'stations' held to facilitate annual confession and communion.[87]

IV

This interaction between élite and popular cultures did not take place in a political or social vacuum. The patronage of popular sports and entertainments practised by men of property presumably played some part in reinforcing vertical ties of deference and clientage. In certain cases, indeed, this was clearly the intention. Conscious intent is most immediately evident in the great civic festivals that were a major part of the culture of urban Ireland in the late seventeenth and eighteenth centuries. The accession of a new monarch and its subsequent anniversaries, royal birthdays, military victories, and similar occasions were marked by elaborate displays of ritual: solemn processions in which leading office holders and citizens marched, accompanied by a military guard, bonfires, fireworks, the ringing of bells, volleys of cannon, and small-arms fire.[88] All this, of course, was spectacle calculated to impress and entertain the populace. Their enthusiastic participation was further ensured by the distribution of free drink, organised in a manner designed to maximise the image of unstinted liberality. When the duke of Ormond made his first entry into Dublin as lord lieutenant in 1665, a conduit was set up in the corn market 'whence wine ran in abundance'. The entry of a later lord lieutenant in 1711 was similarly marked by 'ringing of bells, illumina- tions, wine running in the streets, and all imaginable demonstrations of joy'.[89] By the mid-eighteenth century the arrangements had become more elaborate. On the anniversary of George II's birthday in 1733 the lord lieutenant entertained leading gentry at 'a most magnificent repast, placed in a surprising manner round a fountain in the council chamber, which flowed with wine all the night, from whence several hogsheads of wine were also set a running to the common people, who crowded below to see the illuminations and other curious devices contrived upon the occasion'.[90] At the celebrations of George II's birthday in 1745 several statues were set up at the entrance to the supper room at the Castle, which

> poured a perpetual flow of the choicest wines of all sorts into nick basins
> properly placed to receive them, from whence the liquor was conveyed into
> the lower Castle Yard, where it played off in several fountains of wine during
> the whole of the entertainment, to give the populace an opportunity to drink
> his majesty's health and long life and confusion to his enemies.[91]

Dublin was of course both the kingdom's capital and by far its largest urban centre. Elsewhere civic ritual, and the official largesse that accompanied it, were inevitably less elaborate. But the spirit remained the same. In Killarney the official proclamation of the accession of George I in August 1714 was marked by a bonfire and the firing of vollies, after which the local gentry set up a table for themselves by the bonfire, 'set with bottles and glasses to drink his majesty's health', while providing 'barrels of beer for the soldiers and inferior company'. In Derry the civic authorities celebrated the end of the public quarrel between the king and the prince of Wales in 1720 by inviting 'all estates of men, women, and children in the town (and very numerous they are) to a splendid entertainment of sweetmeats at the Guildhall'. At Carrickfergus in County Antrim a few years later, the governor celebrated the anniversary of the Gunpowder Plot by giving 'to the footsoldiers an hogshead, and to the dragoons a barrel of excellent punch, and the mob as much strong malt liquor as they could make away with'.[92]

These public festivals had their parallels in the private sphere, where land-owners and other men of property employed a similar combination of theatrical representation and calculated display of benevolence to cement the bonds that linked them to their tenants and other dependants. When the eldest son of Dudley Cosby of Queen's County returned in 1724 after three years at the University of Leiden, he was met at the county boundary 'by several gentlemen, friends, and tenants, and garlands and long dancers, and my father invited them all home to dine with him and gave drink and money to the common people and dancers'. When Cosby senior died five years later, his funeral was equally elaborate: 'every creature there that came that had the least tolerable appearance had scarves and gloves, 100 poor were served at the door with bread and ale, and great quantities of victuals of all sorts within, with plenty of wine'.[93] In County Monaghan in 1773 Lord Dartry celebrated his son's fifteenth birthday 'in a very hospitable and princely manner, 150 poor people to dinner, a most magnificent bonfire, a grand dinner and supper, a brilliant ball, and . . . very elegant fireworks'. Twenty children from the school maintained by Lady Dartry attended in their new uniforms, while '160 workmen of several kinds made a solemn procession round the bonfire, with each the instruments of his employment on his shoul-der'.[94]

In addition to such festivals—the domestic equivalent of the royal birthdays, weddings, and anniversaries celebrated by government—there were other occasions for the entertainment of dependants. Elections are generally analysed in terms of the control that a system of open voting allowed landlords to exercise over their tenantry. In practice, however, the exercise of economic power was masked by a facade of reciprocity, as voters dined and drank in an atmosphere of carnivalesque festivity. In County Kerry in 1743 the losing candidate provided '4 tuns of wine, 2 ditto ale, 2 ditto cider, 2 ditto beer, 40 sheep, 20 bullocks, 60 hams, 40 pigs, a hogshead of shrub, 600 fowls, venison, veal, etc.'—all for an electorate of only 300. In the borough of Kinsale in County Cork Agmondisham Vesey in 1765 paid some £645 to four publicans, along with £5 13s. 9d. for a fiddler and £14 9s. 'for beer to the populace'.[95] A less obvious but also important occasion for gentry-sponsored entertainment was provided by the militia. Service in this force, where tenants and other dependants enrolled under the command of their landlord or patron, was in itself an expression of hierarchical social ties. Officers, for their part, were expected to reciprocate by providing regular entertainments for the men under their command. A captain in County Down was severely criticised for his reluctance to pay 6d. rather than 4d. per head to provide with a dinner the company he had raised during the 1745 emergency.[96]

Nor was it only the owners of land who softened economic reality by such means. Others too recognised the value of a well-timed display of sociability and goodwill. When a large new windmill was completed for a Mr Fagan of Mullingar in 1736, he celebrated by inviting the clergy, gentry, merchants, and traders of the town to 'a most elegant entertainment'. After a series of toasts 'two boxes or chests of lemons and oranges, with the just proportion of spirits, etc., were thrown to the millstones . . . [and] immediately ground down to punch through a conduit prepared, which conveyed the liquor into a cistern without side for the use of the populace, who also drank the aforesaid healths with acclamations of joy'.[97] When the new spire of St Patrick's cathedral, Dublin, was completed in 1750, the dean and chapter arranged 'a very plentiful entertainment', at which 'the high table was laid on the top of the spire for such of the workmen and their friends as were entitled there'.[98] Fifteen years later, Hugh Faulkner of Wellbrook in County Tyrone recorded the completion of a weir and mill: 'From eight to nine o'clock we drank whiskey, and from nine to near eleven fought, yet by my management no blood drawn, but several shirts and waistcoats torn'. In all, the construction of the weir had taken '110 men and 20 horses and 15 gallons of whiskey'.[99]

Displays of this kind, whether organised by central or local government, by landowners or by other men of property, had a clear social function. The sponsored festivities rewarded industry, loyalty, and deference, while projecting a general image of benignity and generosity. They thus offered a practical reinforcement of the contemporary ideology of paternalism and deference as the proper guiding principles in social relations. It is important that this should not be idealised. The reciprocity so expressed was a relationship between unequal obligations. The solemn processions that marked state occasions in the larger towns were, among other things, a dramatised representation of a hierarchical social and political order. The same message was conveyed in a local context by the procession of Lord Dartry's workmen, 'with each the instruments of his employment on his shoulder'. Nor were social distinctions forgotten when display gave way to festivity. At the 1714 celebrations in Killarney, the christening of Fagan's mill in Mullingar, and a host of similar occasions there remained a clear division between the quality feasting at their table and the people awaiting the distribution of cheaper forms of liquor. At the same time all these occasions reflect a recognition, however vaguely formulated, that social order did not depend on coercion alone. There was also the necessity of maintaining a level of consensus, goodwill, and mutual accommodation.

Perhaps the clearest demonstration of such a recognition is in the acceptance of occasions of ritualised inversion: points at which the normal constraints of deference were temporarily lifted, permitting the discharge, through forms of licensed aggression, of the tensions and frustrations that inevitably accumulated in a hierarchical and authoritarian society. Such occasions were built into the popular culture of many pre-industrialised societies: the carnivals of southern Europe, with their motif of the world turned upside down, the Shrove Tuesday riots of London apprentices, the aggressive demand for hospitality associated in some regions with a custom like Christmas mumming.[100] It is in this context, for example, that one can best understand the custom observed in Cork city on the day of the installation each year of a new mayor, when boys and young men pelted the official procession and well-dressed passers-by with flour and bran.[101] In Dublin Castle it was the practice, after the customary dinner to mark the anniversary of the rebellion of 1641, to throw open the doors and let in the crowd (according to one account, 'the ladies of the town') to carry off the remains of the food: a custom that neatly combined the themes of licensed plunder and a festive occasion shared in, through official generosity, by all ranks.[102]

Such an analysis, however, can be taken only so far. The greater the potential importance one attaches to such displays of official and private benevolence, the more necessary it becomes to note that many of the occasions involved were fully open to only a section of the population. In the case of two important occasions for the conspicuous display of reciprocity and vertical attachments—election-eering and service in the militia—Catholics were excluded by law up to 1793 from taking any part. Catholic farmers, labourers, and tradesmen may have been happy enough to add their cheers (from throats lubricated by free drink) for the birthday of a landlord's son or the state entry of a lord lieutenant into Dublin. They are likely to have been less enthusiastic about other public occasions for festivity: the anniversary of the accession of George I, sundry military victories over France and Spain, not to mention the anniversaries of the Gunpowder Plot or the providential discovery of the supposed Dublin conspiracy of October 1641. And indeed in 1688 soldiers in James II's catholicised army broke up the traditional celebrations both on 23 October and on 5 November.[103] If a consideration of upper-class patronage of popular amusements and festivities offers a new perspective on the maintenance of social order during the eighteenth century, it also reveals the extent to which the fault lines along which that order was to fracture in the 1790s had been visible long before.

V

Nevertheless, it remains clear that the crisis of the 1790s marked the end of an era in relations between élite and popular cultures. Tom Bartlett has shown how, as early as 1793, the delicate framework of reciprocity and tacit understanding that had up to then governed both the conduct of popular protest and its management by the authorities was irreversibly undermined by new forms of sectarian and political conflict.[104] The same tensions led both government and individual members of the ruling élite to look with new suspicion at the amusements and cultural traditions of the common people. In this case, moreover, the social distance born of bitter political alienation was reinforced by changes taking place in the culture of both rulers and ruled.

The authorities had always imposed some restraints on popular amusements. Under Queen Anne and George I, for example, there had been attempts to prevent gatherings at some of the more important Catholic pilgrimage sites.[105] Later in the century there were sporadic efforts to prevent hurling and other sports on Sundays.[106] An attempt by the sheriff of Dublin in 1789 to prevent bull-baiting on humanitarian grounds had led to a celebrated court case.[107] In the 1790s, however, political crises bred a new suspicion of large popular assemblies, both as occasions of disorder in themselves and as a possible cover for subversive activities. Thus the programme of 'pacification' conducted by the military authorities during the years 1796–8 included the suppression of gatherings for football and other sports.[108] Hostility to popular recreations continued in the tense years following the rebellion of 1798. In March 1805 the under-secretary at Dublin Castle regarded news of a series of meetings to play football in County Meath as 'not at all pleasant. . . ; there is much reason to suspect that there is some mischievous design at bottom'. The gatherings were duly suppressed, despite the protests of those involved 'that they were not doing any harm'. In the same month a magistrate in Dublin dispersed a gathering of nearly 1,000 people assembled to play football and watch a wrestling match at Stoneybatter near the Circular Road. As late as 1814 an attempt by some of the inhabitants of Maghera, Co. Londonderry, to revive the custom, abandoned in 1798, of erecting a maypole was promptly forbidden by a local magistrate.[109]

The spectre of organised, conspiratorial disaffection receded somewhat after 1815. But the wider problem of public order remained acute. Continued high levels of agrarian crime and political unrest led to the formation of the county constabulary in 1822 and of the Irish constabulary in 1836. One result of these moves towards more systematic policing was that the restriction and regimentation of popular amusements, commenced as an emergency measure during the French wars, were continued on an increasingly systematic basis. By the 1830s the designated duties of the constabulary included the suppression of bear-baiting and cock-fighting, the detention of beggars and loiterers, and the prevention of sabbath-breaking amusements. Even where popular festivals were not suppressed, the routine attendance in force of armed constables at fairs, patterns, and horse-races must have done a great deal to inhibit behaviour at these traditional occasions for sport and sociability. In particular, close regulation by the constabulary was by the late 1830s credited with having put an end to the violent clashes between rival factions that had long been part of the explosive vitality of Irish public gatherings.[110]

Nor was it only official attitudes towards popular amusements that were affected in this way. For individual members of the aristocracy and gentry, the confidence that had made possible a relaxed benevolence towards local festive custom was gone forever. Edward Bunting, writing in 1840, attributed the final collapse of support for the music of the harpist to the changes which political and social polarisation had brought to the self-image and manners of the gentry: 'ever since the commencement of the political disputes which have embroiled the latter end of the last, and all that has yet elapsed of the present century, our nobility and gentry have been gradually conforming again to the English model'.[111] The change produced by a new political climate was vividly evident in an incident in Balla, Co. Mayo, in 1842, when a party of May boys came to the house of a Captain Fitzmaurice asking for money for drink. They were dressed in white shirts, with several carrying swords and one—a 'fool or merry man'—equipped with a bladder tied to a pole. Their visit was clearly a burlesque equivalent of the ceremonial procession staged by the journeymen holland weavers in County Armagh almost exactly a century before. On this occasion, however, Fitzmaurice reacted by attempting to seize the swords carried by some of the party as illegal weapons, and the occasion degenerated into an ill-tempered scuffle, followed in due course by prosecutions in the local court.[112]

At the same time it would be a mistake to argue that the breakdown of political relationships was the sole reason for the collapse of gentry support for popular recreations and cultural forms. An increasing separation of élite and popular culture was after all a development seen throughout early modern Europe. The timing and speed of the process varied. In the most economically developed regions, notably in England and France, the withdrawal of the upper classes from customs and recreations which they had formerly shared with those below them was already well advanced by the early seventeenth century. In Russia, on the other hand, it had not been wholly completed even by 1800.[113] Peripheral regions also lagged behind. In Wales, for example, the decisive change in the culture and manners of the gentry came only in the last decades of the seventeenth century, in highland Scotland only after 1700.[114] In Ireland too the rough, unsophisticated manners so often commented on by early Georgian visitors were modified as the century progressed, a process that can be attributed partly to the growth of landed and commercial wealth and partly to the penetration of a provincial society by metropolitan standards of taste and refinement. Duels and heavy drinking, though still more common than in England, were alike reported to have much declined. The proliferation of town houses and country mansions, and the development of a sophisticated Irish tradition of plaster work, glass-making, and other decorative arts, all testified to the dissemination of a new concept of gentility.[115] Where observers in the early eighteenth century had bewailed the lack of a reading public, as many copies of the *Encyclopaedia* were now being sold in Dublin as in London.[116] Against this background it is easy to see how, even without the influence of growing religious and social conflict, the Irish gentry and aristocracy should have begun to find the rough and tumble of participation in the sports and customs of the lower classes increasingly less attractive.

It was not only among the élite, of course, that the late eighteenth and early nineteenth centuries saw a decline in participation in the culture of the lower classes. A similar withdrawal may be seen among the Catholic clergy. By the early nineteenth century the Catholic church was rapidly shedding the self-effacing posture of a semi-legal establishment. Its priests were now prominent local figures, accorded at least a grudging respect by the civil establishment as spokesmen for their congregations. 'The humility or the obscurity of former times', it was claimed in 1834, 'has entirely disappeared. . . . The country priest now copes with the country squire, keeps sporting dogs, controls elections, presides at political clubs, and sits cheek by jowl at public dinners and public assemblies with peers of the land and members of parliament'. With enhanced prestige went a more fastidious attitude to popular beliefs and practices. The priests, it was noted as early as 1819, 'whom circumstances have rendered more objects of consideration', were on that account 'more sensitive to ridicule'. Already by the beginning of the nineteenth century priests were noticeably less willing to lend the sanction of their presence to gatherings at holy wells, the use of supposed relics for magical purposes, or celebrations of the great annual festivals. Over the next two or three decades withdrawal gave way to direct attack. Wakes, keening over the bodies of the dead, patterns and other quasi-religious pilgrimages, the observances on May eve, St John's day, and other festivals—all came under interdict. A reduced tolerance of popular beliefs and rituals was further encouraged by the progress of church reform. Between the 1770s and the 1840s the parochial clergy became better educated, more intensively trained, and more firmly under the control of bishops who were themselves increasingly responsive to the authority of Rome. The tightening of ecclesiastical discipline also reduced social intercourse between clergy and people. Priests were now forbidden to attend wedding banquets, station dinners at the houses of parishioners, horse- races, theatres, public houses, or other places of amusement. The gradual adoption of a distinctive clerical dress provided the outward symbol, as well as being an effective guarantor, of the new social distance between the pastor and his flock.[117]

From one point of view this withdrawal of the Catholic clergy from their former participation in aspects of popular custom and sociability can be seen as removing what had been probably the most important group of mediators between the culture of the common people and that of the social élite. From another perspective, however, the new outlook of the priests reflected changes taking place within the popular culture from whose upper levels they were themselves predominantly drawn. These changes can be attributed to a range of influences: the greater openness to outside influences made possible by improved communications and closer integration with Britain's economic system, the service of tens of thousands of Irishmen in the army and navy during the French wars, the impact of commercialisation on traditional social relationships and on established patterns of work and leisure, the rising living standards observable, even in the supposedly crisis-ridden 1830s and 1840s, among better-off sections of the rural population.[118] Perhaps the most conspicuous early indication of the growth of new attitudes and aspirations was the explosion of demand for elementary education observable from the last two decades of the eighteenth century, and the consequent sharp increase in literacy.[119] This in turn contributed heavily to the beginnings of what was to be a rapid decline in the use of the Irish language.[120] By the 1830s the traditional magical beliefs and rituals of the countryside were also reported to be in decline: the people, in the words of the antiquary John O'Donovan, were getting 'too sensible' to believe in holy wells or fairies.[121] Changing mentalities were also reflected in the extraordinarily rapid pace of politicisation in the 1820s as well as in the increased willingness of dissatisfied individuals to seek an improvement in their condition through emigration.[122]

In the short term the result of all this was to produce a growing division within popular culture itself. On one side there was the culture of the farming population and the urban artisanate: anglicised, politicised, and commercialised. On the other there remained the mental and social world of the rural poor: Gaelic, inward-looking, localised, and subsistence-oriented.[123] In the long term this latter world was to be swept away, as the famine of 1845–50, and the social and demographic changes that followed, brutally cut back the number of labourers, cottiers, and smallholders, and cleared the way for the inculcation into those who survived of new beliefs, values, and standards of behaviour. In the years after the famine, in fact, a new popular culture was taking shape.[124] It was a culture set off from its predecessor not only in being literate, anglicised, and politically aware, but also in its vertical relationships. If the continued political domination of middle-class townsmen and Catholic priests indicates that there was still a need for mediators of a sort, their role was now as political brokers rather than as translators of word or thought. If models of behaviour or consumption still came partly from above, their source was now the urban bourgeoisie. Against such a background there was to be increasingly little place for the patronage from lord and gentleman that had been so important a part of the popular culture of an earlier era.

NOTES

1 Daniel Corkery, *The hidden Ireland: a study of Gaelic Munster in the eighteenth century* (Dublin, 1967), pp. 9, 40–1, 65.

2 L.M. Cullen, 'The hidden Ireland: reassessment of a concept' in *Studia Hib.*, no. 9 (1969). In a later work Cullen has offered some brief but valuable comments on cultural interaction between different social levels: see *The emergence of modern Ireland, 1600–1900* (London, 1981), pp. 98–108, 244–9.

3 See in particular David Dickson, *New foundations: Ireland, 1660–1800* (Dublin, 1987), chap. 4.

4 Brian Boydell, 'Music,1700–1850' in T.W. Moody and W.E. Vaughan (ed.), *A new history of Ireland*, vol. iv: *eighteenth-century Ireland* (Oxford, 1986), pp. 546–7, 558–61; Diarmaid Ó Catháin, 'Dermot O'Connor, translator of Keating' in *Eighteenth-Century Ireland*, ii (1987), pp. 86–7. See also Declan Kiberd, 'Irish literature and Irish history' in R.F. Foster (ed.), *The Oxford illustrated history of Ireland* (Oxford, 1989), pp. 297–305.

5 Tom Dunne, 'Popular ballads, revolutionary rhetoric, and politicisation' in Hugh Gough and David Dickson (ed.), *Ireland and the French revolution* (Dublin, 1990), p. 143.

6 Peter Burke, *Popular culture in early modern Europe* (London, 1978).

7 Ibid., p. 272; J.H. Billington, *The icon and the axe: an interpretive history of Russian culture* (London, 1966), pp. 208–10, 219; Robert Muchembled, *Popular culture and élite culture in France, 1400–1750* (Baton Rouge and London, 1985), p. 42.

8 Peter Burke, *The historical anthropology of early modern Italy: essays on perception and communication* (Cambridge, 1987), chap. 6.

9 D.B. Quinn, *The Elizabethans and the Irish* (Ithaca, 1966); Nicholas Canny, *The Elizabethan conquest of Ireland: a pattern established, 1565–76* (Hassocks, 1976), pp. 160–3.

10 J.J. Hogan, *The English language in Ireland* (Dublin, 1927), pp. 34–6.

11 Nicholas Canny, *The upstart earl: a study of the social and mental world of Richard Boyle, first earl of Cork, 1566–1643* (Cambridge, 1982), pp. 126–8.

12 For a brief review, see Canny, 'Protestants, planters, and apartheid in early modern Ireland' in *I.H.S.*, xxv, no. 98 (November 1986), pp. 105–15.

13 William Petty, *The political anatomy of Ireland* (London, 1691), p. 196; Sir Henry Piers, *A chorographical description of the county of Westmeath, written A.D. 1682* (Dublin, 1786), pp. 108–9.

14 Piers, *Westmeath*, p. 108.

15 N.J.A. Williams (ed.), *Páirlimint Cloinne Tomáis* (Dublin, 1981), pp. 97–8, 101, 105, 109–10, 165.

16 L.M. Cullen, *An economic history of Ireland since 1660* (London, 1972), p. 18.

17 For patterns of landholding in the later seventeenth century, see J.H. Andrews, 'Land and people c.1685' in T.W. Moody, F.X. Martin, and F.J. Byrne (ed.), *A new history of Ireland*, vol. iii: *early modern Ireland, 1534–1691* (Oxford, 1976), pp. 464–6.

18 John Bossy, 'The Counter-reformation and the people of Catholic Ireland, 1596–1641' in T.D. Williams (ed.), *Historical Studies*, viii (Dublin, 1971).

19 This change is difficult to date precisely. David Dickson argues that 'the fundamentals of Christian marriage as defined by the Catholic church were being widely observed by 1640, if perhaps not so obviously so in 1600': 'No Scythians here: women and marriage' in Margaret MacCurtain and Mary O'Dowd (ed.), *Women in early modern Ireland* (Edinburgh, 1991), p. 225. On the other hand, Corish draws attention to continued evidence of 'gross sexual habits' in the 1670s and 1680s: *The Catholic community in the seventeenth and eighteenth centuries* (Dublin, 1981), p. 69.

20 T.C. Barnard, 'Planters and policies in Cromwellian Ireland' in *Past & Present*, no. 61 (November 1973), pp. 39–44.

21 Boyle to Orrery, 18 March 1679 (National Archives, Dublin, Wyche Papers 1/1/30); Ormond to Wyche, 20 November 1678, 7 March 1679 (H.M.C., *Leyborn-Popham MSS* (1899), pp. 242–4).

22 T.C.D., MS 883/1, pp. 255–6.

23 S.J. Connolly, *Religion, law, and power: the making of Protestant Ireland* (Oxford, 1992), chap. 6.

24 [Sir Francis Brewster], *A discourse concerning Ireland and the different interests thereof* (London, 1698), pp. 18–20.

25 *Stat. Ire.*, 6 Anne, c. xi.

26 John Brady (ed.), 'Remedies proposed for the Church of Ireland (1697)' in *Archiv. Hib.*, xxii (1959), pp. 163, 168; William King, archbishop of Dublin, to St George Ashe, bishop of Clogher, 24 February [*recte* March] 1711 (T.C.D., MS 2531, p. 326). The objections to Richardson's scheme may have been, as King believed, a cover for unwillingness to incur trouble and expense, but there seems to be no reason to question Dopping's sincerity.

27 'On barbarous denominations in Ireland', in Herbert Davis (ed.), *The prose works of Jonathan Swift* (14 vols, Oxford, 1939–68), iv, 280–4.

28 'Autobiography of Pole Cosby of Stradbally, Queen's County, 1703–37' in *Kildare Arch. Hist. Soc. Jn.*, v (1906–8), pp. 97–8.

29 Samuel Madden, *Reflections and resolutions proper for the gentlemen of Ireland* (Dublin, 1738), pp. 107–8.

30 David Hayton, 'Anglo-Irish attitudes: changing perceptions of national identity among the Protestant ascendancy in Ireland, *c.*1690–1750' in *Studies in Eighteenth-Century Culture*, xvii (1987), p. 151.

31 W.S. Clark, *The early Irish stage: the beginnings to 1720* (Oxford, 1955), pp. 170–4; J.Th. Leerssen, *Mere Irish and fíor-ghael: studies in the idea of Irish nationality, its development and literary expression prior to the nineteenth century* (Amsterdam and Philadelphia, 1986), pp. 378–9.

32 *Dublin Intelligence*, 12 January 1723. See Ó Catháin, 'Dermot O'Connor'.

33 J.R. Hill, 'Popery and Protestantism, civil and religious liberty: the disputed lessons of Irish history, 1691–1812' in *Past & Present*, no. 118 (February 1988), pp. 102–4.

34 Boydell, 'Music', p. 603; Donal O'Sullivan, *Carolan: the life, times, and music of an Irish harper* (2 vols, London, 1958), i, 125–6.

35 Leerssen, *Mere Irish and fíor-ghael*, p. 383.

36 Clare O'Halloran, 'Irish recreations of the Gaelic past: the challenge of MacPherson's Ossian' in *Past & Present*, no. 124 (August 1989), pp. 69–95.

37 Leerssen, *Mere Irish and fíor-ghael*, pp. 400–33; Brian Ó Cuív, 'Irish language and literature, 1691–1841' in Moody and Vaughan (ed.), *New history of Ireland*, iv, 416–17.

38 Boydell, 'Music', pp. 603–4.

39 Burke, *Popular culture*, chap. 1.

40 Norman Vance, 'Celts, Carthaginians, and constitutions: Anglo-Irish literary relations,1780–1820' in *I.H.S.*, xxii, no. 87 (March 1981), pp. 216–38. For the parallel process among Ulster Presbyterians, see A.T.Q. Stewart, 'The harp new-strung: nationalism, culture, and the United Irishmen' in Oliver MacDonagh and W.F. Mandle (ed.), *Ireland and Irish Australia* (London, 1986), pp. 175–94.

41 David Cairns and Shaun Richards, *Writing Ireland: colonialism, nationalism, and culture* (Manchester, 1988), pp. 25–31, 51–7; Thomas Flanagan, 'Nationalism:the literary tradition' in T.E. Hachey and L.J. McCaffrey (ed.), *Perspectives on Irish nationalism* (Lexington, 1989), pp. 61–78.

42 Burke, *Popular culture*, chap. 2, 'Unity and variety in popular culture'.

43 F.G. James, 'The active Irish peers in the early eighteenth century' in *Jn. Brit. Studies*, xviii, no. 2 (1979), pp. 59–60; J.L. McCracken, 'Central and local administration in Ireland under George II' (Ph.D. thesis, Queen's University, Belfast, 1948), p. 110.

44 J.G. Simms, *The Williamite confiscation in Ireland, 1690–1703* (London, 1956), p. 193.

45 Abercorn to —, 23 March 1714 (P.R.O.N.I., T.2541/1K/1/14).

46 Ó Cuív, 'Language and literature in Irish', pp. 401–2, 414; Oliver MacDonagh, *The hereditary bondsman: Daniel O'Connell, 1775–1829* (London, 1988), pp. 9–10.

47 T.C.D., MS 883/1, pp. 129–30, 16–17.

48 For example, Countess of Cork and Orrery (ed.), *The Orrery papers* (2 vols, London, 1903), i, 157, 215, 319: Lady Llanover (ed.), *The autobiography and correspondence of Mary Granville, Mrs Delaney*, ser. 1 (3 vols, London, 1861), i, 351; Bonamy Dobrée (ed.), *The letters of Philip Dormer Stanhope, 4th earl of Chesterfield* (6 vols, London, 1932), iii, 765–6, 771–2, 924, 945. For upper-class drinking habits, see Elizabeth Malcolm, '*Ireland sober, Ireland free*': *drink and temperance in nineteenth-century Ireland* (Dublin, 1986), pp. 29–49.

49 King to John Pooley, bishop of Cloyne, 1 June 1701 (T.C.D., MS 750/2/2, p. 158).

50 T.C. Barnard, 'Crises of identity among Irish Protestants, 1641–1685' in *Past & Present*, no. 127 (May 1990), p. 47.

51 David Dickson, 'Middlemen' in Thomas Bartlett and D.W. Hayton (ed.), *Penal era and golden age: essays in Irish history, 1690–1800* (Belfast, 1979).

52 Garret FitzGerald, 'Estimates for baronies of minimum level of Irish-speaking amongst successive decennial cohorts: 1771–81 to 1861–71' *R.I.A. Proc.*, C, lxxxiv (1984), p. 127.

53 David Dickson, 'Property and social structure in eighteenth-century south Munster' in L.M. Cullen and F. Furet (ed.), *Ireland and France, 17th–20th centuries: towards a comparative study of rural history* (Paris, 1980), pp. 135–8.

54 For the existence of May poles, bull-baiting, and other sports of English origin, not just in Ulster but in the towns of southern Ireland, see S.J. Connolly, 'Popular culture in pre-famine Ireland' in C.J. Byrne and Margaret Harry (ed.), *Talamh an eisc: Canadian and Irish essays* (Halifax, Nova Scotia, 1986), pp. 14–16.

55 John Dunton, *The life and errors of John Dunton* (2 vols, London, 1818), ii, 563.

56 *The tricks of the town laid open*, printed in Patrick Fagan, *The second city: portrait of Dublin, 1700–1760* (Dublin, 1986), pp. 68–70. An 'abigail' was a lady's maid.

57 Clark, *Early Irish stage*, pp. 144–6.

58 Fagan, *Second city*, pp. 64–6.

59 Art Ó Maolfabhail, *Caman: two thousand years of hurling in Ireland* (Dundalk, 1973), pp. viii, 23–4, 31, 49–51, 100–12.

60 *Pue's Occurrences*, 15–19 July, 9–12, 23–6 August 1746.

61 Ó Maolfabhail, *Caman*, pp. 138, 140.

62 Ibid., pp. 137–40.

63 'Autobiography of Pole Cosby', p. 179.

64 L.P. Ó Caithnia, *Scéal na hiomána: ó thosach ama go 1884* (Dublin, 1980), pp. 27–9.

65 *Dublin Intelligence*, 17 May 1731; Brian Fitzgerald (ed.), *Correspondence of Emily, duchess of Leinster, 1731–1814* (3 vols, Dublin, 1949–57), i, 61.

66 Rev. Toby Caulfield to Kean O'Hara, 4 May 1713 (P.R.O.N.I., T.2812/9/41).

67 *Dublin Daily Advertiser*, 7 May 1737; *Autobiog. and corr. of Mrs Delany*, i, 369, 373; Roger McHugh (ed.), *Carlow in '98: the autobiography of William Farrell of Carlow* (Dublin, 1949), p. 23.

68 *Autobiog. and corr. of Mrs Delaney*, i , 370.

69 O'Sullivan, *Carolan*, i, 43–5.

70 *Autobiog. and corr. of Mrs Delaney*, ii, 368, 559, 580–1.

71 O'Sullivan, *Carolan*, ii, 145–6. According to another account, O'Neill and other harpers performed for 'some Protestant families', but their main patrons were 'old Irish families who had lost their titles or were reduced more or less in their estates': Edward Bunting, *The ancient music of Ireland* (Dublin, 1840), p. 61.

72 Rev. J. Burrows, Diary of a tour in Ireland, 1773 (P.R.O.N.I., T.3551).

73 O'Sullivan, *Carolan*, ii, 150–2; Bunting, *Ancient music*, p. 60.

74 *Autobiog. and corr. of Mrs Delaney*, ii, 365. *Cf.* the complaints regarding the impoverishment of poor families as a result of excessive tea-drinking in *Dublin Daily Post*, 4 June 1739.

75 'The Rosses, County Donegal, in 1753–1754' in *Ulster Folklife*, xix (1973), pp. 22–3.

76 Arthur Young, *A tour in Ireland, 1776–1779*, ed. A.W. Hutton (2 vols, London, 1892), ii, 147.

77 Breandán Breathnach, 'The dancing master' in *Ceol*, iii (1970), p. 117.

78 O'Sullivan, *Carolan*, ii, 158.

79 See above, p. 9.

80 Cullen, *Emergence of modern Ireland*, pp. 102–6.

81 Dáithí Ó hÓgáin, 'Folklore and literature, 1700–1850' in Mary Daly and David Dickson (ed.), *The origins of popular literacy in Ireland: language change and educational development, 1700–1920* (Dublin, 1990), 1–3.

82 See S.J. Connolly, 'Translating history: Brian Friel and the Irish past' in Alan Peacock (ed.), *The achievement of Brian Friel* (Gerrards Cross, 1992).

83 Ó hÓgáin, 'Folklore and literature'; L.M. Cullen, 'Patrons, teachers, and literacy in Irish, 1700–1850', in Daly and Dickson (ed.), *Origins of popular literacy*.

84 *Autobiog. and corr. of Mrs Delany*, iii, 503; James O'Laverty, *An historical account of the diocese of Down and Connor, ancient and modern* (5 vols, Dublin, 1878–95), v, 546. For the social background of Catholic clergymen in general, see L.W. Brockliss and P. Ferte, 'Irish clerics in France in the seventeenth and eighteenth centuries: a statistical study' in *R.I.A. Proc.*, C, lxxxvii, no. 9 (1987), p. 542; S.J. Connolly, *Priests and people in pre-famine Ireland, 1780–1845* (Dublin, 1982), pp. 35–43.

85 W.H. Grattan Flood, 'The diocesan manuscripts of Ferns in the reign of Bishop Sweetman' in *Archiv. Hib.*, iii (1914), p. 117.

86 Connolly, *Priests and people*, pp. 112–13.

87 Ibid., pp. 66–7.

88 For example, see *Dublin Intelligence*, 29 April–11 May 1693, 15 July, 3 October 1708, 31 May 1715, 5 November 1726, 27–30 May 1727; *Dublin Gazette*, 6–10 February, 3–6 November 1711.

89 Thomas Carte, *History of the life of James, first duke of Ormonde* (6 vols, Oxford, 1851), iv, 225–6; *Dublin Gazette*, 3–7 July 1711.

90 *Dublin Gazette*, 30 October-3 November 1733.

91 *Faulkner's Dublin Journal*, 29 October–3 November 1745.

92 Richard Hedges to —, 23 August 1714 (M.A. Hickson, *Selections from old Kerry records, historical and genealogical*, ser. 2, London, 1874, p. 148); William Nicolson, bishop of Derry, to William Wake, archbishop of Canterbury, 3 May 1720 (Dublin Municipal Library, Pearse Street, Dublin, Gilbert MSS, 27, pp. 260–1); *Dublin Intelligence*, 9 November 1728.

93 'Autobiography of Pole Cosby', pp. 168, 181–2.

94 Rev. J. Burrows, Diary of a tour in Ireland, 1773 (P.R.O.N.I., T.3551, p. 90).

95 H.M.C., *Puleston MSS* (1898), p. 327; National Archives, Dublin, Sarsfield Vesey Papers, no. 54(d).

96 Charles Brett to Michael Ward, 4 June 1746 (P.R.O.N.I., D.2092/1/17/21).

97 *Dublin Daily Advertiser*, 27 December 1736.

98 *Esdall's News Letter*, 5 July 1750.

99 Hugh Faulkner to Samuel Faulkner, 12 May 1765 (P.R.O.N.I., Mic. 21/1).

100 Burke, *Popular culture*, chap. 7; G.M.Sider, 'Christmas mumming and the new year in outport Newfoundland' in *Past & Present*, no. 71 (May 1976), pp. 102–25.

101 W.R. Chetwood, *A tour through Ireland in several entertaining letters* . . . (Dublin, 1748), pp. 56–7; Orrery to Swift, October 1735 (*Orrery papers*, i, 137–8).

102 *Autobiog. and corr. of Mrs Delaney*, ii, 481; John Ryder to Sir Dudley Ryder, 25 October [1743] (P.R.O.N.I., T.3228/1/10).

103 Patrick Melvin (ed.), 'Sir Paul Rycaut's memoranda and letters from Ireland, 1686–1687' in *Anal. Hib.*, no. 27 (1972), p. 175; Melvin (ed.), 'Letters of Lord Longford and others on Irish affairs, 1689–1702', ibid., no. 32 (1985), p. 40.

104 Thomas Bartlett, 'An end to moral economy: the Irish militia disturbances of 1793' in C.H.E. Philpin (ed.), *Nationalism and popular protest in Ireland* (Cambridge, 1987), pp. 191–218.

105 Maureen Wall, *The penal laws, 1691–1760* (Dundalk, 1961), pp. 60–2.

106 Ó Maolfabhail, *Caman*, p. 140; Ó Caithnia, *Scéal na hiomána*, pp. 45–9.

107 Archibald Hamilton Rowan, *Autobiography of Archibald Hamilton Rowan, esq.* (Dublin, 1840), pp. 103–10.

108 Ó Caithnia, *Scéal na hiomána*, pp. 524–5.

109 A. Marsden to Rev. W.H. Irwine, 30 March 1805 (National Archives, Dublin, State of the Country papers, 1031/52); Irwine to Marsden, 1 April 1805 (ibid., 1031/53); Luke Brien to —, 10 March [1805] (ibid., 1031/16); W.S. Mason (ed.), *A statistical account or parochial survey of Ireland* (3 vols, Dublin, 1814–19), i, 593.

110 S.H. Palmer, *Police and protest in England and Ireland, 1780–1850* (Cambridge, 1988), pp. 322, 366–7, 406.

111 Bunting, *Ancient music*, p. 67.

112 W. Fitzmaurice to —, 2 May 1842; Petition of John Golding, 16 May 1842 (National Archives, Dublin, C.S.O.R.P., Outrage (1842), 21/10545).

113 Burke, *Popular culture*, pp. 270–81; Muchembled, *Popular culture*, chaps. 4–6; William Monter, *Ritual, myth, and magic in early modern Europe* (Brighton, 1983), chap. 7.

114 Prys Morgan, 'From a death to a view: the hunt for the Welsh past in the Romantic period' in Eric Hobsbawm and Terence Ranger (ed.), *The invention of tradition* (Cambridge, 1983), pp. 49–52; T.C. Smout, *A history of the Scottish people, 1560–1830* (London, 1972), pp. 265–71, 315–16, 322–8.

115 Anne Crookshank, 'The visual arts, 1740–1850' in Moody and Vaughan (ed.), *New history of Ireland*, iv, 499–519. For the change in manners, see Malcolm, *'Ireland sober, Ireland free'*, pp. 45–9; Young, *Tour*, ii, 152.

116 Nicholas Canny, 'Identity formation in Ireland: the emergence of the Anglo-Irish' in Canny and A. Pagden (ed.), *Colonial identity in the Atlantic world, 1500–1800* (Princeton, 1987), p. 209.

117 Connolly, *Priests and people*, pp. 58–74, 108–20, 135–74.

118 Joel Mokyr and Cormac Ó Gráda, 'Poor and getting poorer? Living standards in Ireland before the famine' in *Econ. Hist. Rev.*, xli, no. 2 (1988), pp. 216–22, 229–30.

119 M.E. Daly, 'The development of the national school system, 1831–40' in Art Cosgrove and Donal Macartney (ed.), *Studies in Irish history presented to R. Dudley Edwards* (Naas, 1979), pp. 150–63; J.R.R. Adams, *The printed word and the common man: popular culture in Ulster, 1700–1900* (Belfast, 1987), chaps. 1, 2, 6, 7.

120 FitzGerald, 'Estimates for baronies', pp. 126–8.

121 Connolly, *Priests and people*, pp. 107–8.

122 S.J. Connolly, 'Mass politics and sectarian conflict, 1823–30' in W.E. Vaughan (ed.), *A new history of Ireland*, vol. v: *Ireland under the union*, pt. 1, *1801–70* (Oxford, 1989), pp. 89–93; K.A. Miller, *Emigrants and exiles: Ireland and the Irish exodus to North America* (New York and Oxford, 1985), chap. 2.

123 Some of the evidence for this cultural polarisation is briefly discussed in Connolly, 'Popular culture in pre-famine Ireland', pp. 25–6.

124 For a brief review of the nature of social change in the decades after the famine, see R.V. Comerford, 'Ireland, 1850–70: post-famine and mid-Victorian' in Vaughan (ed.), *New history of Ireland*, v, pt. 1, 372–95.

2

Popular and Unpopular Religion:
A View from Early Modern Ireland

RAYMOND GILLESPIE

The study of 'popular religion' has long been embraced by historians with enthusiasm, but that enthusiasm has been matched by a failure to agree as to what the subject of their study should be. For some scholars the religious needs of the laity were met in the context of the official church, whose ideas spanned both the social élite and the lower ranks of society. The celebration of the mass and its associated devotions has been seen as the centre of lay piety in late medieval England, while after the Reformation the use of the prayer-book has been accepted as sufficient. Those who aspired to a more godly society derived comfort from orthodox puritan spirituality.[1] The alternative and indeed the dominant view among historians has been that popular religion had little in common with the ideas of orthodox religion and thus provides evidence of the division between élites and the lower social orders. The lower orders were perceived to exist in a religious world pervaded by superstition and folk beliefs, and the historians who sought to reconstruct this world drew heavily on early twentieth-century studies by folklorists which recorded esoteric beliefs from all parts of Britain and Ireland.[2] The outcome of this methodology has been a panorama of 'folk beliefs' concerning the supernatural world which did not reflect the official doctrines of Christianity and in many cases were directly opposed to it.[3]

Popular religion, it seems, almost by definition could not conform to the ideas of orthodox Christianity held by the clerical and lay élites in society. Thus for Jean Delumeau in his survey of early modern European Catholicism, the aim of the religious movements styled 'Reformation' and 'Counter-reformation' was 'to christianise the mass of people in the sixteenth, seventeenth, and eighteenth centuries', since 'on the eve of the Reformation the average Westerner was but superficially christianised'.[4] This process of christianisation was seen as the imposition of the religion of the clerical élite on the lay populace. In the case of Catholicism Carlo Ginzberg has used the evidence produced by the Inquisition to study popular ideas of cosmology and witchcraft and their suppression. Such popular beliefs, he has argued, were of considerable antiquity, but under the influence of the new power relationships of the Counter-reformation they had been theologised and consequently demonised and 'later deformed and then expurgated by the superimposition of the scheme of the educated classes'.[5]

This view of religion as a set of power relationships has considerable analytical force and plays a part in understanding how different types of religion worked in early modern Ireland. A process operated by which the élite of an institutional church, who had clearly formed intellectual preconceptions about the nature of belief which were articulated in theological systems, such as the decrees of the Council of Trent, attempted to superimpose these doctrinal positions on an indigenous set of lay ideas about the supernatural which the élite found strange. The decrees of the various Catholic synods in seventeenth-century Ireland required priests to hide sheela-na-gigs, prohibit invocations of the devil, prevent the gathering of 'magical' herbs, and stop the preparation of virility potions. Holy wells and other sites of devotion were also to be controlled.[6] The Franciscan Bernard Gray in the early sixteenth century provided holy water for the cure of cattle, telling those to whom he gave it 'to avoid those charms which some simple-minded people procure from old women and witches, [and] to recite immediately upon his return the Our Father, Hail Mary, and the Creed . . . , and then trusting in God's goodness, to sprinkle the cattle with holy water'.[7]

In more subtle ways too a process similar to Delumeau's christianisation seems to have been undertaken in seventeenth-century Ireland. The traditional lore of Ireland was reshaped by the clergy to remove any non-Christian elements. In Munster the secular priest Geoffrey Keating rewrote the early history of Ireland in his *Foras Feasa ar Éirinn*, making clear that the superhuman stories of the fianna were 'imaginative romances' invented 'for the sake of amusement', and that the fianna were not gods but merely bodyguards for the king.[8] Protestant churches attempted their own brand of christianisation. Presbyterian churches tried to detect those practising divination and issued edicts against sorcery and those who used charms to cure the sick.[9] The Church of Ireland clergy also condemned popular practices of dubious origins, such as astrology, and in the 1690s attempted to make its members into more orthodox Christians through pamphlets and organisations such as the societies for the reformation of manners.[10]

This understanding of popular religion as unorthodox and hence destined to be the victim of changing power relations in the early modern world must not be overstressed. The evidence from Europe of the attempt of both Protestants and Catholics to restructure popular beliefs along lines of doctrinal orthodoxy (for example, through the catechism) suggests that its success was at best problematic.[11] In addition, Ireland provides special problems for those who see power relations between the élite and the populace as central to religious life. Synods might legislate and individual clergy might campaign, but the reality was that the imposition of religiously orthodox systems of belief on most people in early modern Ireland was difficult. All commentators were agreed that the agents of control, the clergy, were in short supply in relation to the people and poorly equipped for their task, both in training and in terms of finance.[12] In the case of Catholicism the imposition of the decrees of the Council of Trent was made more difficult by the fact that it did not have the secular arm of the state to assist it. Furthermore, the main enforcer of power relationships in Catholic Europe, the Inquisition, was absent. Ireland was a long way from the centre of Catholic power in Rome.

I

It seems that to view religious practices and beliefs as a set of power relationships is inadequate for exploring the contemporary understanding of the supernatural world in early modern Ireland. One alternative is to examine religious ideas not from the perspective of the competing institutions but through the eyes of those who came in contact with those religious concepts and adapted them to their own experience and surroundings. In this sense the shaping of religious ideas is not the result of power relationships but the outcome of a dialogue between the doctrinal positions offered as coherent intellectual systems by the various churches on the one hand, and the religious needs of the inhabitants of Ireland on the other. This dialogue was constructed around a series of assumptions common to both sides of the confessional and social divides. All accepted, for example, that God existed, that He was accessible, and that the supernatural world of God, saints, angels, and demons interacted with the tangible world and affected its workings. These commonalities meant that the lines between élite and popular religious culture were often rather more blurred than might be expected. Ideas often associated with lay or popular culture featured in the clerical and élite world. An educated figure such as the Rev. John Keogh of Strokestown in County Roscommon was not only a Church of Ireland clergyman and a correspondent of the Dublin Philosophical Society who believed that all things could be explained rationally; he was also a firm believer that fairy darts were the cause of sudden death in cattle. He based his belief on scriptural texts, the reality of the supernatural world, and the flint arrowheads he had found in the region.[13] This concern with the reality of the supernatural world not only led to a firm popular belief in ghosts as messengers from that world but also prompted some Irish clergy to collect these stories and vouch for their veracity.[14]

What lay behind these expressions of religiosity common to both popular and élite religion was the assumption that God, who was holy and hence radically different from the mundane natural world, was nevertheless at work in that world.[15] This idea was described in the contemporary language of theology as providence. When the inhabitants of early modern Ireland observed the normal workings of their world, or more importantly the abnormal ones, they asked not how it worked but who made it work. Thus Roderick O'Flaherty, writing to William Molyneux in the 1680s about the mysterious Island of Hy Brassil, which according to tradition appeared off the Galway coast at irregular intervals only to disappear again, concluded that whether it was 'land kept hidden by the special providence of God as the terrestial paradise, or some sort of illusion of airy clouds appearing on the surface of the sea, or the craft of evil spirits, is more than our judgment can sound out'.[16]

Questions such as this about strange occurrences in the world often brought doctrinal responses from both clergy and educated laity interested in speculative theology. These were couched in the language of the university, underpinned by biblical commentary, and published in large printed volumes of limited circulation. For the vast majority of the laity the wonder itself was enough, providing evidence for God's working in the world and perhaps conveying a message interpreted through their own experience. Popular religion, both Protestant and Catholic, was a world of wonders. What was important was the source of power behind the wonder: a deceit of the devil or a proof of God. Each religious group laid claim to access to the holy and to the interpretation of wonders. In Catholicism, for example, the context of the wonder or miracle was important. According to the ecclesiastical authorities, if it occurred through a genuine relic used in an approved way, the power was divine. Thus in 1608 the Cistercian abbot of Holy Cross blessed the barren field of a Kilkenny farmer with water into which a relic of the True Cross had been dipped, whereas such actions by laymen were condemned by the Synod of Armagh in 1614.[17] From the Protestant point of view this sort of quasi-magical activity was not the work of God but of the devil. As the violently anti-Catholic pamphleteer Barnaby Rich put it in 1610, Ireland 'do no less abound with witches, and no marvel that it should be so, for the devil hath ever been most frequent and conversant amongst infidels, Turks, papists, and such others that do neither know the love of God'.[18]

The importance of wonders in shaping popular religiosity and the concern to establish their reality as manifestations of the holy can be seen most clearly in the issue of religious controversy. Such controversy was regarded as important in an age when confessional division made it necessary not only to know whether one was a Catholic or a Protestant but also to know why. For some clergy in Dublin this took the form of academic disputation between representatives of different denominations, the Church of Ireland side of the argument usually making its way into print with the intention of showing that Catholicism had been confuted. This sort of activity in the main left the Irish laity unmoved. Only one layman, Sir Christopher Sibthorpe, joined the most celebrated of these clerically dominated controversies.[19] Controversial works appear not to have sold well. When Bishop Bedell imported English controversial works in 1632, he failed to sell them and had to give them away.[20] However, when controversy centred around a more dramatic issue, such as the ability to command the unwelcome supernatural world through exorcism, the response was rather more dramatic. In early 1630 a girl said to be possessed by an evil spirit was brought to the Discalced Carmelite

Fr Paul Browne in Dublin. Browne was arrested and taken to Dublin Castle and the girl given to a Church of Ireland minister called Watson, 'who was regarded as a saint among his own people'. Watson brought her to St Werburgh's, but halfway through a sermon she began to attack those around her. Browne had to be summoned to carry out an exorcism. The exorcism worked and she was 'freed by signs that were evident to everybody present'. The message of the event was clear: Browne had the power to command the devil which the Protestant minister did not have. Browne was accused of witchcraft, arrested, and tried.[21]

Such wonders provoked controversial discussion among the laity, although the clergy tended to ignore them. In 1698, for instance, the bookseller John Dunton, while on a visit to Dublin, was present in a group which included the dean of Killaloe when an incident was related of a ghost pressuring a woman to have her child baptised. The story gave rise to an animated discussion about the theology of infant baptism to which the dean refused to contribute.[22]

This concern with the central point of all popular religion, the manifestation of the holy and its opposite in the natural world, was not a matter of mere curiosity, for it touched on the realities of life in early modern Ireland. Unusual illnesses and diseases were understood in a theological sense: they were either the punishment of God for moral fault, or the result of possession by an evil spirit, or the effect of witchcraft. Thus Thomas Munck, commenting on the state of County Kildare in 1683, observed that the people there 'are much given to credit charms, spells, incantations, [and] divinations, and [they] attribute all diseases not very frequent or common among them to fascination and witchcraft'.[23] Such explanations were not confined to human illness but could be extended to illness in animals, which could be understood as demon possession or witchcraft, and destruction of the harvest by adverse weather was interpreted as a punishment for sin.[24] In all these cases the appropriate response was a religious one—a seeking after the holy to beg forgiveness through fasting and prayer or to oppose external evil with the power of holiness.

For the majority of the inhabitants of early modern Ireland the most pressing religious issue which they had to face was not which set of doctrines was purest or which form of church government most resembled that advocated by the apostles, but rather which religious group could provide access to the power of holiness to counteract the reality of the supernatural world of evil which manifested itself in life-threatening forms. Those forms ranged from the world of the fairies, who stole children or transformed themselves into rats which drank the milk of cattle, through to full-blown witchcraft which caused disease and death.[25] However, God was there not simply to protect but also to be worshipped and to provide a moral framework for the world. Failure to adhere to either of these imperatives not only could result in immediate punishment but also had consequences in the afterlife in the supernatural worlds of heaven and hell. More than anything else, these considerations shaped the religiosity of the inhabitants of early modern Ireland. They not only responded by drawing on ideas offered by the official church but also used more traditional forms of religion, their own reading of sacred texts such as the bible or saints' lives, and their own experience of the world around them, to fashion a religious outlook which met their own needs. Which sources they used depended on how they understood the holy to manifest itself in the secular world, an understanding that varied a good deal in accordance with cultural and confessional backgrounds.

II

The dominant understanding of the nature of the holy in early modern Ireland was that it manifested itself in particular places at particular times, a view most characteristic of both traditional and Counter-reformation Catholicism. A case in point was the consecration at the Eucharist when, through the words *hoc est enim corpus meum*, God Himself became present in the host. The popular understanding of this miracle was at best sketchy. Reports from various parts of Catholic Ireland in the seventeenth century suggest that interpretations of the event varied from the host as a picture of God, through the grace of God, to the manifestation of the Blessed Virgin with the baby Jesus.[26] Whatever the laity may have believed, they treated the Eucharist with considerable devotion. In the early stages of the Reformation in Dublin Edward Staples, Protestant bishop of Meath, claimed that the main preoccupation of the laity was not with changes in church government but with the denial of the sacrament of the altar.[27] This devotion to the Eucharist, of course, was not a new development. The feast of Corpus Christi was well established in late medieval Dublin, for instance.[28] In the seventeenth century eucharistic miracles were reported from Ireland. These varied from one layman who saw a host turn red with blood at the elevation, to priests being miraculously preserved from soldiers at the elevation.[29]

In the popular mind at least, it was easy to associate the power of consecration with a holiness in the consecrator, and some priests came to be seen as holy men. Some religious rituals were perceived by the laity as only valid when a powerful priest was present. Near Dundalk in 1610 it was held that only a priest could baptise. Children were allowed to die unbaptised if a priest were not present.[30] Again in Armagh in the 1640s the Catholic Irish believed that Protestants were not baptised and that they had to be baptised at mass before they could become Christians.[31] This tendency to see the priest as a direct channel to the holy was reinforced by the separation of the priest from his flock by the dress and demeanour demanded by the decrees of the various synods of the seventeenth century.[32] There were practical limitations to this policy. The sporadic enforcement of proclamations banishing clergy meant that in Ulster especially, many clergy had to wear secular dress. Episcopal reports from late seventeenth-century

Ireland suggest that some clergy failed to meet the required standard for less pragmatic reasons, such as frequenting alehouses.[33] But a great many more did maintain an austere existence which gave them a reputation as conveyors of the holy.

The evidence for such powers came in dramatic ways, such as public exorcisms or a reputation as miracle worker. John Dunton, for instance, saw during his visit to Dublin in 1698

> one old friar called Fr Keran, who had been a famous exorcist and excellent good at helping cattle that were overlooked or bewitched (for some of the vulgar are so superstitious to believe this), made sale of holy water which had helpt to cast out devils and of several other consecrated trinkets.[34]

Again, Fr Robert Plunkett, son of the baron of Loughcrew, was described in 1665 as 'not without some fame for working miracles'.[35] The priest with the greatest fame as an immediate channel to the holy was Fr James Finnerty of Tuam. His powers of exorcism and healing were so well known that in 1661 he was summoned to London to treat the queen. The lay perception was that this was power which was given directly to Finnerty and could be passed on. John Digby, son of Kenhelm Digby who was one of the founders of the Royal Society and friend of Charles II's mother Henrietta Maria, fell under the influence of Finnerty in the 1660s. He spent some time with Finnerty in England before going to France to work miracles 'by virtue of some sanctity he derived from Fr Finaghty', and when the power apparently dried up, he followed the priest to Connacht 'to fetch a new stock of the gift'.[36]

Those clergymen who were reputed to have the greatest power and therefore the largest following in Catholic Ireland were the regulars. The body of the Franciscan Micheál Ó Duiblinn, who died in 1652, was reputed to have effected many cures and exorcisms. In County Wexford the Cistercian Fr Canisius was also well known as a miracle worker.[37] In many of these cases the access to the holy came not directly from God but through the invocation of their founding saint. The power of the saint was held to protect his followers. At death many lay people wanted the cord of St Francis or the scapular, and according to the bishops of the province of Cashel in 1632, people placed equal efficacy in the sacraments and the Franciscan habit, and some regarded the Franciscan habit as more important than extreme unction.[38] Many native Irish soldiers going into battle in the 1640s wore a St Francis's girdle under their clothes and carried written prayers to saints in their pockets in the hope of protection.[39] The rationale for such devotion appeared in a sermon at Limerick in 1633 which stated that St Francis went into purgatory at regular intervals to rescue those wearing the habit.[40] Other orders offered unique access to their patron. The Dominicans were reprimanded by the bishop of Cork in the 1630s for calling themselves the Order of the Blessed Virgin Mary, as if they had unique access to her.[41] Even the austere

Jesuits tried to establish a cult of St Ignatius in Munster by reporting pregnancies of barren women, assistance in childbirth, and the conversion of heretics through St Ignatius.[42]

The use of saints as channels of the power of the holy was not unique to the regular clergy, since the cult of the saints was well established in medieval Ireland through relics and hagiography. Stories of saints' lives seem to have circulated widely in sixteenth- and seventeenth-century Ireland, with many prominent families having their own collections of lives, and among the illiterate at a lower level the stories circulated through homilies and in folk traditions.[43] The saint was seen as a friend of God who could be a channel of God's power through miracles. There was a certain degree of functional specialisation among saints. Some were seen as having purely local roles while others had a much wider part to play. In the case of St Patrick a tradition that he would judge and protect the people of Ireland, deriving from the ninth-century *Vita Triparta* and perpetuated through sermons and popular tradition, gave him a national significance. Seventeenth-century Catholic missionaries reported that they had been told by people near Dublin that St Patrick would save them, and when a whale was washed ashore between Dublin and Drogheda in 1683, 'the Irish people called upon St Patrick, [and] some St Dominic and some Colmcille, to save them from the great Leviathan. They thought the day of judgement was at hand.'[44] The same idea of St Patrick as controlling access to heaven for the Irish is contained in a story recorded by the sixteenth-century cleric Edmund Campion, who noted 'that St Patrick, striving with St Peter to let an Irish gallowglass into heaven, had his head broken with the keys'.[45]

The most fundamental role which a saint could play was as protector either of an individual or more commonly of a village or a region. In Munster, according to Jesuit missionaries in 1617,

> on St Valentine's day patron saints, which the Irish call valentines, are drawn for the year. Crowds come to receive them and promised over two hundred thousand acts of devotion, such as saying three Our Fathers or the rosary every day or giving alms once a week.[46]

At the end of the century the Protestant bishop of Cork, Dives Downes, noted that besides celebrating the feast of the patron saint of the diocese, 'in most of the parishes they observe the day of the saint of the parish. The families of O'Sullivan and O'Donegan have their peculiar saints.'[47] In Ulster the evidence is less clear, but the custom of dedicating churches to obscure local saints suggests a practice similar to that of Munster. In Magilligan festivities were held on the feast of St Columcille in 1683.[48] Such local cults were supplemented by more universal figures of holiness, such as Mary or Christ himself represented by crucifixes. The statue of Our Lady at Trim was of both local and national significance, but miraculous crosses at Ballyboggan, Navan, and Sligo are examples of more local attractions.[49] The Church of Ireland bishop of Derry noted in a survey of his diocese that there was a chapel at Agivey where there 'is an image of the Blessed Mary to which there was frequent pilgrimage'.[50] These images constituted less specialised manifestations of holiness which could be appealed to if localised saints failed.

To make local saints relevant to their communities their genealogies and associated place lore were often altered to give them regional significance, or stories were inserted in their lives to give them local connections. In this way communities laid claim to a saint and, by giving him local connections, might appeal to the created local loyalties to provide protection. Thus the same saint could have a number of genealogies relating him to different localities.[51] Of the Irish saints only St Patrick with his national status managed to transcend this fate in the medieval genealogies. Saints were believed to serve as protectors of the region, guaranteeing good harvests and intervening to prevent disaster. They were also invoked to prevent or cure disease. A medical text from Monaghan, in the hands of the Ó Caiside family in the seventeenth century, contained invocations of the local saint Molaise to be used in curing diseases.[52] In County Galway some Jacobite soldiers building shelters in the 1680s were stopped by 'country people . . . telling them some story of a saint who had lived there and [who] after his death visibly punished someone who had presumed to destroy the trees'.[53] Earlier, in 1602, Philip O'Sullivan Beare, on a march from Glengarriff, arrived at the village of Ballyvourney, which was dedicated to St Gobnait, and there he made an offering to the saint, asking for her protection for the rest of his journey.[54] Even after death the saint acted as protector for an individual, and the native Irish annals record the interment of individuals under the protection of the saint to whom the burial ground was dedicated.[55]

The physical manifestations of a saint in any region could vary a good deal. At its simplest there might be a statue of the saint who was the local protector. One late seventeenth-century episode recorded by Jeremy Taylor, bishop of Down and Connor, illustrates the importance of such shrines. At Kilbroney in south Down, rather than distrain his tenants for unpaid rent, the landlord seized the statue of Our Lady of Kilbroney. The tenantry 'thought themselves unblessed as long as the image was away', and quickly paid their arrears of rent.[56] Such statues filled a multitude of roles. On occasion they were taken in procession around the parish to ensure the fertility of land, though this practice was condemned by the synods of Armagh and Dublin in 1614.[57] Such statues could be regarded as direct channels for the supernatural and were often reputed to have been discovered in miraculous ways. A statue found at Dundalk in 1607 'worked such wonders in marvelous and real cures', and at Holy Cross Abbey in County Tipperary a statue of the Blessed Virgin, discovered in miraculous circumstances, also worked marvels.[58] In this way it could be shown that the saint had chosen the community and could be relied on for support.

In addition to statues, most regions had particular places associated with saints. Physical features in the landscape such as church ruins or marked stones were often explained by the presence of a saint to whom there was local devotion, and visits or pilgrimages would be made to such sites to ask for specific favours.[59] William Shee of Kilkenny city, for instance, noted in his prayer-book in 1694, 'My daughter Ellen being very ill, I promised to make a pilgrimage to Our Lady's Island in honour of Our Blessed Lady. This [I] performed.'[60] Such places were regarded as holy, blessed in a special way by a holy man or woman. For this reason prayer said there was considered more efficacious than if offered elsewhere. At Arboe in County Tyrone, for example, three early medieval high crosses were reported in the late seventeenth century to have been brought there by St Patrick, and it was claimed that prayer said there was better than at any common place.[61]

Of these local pilgrimages the most popular was the holy well. This cult spanned all sections of early modern Irish society. The first earl of Antrim visited the holy well at Brideswell in County Roscommon, and town dwellers were as likely to visit wells as were the rural population. Dublin, for instance, had a number of holy wells in or near the city, and it was the custom for people from the surrounding countryside to come to the city on St Stephen's day to visit St Stephen's well.[62] Such wells were usually ascribed to a local saint, sometimes the patron, who is often depicted in his life as striking rock in a Moses-like act to produce water which becomes the well. According to one description from the 1570s, 'Clonsillan and Kellestown, some five miles west of Dublin, have him [St Mochan] for their patron, where under a high rock runneth a spring called St Mochan his well'.[63] In less usual cases these were existing wells blessed by those perceived to have the power of a saint, such as Fr James Finnerty or the Franciscan Bernard Grey.[64] What marked these wells off from the surrounding area were the complex rituals performed there to distinguish the sacred from the profane. These rituals entailed making a number of rounds or stations, usually the sacred numbers three or five, while saying a series of prayers, generally the Pater Noster or the Ave Maria.[65] These were formal prayers for occasions when ritual was important, and although there was another tradition of short, one-sentence prayers derived in part from the litany, this seems not to have operated on such ritual occasions. The formal nature of these prayers is underscored by the fact that while many people knew them, the exact meaning of the prayer was less well comprehended.[66] The significance of these practices, as with most rituals performed by the laity, was probably little understood, and they may well have been seen as imitations of clerical rituals. Their function, however, was to put those who performed them in direct contact with the holy. As John Toland observed at the end of the seventeenth century regarding the practice of leaping through fire on St John's eve, participants thought 'themselves in a special manner blessed by this ceremony, of whose origins, nevertheless, they were wholly ignorant'.[67] The rituals marked the well off and confirmed that its waters had curative powers for both people and animals.[68]

The most powerful access to the holy was of course through the remains of the body of the saint himself or through something with which he had been intimately associated. This cult of relics was well established in late medieval Ireland. Some Irish churches had significant relic collections before the Reformation. Christ Church in Dublin possessed not only a miraculous crucifix and the Bachal Iesu, the staff of Christ reputedly given to St Patrick, but also a miscellaneous collection of thirty-five other relics. In the less exalted location of Rossclogher Castle in County Leitrim Franciso de Cullear, survivor of the Spanish Armada in 1588, noted that the church had not only ornaments but also 'one or two relics'.[69] After the Reformation such relics were scattered into the hands of laymen and augmented by the remains of Catholics martyred in sixteenth- and seventeenth-century Ireland and by passable forgeries of relics destroyed at the Reformation. Besides the physical remains of saints, there were also objects associated with them scattered throughout the countryside. In the early seventeenth century the Book of Durrow, associated with St Columcille, was used by a farmer to cure cattle disease, and 'when sickness came upon the cattle, for their remedy [he] put water on the book and suffered it to rest there a while' before being applied to the livestock.[70]

There was also a continual international trade in relics in the sixteenth and seventeenth centuries. The Dominican church in Sligo town, for instance, acquired relics from France in 1577, and in 1642 a ship forced to land at St Ives in Cornwall while on its way from Bilbao to Ireland was found to be carrying not only rosaries but also some of St Peter's teeth, a vial of Mary Magdalen's tears, and a fragment of the True Cross.[71] Again, in Cavan it was reported in 1614 that some priests had 'brought with them from beyond the seas a cross which they say is of that very cross whereupon Christ was crucified. There came flocking unto them 3 or 4,000 people, and some gave them 6d., some more, some less.'[72]

Such objects constituted direct access to the holy and had a wide range of uses. Most dramatic were the curative powers of relics, either as part of an exorcism or to heal natural infirmities. The relic of the True Cross at Holy Cross abbey in Tipperary was credited with thirty-one miracles in the early seventeenth century. Most of those who availed of its services were drawn from the immediate area of the abbey and from a relatively low social background: two farmers, a piper, two carpenters, and a convicted criminal, for example. Not only did the relic effect cures, but it also protected grain from rats, made barren land fertile, was used for swearing oaths, and provided protection from witchcraft.[73] The True Cross of the Cistercians in Tipperary was not unique. In County Roscommon St Barry's crozier was also used for swearing oaths in the 1680s.[74] In this way relics provided direct access to the holy as part of the interaction between the natural and supernatural worlds.

This traditional perception of the interaction of the natural world with the holy was based on a late medieval understanding of religion founded not on learning but on devotion to saints as protectors and focused on relics and holy places widely dispersed in the community. People were concerned not with how interaction with the supernatural actually worked but with the source of that power in what was totally alien to their world: the power of God. From the point of view of the Counter-reformation clergy this attitude left a good deal to be desired. The clergy were more concerned with learning and with ensuring that the substance and context of the holy were contained within the church and not spread through the community.[75] In part this insistence stemmed from a fear that the populace would make an immediate connection between cause and effect, so that prayer would be seen at the popular level not as petition but as magic. In Dublin during the 1660s, for example, the Jesuits insisted on a novena by the sick person before they would use oil from a lamp burnt before the relics of St Francis Xavier at Mechlin for healing. The clergy also tried to introduce their own channels to the holy in place of more traditional relics. The Agnus Dei, for example, was promoted by the Jesuits, among others, with stories of miraculous cures.[76] It became popular with those exposed to the ideas of Tridentine reform. The brother of the earl of Desmond carried one during the Desmond rebellion, and in the 1640s some men going into battle also carried them.[77] At a more popular level many continued to regard these innovations as simply continuations of an older relic tradition. The fate of the rosary is a case in point. The rosary was introduced into Ireland toward the end of the sixteenth century as an aid to prayer. It was promoted by the Dominicans through their confraternities. By the close of the seventeenth century it was widely diffused, with Luke Wadding, bishop of Ferns, distributing large numbers of rosaries in his diocese to promote prayer. The view of the rosary from a popular perspective was rather different. One commentator in County Galway during the 1690s remarked that

> the women are possessed with this strong fame, that the devil cannot induce them to do any bad action so long as they have the rosary about them (some say in their hands), and . . . they pray to the Virgin Mary to help them.[78]

Thus the rosary became a channel to the holy in the same way as relics, holy wells, and saints in traditional religion were, rather than a means of contemplation advocated by the Counter-reformation movement.

III

The second view of access to the holy in early modern Ireland was that espoused by official Protestantism. Protestants believed that God was at work in the world and that individuals could experience the evidence of the holy, but they argued that this did not happen only at particular times and in special places. Thus they rejected the power of relics and holy sites. While the Catholic sense of the holy held that in the physical buildings of churches people had greater access to the holy, Protestants claimed that the building itself was worth little and that it was the gathered saints in the church which gave validity to communal prayer.[79] The Catholic view of the demarcation of the holy by ritual and tradition was replaced by an individual definition of what was holy through the reading of sacred texts, mainly the bible, and prayer. Some of these ideas were seized by lay Protestants with enthusiasm. When the Protestant army went into battle during the 1640s, it was 'after we had by prayer commended them to God's protection, which in the greatest expeditions was seldom omitted'.[80] The enthusiasm was sometimes excessive. Robert Blair, an early seventeenth-century Presbyterian minister in north Down, on asking a man to examine a sick horse, was told that 'there was need of no other means to be used but prayer whatsoever ailed body and soul, young or old, corn or cattle'.[81] The forms of prayer which Protestants preferred were not the traditional forms favoured by the Catholic laity. Only the Our Father continued to be popular and accepted by all brands of Protestantism in early modern Ireland as a set prayer.[82] Clearly, there were changing fashions in prayer. In the late seventeenth century it was popular among members of the Church of Ireland to use the litany in private prayer, while in the early part of the century the Book of Common Prayer was little used.[83] Many Protestants compiled their own prayers for particular occasions, such as communion services, but in general, outside the liturgy of the Church of Ireland, extempore prayer was the rule among the laity.[84]

In addition to prayer, the bible provided a guide to the world when read, or heard, not as an historical text but as a series of 'types' which could be applied to the world. In the 1580s Andrew Trollop, for example, compared the sins of Ireland to those in Ezekiel 16, and fifty years later, Vincent Gookin saw analogies between the world of Isaiah and Ireland in the 1630s.[85] On a more practical level one man in the late seventeenth century drew up a list of weather prognostications based on biblical texts.[86] Indeed, the bible itself could become a tool in appealing to the holy for guidance, as a number of Presbyterian sessions discovered church members using the bible with keys for prognostications. One guilty party declared that 'he thought there was no harm in it', presumably because he was not appealing to diabolical powers.[87] Rather than leave individuals free to draw their own conclusions from what could at times be an ambiguous text, the clergy felt it their duty to try to constrain lay interpretations of the bible. The Presbyterian minister Robert Craghead observed in the 1690s, 'Do not some rest the scriptures to their own destruction, and the whole duty is it so much as ministers to prevent this danger by explaining these things that are hard to be understood'.[88] Thus the cult of the sermon became important, with lay men and women taking notes of the minister's sermon for reading and reflection later.[89]

There were distinctions between different brands of Protestantism, and also over time the Church of Ireland moved from a puritan position at the beginning of the seventeenth century to a more sacramental one at the end, with consequent changes in ideas about access to the holy.[90] This Protestant position of access to the holy as an individual act involving prayer and meditation produced tensions within popular Protestantism. Contrary to official doctrine, experience suggested that God did manifest Himself in particular places and at certain times. Natural wonders especially produced a tension between 'rational' Protestantism and 'superstitious' Catholicism. One commentator in 1642 experienced such confusion when describing the appearance of two large stars at a battle at Swords which followed the armies about and disappeared after the battle. 'I believe', he noted, 'they were a great encouragement to their [the Protestant] cause and might serve as testimony of Almighty God's assistance. . . . I do not believe in any real assistance of the apparition, yet I will not deny they did appear by the special providence of God, and although of no real assistance, yet may be thought good encouragement to the Protestant cause.'[91]

This tension between a specific view of the manifestation of the holy, as in Catholicism, and a more diffuse view characteristic of Protestantism produced a series of ambiguities within lay Protestants which can be explored through a consideration of the sacraments. Baptism in official Protestant teaching conveyed no supernatural power or protection. It was simply an admission rite to the church or, as the Presbyterians put it, a 'seal of the covenant'. This was interpreted by some Presbyterians near Larne in the 1680s not as the covenant between God and man but as 'supposing their children to be christened into the Solemn League and Covenant'.[92] Detailed statements of what the laity understood by baptism have not survived, but their actions seem to suggest that they felt that more was happening than simply an admission rite. Mothers who were not regular church attenders, or who had been excommunicated for wrongdoing some years earlier, purged their contempt for the church in order to receive baptism for their children. Indeed, certain Independent ministers around Dublin complained in 1659 that after the baptism of their children parents were not seen at the other ordinances such as communion again.[93] This desire for baptism is also revealed in the very short interval between birth and baptism which seems to have prevailed in seventeenth-century Ireland. Both in Derry city during the 1690s and in St John's parish, Dublin, in the late 1650s more than a third of all baptisms took place within two days of birth. Within four days of birth between half and two-thirds of all children had been baptised, and very few were left unbaptised one week after birth.[94] Clearly, Protestant parents saw baptism as more than an admission rite and, in an age of high infant mortality, wanted their children baptised as soon as possible.

The highly diffuse Protestant views of holiness as compared with the more localised ways of accessing the holy in Catholicism created powerful pressures within popular Protestantism on crucial issues such as healing. Protestant clergy held that they did not have the special power of the Catholic clergy, and that God's miraculous intervention in the world, proclaimed by Catholics and evident in the early church, no longer took place.[95] The result was that they could offer no remedies to counteract supernatural manifestations of evil when such were judged to have appeared. When a diabolical ghost haunted the Presbyterian minister of Carnmoney, James Shaw, in 1672, the Antrim Meeting could find no better way of dealing with it than by proclaiming a fast.[96] The response from the Presbyterian Daniel Williams to the haunting of a Dublin house in 1698 was to pray and preach a sermon (on Hebrews 2:18) against it.[97] In such contexts lay Protestants began to devise their own solutions drawing on the bible and experience. In Dublin the Baptist Hirome Sankey tried his hand at exorcism in the 1650s on finding a spirit which could be dislodged only by prayer and fasting as Mark 9:29 required.[98] Perhaps the most dramatic instance of this popular resort to the bible to justify an immediate recourse to the holy came in the healing miracles of Valentine Greatrix in the 1660s. Greatrix, a County Waterford man, experienced what he described as 'an impulse or strange persuasion' that he was able to cure the king's evil, and he began a series of miraculous cures in both Ireland and England. He preached no alternative doctrine and devised no theology of his own, but he was opposed by most of the Irish Protestant clergy, who regarded his actions as superstitious. Greatrix, however, claimed that his power was from God, and used the phrase 'God almighty heal thee for His mercy's sake or for Jesus' sake' in his healing ritual. That ritual was strongly influenced by biblical models. His use of spittle in cures, for example, is reminiscent of Christ's use of spittle in healing a deaf man in Matthew 7:33 and a blind man in Mark 8:23.[99]

The failure of Protestant theologians to explain how the holy could be accessed to counteract illness and other misfortunes led not only to events such as the emergence of Protestant exorcism and miraculous healing on an ad hoc basis but also to a resort by Protestants to channels to the holy which were more traditionally Catholic. Thus, for example, some Protestants took to frequenting holy wells. Richard Dobbs observed in 1683 of Cranfield well in County Antrim that its miraculous properties were 'believed by most of the Irish and many other people'. At least one Protestant, a woman named Mrs Osborne, used it for relief from illness.[100] Again, the form of prayer prescribed by Protestants was so unstructured that some Protestants opted for more traditional forms resembling charms when dealing with certain problems. As the Quaker astrologer Michael Harward noted in the introduction to his 1673 treatise on cattle management, 'the natives and many of our English-Irish lukewarm Protestants, when a disease happens amongst their cattle, do not look for help till some store of them be dead, and then to save those that are kept alive, they make use of those that have charms, enchanted water, enchanted rings, and bells'.[101] If even this failed, resort to more dubious practices was possible. The late seventeenth-century stock book of the Penrose-Fitzgerald estate in County Cork contains the dubious note, 'ABACA-DABRA, these words will cure the shaking ague by writing of it in a piece of paper and put about the sick party's neck'.[102]

IV

The world of popular religion in early modern Ireland was one in which transcendence and immanence were indissolubly intertwined. It was not about purity of doctrine nor about ecclesiastical government. These were matters which preoccupied the clergy but not the majority of the laity. To characterise Christianity as coterminous with a doctrinal system, as Delumeau and others have done, is to miss the central point of popular belief. The laity carved out their own religious role based on a series of devotions set in a particular historical and geographical context. Such devotions were derived not only from the ideas of the church's theologians and parish teaching but also from individual's own experiences and traditions. Thus when religious tensions heightened in the 1640s, these were expressed not in terms of doctrinal dispute but rather in the destruction of what their opponents saw as channels of the holy. The division was not between doctrinal systems but between those who perceived themselves as the agents of God and their opponents, whose power must in consequence be diabolical in origin. Catholics destroyed Protestant bibles and Protestants destroyed Catholic symbols of what they regarded as holy.[103] In 1603, for instance, the vicar of Swords hanged a crucifix on a gibbet.[104] These competing devotional systems which characterised popular religion each implored the assistance of the holy both for the immediate problems of disease, crop failure, or victory in battle and for the longer-term problem of avoiding damnation or eternal torment after death. The tactics used in some cases were very old indeed: imploring the aid of saints through their relics or in special places associated with these holy persons. In other cases the devotions were innovations: Protestants searching the bible for paradigms into which the world could be placed or Catholics using rosary beads as an alternative to a relic. Whatever the clergy of different denominations thought of these practices, they had inadvertently been the instigators of many of them, either through the teachings of the medieval church or through more recent innovations. While doctrine may not have matched the schemes devised by theologians, the devotion was certainly profound, or as one Mayo Franciscan observed of his followers in the 1690s, they 'knew not as much as they do in other countries, [but] they knew enough to be saved'.[105]

NOTES

1 Eamon Duffy, *The stripping of the altars* (New Haven, 1992); Patrick Collinson, *The religion of Protestants* (Oxford, 1982), pp. 189–95; P.S. Seaver, *Wallington's world* (London, 1985).

2 For example, see W.Y. Evans, *The fairy faith in the Celtic countries* (Oxford, 1911); Lady Gregory, *Visions and beliefs in the west of Ireland* (London, 1920).

3 Most impressively in Keith Thomas, *Religion and the decline of magic* (London, 1971).

4 Jean Delumeau, *Catholicism from Luther to Voltaire* (London, 1977), especially chaps. 3 and 4. For the quotations, see pp. 161, 225.

5 Carlo Ginzburg, *The cheese and the worms* (English trans., London, 1980); Carlo Ginzburg, *Night battles* (English trans., London, 1982), p. xviii.

6 P.J. Corish, *The Catholic community in the seventeenth and eighteenth centuries* (Dublin, 1981), pp. 37, 50–1, 69–70.

7 Brendan Jennings (ed.), 'Brussels MS 3947: Donatus Moneyus, De provincia Hiberniae S. Francisci' in *Anal. Hib.*, 6 (1934), pp. 43–4.

8 P.S. Dinneen (ed.), *Foras feasa ar Éirinn: the history of Ireland by Geoffrey Keating* (4 vols, London, 1901–14), ii, 234–7.

9 P.R.O.N.I., D.1759/1A/2, p. 72; D.1759/1E/2, November 1699.

10 For example, see T.C. Barnard, 'Reforming Irish manners: the religious societies in Dublin during the 1690s' in *Hist. Jn.*, xxxv (1992), pp. 805–38.

11 Geoffrey Parker, 'Success and failure during the first century of the reformation' in *Past & Present*, no. 136 (1992), pp. 43–82.

12 For example, see Alan Ford, *The Protestant Reformation in Ireland, 1590–1630* (Frankfurt, 1985), pp. 63–97; Corish, *Catholic community*, pp. 25–30, 49–51.

13 T.C.D., MS 883/1, ff 16–17.

14 Richard Baxter, *The certainty of the world of spirits* (London, 1691), pp. 214–19, 247–9; M.H. Nicholson (ed.), *The Conway letters* (rev. ed., Oxford, 1992), pp. 174–6.

15 For the concept of 'the holy', see Rudolf Otto, *The idea of the holy* (Oxford, 1923).

16 T.C.D., MS 883/1, f. 230.

17 Denis Murphy (ed.), *Triumphalia chronologica monasterii Sanctae Crucis in Hibernia* (Dublin, 1891), p. 127; L.F. Renehan, *Collections on Irish church history*, ed. Daniel McCarthy (2 vols, Dublin, 1861), i, 433.

18 Barnaby Rich, *A new description of Ireland* (London, 1610), p. 9.

19 Declan Gaffney, 'The practice of religious controversy in Dublin, 1600–41' in W.J. Sheils and Diana Wood (ed.), *The churches, Ireland, and the Irish: studies in church history*, xxv (Oxford, 1989), pp. 145–88.

20 E.S. Shuckburgh (ed.), *Two biographies of William Bedell* (Cambridge, 1902), p. 330.

21 Marcellus Glynn and F.X. Martin (ed.), 'The "Brevis Relatio" of the Irish Discalced Carmelites, 1625–70' in *Archiv. Hib.*, xxv (1962), pp. 150–2; Sheffield City Library, Wentworth Wodehouse MSS, Strafford letter books, 5, ff 189–90; *Cal. S.P. Ire.*, *1633–47*, p. 139.

22 John Dunton, *The Dublin scuffle* (London, 1699), pp. 407–10.

23 T.C.D., MS 883/1, f. 297.

24 W.J. Smith (ed.), *Herbert correspondence* (Cardiff, 1968), p. 335; St John D. Seymour (ed.), *Adventures and experiences of a seventeenth-century clergyman* (Dublin, 1909), pp. 23–4.

25 D.B. Quinn, *The Elizabethans and the Irish* (Ithaca, New York, 1966), pp. 86–7; B.L., Sloan MS 900, f. 42.

26 Propaganda Archives, Rome, *Scritture riferite nei congressi, Irlanda*, vol. 2, f. 321; Bodl., Rawl., MS C 439, f. 6.

27 E.P. Shirley (ed.), *Original letters and papers in illustration of the history of the Church of Ireland* (London, 1851), pp. 23–4.

28 Myles Ronan, 'Religious customs of Dublin medieval gilds' in *I.E.R.*, 5th ser., xxvi (1925), pp. 242–6.

29 B.L., Harley MS 3888, f. 128; *Narrative of Edmund Nangle of Cloandarah* (n.p., n.d. [1665]), pp. 8–9. For a collection of host miracles, see Helena Concannon, *The blessed eucharist in Irish history* (Dublin, 1932).

30 Fergus O'Donoghue, 'The Jesuit mission in Ireland, 1598–1651' (Ph.D. dissertation, Catholic University, Washington, D.C., 1981), pp. 89–90.

31 T.C.D., MS 836, f. 40.

32 For example, see Renehan, *Collections*, i, 432; Corish, *Catholic community*, p. 67.

33 Cathaldus Giblin, 'The "Processus Datariae" and the appointment of Irish bishops in the seventeenth century' in Franciscan Fathers (ed.), *Father Luke Wadding* (Dublin, 1957), pp. 541, 543, 547, 548; Corish, *Catholic community*, p. 29; John Hanly (ed.), *The letters of Saint Oliver Plunkett* (Dublin, 1979), pp. 145–6.

34 Dunton, *Dublin scuffle*, p. 333.

35 Hanly, *Letters of Plunkett*, p. 16.

36 *Cal. S.P. Ire., 1666–9*, p. 247; Anselm Faulkner, 'Father O'Finaghty's miracles' in *I.E.R.*, 5th ser., civ (1965), pp. 349–62.

37 'Bonaventure O'Connor to John Colgan, 15 June 1652' in *Catholic Survey*, i (1955), pp. 130–2; Fr Columcille, *The story of Mellifont* (Dublin, 1958), pp. 179–83.

38 Hanly, *Letters of Plunkett*, p. 30; Benignus Millett, 'Calendar of vol. 1 of the *Scritture riferite nei congressi, Irlanda* in Propaganda archives' in *Coll. Hib.*, 6 and 7 (1963–4), pp. 130–3.

39 For example, see Nicholas Bernard, *The whole proceedings of the siege of Drogheda in Ireland* (London, 1642), pp. 53, 84–6; Sankey Cillard, *A continuation of the Irish rebels' proceedings, with our victories over them* (London, 1642), pp. 5–6; B.L., Sloan MS 631, f. 224; *The Protestant wonderment* (London, 1642).

40 O'Donoghue, 'Jesuit mission', p. 244; H.M.C., *Report on the manuscripts of R.R. Hastings* (4 vols, London, 1928–47), iv, 60.

41 Thomas S. Flynn, *The Irish Dominicans, 1536–1641* (Dublin, 1993), p. 254.

42 O'Donoghue, 'Jesuit mission', pp. 153–4, 147.

43 For lay ownership of saints' lives, see Charles Plummer, 'A tentative catalogue of Irish hagiography' in Charles Plummer, *Miscellanea hagiographia Hibernica* (Brussels, 1925), pp. 184, 187, 191, 199, 228, 242, 245; Charles Plummer, 'Latin lives of Irish saints' in *Z.C.P.*, v (1905), pp. 443–4.

44 *Strange and wonderful news from Ireland of a whale* (London, 1683), p. 1; Propaganda Archives, Rome, *Scritture riferite nei congressi, Irlanda*, vol. 2, f. 321.

45 Edmund Campion, 'A historie of Ireland' in *Ancient Irish histories* (2 vols, Dublin, 1809), i, 25.

46 Edmund Hogan, *Distinguished Irishmen of the sixteenth century* (London, 1894), pp. 481–2.

47 T.C.D., MS 562, ff 25v, 61v, 70. For patron days, see Corish, *Catholic community*, pp. 67–8; Robert Dunlop, *Ireland under the Commonwealth* (2 vols, Manchester, 1913), ii, 712.

48 Canice Mooney (ed.), 'Topographical fragments from the Franciscan library' in *Celtica*, i (1946–7), pp. 65–7, 82–4; T.C.D., MS 883/1, f. 219.

49 N.D. White (ed.), *Extents of Irish monastic possessions* (Dublin, 1943), p. 115; Charles McNeill, 'Account of the sums raised by the sale of chattels of some suppressed Irish monasteries' in *R.S.A.I. Jn.*, lii (1942), pp. 14–16; Flynn, *Irish Dominicans*, pp. 42, 85.

50 A.F. O'D. Alexander (ed.), 'The O'Kane papers' in *Anal. Hib.*, 12 (1943), p. 81.

51 Pádraig Ó Riain, 'A methodology in early Irish hagiography' in *Peritia*, i (1992), pp. 157–8; for the multiplicity of local saints, see John Colgan, *Acta sanctorum veteris et majoris Scotiae, seu Hibernicae sanctorum insulae* (Louvain, 1645), sig b1v, b2v.

52 Nessa Ní Shéaghdha, *Catalogue of Irish mauscripts in the National Library of Ireland: fasciculus i* (Dublin, 1967), pp. 85–6.

53 R.H. Murray (ed.), *The journal of John Stevens* (Oxford, 1912), p. 154.

54 Philip O'Sullivan Beare, *Historiae Catholicae Hiberniae*, ed. Matthew Kelly (Dublin, 1850), pp. 244–5.

55 A.M. Freeman (ed.), *The annals of Connacht* (Dublin, 1944), *sub annos* 1537, 1543; William Hennessy (ed.), *The annals of Loch Cé* (2 vols, London,1871), *sub annos* 1527, 1585, 1636.

56 Jeremy Taylor, 'A dissuasion from popery to the people of Ireland' in E. Cardwell (ed.), *Tracts on points at issue between the Church of England and Rome* (Oxford, 1852), p. 466.

57 Renehan, *Collections*, i, 433; M. Comerford, *Collections relating to the dioceses of Kildare and Leighlin* (3 vols, Dublin, 1883–6), i, 248.

58 Murphy, *Triumphalia*, pp. 171–7; T. Crofton Croker (ed.), *The tour of M. de la Boullaye Le Gouez in Ireland, 1644* (London, 1832), p. 33; Henry Fitzsimon, *Words of comfort to persecuted Catholics*, ed. Edmund Hogan (Dublin, 1881), p. 160.

59 Raymond Gillespie, *The sacred in the secular: religious change in Catholic Ireland, 1500–1700* (Vermont, 1993), pp. 10–11.

60 J.F. Ainsworth, 'Survey of records in private keeping' in *Anal. Hib.*, 20 (1958), p. 250.

61 John Richardson, *The great folly, superstition, and idolatry of pilgrimages in Ireland . . .* (Dublin, 1727), p. 6.

62 Colm Lennon, *The lords of Dublin in the age of reformation* (Dublin, 1989), pp. 149–50, 186; B. L., Harley MS 3888, f. 110.

63 Meredith Hanmer, 'The chronicle of Ireland' in *Ancient Irish histories*, ii, 82.

64 Peter Walsh, *The history and vindication of the loyal formulary or Irish remonstrance* (n.p., 1674), p. 713; Jennings, 'Brussels MS 3947', p. 44.

65 The best contemporary collection of rituals is in Richardson, *Great folly*, pp. 64–71.

66 For this lack of understanding, see Edmund Spenser, *A view of the present state of Ireland*, ed. W.L. Renwick (Oxford, 1970), p. 84; Theobald Stapleton, *Catechimus seu doctrine Christiane* (Brussels, 1639), sig b. 1.

67 John Toland, *History of the druids*, ed. R. Huddleston (Montrose, 1814), p. 126.

68 For wells used to cure cattle, see T.C.D., MS 883/1, f. 134.

69 J.C. Crosthwaite (ed.), *The obits and martyrology of Christ Church* (Dublin, 1844), pp. 3–4; Evelyn Hardy, *The survivors of the armada* (London, 1966), p. 94.

70 Gillespie, *Sacred in secular*, pp. 20–1; Denis Murphy (ed.), *The annals of Clonmacnoise* (Dublin, 1896), p. 96.

71 *A true relation of certain passages which Capt. Basset brought us from the west part of Cornwall* (London, 1642), p. 2; Flynn, *Irish Dominicans*, p. 85.

72 H.M.C., *Hastings MSS*, iv, 14.

73 Murphy, *Triumphalia*, pp. 121, 125, 127, 129.

74 T.C.D., MS 883/1, ff 13, 136; MS 883/2, ff 44–5; MS 562, f. 35v.

75 Gillespie, *Sacred in secular*, pp. 21–2.

76 Richard Archdekin, *A treatise of miracles* (Louvain, 1667), pp. 90–2; Fitzsimons, *Words of comfort*, p. 60.

77 J.T. Gilbert (ed.), *A contemporary history of affairs in Ireland* (3 vols, Dublin, 1879), i, 55; B.L., Sloan MS 1449, f. 174.

78 Flynn, *Irish Dominicans*, pp. 54, 239; Bodl., Rawl. MS C 439, f. 6.

79 Robert Craghead, *An answer to a late book entitled a discourse concerning the inventions of men in the worship of God* (Edinburgh, 1694), pp. 96–7.

80 *News from Ireland concerning the warlike affairs in the province of Leinster* (London, 1642), p. 2.

81 Thomas McCrie (ed.), *The life of Mr Robert Blair* (Edinburgh, 1848), p. 63.

82 Craghead, *Answer to late book*, pp. 34–7; Joseph Boyse, *Remarks on a late discourse of William, lord bishop of Derry* (London, 1694), pp. 43–4.

83 H.M.C., *Report on the manuscripts of the marquess of Ormond: new series* (8 vols, London, 1902–20) v, 88, 93; Sir John Harrington, *A short view of the state of Ireland*, ed. W.D. Macray (Oxford, 1879), p. 16.

84 For example, T.C.D., MS 4468; William Hamilton, *The life of James Bonnell, late accomptant general of Ireland* (London, 1703), pp. vi, 149–50.

85 *Cal. S.P. Ire., 1586–8*, p. 424; *Cal. S.P. Ire., 1599–1660*, p. 351; *Cal. S.P. Ire., 1647–60*, p. 182.
86 Notes in volume of bound pamphlets in Dublin City Library, Pearse St., Gilbert collection, 183/1/7F.
87 Presbyterian Historical Society, Belfast, Aghadowey session book, 11 May 1703; Templepatrick session book, f. 52.
88 Craghead, *Answer to late book*, p. 88.
89 For example, see John Bailey, *Man's chief end to glorify God in some brief sermon notes* (n.p., 1689), pp. 21, 32; N.L.I., MS 4201, for a collection of sermon notes.
90 Raymond Gillespie, 'The religion of Irish Protestants' in Alan Ford, James McGuire, and Kenneth Milne (ed.), *As by law established: the Church of Ireland since the Reformation* (Dublin, 1995), pp. 92–4.
91 *Lamentable news from Ireland* (London, 1642), sig A3v–A4.
92 T.C.D., MS 883/1, f. 189.
93 *An agreement and resolution of the ministers of the church associated with the city of Dublin and the province of Leinster* (Dublin, 1659), p. 11; P.R.O.N.I., CR 4/12B/1, pp. 174, 176; D. 1759/2B/2, 3 December 1689; Presbyterian Historical Society, Belfast, Carnmoney session book, p. 46.
94 Richard Hayes (ed.), *The register of Derry cathedral* (Exeter, 1910), pp. 76–106; James Mills (ed.), *The register of St John the Evangelist, Dublin, 1619–99* (Dublin, 1906), pp. 217–35.
95 See, for example, the comments in Henry Leslie, *A discourse of praying with the spirit* (London, 1660), pp. 7–8. For a case study, see Eamon Duffy, 'Valentine Greatrix, the Irish stroker' in Keith Robbins (ed.), *Religion and humanism: studies in church history, xvii* (Oxford, 1981), pp. 251–73.
96 P.R.O.N.I., D.1759/1A/2, pp. 54, 57, 64.
97 Baxter, *Certainty of world of spirits*, pp. 218–20.
98 *Reflections on some persons and things in Ireland by letters to and from Dr Petty* (London, 1660), pp. 101–2.
99 There is a large literature on Greatrix, but the most important work remains his own statement, *A brief account of Mr Valentine Greatrix* (Dublin, 1668).
100 T.C.D., MS 883/1, f. 199; Richardson, *Great folly*, pp. 84–5.
101 Michael Harward, *The herdsman's mate, or a guide for herdsmen* (Dublin, 1673), sig A2.
102 Cork Archives Institute, Cork, U 257/1, f. 29. I am grateful to Toby Barnard for this reference.
103 Raymond Gillespie, 'Destabilising Ulster, 1641–2' in Brian MacCuarta, *Ulster, 1641* (Belfast, 1993), pp. 115–20.
104 Henry Fitzsimons, *The justification and exposition of the divine sacrifice of the mass* (n.p., 1611), p. 122.
105 Bodl., Rawl. C 439, f. 6.

3

The Rise of the Pub: A Study in the
Disciplining of Popular Culture

ELIZABETH MALCOLM

I

In his pioneering study *Popular culture in early modern Europe*, Peter Burke wrote that 'to understand any item of culture we need to place it in context, which includes its physical context or social setting, public or private, indoor or outdoor, for this physical space helps to structure the events which take place in it'.[1] In the past, according to Burke, the main private setting for popular culture was the home, while the main public ones were the church, the tavern, and the market-place. The home, being by definition private, 'virtually escapes the historian of this period', while the church, Burke argued, was most significant as a cultural centre 'in regions where people lived in scattered homesteads, as in Norway, and might not otherwise meet'. Rather, it was the tavern and the marketplace on which Burke concentrated, seeing the latter as more important in northern Europe and the former as more important in the south.[2] Burke was undoubtedly correct to emphasise the determining role of 'physical space', though perhaps he presented this a little too schematically. All the spaces that he mentioned were significant in Ireland: the home, whether it was a big house or a cabin; the church, whether mass rock or cathedral; the tavern, whether shebeen or gin palace; and the marketplace, whether market house or country field. Yet there were important differences between these spaces which Burke did not fully address; not least was the fact that in Ireland some of these spaces were regulated by act of parliament, while others were not.

One of the principal centres of popular culture in Ireland today is the public house. The pub,[3] in both town and country, is the focus of working-class social life, and a good deal of middle–class social life for that matter as well. It is a place to meet, to drink, to eat, to conduct business, to make friends, to play games, to watch television, to listen to music, or simply to pass the time. Yet, in fact, in terms of the variety of its functions and the number of its patrons, the Irish pub has probably passed its peak. In the last twenty or thirty years rising drink prices, better housing, an increase in home drinking, and the competition of other forms

of popular entertainment, notably television, and of other venues, notably licensed clubs and hotels, have led to a fall in the number of people frequenting
pubs.[4] Future historians may well single out the century from about 1850 to about
1950 as the heyday of the pub as a centre of Irish popular culture.

Reliable statistics measuring the popularity of pubs in Ireland are few. But
those which are available, which mainly relate to the towns, suggest that by the
second half of the nineteenth century the pub was the principal centre of male
working-class recreation. A survey conducted in the mid-1870s by the Royal Irish
Constabulary and the Dublin Metropolitan Police showed that on Sundays 30 to
40 percent of the total populations of Cork, Waterford, and Limerick cities
patronised public houses, while in the case of Dublin city the corresponding
figure was 50 percent. These percentages are doubtless inflated: one authority at
the time suggested that cutting them by half would produce a more realistic
figure. Even if halved, though, they remain remarkable.[5] And they are supported
by figures for the numbers of pubs in these cities supplied a few years later to a
house of lords committee investigating intemperance. Cork city had one pub for
every forty adult males; Waterford had one for every thirty-five; while in Limerick in 1876, 19 percent of the houses in the city were pubs, and one person in
every twelve was arrested for drunkenness during the course of the year—the
highest arrest rate of any town in the United Kingdom.[6]

Although, as we shall see, women often ran pubs, they were generally not
themselves regular customers. The Irish pub was until recent times a space largely
reserved for males. Indeed, a feminist critic has characterised pubs as 'female
substitutes': offering 'plentitude, availability, warmth, food, and companionship,
a servicing of male needs'.[7] This interpretation seems to fit nineteenth- and
twentieth-century Ireland in that working-class men consciously went to the pub
to escape their homes and families.[8] The pub offered the comfort and camaraderie
that was so lacking in the urban tenement or the rural cabin. In the countryside
particularly, pubs were often indistinguishable from farmhouses and were regarded as second homes by their customers.[9] In Dublin women and children
usually only entered a pub—then the snug and never the bar—with the family
beer jug to get drink to take home. When therefore we talk about the pub as a
focus of popular culture, we are talking about an essentially male culture. One
could in fact argue that the rise of the pub played a part in separating the sexes
and confining the woman to a purely domestic role. Drink consumption outside
of the pub often entailed a freer and more equal mixing of the sexes.

If pubs attracted more male customers in Ireland a century ago than they do
today, they also offered a greater variety of services and entertainments. As a
result, the publican was a key figure not only in the social life of the country but
in its economic and political life as well. Organisations as varied as trade unions,
young men's societies, and fenian circles all held meetings in pubs. At election
times pubs often served as party headquarters, thus allowing candidates to entice

voters with promises of free drink. One Dublin city publican, referring to the early years of the twentieth century, claimed that 'back then it was the publican who *married* them, *buried* them, and *christened* them'. He was pointing out that in poor working-class areas the publican played a vital role in helping to organise family and community functions, providing both the venue and the drink, the latter often on credit.[10] Besides encouraging games, like billiards and draughts, and allowing gambling on their premises, publicans also frequently organised dances, horse-races, and athletics meetings as a means of boosting their business. Up until 1862 they had been able to sell drink at such gatherings without need of official sanction. Music and singing also seem to have been an important part of the entertainment offered by pubs. The houses that John Devoy frequented in the James's Street area of Dublin, when working as a fenian recruiter in 1865–6, certainly had singing. One was in fact described as a 'singing saloon'. Such saloons had begun to appear in Belfast as early as the 1830s and remained popular until the rise of the music-hall in the 1870s.[11] But by the 1920s Tomás Ó Crohan was complaining that drinking had become 'silent', whereas in his youth in the 1860s and 1870s 'every man that came in [the pub] would not go out without singing a song or telling a tale'.[12]

Pubs fulfilled important economic roles as well as social ones. At fairs and markets deals were often struck in pubs and sealed with drink. Publicans were a major source of credit, particularly in the countryside where cash was often in short supply. They lent money, changed money, and were even accused of counterfeiting money. In Dublin women dealers congregated outside pubs in order to sell their wares to the customers and some also acted as money-lenders. Many pubs also sold groceries as well as drink, and in rural areas some housed post offices, while the publican himself might work as a local tradesman. The sale of drink on its own was often not sufficient to support a family, especially in the more isolated and impoverished parts of the country, and thus the publican found it necessary to diversify his activities. But even in Dublin by the end of the century virtually all pubs, with the exception of a few in the very centre of the city, sold groceries. In addition, throughout the nineteenth century there were spirit-grocer shops in many towns, selling groceries and spirits in small amounts, though only for consumption off the premises. Police and publicans alike complained bitterly that spirit grocers breached their licenses by selling for consumption on the premises, yet while this license existed, publicans were forced into competing with grocers by selling groceries themselves.[13]

Publicans and small shopkeepers, who were often one and the same, had mounted to prosperity and influence on the wave of economic growth that followed the famine. Samuel Clark, in his important 1979 study of the social origins of the land war, wrote of the small-business class, including publicans:

By no means an inconsequential social group even before the famine, in the post-famine period their importance was enhanced still further and they came to rival landowners and clergymen as wielders of local power and patronage. They often enjoyed a social relationship with rural people that was comparable to that of the parish priest.[14]

The bases of the publicans' power were economic and social, but their power was increasingly expressed politically. Even before the famine, however, as Clark suggests, publicans were a far from insignificant political group. During the 1830s they supplied more than 10 percent of voters in towns such as Coleraine, Belfast, Tralee, Youghal, Dundalk, and Derry.[15] This influence continued to grow steadily after the famine. By the 1890s, for instance, more than a third of the Dublin corporation were connected with the drink trade and a quarter were actually publicans. Critics accused the corporation of being controlled by a 'whiskey ring'.[16] Other towns exhibited a not dissimilar pattern. Yet the economic and political roles of the publican in late nineteenth-century Ireland have never been fully explored, while the role of his or her house as a centre for popular culture remains equally obscure. To do justice to all these issues would require a book; this essay will address itself to the last of them.

II

There has been a tendency among historians of popular culture in both England and Ireland to see the period from about 1780 to about 1840 as one of major transition. Prior to 1780 what Burke termed 'traditional culture' still held sway. But in the half-century after 1780 the forces of industrialisation, urbanisation, and evangelicalism combined, in England at least, to eliminate many traditional recreations and entertainments and to prepare the way for the commercialised popular culture of the latter part of the century, seen most notably in the music-hall and in the rise of association football. A rather similar chronology has been suggested for Ireland, though with the growing puritanism of the Catholic church, the introduction of a system of national education, the success of Fr Mathew's temperance crusade, and the famine being singled out as among the main agencies of transformation. The appearance of the Gaelic Athletic Association in the 1880s and the Gaelic League in the 1890s have, under this interpretation, been seen as an Irish reaction against the growing dominance of commercialised English popular culture and as an attempt to return to more genuinely Irish, if carefully sanitised, forms of recreation and entertainment.[17]

Yet in the English context this interpretation has come under challenge. Hugh Cunningham in his 1980 work, *Leisure in the industrial revolution*, looked closely at the period from 1780 to 1880 and argued that 'if such a phenomenon as a "traditional" world of leisure ever existed, which may be doubted, it was destroyed in the sixteenth century by the celebrated combination of capitalism and puritanism'. At the same time he showed that 'many "traditional" sports and customs survived much longer than one might suppose, sometimes after their demise had been celebrated'.[18] These two assertions are not as contradictory as they may at first appear, for Cunningham saw popular culture as highly fluid: constantly under challenge and constantly adapting to survive such challenges. John Golby and William Purdue in their 1984 study, *The civilisation of the crowd*, which covered a good deal of the same ground as Cunningham, also saw a complex process of transition from what they termed 'old' popular culture to 'new' popular culture. Yet 'old' popular culture did not simply disappear. Some aspects survived and indeed thrived in the new commercialised environment of the latter part of the nineteenth century. 'The most obvious instance of adaptability', remarked Golby and Purdue, 'is the inn or alehouse, which was as capable of providing the main community centre for an urban working class as of continuing as a centre for villlage life; it was to be the power house for the development of a great deal of nineteenth-century popular culture'.[19] Cunningham had also singled out the alehouse as a vital centre of popular culture, but he had looked more to its earlier role in rural areas, where 'in the provision of recreation for the poor [it] became increasingly central in the later sixteenth and early seventeenth centuries owing to the erosion of alternative facilities, and in particular of the communal festivities and sports which had flourished in many late medieval parishes'.[20]

These recent English studies would seem to suggest that too much emphasis may have been placed on the late eighteenth and early nineteenth centuries as a critical period of cultural transformation. They would also imply that the pub offers an example of a popular cultural venue which thrived from at least late medieval times, adapting itself throughout four centuries of momentous social change. The obvious question which springs to mind is, Why was the pub so successful in making the transition from traditional to commercial popular culture when other venues and many forms of recreation did not?

There were important differences between the pub and other spaces in which popular recreation and entertainment occurred, which these recent English studies do not sufficiently address. We have already seen that Burke, in considering the 'physical space' in which popular culture thrived, took no account of the fact that increasingly from the sixteenth century, pubs were regulated by the authorities through a system of licenses. His distinctions between public and private, indoor and outdoor spaces are certainly significant, but what set the pub off from the home or the church or the marketplace was that as time passed, it came under more and more rigorous government control. In this context one is driven to wonder how genuinely popular the pub was as a cultural venue. Was it the creation of the populace or rather the creature of authoritarian government? Did it foster genuine popular culture, or did it rather suppress this and substitute

instead officially-approved forms of popular recreation? Perhaps the Irish experience can supply answers to such questions.

The publican was, as we have seen, a key person in many aspects of both town
and country life in post-famine Ireland. But how and when did he or she achieve
this pre-eminence? In examining the development of the pub in Ireland, there
are two particularly critical periods that need to be looked at: first, the years from
about 1600 to 1670, and second, those from about 1780 to 1860. During these
periods, in response to a specific set of problems, successive governments took
decisive action to regulate drinkshops and, in so doing, largely created the pub
as we know it today.

III

In sixteenth-century Ireland one can clearly see Burke's distinction between
indoor and outdoor venues for popular culture in operation, and this applies
particularly to venues for drink consumption. Much popular recreation and ritual
in Gaelic Ireland took place out of doors, while in the pale and the port towns,
dominated by settlers of English descent, there were already special indoor spaces
set aside for drinking and the recreational activities that accompanied it.

Wine was one of Ireland's major items of import throughout the medieval and
early modern periods, and this trade was dominated by the merchant oligarchies
that ruled towns like Dublin, Galway, Waterford, Cork, Limerick, and Carrickfergus.[21] These were powerful groups, often defying the threats of the Gaelic lords
on the one hand and the encroachments of royal authority on the other.[22] From
an early date they sought to control not just the external trade in drink but its
internal production and sale as well. So-called taverns and alehouses seem often
in fact to have been little more than rooms or cellars in merchants' houses. Fynes
Moryson, in his description of the country published in 1617, wrote that in
Dublin and other cities 'they have taverns wherein Spanish and French wines are
sold, but more commonly the merchants sell them by pints and quarts in their
own cellars'. Writing in 1610 with a distinctly jaundiced eye, Barnaby Rich
claimed that in Dublin, 'as they use call every pedler a merchant, so they use call
every alehouse a tavern, whereof there are such plenty that there are whole streets
of taverns . . .'. According to Rich, 'there is almost never a householder in
Dublin (whatsoever trade he otherwise useth) but he will have a blind corner in
his house reserved for a tavern, and this (if he have not a wife of his own to keep
it) shall be set out to one of these women tavern keepers'.[23] Not only the sale of
ale but its production as well seem to have been largely in the hands of women:
even the aldermen's wives, according to Rich, brewed and sold ale.[24]

Prior to the seventeenth century the town authorities did attempt to regulate
the sale of drink. By means of the assize of ale they sought to ensure that drink

was sold at a reasonable price, generally linked to the price of barley or malt. They were also concerned that it should be of good quality and not adulterated. In addition, there were sporadic efforts, mainly in the sixteenth century, to control what went on in drinkshops. In 1528, for instance, the town governors of Galway attempted to stop 'apprentices or Irishmen' from gambling 'at cards, dice, [or] tables [backgammon]' in shops and cellars by ordering that, if caught, the players should forfeit their stakes and the proprietor be fined twenty shillings. In 1565 the Dublin corporation, when fixing the price of ale, passed a resolution forbidding the sale of ale to unmarried women and the keeping of 'hores' in taverns. Clearly, it was feared that drink shops were particularly likely to corrupt the Irish, the young, and women.[25]

Besides attempting to limit the clientele of drink shops to adult English males, the town authorities also became increasingly keen to ensure that such shops were run by respectable individuals, like themselves, and that they supplied food as well as drink and thus provided a useful service for travellers. In 1585 the Galway corporation complained bitterly that the town's taverns were dirty and had 'neither sitting place, cloth, dish, or any other service'.[26] But perhaps the clearest example of an attempt by the town merchants to control the retail drink trade comes from Youghal in County Cork. In 1610 new bye-laws deplored the fact that 'loose and idle people . . . do only address themselves to the keeping of lewd and incontinent tippling alehouses and taphouses, to the great increase of idleness, as is daily manifested'.[27] The corporation therefore decreed that no tradesman could keep a 'common inn, alehouse, or house of entertainment, or in his house sell any manner of wine, aqua vitae, beer, or ale' on pain of a fine of £5. The following year a guild of innkeepers and victuallers was established, with members of the corporation being well represented among its fifteen members.[28] The merchants of Youghal were obviously anxious to stamp out alehouses run by working men and instead to encourage inns, selling food as well as drink, which would be largely under their control.

So, besides regulating the price and quality of ale, which they had been doing since the thirteenth century, and trying to prevent gambling, illicit sex, and the use of alehouses by the young and the Irish, the urban merchant élite was also attempting by the early seventeenth century to determine how many drink shops should be in their towns and who should run them. At about the same time a similar effort was underway in Ulster, where the London companies were specifying how many inns and alehouses they wanted in their new plantation towns. They were concerned at the 'great number of taverns and alehouses' in which the 'poorer sort' spent their 'time and substance' and by which 'much disorder' was created. In 1612 they therefore instructed their agent John Rowley that for the 'more civil and orderly government' of their towns, Coleraine and Derry, the numbers of taverns and alehouses were to be limited: in the case of Coleraine, to three taverns and not more than ten alehouses, and in the case of

Derry, to four taverns and not more than twenty alehouses. Yet these in fact were generous limits: in 1611 Coleraine had only 113 houses built or partially built. J.S. Curl, the most recent historian of the Londonderry plantation, was led to wonder 'what a tiny town like Coleraine, not even half-built, can have been like: almost every other building must have been an alehouse'.[29] The merchants and the planters were soon, however, to have a powerful rival in their attempts to regulate drink shops, and that rival was the crown.

While the towns and the pale and those parts of Munster[30] and Ulster subject to plantation boasted inns, taverns, and alehouses, the picture was rather different in the parts of the country still under Irish control. Neither the production nor the consumption of alcohol in Gaelic Ireland was commercialised. The Irish did not have special indoor spaces set aside for the sale of drink and regulated by their rulers. Much drinking seems to have been what a nineteenth-century observer of rural Ireland termed 'circumstantial' as opposed to regular: that is, it was occasional and linked to certain special events or social gatherings.[31] The Irish lords certainly had access to regular supplies of wine, as they exchanged their cattle and grain for wine supplied by the town merchants or by itinerant traders. But this made wine an expensive commodity and undoubtedly limited its availability. Ale was brewed on a domestic basis and was in fact often supplied to the lords by their tenants as rent. There was also some distilling, though whiskey, which is not mentioned as a drink in Irish sources before the fifteenth century, does not appear to have been widely consumed.[32]

For most of the Irish, though, drinking was linked with special occasions: religious festivals, seasonal celebrations, and the entertainment of guests. Alcohol was not a common article of diet, always available for purchase, as it was in the towns. The medieval Irish economy was to a large degree based on cattle-rearing, and thus the society was a semi-nomadic one, tied to the cycles of the seasonal calendar.[33] Although the lords began building permanent stone tower-houses from the fourteenth century, most Irish dwellings would have been small and often temporary. Thus major popular gatherings to mark special occasions would generally have occurred out of doors at sites like hilltops, springs, river banks, or woods.[34] And a good deal of popular entertainment and drinking would have accompanied such gatherings. The consumption of alcohol therefore had a degree of ritualistic significance among the Irish. It was, for instance, an essential aspect of hospitality, which was a cardinal virtue in Gaelic society. English travellers and settlers frequently complained of the bad roads, the trackless bogs and thick woods, and the lack of inns in rural Ireland, but many were impressed by the hospitality with which they were received by the Irish, whether lord or peasant. About 1620 Luke Gernon, an official based in Limerick, provided a vivid account of the entertainment available for the traveller in an Irish lord's tower-house:

The lady of the house meets you with her train. . . . Salutations passed, you shall be presented with all the drinks in the house, first the ordinary beer, then aqua vitae, then sack, then old ale. The lady tastes it—you must not refuse it. The fire is prepared in the middle of the hall, where you may solace yourself till suppertime—you shall not want sack and tobacco. By this time the table is spread and plentifully furnished with a variety of meats, but ill-cooked and without sauce. . . . They feast together with great jollity and healths abound. Towards the middle of the supper the harper begins to tune and singeth Irish rhymes of ancient making. If he be a good rhymer, he will make one song to the present occasion. Supper being ended, it is your liberty to sit up or to depart to your lodging.[35]

As Gernon left the next morning, he was again formally presented with all the drinks of the house. This is a particularly interesting account, for not only does it illustrate the entertainment available in the lord's castle, but it also clearly shows the ritualistic use of alcohol by the woman of the house to welcome a guest. Drink could thus be used in a ritualistic fashion both outdoors and indoors in Gaelic Ireland.

While the ordinary Irish did not have pubs and seem to have drunk alcohol irregularly and often in conjunction with special occasions, when they had access to the towns, there is evidence suggesting that they made full use of the ready availability of drink. Fynes Moryson wrote:

Neither have they ['the wild Irish'] any beer made of malt and hops, nor yet any ale—no, not the chief lords, except it be very rarely; but they drink milk like nectar, warmed with a stone first cast into the fire, or else beef-broth mingled with milk. But when they come to any market town to sell a cow or a horse, they never return home till they have drunk the price in Spanish wine (which they call the King of Spain's daughter), or in Irish usquebagh, and till they have outslept two or three days' drunkenness. And not only the common sort, but even the lords and their wives; the more they want this drink at home, the more they swallow it when they come to it, till they be as drunk as beggars.[36]

It is hard to decide if Moryson was more outraged by the drunkenness of the Irish or by the fact that upper-class males and females became as drunk as the lower classes. Yet the essentials of this description would fit the reactions of many rural people when faced with the novel prospect of the seemingly unlimited supply of alcohol to be had in towns.

Although pubs are mentioned on numerous occasions in the accounts of English observers, in the records of the town authorities, and in the state papers, what they were actually like, particularly internally, is by no means easy to discover. From the little we know of Irish houses of the period and from descriptions that survive of sixteenth-century English drinkshops, it is possible, however, to hazard a general picture.[37] In rural areas they would have been one-room cabins, and even in the main towns most would have been little more than a room in a private house. English alehouses of the time were of this type, though inns and taverns usually operated on a somewhat grander scale. But in Ireland the distinctions between the various types of drinkshops were often blurred; inns were few and far between; taverns were more plentiful in the ports, although they too may often have been little more than a room in a merchant's cellar. If the drinkshop was a room in a private house, then it was likely to be the kitchen, for an important attraction offered by drinksellers was a warm fire. The furniture was probably basic: at most a trestle table, benches, stools, or a few chairs. The drinkseller would have made his or her own ale and probably beer as well, and such drink would have been consumed from wooden pots holding generally a pint or a quart. Guest rooms were non-existent, and customers wishing to stay the night would probably have simply slept in front of the fire. In sixteenth-century Dublin we know that many such shops were run by women, though according to Rich, they were either employed by men for the purpose or worked on behalf of their husbands. How many independent women brewers or drinksellers there were is unclear, as is how common they were outside Dublin. The entertainment available in such shops, aside from drinking, appears to have been rather limited. There were games and gambling, and there may have been music and dancing. According to the authorities, illicit sex was also on offer, but again it is impossible to tell how common this was.

The impression one gains is that Irish drinkshops were growing in number in the late sixteenth and early seventeenth centuries: they were common in the towns and were increasingly penetrating rural areas. Yet their proprietors seem often to have been poor and the facilities which they offered were fairly basic. To the Irish and particularly to those who had little contact with the towns, drink-shops would have been alien, English institutions with no real role in Gaelic popular recreation.[38] But their growth in number from the latter part of the sixteenth century probably reflected the fact that alternate venues for recreation and entertainment were being progressively eliminated. All the other venues listed by Peter Burke—the home, the church, and the marketplace—were undergoing major changes in Ireland in the century following the 1530s. The Gaelic ruling class was slowly being dispossessed of its lands and castles; the monasteries had been suppressed; and many of the traditional open-air religious or quasi-religious festivals were under attack. Even the Old English merchant élite of the towns found its control of commercial life challenged by the crown in the early seventeenth century. In this era of political and cultural upheaval the humble drinkshop could offer refuge and solace to the dispossessed.[39] It is perhaps not surprising, therefore, that as the crown sought to consolidate its authority, so drinkshops and their proprietors increasingly became targets of official censure.

IV

It was not so much drunkenness, gambling, or immorality that attracted government attention to pubs, though these were regularly condemned; rather, it was
the fear that, particularly in outlying areas, they harboured rebels and were
centres of disaffection. This fear seemed to be vindicated dramatically in 1615
when a conspiracy among a number of disgruntled Ulster lords and their
followers was uncovered. The conspirators aimed to seize a number of the main
plantation towns and to kill Sir Thomas Phillips, one of the largest of the planters
in the new county of Londonderry. The rebellion was planned in an alehouse a
few miles from Coleraine, and according to one informant, the plotters intended
to gather in a tavern in Coleraine and from there to attack the town.[40] The way in
which the conspirators used or intended to use pubs as their headquarters
alarmed the authorities. The need to limit their numbers, to prevent them from
being established in remote spots, and also to ensure the loyalty of their proprietors became pressing, and for the next twenty years there was a series of measures
taken to control them, culminating in Ireland's first liquor-licensing act.

The problem which the government faced was not that there was no licensing
of drink outlets, but rather that there were too many different authorities claiming
a right to issue such licenses.[41] Town merchants, planters, landlords, and government syndicates all attempted to regulate the trade.[42] But drinkshops simply
proliferated, with little check on who operated them or where they were located,
and in the process the crown was deprived of a potentially lucrative source of
revenue.

Even before the 1615 Ulster conspiracy the government had begun steps to
assert its authority over the rapidly increasing number of drinkshops. In 1611 it
was decreed that the 'same laws which restrain the retailing of wines . . . in
England without warrant . . . are also in force in Ireland, and the same penalties
are also incurred there . . .'. Moreover, in Ireland these provisions were to be
extended to include 'the retailing of all sorts of aqua vitae and usquebagh', in
order that 'some reasonable profit may be conveniently raised'.[43] In 1620, on the
king's instructions, Sir Oliver St John, the lord deputy, issued a proclamation
aimed at eliminating the 'divers intolerable mischiefs to the commonwealth of
Ireland' caused by the 'daily increase' in the number of alehouses 'called tippling-
houses'. This proclamation is worth quoting at some length, for it laid down the
basic principles of retail liquor licensing, soon to be enshrined in statutory form:

> no person shall keep any alehouse, &c., within this kingdom but such as shall
> be licensed, and that every person shall upon receipt of his license pay 3s. 6d.;
> and that commissioners shall be awarded under the great seal unto every
> county of this kingdom, to be chosen of the justices of [the] peace with others,
> as the deputy, &c., shall think fit, to consider the number fit to keep alehouses,

who shall yearly, between 1 April and 30 June, assemble at the quarter sessions and make choice of such persons as their ability, &c., they shall know to be fit to keep alehouses, any two or more to be a quorum; the party licensed to enter into recognizances of £10, the condition to be that the party licensed shall observe the assize of bread, ale, and beer, and keep two beds well furnished for lodging strangers, not suffer any common dicing or carding nor harbour suspected persons. . . . And every person acting contrary, &c., to pay 20s. for every month so offending; half to his majesty, the other to the informer . . . , and we command that everyone so licensed shall have some sign, stake, or bush at his door to give notice to travellers that they may receive meat, drink, and lodging for their money.[44]

The clerk of the peace was to attend licensing sessions to record the names of those licensed and to collect their fees. He was to be issued with blank printed license forms so that he could hand these out to those paying the fee. The obvious aim of this proclamation was to establish a standardised procedure throughout the country for licensing alehouses, to be operated by local magistrates. Alehouse proprietors were to be respectable individuals, acceptable to the magistrates and affluent enough to be able to put up a £10 bond and to pay a license fee of 3s. 6d. Their houses were to sell good-quality ale and beer and to provide food and lodging for travellers, thus fulfilling some of the functions more commonly filled in England by inns. They were to be clearly marked by a sign so that travellers would have no difficulty in identifying them. And there was an attempt to prevent their being used by rebels and becoming centres for gambling in which working-men might lose their wages. The proclamation, however, did not set a time limit to the duration of the license, nor did it establish any machinery by which the conditions of the license might be enforced. Presumably, the reward of half of any fine imposed, held out to informers, was intended to encourage unofficial policing.

The measure seems, however, to have had little success in curbing the number of alehouses, for in 1631 another similar proclamation was issued in Dublin by the lords justices. This began by complaining of the 'many mischiefs' arising from the 'excessive number of alehouses . . . in woods, bogs, and other unfit places . . . kept by unknown persons, not undertaken for'—clearly signalling the failure of the earlier proclamation. Concern that such houses were used by rebels was clear, for this proclamation laid down that no visitor was to stay in an alehouse for more than twenty-four hours unless he was ill. Also, this proclamation, unlike its predecessor, specified that licenses were to last for only one year. Thus the alehouse proprietors were liable to have their behaviour scrutinised annually by the magistrates, who had the power to refuse them a further license.[45]

The 1631 proclamation had been issued by the lords justices, but when in 1633 Thomas Wentworth took up the post of lord deputy, he quickly decided that alehouses could only be properly regulated by act of parliament, as they had long been in England. Wentworth personally loathed drunkenness and was also committed to boosting the king's Irish revenue, and for both reasons statutory licensing of alehouses was high on his list of priorities. An 'act for keepers of alehouses to be bound by recognizance' (10 & 11 Chas. I, c. 5), passed in 1635, largely reproduced the wording of the 1631 proclamation, though the fee for a license was raised to 5s. 6d. per annum.[46] Writing to the king in the following year, Wentworth was full of optimism, assuring Charles that the statutory licensing of alehouses would yield an extra £3,000 each year.[47] But even before the troubles of the 1640s there is evidence that Wentworth's optimism was misplaced. Alehouse keepers appear to have continued to operate without licenses, and not just in remote areas, for in 1639 an act was passed to punish offenders against the 1635 act in the county and city of Dublin (15 Chas. I, c. 8).[48] In 1640, out of a total revenue of a little over £84,000, alehouse licenses were only producing £1,500, and wine and whiskey licenses only £1,200.[49]

Although in England the Stuarts, and particularly James I, made various efforts to regulate drinkshops, it was the local gentry and magistrates, notably those influenced by puritanism, who proved most effective in reducing the number of alehouses and in enforcing compulsory licensing. In his history of English alehouses Peter Clark wrote of the seventeenth century:

> The alehouse-keeper was progressively restrained by a strait-jacket of duties and responsibilities. . . . By 1750 the administrative machinery for alehouse regulation had been largely set up and was operating with reasonable efficiency.[50]

The latter statement was probably not true of Ireland much before 1850. During the seventeenth century in Ireland, unlike England, it was the Stuarts and their officials in Dublin who originated the most important regulations aimed at controlling pubs, and who sought to bring a measure of order to the chaotic situation created by the conflicting licensing powers exercised by local authorities. But a coercive system imposed from the top could not hope to work as effectively as local regulation, rigorously enforced.

The Cromwellians directed a good deal of their formidable rhetoric against 'tipplers' and 'disorderly alehouses', and reversing the Stuarts' policy of trying to create a regulated indoor space where drinking could be controlled, they attempted to drive drinking out of doors. Like the Stuarts, they regarded alehouses as centres of disaffection, but unlike the Stuarts, they sought to eradicate the problem in typically heavy-handed fashion by simply abolishing pubs. Attempts to prohibit the sale of drink had the effect of depressing grain prices and thus stirring up opposition among landowners. In December 1653, for instance, Lieutenant Richard Beare, an agent in Cork, was writing to his employer complaining that the proclamation prohibiting the sale of beer and ale had hit the price of grain, and as a result, the tenants were having trouble in paying their rents.[51] In the end, however, the urgent need to boost revenue overcame puritanical objections to alcohol consumption. In 1655 new and heavier duties were imposed on wine imports and on both the production and sale of beer and whiskey, while in 1658 both the customs and excise duties were farmed out to a syndicate. In each case the primary aim was to raise more money with which to finance defence expenditure.[52]

With the Restoration there was a need to reorganise Irish revenues, and thus the early 1660s saw a number of important new measures relating to excise administration and to pubs in particular. The earl of Ormond as lord lieutenant faced much the same problems as Wentworth had thirty years earlier: he wanted to satisfy the Stuarts' seemingly insatiable demand for money, while at the same time reducing the number of small and isolated drinkshops, which were almost impossible to supervise. To these ends two major acts were passed: an 'act for the improvement of his majesty's revenues upon the granting of licenses for selling ale and beer' (14 & 15 Chas. II, c. 18), passed in 1662, and an 'act for the better ordering of the selling of wines and aqua vitae' (17 & 18 Chas. II, c. 19), passed in 1666.[53]

The 1662 act repealed that of 1635, but the preamble to the new act reiterated much of that of the earlier one, suggesting that little had changed in regard to the problem of alehouses. The new act aimed 'to reduce needless multitudes of alehouses to a fewer number, to more fit persons, and more convenient places'. Alehouses were to be licensed by commissioners, appointed by the lord lieutenant from among the magistrates assembled at quarter sessions; licensees were to pay twenty shillings per annum, plus a £10 bond; and the fine for unlicensed selling was fixed at £5. The most notable difference between the 1662 act and its predecessor was the substantial increase in the licence fee: from 5s. 6d. to twenty shillings. In fact, under the Commonwealth the fee had reached thirty shillings per annum. Ormond considered this prohibitive, as many fees were outstanding, and opted instead for twenty shillings. He estimated that there were about 7,000 license-holders in Ireland, but most were 'very poor' and lived in 'remote places'. It was therefore desirable to reduce their numbers, and Ormond felt that a fee of twenty shillings, if properly enforced, would do this, besides yielding some £7,000 a year in revenue.[54]

The other major act passed in the 1660s extended statutory licensing for the first time to shops selling wine and whiskey. Under this measure commissioners were to be appointed by the lord lieutenant to license sellers, and licenses were to run for three years. Wine licenses were to cost from £2 to £40, depending on the location of the shop, while the fee for a license to sell whiskey ranged from ten shillings to £10. License fees were to be paid in two instalments: half at the time of the grant and the other half six months later. The commissioners were to appoint collectors to handle the issuing of licenses and the collection of the fees, and in return for these duties they were to be entitled to one shilling for every license issued.[55]

From the point of view of stamping out illicit drinkshops, regulating who should be awarded a license, and controlling what went on in pubs, the legislation of the 1630s and 1660s left much to be desired. There was no real enforcement machinery beyond the annual licensing sessions held by magistrates, who themselves had an economic interest in encouraging the production and consumption of drink, and the collection of fees by licensing and excise collectors, who seem in many cases to have gained financially from every license issued. Yet, while policing was far from satisfactory, this series of acts and the proclamations preceding them were of considerable importance. Through them by the 1660s a space had been created in Ireland, a space that had not existed at the beginning of the century, in which the government sought to confine and control Irish drinking and its associated recreational activities. The creation of this indoor, public, supervised space was an important step on the road to the disciplining of the Irish pub as a popular cultural venue.

During the seventeenth century, however, many cultural and recreational pastimes continued to be held either out of doors or in the private home. Drinkshops had proliferated in the late sixteenth and early seventeenth centuries in the wake of the spread of English settlement. But they were by no means the dominant popular cultural venue. Much drink consumption still took place in the home or out of doors at religious or quasi-religious festivals, which probably increased in number as the formal structure of the Catholic church was suppressed. Alehouse keepers took advantage of such occasions by erecting tents and supplying drink and often also music.[56] Thus they were not wholly divorced from outdoor popular culture. Alcohol also continued to be brewed or distilled in the home for use at family festivities or in the entertainment of guests. There were commercial distilleries in Dublin, and the distillers got together in the 1660s and again in the 1690s to lobby parliament in defence of their interests. The Dublin brewers were an even more powerful group and received their own royal charter in 1670.[57] The basis of a commercialised, government-regulated drink industry was laid in the seventeenth century, but it was not really until the mid-nineteenth century that government control was fully established.

V

The early eighteenth century could be termed a permissive era in regard to attempts to regulate drinkshops, for very little seems to have been done at either a national or a local level.[58] But from the 1750s an increasingly vociferous chorus of criticism began to be heard. It was aimed not so much against alehouses, as in the previous century, but against houses selling whiskey, whether legally or illegally. This critique gathered pace in the early nineteenth century and after 1829 was boosted by the appearance of societies formed specifically for the purpose of curbing drink consumption. This climate of opinion helped to produce a series of important acts aimed at regulating all aspects of the drink industry and at radically changing Irish drinking habits. This legislation began in the 1790s, reached peaks in the 1830s and 1850s, and was finally consolidated in the 1870s. The proliferation of unlicensed alehouses, their use by rebels, and the government's loss of revenue had been spurs to legislative action in the seventeenth century. In the late eighteenth and early nineteenth centuries the spur was still the number of unlicensed drinkshops and the shelter they offered to members of secret societies, but equally important were the growing popularity of whiskey and the emergence of a vast illegal distilling industry based in the north and west of the country.[59]

As already indicated, whiskey was by no means the most popular form of alcohol in Ireland before the eighteenth century. Ale was most commonly drunk in the sixteenth century, while beer became increasingly popular in the seventeenth. But from about the 1750s spirit consumption began to rise dramatically: at first this was the consumption of imported spirits, but from the 1780s home-produced whiskey rapidly took over from rum, brandy, and gin, and increasingly this was illegally distilled whiskey. Why this sudden rise in spirit consumption occurred puzzled contemporaries. The Irish parliament received many petitions deploring the prevalence of whiskey-drinking, and it debated the problem on a number of occasions, most notably in the early 1790s. These debates led to acts aimed at curbing the explosive growth of spirit consumption by increasing spirit duties and to measures aimed against illicit distillers. And they also led to actions both inside and outside parliament to control the occasions at which drinking occurred. Attacks on popular culture launched in the early nineteenth century, and especially attacks on wakes, patterns, and fairs, almost invariably singled out drunkenness and fighting resulting from drunkenness as among the main abuses needing to be stamped out. And in fact the reformers may well have been correct in seeing popular festivals as both more frequent and more riotous than they had been in the past.[60]

If the growing popularity of spirits from the late eighteenth century fueled the campaign against popular culture, it also directed increasingly critical attention at the shops retailing drink. Many of the petitions received by the Irish parliament between 1760 and 1790 complained not only of the popularity and cheapness of spirits but of the proliferation of 'dramshops'.[61] The cost of spirit licenses had actually been reduced in 1775 to between £3 and £5, depending upon the location of the house (15 Geo. III, c. 15), while from 1785 grocers were permitted to sell spirits for consumption off the premises (25 Geo. III, c. 8; 30 Geo. III, c. 11).[62] It is not clear exactly how many alehouses and dramshops there were in Ireland in the eighteenth century. In parliament in February 1791 Henry Grattan claimed that there were about 8,000 licensed spirit shops in the country, but that 90,000 houses actually sold spirits.[63] It is impossible to tell how accurate these figures are, but there is no doubt that illicit selling of whiskey, like illicit production, was being conducted on a huge scale. It is certainly no coincidence that the Irish word 'shebeen' first entered the English language toward the end of the eighteenth century; the need for a special word in English is a clear indication of the growing significance of the phenomenon.[64]

A serious attempt to regulate shebeens and public houses in general was launched in the 1790s. In 1791 a new licensing act (31 Geo. III, c. 13) began by complaining that the 'use of spiritous liquors prevails to an immoderate excess, to the great injury of the health, industry, and morals of the people', and it went on to increase spirit-license fees dramatically, to between £4 and £20, depending on whether the shop was in a town or in a rural area. Moreover, no house could be licensed for the sale of whiskey unless it had at least two hearths. Besides trying to reduce the number of dramshops by increasing the license fee, parliament was also obviously attempting to disqualify the poorest one-hearth cabins from holding a license. Another important act passed in 1792 (32 Geo. III, c. 19) aimed to encourage the sale of beer while curbing illicit trading. Publicans in Dublin, Cork, Waterford, and Limerick could obtain a reduction of their license fee if they sold more than seventy-five barrels of beer each year. But at the same time they were not permitted to sell spirits before one o'clock on Sundays or before sunrise on other days. Fines for unlicensed selling were increased substantially, to £40 in Dublin and £20 elsewhere. This act also made it illegal to pay workmen's wages in pubs, to pay wages in spirits, or to stop wages in order to recover drink debts. In addition, it allowed the appointment in Dublin of parish overseers, who were to be responsible for seeing that pubs operated in an orderly manner. A further act (36 Geo. III, c. 40), passed in 1796, obliged vestries throughout the country to appoint such overseers.[65]

But what was a late eighteenth- or early nineteenth-century Irish shebeen like, and what entertainment or recreation did it offer its customers? There are numerous references to shebeens, particularly in parliamentary papers, in temperance propaganda, and in newspapers, but such references are usually too brief to allow one to visualise the interior of such an establishment. In order to do that, we must turn to contemporary literature. Anthony Trollope, although an Englishman, travelled extensively in Ireland on post-office business in the 1840s and 1850s. More than most people, Trollope would have been familiar with Irish hotels, inns, pubs, and also, apparently, shebeens. In his first and arguably his best Irish novel, *The Macdermots of Ballycloran*, published in 1847, he provided a vivid description of a shebeen in Mohill, Co. Leitrim, in the 1830s:

> The house, or rather cabin, consisted only of two rooms, both on the ground, and both without flooring or ceiling; the black rafters on which the thatch was

lying was [*sic*] above, and the uneven soil below; still, this place of entertainment was not like the cabins of the very poor: the rooms were both long, and
as they ran lengthways down the street, each was the full breadth of the house:
in the first sat the widow Mulready, a strong, red-faced, indomitable-looking
woman about fifty. She sat on a large wooden seat with a back capable of
containing two persons; there was an immense blazing fire of turf, on which
the water was boiling in a great potato pot, should any of her guests be able to
treat themselves to the expensive luxury of punch. A remarkably dirty small
deal table was beside her, on which were placed a large jar containing a quantity
of the only merchandise in which she dealt, and an old battered pewter
measure in which she gave it out. . . . There was a door at the further end of
the room, which opened into the one where Mrs Mulready's more known and
regular visitors were accustomed to sit and drink, and here rumour said a
Ribbon lodge was held; there was a fire also here, at the further end, and a long
narrow table ran nearly the whole length of the room under the two windows,
with a form on each side of it. Opposite this was Mrs Mulready's own bed,
which proved that whatever improprieties might be perpetrated in that house,
the careful widow herself never retired to rest till they were all over.[66]

Trollope clearly thought that the entertainment provided by shebeens was very
limited. He accepted the official view that they were little more than drinking
shops and havens for Ribbonmen. Later in the novel he portrayed drunken illicit
distillers and Whiteboys planning the murder of a revenue-police officer in
Widow Mulready's house. He also drew an implicit contrast between the illegal
shebeen and a legal 'whiskey shop'. Mrs Mehan's shop hosted a wedding attended
by, among others, the priest and the revenue officer. After the ceremony in the
front room of the shop there was a plentiful meal, music played by a fiddler, wild
dancing, and much drinking in the kitchen.[67] Mrs Mehan's shop, like Mrs
Mulready's, had two rooms: a more public outer room and a more private inner
one. But whereas the Mulready sanctum was used to plan a death, in the Mehan
kitchen life and its pleasures were celebrated. Yet clearly, the dichotomy constructed in this novel between the legal and the illegal drinkshop was more
ideological than real. Not all shebeens harboured potential murderers, and many
of them must have shared the gaiety of Mrs Mehan's house. Trollope's portrayal,
however, reflected the official view that shebeens were threatening places, best
done away with and replaced by well-regulated, government-licensed houses.

The legislation of the 1660s had left the relative roles of magistracy and excise
in the issuing of retail licenses far from clear, but the 1791 licensing act clarified
the situation by specifying that the excise could not issue a license to sell spirits
without a magistrate's certificate testifying to the good character of the applicant
and the suitability of his or her house for the sale of drink.[68] A number of acts of
parliament were passed over the following seventy-five years seeking to tighten

the magistracy's control over the issuing of retail licenses.[69] But complaints at the laxity of magistrates and at the excessive number of licensed houses continued even after 1850. In Dublin and Belfast the power to license public houses was vested in the recorder in an attempt to ensure firmer control. Sir Frederick Shaw, recorder of Dublin for nearly fifty years up to 1876, decided in the 1850s that the city had enough pubs, and thereafter he refused to approve any new public-house licenses. This policy forced up the value of the existing pubs and also obliged aspiring drink retailers to take out a spirit-grocer's license, which allowed sale of spirits only for consumption off the premises, and which up until 1872 could be had from the excise without a magistrate's certificate. The licensed trade in Dublin, and in Belfast too when the policy was applied there from the 1860s, thus became divided between relatively affluent publicans, anxious to establish their respectability and increasingly influential in local politics, and spirit grocers, who were poorer and who found it difficult to make a reasonable living without breaching the very restrictive conditions of their license.[70]

Despite the actions of recorders in some of the cities, it was not in fact the zeal of magistrates that enforced the increasingly rigorous provisions of the licensing laws. Magistrates, as we have seen, were certainly crucial in England, but in Ireland the major turning point came in the 1830s with the emergence of an efficient national police force. Early attempts to employ constables, watchmen, and parish overseers to police drinkshops do not seem to have been very success-ful,[71] but several major licensing acts passed in the 1830s gave the newly-consoli-dated Irish constabulary considerable powers to enforce laws against shebeens and illegal selling by licensed publicans and spirit grocers.

Under Perrin's act of 1833 (3 and 4 Wm IV, c. 68) magistrates were empowered to close pubs if a riot was feared, and constables could enter licensed premises during closing hours and eject drinkers found there; in 1836 (6 and 7 Wm IV, c. 38) drinking and gambling in pubs during closing hours were outlawed, and publicans were forbidden to display political emblems or to allow illegal organi-sations to meet on their premises. In 1839 (2 and 3 Vic., c. 79) magistrates were empowered to issue search warrants to constables to enter any unlicensed prem-ises where it was suspected that spirits were being sold; while in 1845 (8 and 9 Vic., c. 64) this provision was extended to spirit-grocer shops. By these various acts the police were in effect given power to enter and search any house, licensed or unlicensed, that was suspected of breaching the licensing laws, though in the case of unlicensed premises a search warrant from a magistrate was required. Under Perrin's act it was also an offence to refuse to admit or even delay to admit a constable onto licensed premises. The 1836 act in addition gave police a role in the licensing of publicans when it specified that applicants for a license required not only a certificate from the magistrates but a similar certificate from a chief constable or two parish overseers. In 1854 (17 and 18 Vic., c. 89) this provision was extended when all applicants were required to give twenty-one days' notice to the police before the licensing sessions, and the police were empowered to lodge objections to applications. By this act the police were in effect given a power of veto over pub-license applications.

By the end of the century the single subject occupying most space in the Royal Irish Constabulary's (RIC) guide for constables was enforcement of the licensing laws.[72] Although the police may not always have been as enthusiastic about prosecuting illicit traders as the temperance lobby wished, nevertheless, there is little doubt that the more rigorous licensing laws, and particularly those introduced from the 1830s onwards, could never have been enforced without the simultaneous creation of a centrally-controlled, national police force. The Irish magistracy had proved either unwilling or unable to curb illicit trading. In the late 1850s the constabulary took over responsibility for putting down illicit distillation as well, after the ineffectiveness of the magistrates and the old revenue police had been revealed by a parliamentary enquiry.[73] The transfer of licensing powers to judges in some of the cities was a measure further highlighting the inadequacies of the Irish magistracy. By these various means, however, from the 1830s an effective system for enforcing legislation to regulate pubs was at last created.

Yet while the public house as an indoor drinking space was being progressively hedged around by a vast amount of complex legislation, before 1850 much drinking continued to take place out of doors at periodic festivals, fairs, and sports meetings. The publican was by no means totally confined to his house, for in rural areas particularly, he could do a good deal of business at such gatherings. Thus, well into the first half of the nineteenth century the publican straddled the worlds of both government-sanctioned, indoor drinking and outdoor, unregulated popular festivals. And in so doing, he rubbed shoulders with both the illicit distiller and the shebeen keeper.

Publicans were often accused by their critics of promoting outdoor gatherings themselves, like dances, horse-races, and, in Ulster, Orange marches, as a means of drumming up business.[74] They were certainly to the fore at patterns and fairs, erecting their tents[75] side by side with those of shebeen keepers, selling drink and food, and often providing pipers and fiddlers to encourage dancing. Thomas Crofton Croker gives a vivid picture of the tents at the pattern held at Gougane Barra, Co. Cork, on St John's eve in 1813:

> whiskey, porter, bread, and salmon were sold in booths or tents resembling a gipsy encampment, and formed by means of poles or branches of trees meeting at angles, over which were thrown the proprietor's great coat, his wife's cloak, old blankets, quilts, and occasionally a little straw. Above the entrance of each was suspended the name of the owner if he happened to possess a license; when this was not the case, a jug, a bottle, or pipe were displayed to indicate that spirits and porter might be had within. . . . Almost every tent had its piper, and two or three young men and women dancing the jig. . . .[76]

It is interesting to note that unlike in licensed pubs, the sexes mixed freely at these outdoor gatherings, drinking and dancing together. Drink tents could often be quite numerous. The Halls quote an account of the pattern held on St Declan's day at Ardmore, Co. Waterford, which shows that at its height the pattern was attended by some 12,000 to 15,000 people, who were served by sixty-four tents.[77]

From the 1830s, however, as the government was tightening the regulations applying to licensed drinkshops, it also began to take upon itself powers to regulate drink-selling at fairs, patterns, and other popular outdoor festivals. An important licensing act passed in 1836 (6 and 7 Wm IV, c. 38) was strongly supported by the reforming under-secretary at Dublin Castle, Thomas Drummond, who in the same year was closely involved in the reorganisation of the Irish constabulary.[78] This specified that licensed traders had to close their outdoor booths from 6 p.m. to 9 a.m. in summer and from 3 p.m. to 9 a.m. in winter. Accounts of patterns suggest that drinking and fighting were at their height in the late afternoon and early evening, after the day's devotions had been completed. Restricting drinking to daylight hours would also doubtless have made it easier for the police to control any disorder. Finally, in 1862 publicans selling at fairs and races were required to take out an occasional license, which could not be issued by the excise without a magistrate's certificate (25 Vic., c. 22), and in 1863 the hours of trade for an occasional license were fixed at from sunrise till one hour after sunset, though in the case of public dinners or balls the hours could be extended with a magistrate's consent (26 and 27 Vic., c. 33). Clearly, such legislation was intended to curb popular outdoor recreation and not the indoor gatherings of the upper and middle classes.

Restrictions on the supply of drink to outdoor gatherings were used from the 1830s onwards as part of a campaign to discourage such occasions. Donnybrook fair in Dublin and the Easter Monday celebrations held on Cave Hill above Belfast were both finally stamped out in the 1860s. Refusing occasional licenses for such gatherings and strict enforcement of the licensing laws by the police played a major role in their demise.[79] By the 1860s and 1870s, in fact, contemporaries were recognising that the suppression of popular festivals had deprived the Irish of many traditional modes of recreation and that the pub had benefited as a consequence. Frederick Falkiner, who succeeded Shaw as recorder of Dublin, declared in 1877 that he wanted 'to see the people getting more pleasure, but they have none almost now, so far as I can see, except drinking. . .'. Even in the pubs, though, Falkiner felt there was little entertainment: 'they have not the amusements that the French have, of dominoes and backgammon'. Captain George Talbot, the assistant commissioner of the DMP, largely agreed with Falkiner. He summed up Dublin working-class recreation as drinking on Saturday evening after having been paid and going for walks to the Phoenix Park or to Kingstown (Dun Laoghaire) on Sunday and drinking in the pubs there. Talbot, unlike

Falkiner, however, was not condemning such forms of recreation; as a young man, he said, he had often done the same himself.[80]

After 1850 the Irish pub entered upon its heyday. The number of pubs stabilised and remained at around 16,000 to 17,000 for the next half-century. With the dramatic decline in the population beginning in the 1840s, however, the ratio of pubs to people actually rose substantially: from one per 613 in 1841 to one per 336 in 1871, to one per 249 in 1901.[81] In England from the late eighteenth century breweries began to buy up or invest in pubs, giving rise to the phenomenon of the tied house. By 1900 fully 75 percent of English pubs were tied to breweries. This connection helped to finance the development of the gin palaces of the 1830s and the neo-gothic temples of the 1880s and 1890s.[82] But Irish breweries showed little inclination to involve themselves directly in the retail trade. Irish pubs therefore usually remained as small independent businesses. Drink palaces did appear in the major cities, most notably the Crown Liquor Saloon in Belfast and the Irish House, the Long Hall, Ryan's, and Lynch's in Dublin, but these were far from typical Irish pubs.[83] Unlike English pubs, few Irish ones were purpose-built; many were converted houses or shops, and their fittings were strictly functional. Also, unlike English pubs, many went by the name of the present or past publican, emphasising the fact that one individual ran the house. Entering the house therefore entailed entering into a relationship with that individual. Irish publicans were therefore more independent and generally retained more local influence than their English counterparts.

Mass-Observation's pioneering study of the pubs of Bolton, Lancashire, in the 1930s began with the comment that the pub was 'the only kind of public building used by large numbers of ordinary people where their thoughts and actions are *not* being in some way arranged for them. . .'.[84] This essay would suggest that such a claim was not true of Irish pubs nor of English ones either. The Irish drinkshop had been singled out by governments beginning in the early seventeenth century as a dangerous institution, threatening the stability and income of the state on the one hand, and undermining the morals of the people on the other. But by the late nineteenth century, after a vast amount of complex legislation, it had been transformed into an accepted and indeed vital part of social and economic life, with the publican as a respectable and often influential local figure. Even the Catholic church, while condemning intemperance, recognised that the publican and his house served vital and valuable functions in the community.[85]

In Ireland the pub had been disciplined principally by legislation at the national level, enforced at first not very effectively by magistrates and excise officers, and then from the 1830s far more rigorously by the new Irish constabulary. At the same time that the authorities were shaping the pub into a controlled and well-ordered environment, they were attempting to suppress many alternate popular cultural venues. Complaints by police and magistrates in the 1870s that the Irish, in the cities at least, were totally ignorant of either indoor or outdoor games and seemed only to find recreation in pub-drinking are thus deeply ironic, for it was such people who had played an important role in elevating the pub to its central place in Irish leisure activities.

The creation of the pub and the suppression of other venues led to a shift in drinking from outdoors into the confined and regulated space of the government-licensed drinkshop. Peter Burke's emphasis on the determining role of physical space in shaping popular recreation is surely well placed, for in restricting drinking to a clearly designated and controlled space, the authorities succeeded in disciplining it. The drinker could drink only at certain times; what he drank and what he paid for it were regulated; drunkenness and fighting could lead to his ejection from the pub; the types of games which he could play were limited, while even singing and dancing might be barred; and both the people and organisations that he could meet with in the pub were controlled. Mass-Observation's emphasis on the freedom which the pub offered its customers was misplaced. At the outdoor festival, up to the 1830s at least, none of these prohibitions would have applied, but efforts made thereafter to discipline outdoor drink consumption as well helped to undermine the popularity of such festivals. It is hardly surprising to find that after 1850 drink, and particularly whiskey, consumption declined in Ireland. While increased taxation certainly played a part in this, the restrictions placed on drink venues were also without doubt important.

The creation of the pub was, however, a very slow and complex process, and even after 1850, especially in rural Ireland, regular pub-drinking was by no means the only drinking pattern evident. Although many of the larger outdoor festivals had disappeared or were in serious decline, irregular, heavy drink consumption at fairs, wakes, or weddings was still common. Thus the recent tendency among English historians of popular culture to stress the resilience and adaptability of many traditional customs and institutions would seem appropriate to Ireland as well. In the Irish context also, too much emphasis should not be placed on the half-century after 1780 as the period of most critical change. The concept of the public house, licensed by central government and regulated by the local authorities, was introduced into Ireland in the seventeenth century, and many of the basic principles of its operation were set out in statute form in the 1660s. The most important innovations of the years between 1780 and 1850 were the creation of an effective machinery for enforcing such statutes and, through this, the suppression of the vast industry producing and selling drink illicitly. Regulated to the government's satisfaction, with its illegal rivals largely suppressed, and enjoying at least the acquiescence of the Catholic church, the pub was thus able to emerge after 1850 as the principal Irish recreational venue.

NOTES

1 Peter Burke, *Popular culture in early modern Europe* (London, 1978), p. 108.

2 Ibid., pp. 108–11.

3 I am using the terms 'public house' and 'pub' fairly loosely. For the etymology of the word 'public house', see the *O.E.D.* and Peter Clark, *The English alehouse: a social history, 1200–1830* (London and New York, 1983), pp. 5–6, 195.

4 Phil Davies and Dermot Walsh, *Alcohol problems and alcohol control in Europe* (London, Canberra, and New York, 1983), pp. 90–106. For a study that found pubs still the focus of social life in Ennis, Co. Clare, in the 1980s, see Chris Curtin and Colm Ryan, 'Clubs, pubs, and private houses in a Clare town' in Chris Curtin and T.M. Wilson (ed.), *Ireland from below: social change and local communities* (Galway, n.d.), pp. 128–43.

5 For a discussion of this survey and the context in which it was made, see Elizabeth Malcolm, *'Ireland sober, Ireland free': drink and temperance in nineteenth-century Ireland* (Dublin, 1986), p. 234.

6 *Fourth report . . . from the select committee of the house of lords on intemperance*, pp. 443, 445, 459, 495–6, H.L. 1878 (338), xiv, 443, 445, 459, 495–6; *Report from the select committee on sale of intoxicating liquors on Sunday (Ireland) bill*, pp. 227–8, 270, H.C. 1877 (198), xvi, 244–5, 287.

7 Valerie Hey, *Patriarchy and pub culture* (London and New York, 1986), p. 30.

8 There is ample evidence of this attitude in K.C. Kearns, *Dublin tenement life: an oral history* (Dublin, 1994), pp. 49–54.

9 Robert Lynd, *Home life in Ireland* (London, 1909), p. 276; Henry Glassie, *Passing the time: folklore and history in an Ulster community* (Dublin, 1982), pp. 80–1.

10 Quoted in Kearns, *Dublin tenement life*, p. 118.

11 John Devoy, *Recollections of an Irish rebel* (reprint, with introduction by Seán Ó Lúing, Shannon, 1969, of orig. ed., New York, 1929), pp. 165–6, 168; John Gray, 'Popular entertainment' in J.C. Beckett *et al.*, *Belfast: the making of the city, 1800–1914* (Belfast, 1983), pp. 103–4.

12 Quoted in Robin Flower, *The western island or the Great Blasket* (Oxford, 1944), p. 16.

13 There is no substantial study of the role of pubs and publicans in post-famine Ireland, but the following works contain useful information: *Annual report of the committee of the Licensed Grocers and Vintners' Protection Association of Dublin* (Dublin, 1898); *Report from the select committee on the sale of liquors on Sunday (Ireland) bill*, pp. 74–104, H.C. 1867–8 (280), xiv, 632–62; *Minutes of evidence taken before the royal commission on liquor licensing laws . . .*, pp. 36, 79, 201, 247 [Cd 8980], H.C. 1898, xxxviii, 570, 613, 735, 781; Charles McGlinchey, *The last of the name*, ed. Brian Friel (Belfast and Dover, N.H., 1986), pp. 62–3; K.T. Hoppen, *Elections, politics, and society in Ireland, 1832–1885* (Oxford, 1984), pp. 53–4, 430–2; Malcolm, *'Ireland sober, Ireland free'*, pp. 206–9.

14 Samuel Clark, *Social origins of the Irish land war* (Princeton, N.J., 1979), p. 128. For a recent study of publicans and grocers in Thomastown, Co. Kilkenny, that challenges Clark's interpretation, see P.H. Gulliver, 'Shopkeepers and farmers in south Kilkenny, 1840–1981' in Marilyn Silverman and P.H. Gulliver (ed.), *Approaching the past: historical anthropology through Irish case studies* (New York, 1992), pp. 189–200.

15 Hoppen, *Elections*, pp. 40–1, 52.

16 *Annual report Licensed Grocers, Dublin*, pp. 36–8; M.E. Daly, *Dublin—the deposed capital: a social and economic history, 1860–1914* (Cork, 1984), pp. 205–6, 218.

17 For a description of the decline of English popular recreations, see R.W. Malcolmson, *Popular recreations in English society, 1700–1850* (Cambridge, 1973); for Ireland, see Elizabeth Malcolm, 'Popular recreation in nineteenth-century Ireland' in Oliver MacDonagh, W.F. Mandle, and Pauric Travers (ed.), *Irish culture and nationalism, 1750–1950* (London and Canberra, 1983), pp. 40–55. The present essay revises some of the ideas expressed in my earlier article.

18 Hugh Cunningham, *Leisure in the industrial revolution, c.1780–c.1880* (London, 1980), pp. 15,

22. Cunningham's point about the persistence of popular culture and the dangers of prematurely celebrating the demise of a particular custom is reinforced in the Irish context by Estyn Evans, who warned that 'it is rarely safe to speak of old customs as extinct in rural Ireland. It has more than once been my experience to come across habits and beliefs which were described as dead half a century ago.' See E.E. Evans, *Irish heritage: the landscape, the people, and their work* (Dundalk, 1942), p. 174.

19 J.M. Golby and A.W. Purdue, *The civilisation of the crowd: popular culture in England, 1750–1900* (London, 1984), p. 40.

20 Cunningham, *Leisure*, pp. 15–16.

21 H.F. Kearney, 'Select documents, xvi: the Irish wine trade, 1614–15' in *I.H.S.*, ix, no. 36 (September 1955), pp. 408–42; Anthony Sheehan, 'Irish towns in a period of change, 1558–1625' in Ciaran Brady and Raymond Gillespie (ed.), *Natives and newcomers: essays on the making of Irish colonial society, 1534–1641* (Dublin, 1986), p. 117.

22 Sheehan, 'Irish towns', pp. 93–119; Gearóid MacNiocaill, 'Socio-economic problems of the late medieval Irish town' in David Harkness and Mary O'Dowd (ed.), *The town in Ireland* (*Hist. Studies* xiii, Belfast, 1981), pp. 7–21; Colm Lennon, *The lords of Dublin in the age of reformation* (Dublin, 1989).

23 Moryson quoted in C.L. Falkiner (ed.), *Illustrations of Irish history and topography, mainly of the seventeenth century* (London, New York, and Bombay, 1904), p. 226; Barnaby Rich, *A new description of Ireland wherein is described the disposition of the Irish whereunto they are inclined* (London, 1610), pp. 70, 72.

24 Rich, *New description*, pp. 70–1. The records of the Dublin corporation suggest that in the fifteenth century the majority of brewers were female: 'brewesteres' was the term used to describe them in the corporation records in 1470. Peter Clark found that in England too in the late medieval period the ale industry was dominated by women, or 'ale-wives' as they were commonly called. See J.T. Gilbert (ed.), *Calendar of ancient records of Dublin* (Dublin, 1889), i, 342; Clark, *English alehouse*, pp. 21–2.

25 *Stat. Ire.*, i, 14–15; Gilbert, *Calendar*, ii, 38–9; i, 288; M.D. O'Sullivan, *Old Galway: the history of a Norman colony in Ireland* (Cambridge, 1942), p. 444.

26 O'Sullivan, *Old Galway*, p. 439.

27 Richard Caulfield (ed.), *The council book of the corporation of Youghal, from 1610 to 1659, from 1666 to 1687, and from 1690 to 1800* (Guildford, Surrey, 1878), p. 7.

28 Ibid., pp. 7, 20. As Youghal had a total population of around 2,000 in 1600, up to twenty inns would seem in fact quite a generous supply. See Sheehan, 'Irish towns', pp. 100–1.

29 J.S. Curl, *The Londonderry plantation, 1609–1914* (Chichester, Sussex, 1986), pp. 54, 433. In his book Curl includes a picture-map of Newtown Limavady in 1622, which shows perhaps the only illustration of an Irish inn from this period. Inns were certainly encouraged by the plantation authorities and were recorded in towns such as Armagh, Omagh, Belturbet, Virginia, and Lifford, where they were expected 'to give entertainment to passengers'. See Philip Robinson, *The plantation of Ulster: British settlement in an Irish landscape, 1600–70* (Dublin and New York, 1984), p. 173.

30 Michael McCarthy Morrogh, 'The English presence in early seventeenth-century Munster' in Brady and Gillespie, *Natives and newcomers*, p. 179.

31 This term was used by T.W. Russell, a temperance agent in the 1860s and 1870s and from the 1880s a unionist MP representing County Tyrone. See *Fourth report . . . from the select committee of the house of lords on intemperance*, pp. 354, 396, H.L. 1878 (338), xiv, 354, 396.

32 I would like to thank Dr Mary O'Dowd for information on the role of alcohol in late medieval and early modern Gaelic society. For the consumption of whiskey in Ireland at this time, see Malcolm, *'Ireland sober, Ireland free'*, pp. 2–5.

33 Kenneth Nicholls, *Gaelic and Gaelicised Ireland in the middle ages* (Dublin, 1972), pp. 114–18; K.W. Nicholls, *Land, law, and society in sixteenth-century Ireland* (O'Donnell lecture, Cork, 1976), p. 9; Mary O'Dowd, 'Gaelic economy and society' in Brady and Gillespie, *Natives and*

newcomers, pp. 128–31; Nerys Patterson, *Cattle lords and clansmen: the social structure of early Ireland* (2nd ed., Notre Dame, Indiana, and London, 1994).

34 Máire MacNeill, *The festival of Lughnasa: a study of the survival of the Celtic festival of the beginning of harvest* (reprint, Dublin, 1982, of orig. ed., London, 1962), pp. 67–70.

35 Quoted in J.P. Myers, Jr. (ed.), *Elizabethan Ireland: a selection of writings of Elizabethan writers on Ireland* (Hamden, Conn., 1983), p. 253.

36 Quoted in Falkiner, *Illustrations*, p. 229. Another example of this phenomenon was seen in Moneymore, Co. Londonderry, where a new agent, appointed in 1615, set up his own brewery, paid his workmen in beer, and allowed alehouses to proliferate in the town. In 1618 a delegation of the inhabitants went to London to complain to the London companies that the Irish from the surrounding areas had flocked to the town to drink unchecked and that brawling had become almost constant (Curl, *Londonderry plantation*, p. 178).

37 For information on Irish houses during the late medieval and early modern periods, we have to turn to the evidence of archaeology. See Ann Hamlin and Chris Lynn (ed.), *Pieces of the past: archaeological excavations by the Department of the Environment for Northern Ireland, 1970–86* (Belfast, 1988), pp. 78–84; T.B. Barry, *The archaeology of medieval Ireland* (London and New York, 1987), pp. 73–4, 81–2. For English alehouses of this period, see Clark, *English alehouse*, pp. 164–7.

38 Herbert Hore and James Graves (ed.), *The social state of the southern and eastern counties of Ireland in the sixteenth century . . .* (Dublin, 1870), pp. 141–3.

39 It is interesting, for instance, to note how many seventeenth-century Irish poets patronised drinkshops, when their predecessors would have been more commonly found in the tower-houses of the Gaelic lords. Dáibhidh Ó Bruadair (*ca.* 1625–98) was not alone in finding consolation in the 'gaily lighted ale-shops' of Cork, with their many 'quarts and pints'. See John MacErlean (ed.), *The poems of David Ó Bruadair* (London, 1913), ii, 77.

40 Raymond Gillespie, *Conspiracy: Ulster plots and plotters in 1615* (Belfast, 1987), pp. 15–17. It was probably no coincidence that in 1623 Phillips was proposing that no alehouses should be allowed 'in remote places' in Ulster, and that no 'beverage maker' should be allowed 'to dwell but in towns and villages under some British gentleman'. See *Cal. S.P. Ire., 1615–25*, pp. 411–12.

41 Victor Treadwell, 'The establishment of the farm of the Irish customs, 1603–13' in *E.H.R.*, xciii, no. 368 (July 1978), pp. 580–602; Malcolm, *'Ireland sober, Ireland free'*, pp. 7, 11–16; Sean Reamonn, *History of the revenue commissioners* (Dublin, 1981), pp. 4–6.

42 Caulfield, *Youghal council book*, pp. 49, 12; Aidan Clarke, *The Old English in Ireland, 1625–42* (London, 1966), pp. 49–50, 57–8.

43 *Cal. Carew MSS, 1603–24*, pp. 207, 161; *Cal. S.P. Ire., 1611–14*, pp. 249–50; *Commons' jn. Ire.*, i, 56.

44 This proclamation does not appear to survive among the state papers, but it was obviously sent to town councils and magistrates, and thus it is to be found in the council book of Youghal corporation. See *Cal. S.P. Ire., 1615–25*, p. 282; Caulfield, *Youghal council book*, pp. 75–7.

45 Caulfield, *Youghal council book*, pp. 171–2.

46 *Commons' jn. Ire.*, i, 116; *Stat. Ire.*, ii, 151–2.

47 William Knowler (ed.), *The earl of Strafford's letters and dispatches, with an essay towards his life, by Sir George Radcliffe* (Dublin, 1740), ii, 8.

48 *Stat. Ire.*, ii, 202.

49 *Cal. S.P. Ire., 1647–60*, pp. 234–5, 352–3; *Cal. S.P. Ire., 1633–47*, pp. 299, 318.

50 Clark, *English alehouse*, p. 181.

51 P.H. Hore, *History of the town and county of Wexford* (London, 1906), v, 311–12; T.C. Barnard, *Cromwellian Ireland* (London, 1975), pp. 40–1; Historical Manuscripts Commission, *Report on the manuscripts of the earl of Egmont*, vol. i, pt. ii (London, 1905), p. 530.

52 *Cal. S.P. Ire., 1647–60*, pp. 812, 858–9.

53 *Stat. Ire.*, ii, 511–12; *Stat. Ire.*, iii, 185–9.

54 *Cal. S.P. Ire., 1660–62*, p. 637.

55 *Commons' jn. Ire.*, i, 722, 749; E.B. McGuire, *Irish whiskey: a history of distilling, the spirit trade, and excise controls in Ireland* (Dublin and New York, 1973), pp. 101–2.

56 See Sir Henry Piers's account of drink being sold after a pilgrimage in County Westmeath in the 1680s, in Edward MacLysaght, *Irish life in the seventeenth century* (2nd ed., Cork, 1950), pp. 163–4.

57 *Cal. S.P. Ire., 1669–70*, pp. 288–90.

58 This is not to say, however, that Irish drinking habits and drinkshops lacked critics. See, for instance, [Samuel Madden], *Reflections and resolutions proper for the gentlemen of Ireland, as to their conduct for the service of their country . . .* (Dublin, 1738), pp. 47–8, 68–71, 203.

59 This industry will not be treated in any great detail here, as it has been examined at length elsewhere. See, for example, K.H. Connell, *Irish peasant society: four historical essays* (Oxford, 1968), pp. 1–50; McGuire, *Irish whiskey*, pp. 388–432; Malcolm, 'Ireland sober, Ireland free', pp. 31–8.

60 S.J. Connolly, *Priests and people in pre-famine Ireland, 1780–1845* (Dublin, 1982), p. 166; P.J. Corish, *The Catholic community in the seventeenth and eighteenth centuries* (Dublin, 1981), pp. 50–1, 111–14.

61 See, for instance, the petition from the corporation of Dublin brewers received in 1760, in *Commons' jn. Ire.*, iv, 204–5, and the petition from the grand jury of the city of Dublin received in 1785, *Commons' jn. Ire.*, v, 346.

62 McGuire, *Irish whiskey*, pp. 158, 160–2.

63 *Commons' jn. Ire.*, iii, app. xcix; v, app. lxxxiv; *Parl. reg. Ire.*, xi, 68.

64 *O.E.D.*

65 *Stat. Ire.*, xv, 560–70; McGuire, *Irish whiskey*, pp. 160–1.

66 Anthony Trollope, *The Macdermots of Ballycloran* (reprint, New York, 1988, of 5th ed., London, n.d.), pp. 75–6.

67 Ibid., pp. 111–24. For a useful discussion of the political limitations of Trollope's view of Ireland in this novel, see Conor Johnston, '*The Macdermots of Ballycloran*: Trollope as a conservative-liberal' in *Eire-Ireland*, xvi, no. 2 (Summer 1981), pp. 71–92.

68 McGuire, *Irish whiskey*, p. 121; *Parl. reg. Ire.*, xiii, 469.

69 By the early 1870s there were, in all, fourteen different types of retail-liquor license, five of which required a magistrate's certificate. For helpful digests of the voluminous Irish licensing legislation of the nineteenth century, see Andrew Reed, *The liquor licensing laws of Ireland* (Dublin, 1889); M.B. Kavanagh and A.W. Quill, *The licensing acts, 1872–1874, and an appendix of all the statutes regulating the sale by retail of intoxicating liquors in Ireland and the management of licensed houses* (Dublin, 1875).

70 *Report from the select committee on sale of intoxicating liquors on Sunday (Ireland) bill*, pp. 63, 117, 236, H.C. 1877 (198), xvi, 80, 134, 253; *Report from the select committee on public houses*, p. 141 [C 367], H.C. 1854, xiv, 405.

71 S.H. Palmer, *Police and protest in England and Ireland, 1780–1850* (Cambridge, 1988), pp. 121–2; Brian Henry, *Dublin hanged: crime, law enforcement, and punishment in late eighteenth-century Dublin* (Dublin, 1994), pp. 137–53.

72 In its various forms it took up over 10 percent of the book. See Andrew Reed, *The Irish constable's guide* (3rd ed., Dublin, 1895).

73 *Report from the select committee . . . appointed to consider . . . extending the functions of the constabulary in Ireland to the suppression or prevention of illicit distillation*, H.L. 1854 (53), x.

74 Anon., 'Irish dancing fifty years ago' in *Dublin University Magazine*, lxii, no. 370 (October 1863), p. 430; *Third report from the select committee appointed to inquire into . . . Orange lodges . . .*, pp. 288–9, 348, 384, H.C. 1835 (476), xvi, 288–9, 348, 384.

75 For a vivid description of the tents of Donnybrook fair, see Jonah Barrington, *Personal sketches of his own times* (3rd ed., London, 1869), ii, 329–31.

76 T.C. Croker, *Researches in the south of Ireland*... (reprint, Shannon, 1969, of orig. ed., London, 1824), p. 280.

77 S.C. Hall and A.M. Hall, *Ireland, its scenery, character, &c.* (London, 1841), i, 284. Inglis saw twenty or more tents at a pattern in the Joyce's country in Connemara in 1834, while Thackeray saw fifty at the foot of Croagh Patrick in 1842. See H.D. Inglis, *Ireland in 1834: a journey throughout Ireland during the spring, summer, and autumn of 1834* (London, 1834), ii, 49–50; [W.M. Thackeray], *The Irish sketch-book* (London, 1843), ii, 102.

78 Drummond had personally ridden out to the Phoenix Park to close the drink booths that generally opened there on Sunday afternoons and evenings. See R.B. O'Brien, *Thomas Drummond, under-secretary in Ireland, 1835–40: life and letters* (London, 1889), pp. 246–8; Galen Broeker, *Rural disorder and police reform in Ireland, 1812–36* (London and Toronto, 1970), pp. 219, 225–7.

79 Fergus D'Arcy, 'The decline and fall of Donnybrook fair: moral reform and social control in nineteenth-century Dublin' in *Saothar*, 13 (1988), pp. 7–21; Gray, 'Popular entertainment', pp. 99–101.

80 *Report from the select committee on sale of intoxicating liquors on Sunday (Ireland) bill*, pp. 31, 67, 69, H.C. 1877 (198), xvi, 48, 84, 86.

81 Wilson, *Alcohol*, pp. 403–5.

82 Mark Girouard, *Victorian pubs* (London, 1975); Brian Spiller, *Victorian public houses* (Newton Abbot, Devon, 1972).

83 Girouard, *Victorian pubs*, pp. 240–4; Jeanne Sheehy, *The rediscovery of Ireland's past: the Celtic revival, 1830–1930* (London, 1980), pp. 70, 76.

84 Mass-Observation, *The pub and the people: a worktown study* (reprint, London, 1987, of orig. ed., London, 1943), p. 17.

85 Elizabeth Malcolm, 'The Catholic church and the Irish temperance movement, 1838–1901' in *I.H.S.*, xxiii, no. 89 (May 1982), pp. 1–16.

4

The Irish Rogues

NIALL Ó CIOSÁIN

Many studies of early modern rural popular culture have taken as their starting point the small, cheap printed books which circulated among peasant readers. These were sold by travelling pedlars along with other goods and were bought by them from urban printers who specialised in that market. These books have many advantages as a source for the social historian: they have survived in quantities which are large enough to be representative, but not so large as to preclude an overall survey. Thus Mandrou for France, Spufford for England, and Adams for Ulster attempt to characterise the printed corpus as a whole. They point to the proportions of religious material as against secular, for example, or of 'escapist' as against 'realist', chart changes over time in these proportions, and construct a 'popular print culture' thereby.[1]

Such an approach, while indispensible as a starting point, does not satisfactorily elucidate the question of such texts as a guide to a 'popular' culture. Many chapbooks in the seventeenth and early eighteenth centuries were aimed at an urban bourgeois audience rather than at the rural peasantry frequently assumed by historians; and a totalising approach, while appropriate for a survey of printed output, tends to falsify the experience of the majority of readers, who saw books only infrequently and may have read a single text, or a few texts, intensively over a long period.[2]

In other words, these studies tend to conflate popular printing with popular culture and to stress production of texts rather than consumption or reception. For a peasant readership there is little direct evidence of reception. In the pre-famine period in Ireland there are few of the lower-class or autodidact autobiographies which give some evidence of popular styles of reading elsewhere.[3] Some clues can be got from a knowledge of the wider cultural context, from the worldview which the readers brought to bear on the texts. The ways in which the texts were adapted from their sources for a popular audience can also offer a guide to reading practices. Conversely, the manner of reception of the printed text will tell us more about the wider culture as an interpretative framework.

One way of doing this is to take a single text or a group of related texts and to follow them through the various formats of production and manners of reception. The text used here is *A history of the most notorious Irish tories, highwaymen, and rapparees*, better known as *Irish rogues and rapparees*, or simply *Irish rogues*, by J. Cosgrave, first published in the mid-eighteenth century and frequently reprinted. It is a collection of lives of highwaymen and robbers, all Irish and mostly operating in Ireland, and is the principal Irish example of the literature of criminality which was a strong feature of popular print in Western Europe. Unfortunately, nothing is known about Cosgrave, but his text is a particularly revealing one: its characters are historical figures from the Irish seventeenth century, presented in a framework derived from European learned and popular criminal biography. Comparison of *Irish rogues* with its sources and with the various types of criminal literature can give an idea of the reception of the text; other clues can be got from the changing format of the book and from the general context of eighteenth- and nineteenth-century Gaelic and popular culture; and finally, like much of the popular culture and folklore which has survived, it was rediscovered, reconstructed, and used by nineteenth-century bourgeois nationalism.

In this respect *Irish rogues* illustrates the fact that 'popular' culture cannot easily be distinguished from 'elite' or 'learned' culture on the grounds of content, but that broader practices need to be borne in mind. As Chartier has expressed it, 'the "popular" cannot be found readymade in a set of texts that merely require to be identified and listed; above all, the popular qualifies a kind of relation, a way of using cultural products as legitimate ideas and attitudes'.[4]

The earliest surviving edition of *Irish rogues* dates from 1747; printed in Dublin, it is described as the 'third edition'. A 'tenth edition' was printed in Dublin in 1782, and also a 'twelfth'. It was a standard text of popular literature by the early nineteenth century, appearing frequently in catalogues and surviving in many editions.[5] *Irish rogues* is also conspicuous in accounts by contemporaries of popular literature in Ireland, picked out presumably because of its subversive nature. It was first mentioned by name at the beginning of the nineteenth century as being read in peasant schools and as part of the background to the rebellion of 1798. Thereafter, it was among the texts most frequently cited by commentators on 'the state of Ireland'.[6]

The use of these books in schools is confirmed by some surviving documentation as well as by the recollections of some of those who were educated in hedge schools. It is recorded as having been in use as a reader by a fourteen-year-old child in a school in west Kerry in the 1790s. There is also the well-known description of a more general readership by the folklorist Crofton Croker in the 1820s: 'A history of rogues and rapparees is at present one of the most popular books among the Irish peasantry and has circulated to an extent that seems almost incredible; nor is it unusual to hear the adventures and escapes of highwaymen recited by the lower orders with the greatest minuteness and dwelt on with the greatest fondness'.[7]

Irish rogues has been approached in a number of different ways. Sometimes it is treated as a series of factual accounts, illustrating social conditions in the late seventeenth and early eighteenth centuries. This is less than appropriate to these slightly fantastic stories, which are mainly invented or taken from elements of the hero type in traditional oral culture.[8] Nevertheless, it should be pointed out that the real historical figures on whom most of these texts are based fit the category of bandits or brigands which existed in other European countries at roughly the same point in state-formation, when, as Connolly puts it, 'central government aspires to maintain a uniform rule of law throughout its territory but has not yet developed the resources to do so effectively'. The brigands represented older, local power structures struggling against the imposition of central law, and frequently operated in conjunction with local élites.[9]

The terminology of the Irish phenomenon is also typical. 'Bandit' means literally 'banished', in other words, an outlaw; as Davis points out in his study of Italy, this is 'a condition, not a crime'. In Ireland the equivalent was 'tory', from the Irish '*tóraighe*', meaning 'wanted' or 'one who is searched for', again a condition rather than a crime in itself. The tories were originally the outlaws of the late seventeenth century, but the term survived (see below), not least in the title of Cosgrave's book (and despite its use as a term in British politics from the later seventeenth century).[10]

By the same token the strictures that have been made in the European historiography about romanticising the historical bandit as a 'primitive rebel' engaged in social protest, also apply to Ireland. As Blok and others have pointed out, the description of such figures by Hobsbawm involves the confusion of a popular myth of the bandit with the historical reality.[11] In the case of the chapbook literature we are looking primarily at mythical figures or constructs and not at real historical events. We need, then, to look at the literary conventions which underlie these constructs.

One strand of the genealogy of criminal biography comes from the representation within 'official' culture of those who were outside it or marginal to it. This genre originated in discussions of the poor and beggars in the sixteenth century and had been extended to criminals by the seventeenth. It represented these groups in structural terms as 'countercultures' which parallelled or were inversions of conventional society. Thus beggars or robbers were shown as forming organised hierarchies, with a leader such as the 'king of the beggars', with their own rules, rituals, and laws, and frequently featuring an alternative language such as beggars' cant or thieves' slang. England, France, Germany, and Italy all had traditions of this *Liber vagatorum* literature; sixteenth-century English examples include the *Fraternity of vagabonds* (1561) by John Awdeley, which divides beggars into nineteen 'orders', giving a slang term for each one; and *A caveat or warning for common cursetors, vulgarly called vagabonds* (1566) by Thomas Harman, which explains the tricks and cheats used by thieves, beggars, card tricksters, and the like. These books were read partly as explanations and taxonomies of groups which were on the margins of society, and partly as practical guides to dealings with them.[12]

This strand of the genealogy continues in the picaresque novel of the sixteenth and seventeenth centuries, which shares the concern with the marginal and criminal. Indeed, the rapidity of the spread of picaresque from its sixteenth-century origins in Spain throughout Europe in the early seventeenth century is partly accounted for by the way in which it fused with the earlier *Liber vagatorum* tradition, incorporating elements such as the glossary of slang. It differed from the *vagatorum* literature by being a narrative and concerned with one rogue rather than an entire class of rogues. In this way picaresque shifted the literature of criminality away from the purely taxonomic and towards the biographical or even the autobiographical, since the hero is usually the narrator in the picaresque novel.

English translations of Spanish picaresque novels began to appear in the late sixteenth century, beginning with *Lazarillo de Tormes*, one of the two earliest Spanish examples, which was published in London in 1576. By the mid-seventeenth century original English works were being published, such as *The English Gusman* (1652) by George Fidge, whose title echoes *Guzman De Alfarache*, the other earliest Spanish text. The best-known example of English picaresque was *The English rogue described in the life of Meriton Latroon* (1665) by Richard Head.[13]

Finally, the specifically criminal literature which proliferated in the late seventeenth and early eighteenth centuries, and from which the chapbook literature was derived, sprang from concerns similar to those of *Liber vagatorum* and picaresque, and shared some of their characteristics. It was concerned mainly with condemned criminals, often being produced to accompany the execution of a specific criminal. Amid the vast mass of printed material it is convenient to isolate three recurring textual forms and two types of criminal.

The forms are the 'trial', the 'last speech', and the 'confession' or 'life'. The 'trial' was a straightforward account of the court proceedings leading to condemnation. The 'last speeches' were highly stylised productions in which the repentant criminal denounced his (or her) past life as immoral and told the crowd (or the reader) to benefit by his example. In this way the last speech, when sold at executions, formed part of the wider ritual of the public execution, or when sold elsewhere, served to bring that ritual to a wider print audience.[14] The 'confession' or 'life' was an account of the crimes of the condemned, often in his own voice. These accounts, according to Linebaugh, 'minimise the repenting tone' of the last speeches and provide instead a detailed description of the crimes themselves. Although these are not entirely fictionalised accounts, they have certain similarities to fictional criminal biography and provided a source for the latter which needed little adaptation. The different forms were frequently combined, giving pamphlets with titles like 'The last speech and confession of . . .' or 'The trial and last speech of . . .'. One publication which combined all three was the *Account* of the ordinary (chaplain) of Newgate prison, a serial publication of the last speeches and lives of condemned prisoners in that institution, which was printed from the seventeenth century right through the eighteenth.[15]

As for the types of criminal, two broad categories in particular are picked out by Du Sorbier and Faller, the most thorough students of the English material.[16] On the one hand, there were murderers (particularly those who murdered close relatives), whom Du Sorbier calls '*escrocs célebres*', criminals who are condemned outright but who fascinate as well as horrify. On the other hand, there was the highwayman/robber who, although feared in practice, is condemned much less unequivocally, and who is sometimes even '*un héros populaire*'.

Among these categories of text and character the 'confession' or 'life' of the highwayman/robber is the combination which produces probably the most admiration and the least condemnation. It is also the form which follows most closely in the line of the picaresque and the vagabond literature. It has the fascination of the picaresque with the ingenious rogue and his tricks, and contains many of the practical and taxonomic features of the vagabond literature. Titles such as *The life of Martin Bellamy . . ., necessary to be perused by all persons in order to prevent their being robbed for the future* and *A genuine narrative of all the street robberies committed . . . by James Dalton . . ., to which is added a key to the canting language taken from the mouth of James Dalton*, both printed in London in 1728, are representative.

Robbers' lives such as these became the basis of large collections of criminal biography in the early eighteenth century, of which the best known were Alexander Smith's *Complete history of the lives and robberies of the most notorious highwaymen* (1713–14) and Charles Johnson's *A general history of the lives and adventures of the most famous highwaymen* (1734). These were large bound volumes costing several shillings, as opposed to perhaps a halfpenny for the single-sheet last speeches, and were clearly aimed at a more prosperous readership of the 'middling sort' and the ruling elite.[17]

Printed production in Dublin of criminal literature was very active in the same period and was closely integrated with English and European production. Some of the better-known London criminals, such as Jonathan Wild and Jack Sheppard, had their last speeches and lives reprinted in Dublin, and a translation of a life of the French smuggler Mandrin, one of the two principal figures in eighteenth-century criminal biography in France, had a specific Dublin edition in 1755. Many trials and last speeches of Irish criminals were also produced, particularly in the period 1710–30. The demand for them may be illustrated by the fact that differing versions of the same criminal's supposed speech were produced by different printers. A 'last speech' of 1725 claimed that 'I had no thought of making a speech had I not heard a false and scandalous paper cry'd about, called my speech, printed by one Brangan . . .'.[18] The genre became so common in Dublin that it was parodied, as, for example, in *The last speech and dying words of J-n A-b-kle, author of the Weekly Journal* (*ca.* 1725), which is an accusation of plagiarism, i.e., robbery of verse. There was also a market for the larger collections in Dublin, as a letter to the *Dublin Weekly Journal* in 1725 complained: 'The biographers of Newgate . . . have been as greedily read by the people of the better sort as the compilers of the last speeches and dying words by the rabble'.[19]

Cosgrave's *Irish highwaymen, tories, and rapparees*, therefore, which probably first appeared in the 1740s, was intended as an Irish counterpart to the works of Smith and Johnson and echoes their titles.[20] This is confirmed by the fact that it borrowed most of the (few) Irish criminals who appeared in those books: Patrick Fleming, William Maguire, and Richard Balf. (There was one Irish robber in Smith's collection whom Cosgrave did not take, Patrick O'Brien, and I will argue that this was a significant omission.) The debt to Smith and Johnson is underlined by the fact that certain editions of Cosgrave, needing to fill out the volume to 108 or 144 pages, included non-Irish lives from these books, such as Gilder Roy (Scottish) and Captain Martel (an English pirate). Because of this influence half of the figures in the first edition are highwaymen who spent most of their careers in London and were executed there.

Irish rogues differs from its prototypes in two ways, however. First, it seems to have been printed from the beginning in a small format, probably selling at 3d. or 6d. Second, most of the characters and stories are rural, as opposed to the urban, particularly London, flavour of the English collections. The initial intended audience, as the writer to the *Weekly Journal* suggests, was equivalent to the English 'middling sort', including tenant farmers who were very likely to be literate, given the increasing commercialisation of the agricultural economy by the mid-eighteenth century. That these readers were fairly comfortable is suggested by the preface, which, in addition to a moral warning, has a taxonomic/practical dimension. It claims to have 'no other design than to discourage young men from falling into such bad company as may lead them into a shameful way of living', and it also promises to be 'of service to honest men who happen to have dealings with such cattle as are here treated of'. These 'honest men' no doubt included pasture farmers, who would be interested in the techniques of horse-, cow-, and sheep-stealing described in the life of Charles Dempsey.

By the early nineteenth century, as Crofton Croker maintained, the book was read mainly by a lower-class audience, since the price had remained stable or dropped. The preface was no longer included in early nineteenth-century editions, and it therefore seems likely that the lives were read in a more straightforwardly admiring way.

Cosgrave's *Irish highwaymen* contains the following characters:

	Death	No. of pages	Source
Redmond O'Hanlon	1681	30	a
[Captain Power]		4	
John MacPherson	*ca.* 1678	2	
Patrick Fleming	1650	6	b
William Maguire		4	b
Richard Balf	1702	10	b
James Butler	1716	4	b
John Mulhoni	1722	6	c
James Carrick	1722	6	
Charles Dempsey	1735	17	
[Manus MacOniel]		$4/20^{21}$	
[James MacFaul]		15	
[William Peters]	1756	16	
[Paul Liddy]	1780		

The names between brackets are not in the earliest editions.

a: *Count Hanlan's downfall* (1681) and *The life and death . . . of Redmond O'Hanlon* (1682).

b: Smith, *Complete history*, or Johnson, *General history*.

c: *A compleat and true account of all the robberies committed by James Carrick, John Mulhoni, etc.* (London, 1722). This is the source for the life of Mulhoni, but not for that of Carrick, in whose voice the narrative is placed.

The life of Redmond O'Hanlon is the first and longest of the lives and is worth examining in detail, as it is representative of both the tone and the production of the book. It was also the most successful and seems to have been the only one to have been taken up and reprinted singly and outside Ireland: there were editions in London in 1819 and in Glasgow in about 1840.[22]

O'Hanlon was and remains the best known of the tories of the seventeenth century; he was active in south Ulster in the late 1670s and early 1680s. Tories were bandits who flourished particularly in the disturbed aftermath of the Cromwellian and Williamite settlements. As noted earlier, toryism was not exclusively the product of changes in Irish society during the seventeenth century but was similar to European banditry in general; in Ireland, however, the disjunction between traditional hierarchies and central government was probably more pronounced than elsewhere. Some at least of the tories were displaced landowners who refused or were unable to emigrate or become tenants. It is likely that the real O'Hanlon was a member of such a gentry family.

It is fairly clear that the historical O'Hanlon was different from the popular myth of the bandit-hero leading a gallant band for the protection of the poor. He made peasants pay him tribute money, for instance, and offered to turn his colleagues over to the law in return for a few years' protection.[23] By the mid-eighteenth century, however, the myth had already been firmly established. In Cosgrave's text O'Hanlon fulfills many of the criteria set out by Hobsbawm for the bandit-hero:[24]

- He robs from the rich and gives to the poor: 'he was naturally of a very generous disposition, frequently giving share of what he got from the rich to relieve the poor in their necessities'.

- He is a master of disguise: 'he understood the art of dissimulation, or disguising himself, as well as any man, sometimes appearing like an officer, sometimes like a country gentleman, and sometimes like a footman, and could alter the tone of his voice at pleasure'.

- Being invulnerable, he dies through treason: 'he died at last by the hand of his foster-brother, who, for the sake of the large reward offered for Redmond's head, caused his wife to lay a wile for him, and she betrayed him under the pretence of giving him some refreshment'.

The gradual mythification of O'Hanlon can be seen in the differences between Cosgrave's account and previous ones. The earliest text about O'Hanlon is a pamphlet of 1681, the year of his death, and is very much a factual piece of newsreporting, describing in seven pages his betrayal by his foster-brother, his capture, and death.[25] The following year, a longer, twenty-three-page text appeared, *The life and death of the incomparable and indefatigable TORY Redmond O'Hanlyn, commonly called Count Hanlyn.*[26] This work already begins the fictionalising process by treating O'Hanlon as a conventional picaresque hero, giving him, for example, a remarkable birth, predicted to his mother by a fortune teller: he was born with a 'T' on his chest, which was interpreted by neighbours as a cross without a head and as a sign that O'Hanlon would be a martyr. In fact, the author tells us, it stood for thief or tory. Moreover, O'Hanlon was born 'in the year 1640, the year preceding the last Irish rebellion, as if fate had sent him a harbinger to the confusion and mischief following, or as if the birth of so great a man ought to be attended by no less than a universal conflagration'.

The picaresque intention is made explicit early in the narrative, when the author declares that 'the Spanish Guzmond, the French Duval, and the English Rogue were but puisnes in the profession' compared to O'Hanlon. In this text O'Hanlon begins his career early by robbing his school friends, his teacher, and then his parents. The second half of the narrative (pp. 13–23) consists of a series of classic rogue stories in which O'Hanlon outwits soldiers, goes about in disguise, and has narrow escapes. He is summed up as 'naturally bold but not cruel, shedding no blood out of wantonness . . .; had his inclinations been virtuous, as his parts were quick, he might have proved a good subject to his king and serviceable to his country'.

O'Hanlon is therefore already free from condemnation in a text which appeared one year after his death. Half a century later, using the 1682 text as his principal source, Cosgrave completed the process of constructing a bandit-hero by altering the story in two ways.[27] First, the narrative is dehistoricised to a large extent. No birthdate is given, and there is consequently no mention of the 1641 rebellion. An episode is altered in which, after the Restoration, O'Hanlon goes straight for a few years, becoming a collector of poll money and hearth tax, not an occupation likely to make a man popular. In Cosgrave's version 'Redmond was presented with the king's protection for three years', without a date or the king's name being given.

Second, the features of the picaresque unsuitable to the bandit-hero are dropped. There is no birthmark, and a note in some editions explicitly denies that there was one: this is 'a story and a fiction'. In particular, O'Hanlon's youthful wickedness is omitted, and he becomes an outlaw in adult life by 'happening to be at the killing of a gentleman in a quarrel'. This is close to another of Hobsbawm's criteria of social banditry: 'A man becomes a bandit because he does something which is not regarded as criminal by his local conventions but is so regarded by the state or by local rulers'.[28]

Before this, Cosgrave supplies an important new beginning:

> Redmond O'Hanlon was the son of a reputable Irish gentleman who had a considerable estate. . . . The nation being reduced by the English forces, several Irish families who had a hand in the wars of Ireland were dispossessed, and their lands forfeited; by which means a very great alteration was made in this family, and several of the O'Hanlons were obliged to travel in hopes of retrieving their fortunes . . . ; poor Redmond [was] in this unhappy condition.

Here we move away from the notion that the individual personality is the source of crime, and towards an explanation which locates it in social conditions. The particular social condition in question—dispossession—underlies, I will argue below, many of the lives in the collection.

Comparison of O'Hanlon's life with its probable sources, then, shows a glamourising tendency at work. The same process can be seen in the other case in which Cosgrave adapted (rather than reproduced) an identifiable source. This is in the lives of John Mulhoni and James Carrick. The life of Mulhoni derives fairly directly from *A compleat and true account of all the robberies committed by James Carrick, John Mulhoni, and their accomplices . . .*, a pamphlet published in London in 1722. This is made explicit by Cosgrave, who refers to 'our author' [i.e., his source] at the beginning of Mulhoni's life. The episodes follow in the same order as in the London pamphlet; what is excised is the moral reflection or terminology which occurs from time to time in the London text, such as '[we were] enjoying the fruits of our wicked labours without the wonted inquietudes that are the consequences of them'. This type of observation serves not only to introduce a moral dimension but also to distance the reader from the action occasionally. The absence of these qualities in the Cosgrave text suggests a more straightforward identification between the reader and the hero.

Cosgrave's life of Carrick, strangely enough, is not taken from the same source; it may nevertheless be compared with it, and it proves to be entirely different. The contrast between the two is most marked at Carrick's imprisonment and execution. In the London texts he presents the appropriate spectacle of repentance and makes a classic moralising 'last dying speech': 'I have made such reflections on my past life in this vale of sorrow and misery as will, I trust, fit me for those heavenly mansions . . . , desiring all those that are left behind me and have been followers of the like evil courses . . . that they will amend their lives by my example'. None of this happens in Cosgrave's version. Not only does Carrick not repent, he pays no attention to priests or chaplains, none of whom

> could make him refrain from certain lewd women then in confinement . . . ; his thoughts seemed more fixed on them than on eternity. . . . At the place of execution he looked about him and smiled at all he knew there, giving himself a genteel air in fixing the rope, and laughing and giggling all the while Mr Purney was at prayers . . . ; even at the fatal tree he had continually some ridiculous gesture or other to amaze the spectators rather than to beg the forgiveness of God and exhort the people to take warning by his untimely end.

When the prison chaplain remonstrates, Carrick 'replied that he had received the sacrament in his own way and had prepared himself according to his own opinion'. Cosgrave's comment on this unconventional end, while moral, is equivocal: 'Any impartial reader may judge whether he was duly prepared to leave the world'.

The absence of explicit condemnation is a feature of the collection as a whole; this is fundamentally a collection of heroes. Despite the claim in the preface that the book has 'no other design than to discourage young men from falling [into] such company as may lead them into a shameful way of living', there is little evidence of such an intention in the lives themselves. Only one of the characters, Captain Power, makes a conventional 'last dying speech', 'desiring all young men to shun the company of lewd women'. Even this speech is equivocal, however; Power had been betrayed by a woman with whom he had been drinking, and this is one of the reasons women should be avoided:

> 'By women', said he, 'was I enticed to continue in sin, and by a woman was I at last betrayed, though she pretended to be my friend', which speech melted the spectators into tears.

Before this, in any case, Power has been described as generous to the poor, at one point helping a tenant who was in arrears with his rent.

The forms of explanation of criminal behaviour invoked by Cosgrave also fall well short of outright condemnation. A tendency to crime is either innate or developed in early life, after which the criminal can never break away from it. The life of James Carrick begins: 'When a vicious inclination is settled in the nature of man, no education, no learning, no rules of morality are sufficient to alter his temper'; in the life of John MacPherson, 'When vice has settled in the bone, no medicine that can be applied to the flesh can expel it'. This deterministic explanation comes close to absolving the criminal by implication: 'Want of precaution in the beginning often lays men under difficulties they can never surmount'—in the life of MacPherson. The criminal is thus no longer a moral agent, the reader does not have to condemn him completely, and this leaves the way open to an admiration, if not for crime itself, at least for the ingenuity of its execution. The cleverness of the criminals is therefore emphasised. William Peters, for example, 'had a political genius and would have made a great proficiency in learning if he had rightly applied his time'.

In a more general way Cosgrave's favourable attitude can be seen by setting the lives within the typology constructed by Faller in his recent study of English criminal biography. In his discussion Faller conveniently uses Smith's *Complete history*, one of the English prototypes and sources for Cosgrave. Faller distinguishes three types of criminal (or more precisely, criminal action).[29] The hero is the most positive—he is 'gallant, witty, judicious in his selection of victims, he uses the minimum force necessary . . . , [and] though an outlaw, he maintains a sense of social justice'. The second type, the brute, is the most negative—he is violent and inflicts the maximum suffering on his victims. He does not observe basic social norms and sometimes lives outside society altogether. The classic example in Smith is Sawney Beane, who lives in a cave in sixteenth-century Scotland, robbing and then eating passersby. The third type, the buffoon, is morally neutral and is used for humourous effect, usually playing tricks on his victims.

All three types are found in Smith's *Complete history*, but in *Irish rogues* the brute is completely absent. There is no inhuman figure or even any episode in which a particularly nasty punishment is inflicted on a victim. Moreover, although there is a 'brutish' Irish highwayman, Patrick O'Bryan, in Smith's collection, he is not used by Cosgrave. (O'Bryan rapes and then murders a young woman while robbing a house.)

On the other hand, Cosgrave does include two buffoons taken from Smith: Patrick Fleming, whom Faller uses to exemplify the prototypical buffoon, and William Maguire, alias Irish Teague, whose comic value lies in his Irish speech and bulls. The flavour of these characters may be gauged from an episode in the life of Maguire: he robbed a lady on the highway by asking her to lend him money. She replied that that was not lending but robbing, to which Maguire answered: 'By my shoul and shalvation, Madam, I am stranger upon the country, and I want your monies, and what's lying good for; af you lend it to me, I won't give it to you again, and af I rob you, I will keep it, and that's all the difference I make between robbing and borrowing. . .'. The buffoon, however, is morally neutral, more of a cartoon figure than a real criminal, and the presence of two in Cosgrave does not alter the generally positive attitude to crime. These buffoons, moreover, are omitted from some of the cheaper nineteenth-century versions. As the text moved down the price range and the social scale, the brute was still absent, the buffoon declined, and the figure of the hero became even more dominant.

The positive view of criminals, in particular the absence of brutes, becomes even more striking when we bear in mind the extent to which *Irish rogues* derives from English models, during a period in which the brute and the buffoon were precisely the two most powerful representations of the Irish. Hayton has shown that the representation was in transition 'from barbarian to burlesque', from brute to buffoon in Faller's terminology, in the late seventeenth and early eighteenth centuries, but both images were present throughout the eighteenth.[30]

Fleming and Maguire are versions of the Irish buffoon or rogue image. Fleming derives from the picaresque, which in its English form had an occasional Irish dimension. Head's *The English rogue*, the best-seller of the genre, explains its hero's roguery by his being born in Ireland, though of English parents: 'Neither shall I much thank my native country [i.e., Ireland] for bestowing on me such principles as I and most of my countrymen drew from that very air. The place, I think, made me appear a bastard in disposition to my father.'[31] Maguire, on the other hand, fits neatly into the comic genre of English representations of Irish (or Hiberno-English) speech. Maguire's alias is Irish Teague, and Teague was one of the stock names for the comic Irishman; the classic text which established the genre, a joke book of *ca.* 1680, was known as *Teague-land jests.*[32]

The Irish/barbarian image was not only part of the general culture, particularly after the 1641 rebellion, but was also sometimes used explicitly in English criminal biography. One of the lives of Jonathan Wild published in London just after his execution traces his genealogy to 'his great-grandfather's father, whose name was Patrick MacJudas Wild, and lived in a cave on the mountains of Newry in Ireland. . . . [Patrick and his family were] in nature savage beasts, not only void of religion, government, etc., but also of Christianity universally . . . ; they lived by robbing the travellers as they passed on foot over the mountains of Newry.'[33]

In constructing an Irish counterpart to English collections of criminal biography, Cosgrave therefore accepts the Irish buffoon/rogue figure while completely rejecting that of the Irish brute. None of the editions of *Irish rogues* includes a brute figure even though these were easily constructed by someone less favourably disposed to outlaws: the figure of William Crotty, a Waterford rapparee, as described by J.E. Walsh in 1847, is a pure brute, right down to the comparison with his Scottish prototype:

Men from the woods and mountains infested the neighbourhood of populous towns, having holes and dens from which they issued to commit their depredations, and to which they retired, like wild beasts to their lair. . . . Such was the mode of life of Crotty. . . . Crotty was reputed to be a cannibal, and he was believed to fill [his cave] with stores of human flesh on which he fed. Hence he was called the 'Irish Sawny Bean' after the Highland robber of that name, who is said to have had a taste for the same diet.

Crotty was executed in 1742 and was therefore well within the timescale of the later editions of *Irish rogues*.[34]

So much for the absence of negative qualities. In terms of positive ones Cosgrave's characters are presented very favourably. Some are handsome and strong: Paul Liddy was 'a very handsome, well-set young man, about six feet high and every way proportionable, and in strength outvied most of his age in the kingdom'. John MacPherson 'was always a leading man at hurlings, patrons, and matches of football, and acquired such fame by his wondrous activity that no single person dared oppose him at any exercise. He was accounted in his time the strongest man in the kingdom'. Other accomplishments are listed: James Butler 'spoke Latin pretty fluently', and two were musicians: as MacPherson 'was carried to the gallows, he played a fine tune of his own composing on the bagpipe, which retains the name of MacPherson's tune to this day', and William Peters 'composed several songs and put tunes to them, and by his skill in music had gained the favour of some of the leading men's sons in the country, who endeavoured to get him reprieved'.

Most importantly of all, these criminals were 'gentlemen', either of good birth or capable of correct behaviour. O'Hanlon, as we have seen, was 'the son of a reputable Irish gentleman', Captain Power, 'a genteel robber', 'was the younger son of a worthy gentleman'; Paul Liddy, 'a gentleman robber', 'was the son of very reputable parents who had him educated after a genteel manner by the best masters in the country'; and so on. They therefore have a relatively exalted code of behaviour: Paul Liddy, when engaged in highway robbery, 'always behaved agreeably to his education, more like a gentleman than any of his comrades'; MacPherson 'was very cautious of striking unless in his own defence'; Peters was 'very diverting in company and could behave before gentlemen very agreeably'.

If, as Lusebrink argues, the popular literature of crime represents '[*la*] *mise en cause fondementale* [*de la justice*] *par une fraction importante de la population*', the good breeding of the criminals, in a society in which deference was still very strong, was certainly a major factor in legitimising the challenge to central authority. Moreover, they are not simply gentlemen but also leaders, and they frequently control entire alternative power structures. In the French eighteenth-century popular literature Mandrin commands a 'captain', 'lieutenants', and 'soldiers' while issuing laws and levying taxes. Similarly, in *Irish highwaymen*

O'Hanlon is described as 'protector of the rights and properties of the benefactors, and captain-general of the Irish robbers'; he issues his own laws, levies tolls on pedlars, 'who acknowledged his jurisdiction', and even sent one individual, who had been robbing in his name, to the gaoler of Armagh, with instructions to try him at the next assizes.[35]

This theme is found throughout Cosgrave's lives. Fleming greeted his highway victims with the declaration, 'I am the chief lord of the county and collector of the road, and you shall pay tribute to Patrick Fleming'. Paul Liddy was the 'captain' of three bands, with 'subalterns' and a 'brigade of twelve of the most resolute fellows among them, whom he was to command in person'. Charles Dempsey, as well as having a network of cattle stealers throughout the country under his command, set up an alternative educational system for rustlers: 'He had likewise never less than four apprentices at a time, who were always bound for the term of seven years and paid a pretty round sum for learning his art and mystery, in which he had such a great skill that boys were sent to him all the way from the county of Kerry to be bound'.

Here the taxonomic aspect of the *Liber vagatorum*/picaresque tradition is being used not to explain marginal people to conventional society but implicitly to question that society and the forms of power within it.[36] The hierarchies among highwaymen, although similar to, even mirror images of, those of the state, are clearly in opposition to that state and to the extension of its power; soldiers and tax collectors are favourite targets. The legitimacy of this opposition is therefore derived not from a critique of the state or of its structures of power but from the social position of the bandit himself and his command over an alternative structure: it is a reaction of traditional hierarchies to new ones, and typical of 'pre-modern' political protest.

In Ireland, where the personnel of the landed classes had changed enormously during the seventeenth century, the break between the old and the new was very marked. The older ruling class, now mostly dispossessed, either emigrated, became tenants on or near their old estates, or became outlaws. The post-dispossession context of Cosgrave's text is underlined by the fact that the first and longest life is that of Redmond O'Hanlon, in many ways the prototypical tory. None of the other figures is, strictly speaking, a tory; the emphasis on noble blood, however, implies this background, and some of the figures have typically tory names. *Irish rogues* contains a Captain Power, and the principal tory of Munster, according to Prendergast, was Colonel Power;[37] and Charles Dempsey's father is described in the text as 'a man of note among the rapparees of King James' time'.

The ideological context of these texts, the principle which legitimises the challenge to authority, is nobility of blood and the rightful ownership of land.[38] The initial appeal of the book was probably to surviving members of Catholic gentry families who had lost their land. Its becoming a part of chapbook literature by the late eighteenth century indicates a generalisation of the feeling of dispossession among the population at large (or at least among tenants).

If the historical phenomenon of banditry or brigandage can be related to the development of the state, so too can a major part of the appeal of bandit literature to readers. The figure of a bandit, free from conventional restraints on behaviour, appealed to a readership in proportion as that readership became subject to social and legal restraints in ever-increasing areas of their lives. In eighteenth- and nineteenth-century Ireland, as elsewhere, this meant greater contact with a state apparatus. Besides explaining much of the popularity of the literature, this hypothesis fits the chronological pattern of readership. A minor-gentry/middle-class audience in the eighteenth century would already have been in regular contact with state authority; an audience lower down the social scale would arrive at that point in the early nineteenth.

An anti-authoritarian, anti-state ideology in nineteenth-century Ireland was very likely to be nationalistic (and sometimes Catholic) in tone, and during the century we find tories and rapparees being idealised and used as proto-nationalist figures in Anglo-Irish élite literature, especially in novels and poetry. The original source in many cases was *Irish rogues*.[39]

One of the earliest cases is instructive—John Banim's *The Boyne water* (1826), a novel set in the Williamite wars of 1689–91. The plot establishes a number of symmetries on each side of the conflict, and 'rapparees' are used on the Catholic side in symmetry with 'Orangemen' on the Protestant. Using as a base Cosgrave's life of Charles Dempsey, a horse-stealer known as 'Cahir na Gappul', in which 'Charles' father was a man of note among the rapparees in the reign of King James', Banim calls one of his principal rapparees 'Rory na Gappul', and Rory is also skilled at dealing with horses, which he tames by whispering to them. When explaining this gift, Rory calls it 'a little bit of a secret that I had from the father before me, and I'll leave to this son that is to come after me', and he points (presumably) to Charles.

Cosgrave's life of Dempsey is principally a list of horse-stealers' tricks. Banim turns this fairly amoral rogue into a representative of Catholics in Ireland, and he thus set a precedent which was much followed. The precedent also concerned terminology: with the increasing political integration of Ireland with Britain following the Act of Union of 1800, the word 'tory' could no longer be used in the original sense. As Banim put the point, it 'has since become the honourable appellation of honourable men'.[40]

Later in the century, possibly owing to the increasing association between Irish nationalist politics and the Whig party, the original tories had become positively evil compared to the virtuous rapparees. The positive presentation of the rapparee at the expense of the tory reached a peak in William Carleton's novel *Redmond Count O'Hanlon, the Irish rapparee*, of 1862:

At this period the country was overrun and ravaged by lawless bands of rapparees and the still more atrocious body of tories, the latter of whom spared neither life nor property in their merciless depredations. With them religion, of which they were as ignorant as the brutes around them, was no safeguard whatsoever. The Catholic was robbed and slaughtered with as little remorse as the Protestant, whilst among the rapparees, on the other hand, there was moderation and forbearance.

Indeed, Carleton's rapparees had become Victorian gentlemen:

It is singular to reflect upon the strange perversion and involution of moral feeling by which this terrible confraternity was regulated. The three great principles of their lawless existence were such as would reflect honour upon the most refined and the most intellectual institutions of modern civilisation. These were, first, sobriety; secondly, a resolution to avoid the shedding of human blood; and thirdly, a solemn promise never to insult or offer outrage to woman, but in every instance to protect her.

The preference for rapparees rather than tories reverses the original preference, '*tóraigh*', 'hunted', being less derogatory than '*ropaire*', literally 'a stabber'. In any case, the later nineteenth-century figure is always a 'rapparee'.

Carleton had read *Irish rogues* in his youth in County Tyrone, and he recycles much of it in the novel: O'Hanlon's followers, in defiance of space and time, consist of all the figures in *Irish rogues*, who relate some of their adventures, which Carleton has taken from Cosgrave.[41] Banim in 1826 used the rapparee to represent Catholic Ireland in a novel which argued for the reconciliation of Catholic and Protestant Irishmen. By mid-century, however, nationalist politics had become more closely fused with Catholicism, and the Catholic rapparee becomes an overall national figure. In the nationalist ballad poetry of the later nineteenth century the rapparee becomes almost a stock motif, representing the continuity of a 'national spirit' after the defeats of the seventeenth century. There are rapparee poems by Charles Gavan Duffy (1850), P.D. Joyce (*ca.* the 1870s), P.J. McCall (1894), and William Rooney, all of which depict the rapparee fighting against 'sassenachs' and 'saxons'. Gavan Duffy's gloss is typical:

A multitude of the old soldiers of the Boyne, Aughrim, and Limerick preferred remaining in the country at the risk of fighting for their daily bread; and with them some gentlemen, loath to part from their estates and sweethearts. The English army and the English law drove them by degrees to the hills, where they were long a terror to the old and new settlers from England and a secret pride and comfort to the trampled peasantry, who loved them even for their excesses.[42]

Irish rogues was taken up in the literary nationalism of W.B. Yeats as representative of the 'Celtic' temperament. He read the text in the early 1890s in preparation for a book on 'Irish adventurers' which in the end was never published. Finally, in the post-independence period highwaymen and rapparees became, along with Irish soldiers in eighteenth-century Europe, a staple of nationalist children's literature. A good example is *The highwayman in Irish history* (1932) by the appropriately-named Terence O'Hanlon. This was a reprint of a series of articles from a children's magazine, *Our Boys*, and was also based to a large extent on *Irish rogues*. The introduction indicates the tone and the debt to the original texts:

> There was a time when Irish boys were free to choose their own school readers . . . ; being sturdy lads, born into a heritage of suffering and persecution, the spirit of resistance burning in their veins, it is not surprising that the reading book they liked best was a cheap little work containing an account of daring deeds of famous Irish outlaws, rapparees, and highwaymen.[43]

The meaning of the figures in *Irish rogues* evolved over time, appearing in printed forms destined for different audiences in different periods, whether minor gentry, peasant, or bourgeois. This study has concentrated on the styles of reading which can be inferred from the texts themselves, on a reception which is inscribed in them. It remains to confirm, modify, or add to such readings from other sources.

NOTES

1 R. Mandrou, *De la culture populaire aux XVIIe et XVIIIe siècles: la bibliothèque bleue de Troyes* (Paris, 1964); M. Spufford, *Small books and pleasant histories: popular fiction and its readership in seventeenth-century England* (London, 1981); J.R.R. Adams, *The printed word and the common man: popular culture in Ulster, 1700–1900* (Belfast, 1987).

2 The debate is summed up in J.L. Marais, 'Littérature et culture 'populaires' aux XVIIe et XVIIe siècles: réponses et questions' in *Annales de Bretagne et des Pays de l'Ouest*, t.87 (1980), pp. 65–105.

3 E.g., in D. Vincent, *Literacy and popular culture: England, 1750–1914* (New York, 1989).

4 R. Chartier, 'Culture as appropriation: popular cultural uses in early modern France' in S. Kaplan (ed.), *Understanding popular culture* (1984), p. 233.

5 According to M.G. Jones, *The charity school movement: a study of eighteenth-century puritanism in action* (Cambridge, 1938), p. 83, *Irish rogues* was found by inspectors of the Society for the Promotion of Christian Knowledge in the 1720s, but there does not appear to be such a description in the S.P.C.K. documents cited by Jones.

6 W. Stokes, *Projects for re-establishing the internal peace and tranquillity of Ireland* (Dublin, 1799), pp. 41 ff; R. Bell, *A description of the condition and manners . . . of the peasantry of Ireland such as they were between the years 1780 and 1790* (London, 1804), pp. 40–1. Later descriptions include H. Dutton, *A statistical survey of the county of Clare . . .* (Dublin, 1808); *Fourteenth report from the commissioners of the Board of Education in Ireland*, H.C. 1813–14 (47), v, appendix (letter from R.L. Edgeworth); J. O'Driscol, *Views of Ireland: moral, political, and religious* (2

vols, London, 1823), p. 80; J.E. Walsh, *Sketches of Ireland sixty years ago* (Dublin, 1847), chap. 9; W.R. Wilde, *Irish popular superstitions* (Dublin, 1852), p. 86.

7 P. De Brún, 'Some documents concerning Valentia Erasmus Smith School, 1776–95' in *Kerry Hist. Soc. Jn.*, xv-xvi (1983), pp. 70–82; *First report of the commissioners of Irish education inquiry*, H.C. 1825 (400) xii, appendix 261; T. Crofton Croker, *Researches in the south of Ireland . . .* (London, 1824), p. 55.

8 D. Ó hOgáin, *The hero in Irish folk history* (Dublin and New York, 1985), pp. 178–92; S. Ó Catháin, *Irish life and lore* (Cork, 1982), chap. 1.

9 S.J. Connolly, 'Violence and order in the eighteenth century', in P. O'Flanagan, P. Ferguson, and K. Whelan (ed.), *Rural Ireland, 1600–1900: modernisation and change* (Cork, 1987), pp. 42–61; J.A. Davis, *Conflict and control: law and order in nineteenth-century Italy* (London,1988), chap. 3.

10 Davis, *Conflict and control*, p. 73. An example of seventeenth-century use of the terminology appeared in *The true domestick intelligence*, London, 16 January 1680: 'Letters from Ireland inform us that one O'Hanlan, with several banditi or tories, hath long infested several places of that countrey . . .' (quoted in K. McMahon, 'The O'Hanlon letter' in *Seanchas Ardmhacha*, x [1980–1], p. 38).

11 E.J. Hobsbawm, *Primitive rebels: studies in archaic forms of social movement in the 19th and 20th centuries* (Manchester, 1959); idem, *Bandits* (London, 1969); A. Blok,'The peasant and the bandit: social banditry reconsidered' in *Comparative Studies in Society and History*, xiv (1972), pp. 494–503.

12 R. Chartier, 'The literature of roguery in the *Bibliothèque bleue*' in idem, *The cultural uses of print in early modern France* (Princeton,1987), pp. 265–342; F. Du Sorbier, *Récits de gueuserie et biographies criminelles de Head à Defoe* (Berne, 1983), chap. 3. A number of books look at the English vagabond literature, e.g., F. Aydelotte, *Elizabethan rogues and vagabonds* (Oxford, 1913).

13 A.A. Parker, *Literature and the delinquent: the picaresque novel in Spain and Europe, 1599–1753* (Edinburgh, 1967), chaps. 4–5, quote on p. 100; H. Sieber, *The picaresque* (London, 1977), chap. 3; Du Sorbier, *Récits*, chap. 1; idem, 'La biographie criminelle Anglaise: formes narratives et circuits de diffusion' in *Dix-Huitième Siècle*, no. 18 (1986), pp. 155–68; R. Head and F. Kirkman, *The English rogue* (London, 1928).

14 J.A. Sharpe, ' "Last dying speeches": religion, ideology, and public execution in seventeenth-century England' in *Past & Present*, no. 107 (1985), pp. 144–67; H.J. Lusebrink, 'La letteratura del Patibolo: continuità e transformazioni tra '600 e '800' in *Quaderni Storici*, xlix (1982), pp. 285–301.

15 P. Linebaugh, 'The ordinary of Newgate and his *Account*' in J.S. Cockburn (ed.), *Crime in England, 1550–1800* (Princeton, 1977), pp. 246–69, quote on p. 264. See also M. Harris, 'Trials and criminal biographies: a case study in distribution' in R. Myers and M. Harris (ed.), *Sale and distribution of books from 1700* (Oxford, 1982).

16 Du Sorbier, *Récits*; L.B. Faller, *Turned to account: the forms and functions of criminal biography in late seventeenth- and early eighteenth-century England* (Cambridge, 1987).

17 P. Rawlings, *Drunks, whores, and idle apprentices: criminal biographies of the eighteenth century* (London, 1992), intro., pp. 3–4.

18 *The last speech of J[onathan] W[ild]*, *the notorious thief taker* (Dublin, 1725); H. Bleackley and S.M. Ellis, *Notable British trials: Jack Sheppard* (London, 1933), p. 128; *Authentic memoir of the remarkable and surprising exploits of Mandrin, captain-general of the French smugglers . . .* (Dublin, 1755); *The last speech and dying words of Elinor Sils . . .* (Dublin, 1725); *A catalogue of the Bradshaw collection of Irish books in the University Library, Cambridge* (3 vols, Cambridge,1916), i, 121–5, 701–2; E. MacLysaght, *Irish life in the seventeenth century: after Cromwell* (London, 1939), appendix H.

19 *Dublin Weekly Journal*, 29 May 1725.

20 I used Smith in a slightly censored reprint: A. Smith, *A complete history of the lives and robberies*

of the most notorious highwaymen ... (ed. A.L. Hayward, n. p., 1926). Some of the lives from Johnson are found, also censored, in J.L. Rayner and G.T. Crook (ed.), *The complete Newgate calendar* (London, 1926).

21 This varies in different editions.

22 The Glasgow edition is dated to *ca*. 1840 in T.W. Moody, 'Redmond O'Hanlon', *Proceedings of the Belfast Natural, Historical, and Philosophical Society*, 2nd ser., i, pt i (1935–6), pp. 17–33.

23 Connolly, 'Violence and order', p. 43; McMahon, 'O'Hanlon letter'.

24 Hobsbawm, *Bandits*, pp. 42–3.

25 *Count Hanlan's downfall, or a true and exact account of the killing of that archtraytor and tory Redmond O Hanlan* ... (Dublin, 1681).

26 Dublin, 1682.

27 There may have been intermediate versions, but I have never seen any references that would point to the existence of such versions.

28 Hobsbawm, *Primitive rebels*, p. 15.

29 Faller, *Turned to account*, chap. 6.

30 D.W. Hayton, 'From barbarian to burlesque: English images of the Irish, *c*. 1660–1750' in *Irish Economic and Social History*, xv (1988), pp. 5–31.

31 *English rogue*, p. 6.

32 B. Earls, 'Bulls, blunders, and bloothers: an examination of the Irish bull' in *Béaloideas*, lvi (1988), pp. 1–92.

33 *The life and glorious actions of the most heroic and magnanimous Jonathan Wild, generalissimo of the prig forces in Great Britain and Ireland* ... (London, 1725), p. 4.

34 Walsh, *Ireland sixty years ago*, p. 88; C. Maxwell, *Country and town in Ireland under the Georges* (Dundalk, 1949), p. 288.

35 H.J. Lusebrink (ed.), *Histoires curieuses et véritables de Cartouche et Mandrin* (Paris, 1984), intro., pp. 21, 40.

36 Thus, although there are a few references to 'the canting language', there is no glossary or other attempt to explain it; indeed, it is assumed that the reader knows what is being referred to.

37 J.P. Prendergast, *Ireland from the restoration to the revolution, 1660–1690* (London, 1887), p. 79.

38 This is entirely missing in the 1819 London edition of O'Hanlon's life, where, although favourably presented in a text largely derived from Cosgrave, he is described as 'of rather mean extraction'. See *The Irish freebooter, or surprising adventures of Captain Redmond O'Hanlon* ... (London, 1819).

39 For similar cases in Europe, see F. Egmond, 'The noble and ignoble bandit: changing literary representatives of West-European robbers' in *Ethnologia Europaea*, xvii (1987), pp. 139–56.

40 J. Banim, *The Boyne water: a tale by the O'Hara family* (3 vols, London, 1826), i, 232, 238.

41 William Carleton, *Redmond Count O'Hanlon, the Irish rapparee* (Dublin and London, 1862), pp. 50, 87, 92.

42 C.G. Duffy, 'The Irish rapparees' in M. McDermott (ed.), *The new spirit of the nation*; P.D. Joyce, 'Will of Glenore' in *Ballads of Irish chivalry* (Dublin, 1908); P.J. McCall, 'Redmond O'Hanlon' in *Songs of Erin* (Dublin, 1894); W. Rooney, 'Song of the rapparee' in *Poems and ballads* (Dublin, n.d.).

43 M.H. Thuente, *W.B. Yeats and Irish folklore* (Dublin, 1980), chap. 5, 'Rakes and rapparees: Irish adventurers'; T. O'Hanlon, *The highwayman in Irish history* (Dublin, 1932), pp. 1–2.

5

Swine-Tax and Eat-Him-All-Magee:
The Hedge Schools and Popular Education
in Ireland

J.R.R. ADAMS

The schools were conducted by men of sound and serious scholarship. Most of them were poor, but they taught mathematics and the classics of an advanced standard and cultivated poetry-making in the Irish language.[1]

> First, vulgar branches to corporify—
> I teach calligraphy, brachygraphy,
> The analytic art that boobies vexes,
> By counting fives and tens with vees and eckses:
> Vertiginous trochilics, and gnomics,
> I teach to harmonise with geoponics.
> Then selenography—celestial physics,
> The differential calculus and quizzics.
> By loxodromics or dynamics deep,
> I measure land, or else I sail a sheep:
> By Milton's Euclid I adjust to hairs,
> Five-sided trigons, and three-corner'd squares.
> Next trace crinigerous comets and erratics
> In rectilinear curves, by hydrostatics.
> Show obfuscations of the prime meridian,
> By CHRONONHOTONOMICRONMAGWIDGEON.[2]

There are two popular images of the Irish hedge schools of the eighteenth and early nineteenth centuries. One, represented by the first quotation above, runs roughly as follows. A peasantry brutally forbidden any form of education by a harsh system of penal laws is nevertheless eager for knowledge. As a result, every parish abounds with intent groups of scholars clustered behind a hedge at the feet of a tatterdemalion schoolmaster imparting the wisdom of the ages. The hills teem with peasants, each owning little more than a mended spade, who nevertheless are able to quote faultlessly from the Greek and Roman classics and to indulge in learned logical arguments. The second image, from a poem by George

Dugall (himself a hedge schoolmaster), is entirely different. The hedge schools are run by semi-illiterate pedants who amaze an ignorant peasantry with their high-flown and fantastic diction.

What exactly were hedge schools? First, they were totally independent of any kind of authority other than market forces and the ire of the parents. Excluded from this definition, therefore, are all schools run by churches, education societies, or the state. Second, they were run by teachers who themselves had received no formal training. Third, they were not necessarily held literally behind a hedge or even in rural surroundings. Fourth, they were intended entirely for the lower orders, and excluded therefore are schools specifically catering for the middle classes.

The origins of the hedge schools are obscure. In one sense they had always existed: before the days of universal state-funded education there would always have been people, themselves of humble station, who for a small fee would have taught some of the children of neighbours to the best of their ability. To some people knowledge has always had a magical quality and has been seen as the key to something better. But documentation before the late eighteenth century is scanty, to say the least. Such humble establishments left no records and taught few people who made their mark on history. It is somewhat fanciful to trace their story back to the bardic schools or the early Christian monasteries. It is equally fanciful to link them with the seventeenth-century Irish colleges on the continent of Europe.

The first glimmerings of what can be recognised as the hedge schools of Ireland are found in a late seventeenth-century chapbook version of *The seven wise masters of Rome*, collected by Samuel Pepys, who took time off from his official duties and from writing his diary to amass a substantial number of popular publications between 1661 and 1688. The preface of this little book makes the claim that 'of all histories of this nature, this exceeds, being held in such esteem in Ireland that it is of the chiefest use in all the English schools for introducing children to the understanding of good letters'.[3] This statement strikes a chord which resonates through the whole history of hedge schools right up to the early nineteenth century, and it should be noted that it predates the penal laws.

Nevertheless, the penal laws were of some importance in the history of hedge schools. One of the main laws in this respect was 'An act to restrain foreign education', passed in 1695. While the main provisions of this law were of little interest to the common person (how many of them intended to send their sons abroad to be educated?), section 9 was of at least potential importance:

And whereas it is found by experience that tolerating and conniving at papists keeping schools or instructing youth in literature is one great reason of many of the natives of this kingdom continuing ignorant of the principles of true religion and strangers to the scriptures, and of their neglecting to conform themselves to the laws and statutes of this realm, and of their not using the English habit and language, to the great prejudice of the public weal thereof: be it further enacted by the authority aforesaid that no person whatsoever of the popish religion shall publicly teach school or instruct youth in learning, or in private houses teach or instruct youth in learning within this realm from henceforth, except only the children or others under the guardianship of the master or mistress of such private house or family, upon pain of twenty pounds and also being committed to prison, without bail or mainprize, for the space of three months for every such offence.[4]

This was followed in 1703 by another act—an act 'to prevent the further growth of popery'[5]—and in 1709 by an act extending the system yet further, deeming any Catholic who taught as an assistant to a Protestant schoolmaster to be a 'popish regular clergyman' liable to the same punishments. Apparently, schoolmasters, when prosecuted by presentment of the grand jury, were absconding to other counties and starting all over again.[6] These laws bore heavily on the education of Catholics and remained in force until 1782. In that year an act was passed permitting 'papists or persons professing the popish religion' to teach school and repealing the relevant portions of the above acts.[7] It was considered that the restrictions were 'too severe and have not answered the desired effect'. There were exceptions: the liberalising act of 1782 did not apply to any schoolmaster who did not take the oath of allegiance, or to any Catholic schoolmaster who accepted Protestant pupils, or to any Catholic schoolmaster who assisted a Protestant one or did not obtain a license from the local Protestant bishop. This, then, was the legal background, apart from a few more minor acts of parliament. The degree to which the penal laws were applied, however, varied from place to place and from time to time. What, then, was the position?

Evidence is hard to find, particularly in the earlier period. During the reign of Queen Anne Presbyterians—who suffered under penal laws as well—were forced to complain that it was

> a great grievance to us that the education of our youth is extremely discouraged by our being deprived in many places of the liberty of entertaining common schoolmasters of our own persuasion. . . . And even many of those who teach only to read and write in country parishes are prohibited and persecuted, to the great prejudice of children and discouragement of parents who are conscientiously concerned for their education.[8]

Things were of course even harder for the Catholics. In 1731 the Church of Ireland bishop of Derry rather triumphantly declared, 'There are not any popish schools; sometimes a straggling schoolmaster sets up in some of ye mountainous parts of some parishes, but upon being threatened, as they constantly are, with a warrant or a presentment by ye churchwardens, they generally think proper to withdraw'.[9] But things were probably occurring in 'ye mountainous parts' that the good bishop did not know about. Elsewhere in Ireland in the early eighteenth century there is evidence of active persecution of 'popish schoolmasters'.[10] As the eighteenth century progressed, however, the penal laws seem to have been applied with less and less rigour.

Before we discuss the hedge schools proper, it is as well to look at the alternatives open to the non-elite. The oldest of these alternatives were the parish schools established under a law of Henry VIII.[11] This enjoined every clergyman in Ireland to keep or cause to be kept a school within his parish. It is clear that not all clergymen complied, and it is also clear that the clergy do not seem to have been generous in their support. In 1810 it was noted that there was a custom, evidently of long standing, that in those parishes where the clergy did comply, the incumbents paid a stipend of forty shillings per annum to the master.[12] The religious makeup of the schools in the eighteenth century is not known. By the early nineteenth century most of the schools were connected with one or another of the education societies, and their character therefore depended on the policies of those bodies. Various other schools, such as the Erasmus Smith schools, were founded in the seventeenth and eighteenth centuries; the best known of these were the charter schools.

The charter schools were organised by the Incorporated Society for Promoting English Protestant Schools in Ireland, which received its charter in 1733. As the title suggests, these schools were expressly intended for use as proselytising institutions and as part of the political governance of Ireland. The first school was opened at Monasterevin in County Kildare in 1734, and seven more were erected in the following three years. They were financed by donations from the clergy and gentry as well as by an annual grant of £1,000 from the crown. This was augmented in 1745 by an act compelling hawkers and pedlars to take out licenses, the proceeds of which were transferred to the society, giving a further grant of £1,000 annually. More schools were built, and by 1769 these amounted to fifty-two schools and five nurseries.

It was conceived that the 'popish' children would be better instructed away from the influence of their parents and other relatives, and to this end they tended to be transported to areas remote from their own and largely kept inside the walls. This naturally caused some difficulties in filling the schools, so that the society built nurseries in order to keep up a constant supply. In the 1780s they were visited by John Howard, appropriately enough a penal reformer, and the picture which he painted of both the educational standards and the living conditions was horrifying. Reading was neglected in favour of making the children work for their master's benefit, and they were ill-clothed and almost starved.

At the time of the education inquiry of 1824 there were thirty-four schools containing just over 2,000 children, and the dreadful reputation of the schools has tended to obscure the fact that they were never an important part of the Irish elementary-education scene. One of the stated objectives of the schools was the eventual apprenticeship of the children, with added inducements for marrying Protestants, but the education commissioners found that over the previous ninety years the charter schools had received £1,027,715 from parliamentary grants, and that a total of 12,745 children had been apprenticed, of whom a large proportion did not have very good skills.

The mass extension of schools under the direction of education societies did not really get under way until the early nineteenth century. To take the societies in chronological order of foundation, the Association Incorporated for Discountenancing Vice and Promoting the Knowledge and Practice of the Christian Religion was founded in 1792. Originally, this strongly Anglican body contented itself with distributing bibles, tracts, and other literature at reduced prices. In 1800 the society was incorporated by act of parliament and in the following year received a grant from government. Encouraged by this, it decided to apply funds to the support of schools, especially those parish schools established under 28 Henry VIII, c. 15. These schools were of course strongly Protestant in character and curriculum but were well attended by Catholics; in 1822 there were on the books 6,200 Protestants and 5,334 Catholics.[13]

The next society of importance was the London Hibernian Society for Establishing Schools and Circulating the Holy Scriptures in Ireland, originating in 1808. Its character can be gleaned from the following declaration:

> The great body of the Irish wander like sheep that have no faithful shepherd to guide them. Legendary tales, pilgrimages, penances, superstitions, offerings, priestly domination, the notorious habit of reconciling sanctimonious accents and attitudes with abandoned practices, and all that shocks and disgusts in the mummery of the mass house cannot fail to fix a mournful sentiment in the heart of every enlightened and pious observer.[14]

This set of structures came from a society which positively disavowed that its object was to make proselytes from the Catholic to the Protestant religion![15] Nevertheless, there were many Catholic children on the books in 653 schools, containing altogether 61,387 scholars in 1823. There were even some Catholic masters,[16] which shows, perhaps more than anything else, the widespread desire for education. The schools were in general common cabins or mere hovels, and the masters were drawn from the 'lowest ranks of the peasantry and have themselves but very little education'.[17] To read between the lines, it looks as if some hedge schoolmasters had found a slight additional source of income. As will be seen later, there were often no scruples about the precise nature of the religion taught, if any.

The next important society to be founded was the Sunday School Society for Ireland, established in 1809. By 1825 it had 1,702 schools and 150,831 scholars on the books, though it restricted aid to the provision of such works as testaments and spelling books.[18] It seems that as in the case of other schools, Catholics attended in order to gain basic literacy. But the most important organisation of this kind was the Society for the Education of the Poor of Ireland, more commonly known as the Kildare Place Society. This body was founded in 1811 and had as its great aim the establishment of schools which both in their government and their educational policies should be uninfluenced by religious considerations, and in which the bible, without note or comment, should be read by all who had attained sufficient proficiency in reading. All catechisms and works of religious controversy were to be excluded. A government grant was first given in the parliamentary session 1814–15. By 1830 there were 1,634 schools in connection with the Kildare Place Society.[19] Though at first the society was well regarded by the Catholic clergy, it gradually became an object of suspicion as a largely Protestant organisation, a suspicion heightened by the simultaneous connection of some of its schools with other educational bodies of a more proselytising nature. Nevertheless, it had a great effect on popular education, with large numbers of pupils of every religious persuasion. In matters of religion it attempted a compromise which in the end offended both sides: the evangelical Protestants thought that there was not enough religion, and the Catholic clergy believed that what religion there was was too Protestant in conception. The parliamentary grant was discontinued with the advent of the national system in 1831.

But one of the society's triumphs was its publishing ventures. Commencing in 1817, it published about eighty little books, of an improving but entertaining nature, which were sold at the same price as the popular literature commonly read. The books were a great success: by 1831 some 1,465,000 volumes had been distributed; some had been sold, some sent as complete libraries to each Kildare Place Society school, and some dispatched as libraries to other bodies.[20] Of these books, twelve were of a non-sectarian nature, ten were 'instructive of arts or economy', ten were works on natural history, and thirty-two were books of voyages and travel. There was also a miscellaneous batch of fifteen titles, including fiction. The effect of these books was enormous. For the first time the ordinary Irish reader had access to sound material for the same price as he or she was used to paying for such works as *The seven champions of Christendom*, and the little books were to be found everywhere. Despite the pious hopes of the society, however, they seem to have supplemented the traditional fare instead of supplanting it.

This discussion raises the question of the nature of the books commonly used in the hedge schools themselves. There are a number of sources to inform us, and luckily these form a fairly coherent picture. Three contemporary listings will illustrate this coherence, though as we will see later, these listings tend to record only the more picturesque of the volumes. Hely Dutton, writing in 1808, gave a picture of what was read, apart from a few 'universal spelling books':

History of the seven champions of Christendom. [History of] Montelion, knight of the oracle. [History of] Parismus and Parismenes. [History of] Irish rogues and raparees. [History of] Freney, a notorious robber, teaching them the most dexterous mode of robbing. [History of] the most celebrated pirates. [History of] Jack the bachelor, a notorious smuggler. History of fair Rosamond and Jane Shore, two prostitutes. [History of] Donna Rosina, a Spanish courtesan. Ovid's art of love. History of witches and apparitions. The devil and Dr Faustus. Moll Flanders, highly edifying no doubt. New system of boxing by Mendoza, &c., &c.[21]

The second list was furnished by Henry Cooke, the Presbyterian minister, as he then was, in his evidence to the commissioners on Irish education in 1824. Cooke (*ca.* 1788–1868) had himself been educated in hedge schools:

I recollect one book being common in the schools, called the *Lilliputian magazine*; another, the *Youth's instructor*, those were good books. . . . I recollect reading a book called the *Seven champions of Christendom* and *Destruction of Troy*; I recollect reading *Hero and Leander*, *Gesta Romanorum*, and *Seven wise masters*; I recollect having read the *Chinese tales*; I recollect having read the romance called *Parismos and Parismenes* and *Don Belianis of Greece*; another extravagant tale I recollect having read [is] the *History of Captain Freney*, a robber; I perfectly and distinctly recollect . . . *Valentine and Orson* . . . , *Irish rogues and raparees*, and a book called the *History of Redmond O'Handlon*.[22]

The third list comes from William Carleton's *Traits and stories of the Irish peasantry*. Carleton (1794–1860) was also educated at a hedge school and was indeed for a time a hedge schoolmaster himself:

The books of amusement read in these schools . . . were the Seven champions of Christendom, the Seven wise masters and mistresses of Rome, Don Belianis of Greece, the Royal fairy tales, the Arabian nights entertainments, Valentine and Orson, Gesta Romanorum, Dorastus and Faunia, the History of Reynard the fox, the Chevalier Faublax; to those I may add the Battle of Aughrim, Siege of Londonderry, History of the young Ascanius . . . , and the Renowned history of the siege of Troy, the Forty thieves, Robin Hood's garland, the Garden of love and royal flower of fidelity, Parimus [*sic*] and Parismenus, along with others, the names of which shall not appear on these pages.[23]

These little volumes were part and parcel of the wares carried around the countryside by the travelling chapmen of the eighteenth and early nineteenth centuries,[24] and indeed the books found in the schools were, with few exceptions, probably tattered copies of those to be found in homes generally. This is confirmed by the lists of publications sold to chapmen by the Belfast bookseller James Magee. His 1777 list contains, *inter alia, The complete history of Valentine and*

Orson, *Arabian tales, Seven champions, Parismus and Parismenes, Lilliputian magazine, Seven wise masters, Reynard the fox, Moll Flanders, Irish rogues,* and *Garden
of love, or flower of fidelity*, these works amounting to about a quarter of the whole
list.[25]

It must be said, however, that the list given in the 1825 report of the commissioners for Irish education, while it certainly mentions the works above, also
shows that in the four counties surveyed by them (in what manner we know not),
the extent of the books was much wider. Indeed, religious works of many kinds
formed the largest grouping.[26] Naturally, these were not the sort of books to
attract either fond memory or the ire of the respectable. The commissioners' list
also fails to record school textbooks proper.

It is worthwhile examining in detail some of the books available, especially
those used as readers and in teaching literacy. Though oral literature of all kinds
still pervaded the countryside, the matter circulated in printed form (and widely
disseminated) should not be ignored. In fact, as so much attention has been placed
on oral tradition, this printed matter should be emphasised. In particular, any
material which expanded the imagination is of importance. In this respect the
chivalric and neo-chivalric novels are of great significance. The fact that in later
years those who had attended hedge schools remembered them and their titles
with such vividness testifies to the effect which they had on the youthful
consciousness.

One of the oldest of these tales is *The famous testament of the seven wise masters
of Rome*. This is believed to be of ancient Indian origin, reaching Europe during
the middle ages and first printed in English in the early sixteenth century.
Somewhat reminiscent of the *Arabian nights*, the book concerns the son of an
emperor who has spurned advances from his stepmother. The stepmother attempts to get her stepson executed and retails to her husband every night a tale
about sons dispossessing their fathers and treacherous counsellors. The boy's
tutors—the wise masters—in their turn retail stories to the emperor concerning
the duplicity of women. Like many of the versions of stories current in the hedge
schools, whatever historical period is ostensibly dealt with, there is an overwhelming air of medieval chivalry about the plot. In this case the emperor's second wife
is daughter to the king of Castille, and there are the usual barons and knights.
Also like many of these stories, there is a heavily symbolic air, which, despite being
spelt out in case it should be missed, was probably ignored by the children (and
adults) who read it in the eighteenth and early nineteenth centuries. In this
particular story the emperor signified the world, whose son represents mankind.
Mankind lost his real mother (reason and divine grace) and fell into the hands of
the stepmother (sin). The seven wise masters represent the seven liberal sciences,
intended 'to give him wholesome instructions'.[27]

Another of the early works, traceable well back into the medieval period, is the
History of Reynard the fox. Though it claims to be in the fable tradition, it can be

read, and almost certainly was read by an unsophisticated audience, as a mock-epic. It certainly had racy passages, which the godly would not have been too pleased to have read by children, at least by the nineteenth century when people worried more about such things. The following story is intended to convey the message that one should not venture on an undertaking against 'cunning, crafty men'. Tybart the cat has been tricked by Reynard into a trap laid by a priest for himself:

> The cat all this while making a flouncing to and fro to get loose, awakened the parson, who, supposing that it was the fox that had been taken, alarmed his whole family, and ordering Dame Jollock, his wife, to light up an offering candle, he leaped out of bed and ran downstairs, being followed by Martinet, his son, and others, who laid so unmercifully on Tybert that they not only woefully bruised him, but Martinet, thinking at one blow to deprive him of life, beat out one of his eyes, which the cat perceiving and finding what danger he was in, taking a desperate leap between the naked priest's legs, with his claws and teeth caught hold of his genitals and brought them clear away, which made him a perfect eunuch; this Dame Jollock seeing, cried out most piteously and swore she would rather have lost ten years' offerings than one small morsel of those precious jewels, cursing her hard fortune, and the time the gin was ever placed there, to occasion this loss and sorrow, saying to her son, see, Martinet, thy father's delight and my jewel taken away by the cursed cat, so that now it is quite spoiled, and though he may be recovered and live long, yet he can never be recovered to my satisfaction or be any ways useful to me, but it is spoiled to his shame and my utter loss, O woe is me.[28]

Another of the medieval tales, and one of the most popular, was *Valentine and Orson*. It is one of the constants on every list of popular material in Ireland. First printed in Lyons in 1489, it went through frequent editions in English from the sixteenth century onwards. The story concerns two sons of the emperor of Greece who are by mischance born in a forest. Orson, as his name would suggest, is brought up by a bear as a wild man, and Valentine is found and brought up by King Pepin, the father of Charlemagne. There are stirring adventures of many kinds, involving everything from dwarfs to giants, ogres to knights. The preface indeed commended itself to country readers, though hardly in flattering terms: 'it gives also a working to the minds of dull country swains, and, as it were, leads them to search for martial atchievements [*sic*], befitting many pastimes'. The preface also has a passage that anticipates the modern blurb:

> If you desire to see the care and trouble of kings, here they are; if for courtly tournaments and combats of princes, here they are; if you desire to know the battles of martial champions, here they are; if of travels of knightly adventures, here they are; if of the sorrows of distress'd ladies, here they are; if of strange

birds and savage education, here they are; if of friends long lost and their joyful
meeting again, here they are; if of charms and enchantments, here they are; if
of long captivities and imprisonments, here they are. . . ."[29]

There can be no doubt as to the source of the popularity of this kind of thing in
the countryside, and by natural extension, in the hedge schools. Indeed, in many
ways it could be said that the hedge schools were in advance of the 'proper' schools
of the nineteenth century in encouraging reading ability by letting the children
read something interesting, though of course this was by default rather than as
part of a conscious policy.

Following these genuinely medieval romances with their heavily symbolic
overtones came the pure escapism of the neo-chivalric romances of the late
sixteenth and seventeenth centuries. Of these, by far the most popular was the
Seven champions of Christendom, one of the most frequently mentioned hedge-
school books. It is not hard to see the appeal of this story, written by the hack
Richard Johnson and first published in 1596/7. The heroes of this story were
seven saints (St George, St Denis, St James, St Anthony, St Andrew, St Patrick,
and St David) who had their marvellous adventures 'not long after the destruction
of Troy'—a potent era in which to place the story, and one strictly fantastic. The
protagonists become involved in a number of exciting adventures, conquering
giants, knights, and ogres, with St Patrick himself playing a prominent part.
These exertions are punctuated by others, such as the episode in which they rest
their weary heads 'on their ladies' soft bosoms, solacing in such rapture of
pleasure that no pen can express'. Indeed, there are a few passages in this story,
as in the others, which make one understand the dislike expressed for them by
the early nineteenth-century educational reformers. It was not just the apparent
uselessness of the stories, conveying absolutely no accurate information about the
exports of Peru, that they did not like, but such passages as the following, in which
the knightly saints come across in Provence

> a beauteous virgin lying on her back in an indecent posture, and coming near,
> they perceived her staked to the ground by the hair of her head, her arms and
> hands stretched out and tied to two hollow shrubs, and her legs fastened very
> wide asunder, in a manner as if she had been stretched on a rack.[30]

This passage is indeed the stuff of pornography, even if lacking in explicit sex.
Nevertheless, apart from such episodes as this, the *Seven champions of Christendom* is an exciting and adventurous story. One of its most interesting aspects, apart
from its undoubted popularity in its own right, is the connection between its text
and the mummers' plays so popular in Ireland and elsewhere. The concept of St
Patrick as a noble knight is central to the mummers' plays.

Another of the late sixteenth-century neo-chivalric tales often mentioned in
connection with the hedge schools was *Don Belianis of Greece*, first published in

1598. In format its plot conforms to the norm for these stories, containing the varied adventures of Don Belianis, son of the emperor of Greece, including an outing to Ireland, where he takes service under the high king, Owen Roe O'Neill. He wages war against the prince of Ulster, who is aided by McGuire, father to Peter, Knight of the Keys, and the giant Fluerston from the Carlingford mountains. All ends well as usual, and the story, like others, illustrates the very non-historical and purely fanciful settings of these tales, in which characters from real life and imaginary persons of all kinds play out their wars in a setting of knightly chivalry, surrounded by magic.

As previously mentioned, these stories would have been of real use in the teaching of literacy, probably of more use, if conveying less practical information, than the dry-as-dust material that succeeded them when the national system of education became entrenched. As early as the seventeenth century this fact was recognised by the eminent English geographer and religious writer Peter Heylyn in his *Cosmography*, just at the very end, where he has a whimsical section on the unknown parts of the world, including 'the lands of chivalry':

> And yet I cannot but confess (for I have been a great student in these books of chivalry) that they may be of very good use to children or young boys in their adolescency. For besides that they divert the mind from worse cogitations, they perfect him that takes pleasure in them in the way of reading, beget in him an habit of speaking, and animate him many times to such high conceptions as really may make him fit for great undertakings.[31]

The genres of popular literature most commonly attacked by the critics of hedge schools, apart from the romances already mentioned, were biographies of highwaymen, prophecies, and seditious works generally. Of all the biographies of highwaymen, by far the most popular were the *Life and adventures of James Freney* and John Cosgrave's *Genuine history of the lives and actions of the most notorious highwaymen*, better known as *Irish rogues and raparees*. These volumes formed in many ways a more modern counterpart to the older works of chivalry, and indeed some attempt was made to create the image of a knight of the road, with, in Freney's case at any rate, a notable lack of success, to modern eyes at least. Freney, besides indulging in some adventures of a Robin Hood nature, was not above embarking on robbery with violence. Indeed, burglary was as prominent as highway robbery, and perhaps the authorities had some cause for alarm at the widespread circulation of these books. A youth was hardly likely to get on a horse, in the manner of Don Quixote, and go looking for giants, but some breaking and entering at the local big house was not entirely out of the question. There is even some evidence for this point of view:

> Whereas on Thursday night last, between the hours of nine and ten o'clock, after all the servant-men, who slept in the outhouse, had retired to the beds,

except the butler, a desperate set of fellows entered Doctor Lill's house of Barn-hill in the county of Tyrone and in a most outrageous manner abused and desperately cut his butler, who had given them opposition; and had it not been for the cries and shouts of the family, which were heard by the neighbours of Stewarts-Town, who humanely ran to their assistance, they would have gained their ends and perhaps would have committed murder, as they fired a shot at Mrs Lill, who was calling out of the window for help; but fortunately, the shot missed her and broke the pane of glass next to where she was standing. Two of the fellows who entered the house had black faces, one of which had a shirt on, hanging from the top of his head, leaving his face open to the mouth. The third was a well-looking fellow, about 5 feet 9 inches high, seemed to be between thirty and forty years of age; he had on a brown jacket and striped waistcoat—sailor-like; was not disguised; said he was called the 'bold Capt. Freney'.[32]

This was in 1790, long after the era of the real Captain Freney. The disguise of the would-be robbers is interesting, as it is reminiscent of those used by the various agrarian secret societies and later by the mummers as costume during their plays—at least by those mummers who were not too concerned to devise more elaborate costumes.

Of course, besides the chivalric romances, religious works, tattered newspapers, odd volumes of novels, and so on, which were used as aids to literacy, there were schoolbooks proper, generally spelling books and arithmetics. The list of books carried by the chapmen who were the customers of the Belfast bookseller James Magee in 1750 included Edward Cocker's *Arithmetic* and Thomas Dyche's *Spelling dictionary*.[33] In 1777 they were carrying George Fisher's *Arithmetic*, David Manson's *Spelling book*, John Gough's *Practical arithmetic*, David Manson's *Pronouncing and spelling dictionary*, Isaac Watt's *Compleat spelling book*, Thomas Dilworth's *New guide to the English tongue* (a spelling book), Thomas Dyche's *Spelling dictionary* and Daniel Fenning's *Universal spelling book*.[34] These titles give some idea of the type of schoolbook to be found in the schools. It was not worth the chapman's while to carry works on history, geography, or the classics, though these of course were often taught. There was a natural progression of favourites as well. In arithmetic Cocker can be seen to have been superseded by Gough, for instance, as Gough was himself superseded in the early nineteenth century by James Thomson.

That these sorts of books continued to be in common use into the nineteenth century is confirmed by the writers in Shaw Mason's *Statistical account*. One writer commented:

> The books used in these seminaries are in general of an indifferent description; they are furnished with useful spelling books and dictionaries published a few years ago in Belfast by a schoolmaster of the name of Manson; but when they

have learned to read, their attention is directed to the biography of robbers, thieves, and prostitutes, the reveries of knights errant and crusaders, a seditious history of Ireland, tales of apparitions, witches, and fairies, and a new system of boxing.[35]

This is the standard rhetoric of contemporary writers, but despite the dismissive note generally sounded, there is no reason why a diet of such works should not have provided a reasonably good standard of literacy along with enjoyment, given a capable schoolmaster (and one who was not too much of a flogger).

What kind of person was the hedge schoolmaster? The figure of tradition is certainly well known. The reality was somewhat different, in that anyone from a man with the highest attainments to the lowest could open a school and hope to attract pupils. To take the lowest first, we have the following advertisement from 1795:

MURDER! ! !

Whereas on Thursday morning the 24th inst. William Donaldson of Bally-harry was murdered at Newtownards, with many circumstances of savage barbarity, by Pat Beatty and Thomas M'Neight. Through the active and spirited exertions of the inhabitants of Newtownards, Beatty was taken, but M'Neight has eluded their most diligent searches. M'Neight is about 30 years of age, about 5 feet 10 inches high, well made, has black woolly hair and a wild, unsettled look. He is nearly deprived of the use of the fingers and thumb of the right hand, which are shrivelled up and contracted from his having fallen into a furnace of boiling lye. He can, however, write tolerably with them and earned his livelihood by teaching school and as a day labourer. He is a man of noted bad character and has long been the pest and terror of this town and neighbourhood.[36]

This description pointed to schoolmastering at the lowest possible level, with a teacher who was certainly a terrifying figure, probably very little better educated than the pupils whom he was attempting to teach. The level above this would have been the teacher with some pretence to learning, but only a pretence, who kept the peasantry in awe by utilising a supposedly learned and half-understood vocabulary. This was the type of schoolmaster most often satirised, not least by the more literate hedge schoolmasters themselves. Such a teacher was Bugbear, the 'hero' of George Dugall's poem 'Bugbear & Clodpate'. Bugbear, the 'knight of the didactic switch', is out of a place for haunting the dram-shop and the stew. Meeting Clodpate, he dazzles him with a display of erudition, of which the sample quoted at the head of this essay gives a fair example. He gains a school, where, well versed in such arcana as 'swine-tax and eat-him-all-Magee' (syntax and etymology), he proceeds to stock the neighbourhood with fools. Bugbear is a hedge schoolmaster of literature, but the stereotype was so widespread (it was repeated by writers such as Dugall and Carleton, who were speaking from experience) that it was probably true to some extent. And how could it not be? Societies where literacy is valued but relatively hard to attain tend to breed such people, as witness the 'babu English' of India. This problem would also have been encouraged by the high-flown language of many of the books used. Carleton commented on this feature himself:

> That a great deal of ludicrous pedantry generally accompanied this knowledge is not at all surprising when we consider the rank these worthy teachers held in life and the stretch of inflation at which their pride was kept by the profound reverence excited by their learning among the people. It is equally true that each of them had a stock of crambos ready for accidental encounter which would have puzzled Euclid or Sir Isaac Newton himself; but even these trained their minds to habits of acuteness and investigation. When a schoolmaster of this class had established himself as a good mathematician, the predominant enjoyment of his heart and life was to write the epithet Philomath after his name.[37]

At the top of the hedge-school tree was the genuinely educated man. Tradition has such masters concentrated in Munster, but they were to be found everywhere, though rare and highly valued. Frank Glass, a hedge schoolmaster in County Londonderry at the end of the eighteenth century ('a pure Milesian, short of stature, fiery in temper, with features exhibiting a strange combination of cunning, thought, and humour'), who swore at his pupils and taught them to swear, was an excellent scholar.[38] His love for the classics, especially Horace, was almost a passion.

In the parish of Dungiven, Co. Londonderry, the local rector noted in the early nineteenth century that in the lowlands the inhabitants were 'in general an educated people, that is, they can all almost read and write and understand a little of arithmetic'. But in the mountains

> the few who receive any kind of instruction surmount by ardent zeal and persevering talent every obstacle to knowledge and often arrive at attainments in literature of which their wealthier and more favoured neighbours never dream. They have more peculiarly a taste for and facility in acquiring langauges which is very remarkable; every one who converses with a mountaineer acquainted with the English language must be struck with the singular precision and eloquence of his expressions, which have rather the air of a written than of a colloquial style. . . . Even in the wildest districts it is not unusual to meet with good classical scholars; and there are several young mountaineers of the writer's acquaintance whose knowledge and taste in the Latin poets might put to the blush many who have all the advantages of established schools and regular instruction.[39]

Thus the hedge schoolteachers were, as one would expect, a varied bunch. Some were, as one writer put it, 'almost in as great a need of instruction as themselves'.[40] Others had a barely held knowledge of badly understood, or misunderstood, higher things but maintained prestige mainly by bluff. Some were no doubt perfectly competent teachers, and others, probably very few, were capable of imparting an education that could enable at least some of their pupils to pass on eventually to university, as in the case of Henry Cooke. How were they trained?

The basic form of training of the hedge schoolmaster was well described by William Carleton.[41] When the parents of a boy decided that 'he was particularly cute at the larnin', they had three ambitions: that he should be either a priest, a clerk, or a schoolmaster. Once this issue had been decided, he was set aside from every class of labour in order to pursue his studies. Every effort was made to provide him with clothes and books. The pupil remained at the local school until he decided that he had completely drained the master of his knowledge. Carleton described a contest with the master, though this was by no means universal. The pupil, by now confident of his powers, sent a challenge to the master, and a public exhibition of learning took place. If the pupil were not judged the victor in learning over his master, he resumed his studies under him, but if he were victorious, he sought out a fresh schoolmaster. Another challenge ensued, and if defeated, he became his pupil, staying at night with the neighbouring farmers, whose sons he instructed in lieu of payment for the hospitality. He was denominated a 'poor scholar'—an emotive term which ensured him the respect of all. In this manner he proceeded around the country, drinking in whatever knowledge he could find for three or four years, returning eventually to his native place to send another challenge to his old schoolmaster, and, if this was successful, he drove him from his situation. The vanquished schoolmaster then sought out a new district and proceeded to mount a series of challenges of his own. The terms for victory and defeat were 'sacking' and 'bogging'. It is unclear how common this practice was. One suspects that ejectment was possible only if the local master was not popular with the parents involved.

For those with higher ambitions the aim of the poor scholar was to go to the schools of Munster, held to be the centre of classical education. Carleton himself set out on an abortive journey of this kind and found that the satchel on his back, obviously filled with books, immediately identified him as a poor scholar. This recognition assured him of kindness and hospitality along the route from the common people, who held him in great esteem.[42] Thomas Crofton Croker described such persons as well. According to him, they were generally the sons of reduced farmers and natives of Ulster and Connacht, who, having acquired all the learning that the local master could give them, ranged 'through the bogs of Munster' to complete their knowledge of Latin and acquire Greek. Apparently, the master whose school they were currently attending gained little but glory from their presence.[43]

Such poor scholars sometimes aspired to the priesthood, sometimes to be hedge schoolmasters in their turn. Those who became schoolmasters then had to find a school. At times, as Carleton described, they would drive out a less able schoolmaster. A public contest of wits, however, would not have been universally necessary. It would have been sufficient to set up another school nearby and to wait for pupils, or rather the parents, to transfer allegiance. This happened to one of Carleton's teachers, Charles McGoldrick of Tulnavern, Co. Tyrone. His classical school lasted about three years, and Carleton had progressed only as far as Ovid's *Metamorphoses*, Justin, and the first chapter of John in the Greek testament when all his Protestant scholars left him because a Presbyterian had opened a rival school in Augher. McGoldrick then disappeared.[44] Schoolmasters were indeed a peripatetic breed, perpetually pulling up stakes and moving to greener pastures, or being supplanted by an apparently better master. The lives of those who went to hedge schools, such as Carleton and Henry Cooke, show a succession of masters and schoolhouses.

The income of the hedge schoolmaster was small. Fees were charged quarterly. 'Readers' and 'spellers' were charged from one shilling and sevenpence up to as much as five shillings in the best schools. 'Writers' were charged between two shillings and twopence and four shillings per quarter. Arithmetic could cost from three shillings and fourpence to eight shillings. The most common sums were two shillings and twopence for spelling and reading, three shillings and threepence for writing, and four shillings and fourpence for arithmetic. Latin, in those schools where it was taught, was dearer—about eleven shillings. One writer noted in the early nineteenth century that these terms had been stable for about fifty years.[45]

Several factors affected the schoolmaster's ability to earn a decent living. The first was obviously the number of children at his school. If too few came, he was forced to flit to new ground. This would also happen if another school appeared in the neighbourhood and for some reason attracted his pupils away. The number of pupils, on average, was about forty. Another factor was the seasonality of attendance. On the positive side he often received fuel, butter, eggs, and so on as part payment, and he frequently stayed free of charge in a parent's house or at a number of houses in rotation. Many earned a pittance. In County Sligo

> many of these poor schoolmasters do not earn sixpence per day by their continual labours, from the small allowance paid to them and in many cases promised but not paid; so that they are often obliged to have recourse to the magistrate to recover their miserable wages of 1s. 8d. per quarter. They could not subsist at all in this state, but that they make a practice of going home with some of the children daily or weekly, where they get their food or bread.[46]

There were other occasional sources of income. The schoolmaster was 'the general scribe of the parish, to whom all who wanted letters or petitions written, uniformly applied'.[47] Remuneration for these services could be either in kind or in cash. Thus the Irish hedge schoolmaster eked out his often precarious existence. In what sort of accommodation did he do so?

At the basic level the hedge school would have been just that. In 1775 Richard Twiss observed near Dunleer 'about a dozen bare-legged boys sitting by the side of the road, scrawling on scraps of paper placed on their knees; these boys, it seems, found the smoke in their school or cabin insufferable'.[48] It should be noted that there was no suggestion here that these outdoor arrangements were permanent, but merely that it was more pleasant outdoors than inside that day. Indeed, common sense suggests that in the Irish climate a school without even a roof over its head would have been comparatively rare, at least after the early period of persecution. No doubt on warm days children in many schools would have copied the example of those of Dunleer and preferred the fresh air.

The most primitive form of schoolhouse was well described by Carleton:

> The manner of building hedge schoolhouses being rather curious, I will describe it. The usual spot selected for their erection is a ditch on the roadside, in some situation where there will be as little damp as possible. From such a spot an excavation is made equal to the size of the building, so that when this is scooped out, the back side-wall and the two gables are already formed, the banks being dug perpendicularly. The front side-wall, with a window on each side of the door, is then built of clay or green sods laid along in rows; the gables are also topped with sods, and perhaps a row or two laid upon the back side-wall if it should be considered too low.[49]

The roof was then erected and thatched, leaving a hole in the middle to let the smoke from the fire escape, and the school was then ready for business. Such a structure could have been erected in a day. Carleton also described the interior, with its pile of turf, added to every day by the pupils, who were each supposed to bring two turves. The children sat on round stones, some capped with a straw collar, others with springy material cut from the bog. Most pupils had to sit on the floor. Hats were hung on wooden pegs driven into the walls.

This was one of the commonest types of school. Many such structures existed in the parish of Maghera, Co. Londonderry, where they were described as

> in general wretched huts built of sods in the highway ditches, from which circumstances they are denominated hedge schools. They have neither door, window, nor chimney, a large hole in the roof serving to admit light and let out the smoke which issues from a fire in the middle of the house. A low narrow hole cut in the mud wall on the south side of the hut affords ingress and egress to its inhabitants.[50]

Many temporarily vacant buildings were pressed into service, though some schools would have been purpose-built. Generally, they were wretched erections. Henry Cooke's school in County Londonderry (or rather one of them) had two windows, one blocked with earthen sods and the other unglazed. The furniture consisted of one table, one stool (appropriated by the schoolmaster 'to save him . . . from the colic'), and a quantity of stones.[51] Barns were often used. The most comfortable of the schools were those held in a room of the schoolmaster's own house or in a house belonging to one of the parents. There at least was found a continuity of warmth, with a fire constantly alive.

Hedge schools, though not in the strict sense, existed in the towns as well. Carleton, referring to the time when he was a young man very early in the nineteenth century, remarked:

> I have reason to feel convinced . . . that half a century ago there were nearly as many 'hedge schools' in Dublin as there were of all other classes put together. In other words, that nearly one-half were hedge schools taught in private rooms by men who were unworthy to be compared with the great body of the country hedge schoolmasters of Ireland. They were for the most part, if not illiterate, excessively and barbarously ignorant. Nay more, I knew one instance in which the master actually went round with his scholars, as they used to do in the country, and as I myself did at Newcastle.[52]

Schools of this nature existed in Belfast as well, where a writer commented in 1795 on the large number of day-schools, available to nearly everybody because of their low rates, which were to be found in nearly every street.[53] Indeed, every town must have had such schools.

Life in the schools was naturally varied, depending on the learning and disposition of the schoolmaster, the nature of the building, and the state of the weather. One of the best descriptions was furnished by Carleton.[54] He pictured one of the ruder schools, built into a ditch, as described above. In a ring of children sits the schoolmaster upon a deal chair, bearing a broad ruler, the emblem of his power. In a corner there is the pile of turf with its daily contributions. Along the walls are a number of round stones as make-do seats. The floor is strewn with the tops of quills, pens, broken slates, and tattered leaves of books. Some of the children are playing, others employed in writing their copies, seated on the ground with the paper placed on a piece of planed deal. The older boys are working at their arithmetic sums. The bigger boys are near the master, and there are a few girls, the daughters of the more respectable farmers, who do not want their daughters to be entirely illiterate in order to increase their marriageability.

The school is alive with the buzz of teaching, some of the children rehearsing their lessons, some being taught by the master. Carleton approved of all this hurly-burly, as opposed to the more rigid discipline imposed on the latter-day official schools, for he felt that a child was capable of more intense study and abstraction in the din of a rowdy schoolroom than when forced to sit in silence. Children who went too far were being punished. One perhaps was wearing the 'soogaun'—a straw collar around the neck—which served in place of a dunce's cap. If the summer's day was fine, the children were stretched outside on the grass.

At Easter and Christmas there was the excitement of the 'barring out'. The master was sent on a fool's errand and then the door was barred against him; he was not permitted to re-enter until a vacation had been extorted. It was part of the fun that the teacher had to make every effort to get in again. If he did, the children had no claim to a long vacation and were indeed liable to correction. There were undoubtedly masters with whom it would have been unwise to try tricks of this kind, such as the master who for his own mere amusement would go out to the nearest thorn hedge, cut a branch, arrange the children in a circle with their naked legs pointing inwards, and proceed to sweep the branch round and round against their flesh until a ring of blood was visible on the ground where they sat. Corporal punishment was general in the schools, but seldom cruelty of this nature. Such a schoolmaster would almost inevitably have found the child's elders intent on retribution in kind.

The schools were best attended in summer, less well attended in spring and harvest for obvious reasons; in winter, if the building was wretched, they were often deserted. To judge from the figures quoted in the various reports comprising Shaw Mason's *Statistical account*, about one-third of the pupils were female, a rather surprising figure given the anecdotal evidence emphasising male attendance.[55]

One of the most remarkable things about the hedge schools was their non-denominational makeup. Pollock, the teacher of Henry Cooke, had a typical hedge-school attitude to religious education which would do credit to the most fervid advocate of integrated education, though it probably stemmed from self-interest rather than idealism. Catechisms were enforced without exception and without distinction. The *Shorter catechism* of the Westminster divines, the *Church catechism*, and the *Christian doctrine of the Roman Catholics* were taught to members of the respective sects. No child was suffered to escape.[56] Cooke himself in later years did not see any great harm in this practice. He gave evidence on the matter to the education commissioners in 1824:

Were children of all religious persuasions educated promiscuously in the schools?—Yes, and so far as I recollect my own observations at the time or those of others, I never heard the least objection, or any idea of impropriety in it, or evil that might arise from it.

Did the children receive religious instruction in the school according to the doctrine of their respective churches?—To a certain extent . . . ; invariably, the catechisms of the churches to which the children belonged were taught in all the English schools where I was educated.

Who taught the catechism?—The schoolmaster.

Did he make any scruple in teaching the catechism of a church of which he was not a member?—None at all; three catechisms were taught in the same school. . . .[57]

Did that various knowledge of the catechisms confound your religious belief?—I do not think it did in any degree.

Here, then, we have the hedge schools of Ireland, some bad, some good, some excellent, but all testifying to the strong desire of ordinary Irish people to see their children receive some sort of education. Here were schools where Protestant and Catholic rubbed shoulders, where hard-won literacy and sometimes more was gained (though lack of opportunity often meant that it was largely lost again), and where children learned to read from works of adventure. This was a far cry from the ultimately segregated classes and dull readers of the national schools which began to supplant them in the 1830s. It is easy to be sentimental about them, for many a child's schooling was nasty, brutish, and short, but for many others it was the opening to a wider world. Much has not been covered in this account: the Gaelic scholarship of many of the schoolmasters, for instance, and the many excellent poets in Irish. What has been emphasised is the experience of the majority of children at these schools. One haunting thought remains: Did the love of the hedge schoolmasters for long portmanteau words, flung together from English, Latin, and Greek, find a distant echo in the work of another Irishman —James Joyce?

NOTES

1 P.J. Dowling, *The hedge schools of Ireland* (2nd ed., Cork, 1968), blurb on rear cover. This book, first published in 1935, remains the standard work.

2 George Dugall, *The northern cottage, book I, and other poems* (Londonderry, 1824), p. 50.

3 Margaret Spufford, *Small books and pleasant histories: popular fiction and its readership in seventeenth-century England* (London, 1981), p. 74.

4 *An act to restrain foreign education* (7 William III, c. 4).

5 *An act to prevent the further growth of popery* (2 Anne, c. 6).

6 *An act for explaining and amending an act intituled an act to prevent the further growth of popery* (8 Anne, c. 3).

7 *An act to allow persons professing the popish religion to teach school in this kingdom* (21 & 22 Geo. III, c. 62).

8 J.A. McIvor, *Popular education in the Irish Presbyterian church* (Dublin, 1969), pp. 26–8.

9 Dowling, *Hedge schools*, pp. 48–9.

10 W.P. Burke, *The Irish priests in the penal times (1660–1760)* (Waterford, 1914), pp. 301–2, 386–8, 394–6.

11 *An act for the English order, habit, and language* (28 Henry VIII, c. 15).

12 *First report of the commissioners on education in Ireland*, H.C. 1825 (400), xii, 37 (hereafter cited as *First report*).

13 *First report,* p. 33.
14 Ibid., p. 66.
15 Ibid., p. 69.
16 Ibid., pp. 67, 81.
17 Ibid., p. 81.
18 Ibid., p. 62.
19 R.M. Martin, *Ireland before and after the union with Great Britain* (2nd ed., London, 1848), p. 210.
20 H.K. Moore, *An unwritten chapter in the history of education* (London, 1904), pp. 247–8.
21 Hely Dutton, *Statistical survey of the county of Clare* . . . (Dublin, 1808), pp. 236–7.
22 *First report,* appendix, p. 820.
23 William Carleton, *Traits and stories of the Irish peasantry* (4th ed., 5 vols, London, 1836), ii, 235–6.
24 J.R.R. Adams, *The printed word and the common man: popular culture in Ulster, 1700–1900* (Belfast, 1987).
25 Ovid, *Ars amandi, or Ovid's art of love* (Belfast, 1777), pp. 179–80.
26 *First report,* appendix, pp. 553–9.
27 *History of the seven wise masters* (Dublin, 1814), p. 1.
28 *The most pleasing and delightful history of Reynard the fox* (Belfast, 1814), pp. 30–1.
29 *The history of Valentine and Orson* (Belfast, 1782), p. ii.
30 Richard Johnson, *The illustrious and renowned history of the seven champions of Christendom* (Dublin, *ca.* 1840), p. 61.
31 Peter Heylyn, *Cosmography in four books* (6th ed., London, 1682), p. 562.
32 *Belfast News-Letter,* 28 December 1790.
33 Robert Russell, *Seven sermons* (Belfast, 1750), p. 176.
34 Ovid, *Ars amandi,* pp. 179–80.
35 W.S. Mason (ed.), *A statistical account or parochial survey of Ireland drawn up from the communications of the clergy* (3 vols, Dublin, 1814–19), i, 598–9.
36 *Belfast News-Letter,* 6 October 1795.
37 Carleton, *Traits and stories,* ii, 151–2.
38 J.L. Porter, *The life and times of Henry Cooke* (London, 1871), pp. 6–7.
39 Mason, *Statistical account,* i, 313–14.
40 Ibid., p. 5.
41 Carleton, *Traits and stories,* ii, 151–2.
42 Ibid., pp. 152–3.
43 T.C. Croker, *Researches in the south of Ireland* . . . (London, 1824), pp. 326–7.
44 William Carleton, *Life of William Carleton* (2 vols, London, 1896), i, 38.
45 Mason, *Statistical account, passim.*
46 Ibid., ii, 374.
47 Carleton, *Traits and stories,* ii, 222.
48 Richard Twiss, *A tour in Ireland in 1775* . . . (London, 1776), pp. 73–4.
49 Carleton, *Traits and stories,* ii, 197–8.
50 Mason, *Statistical account,* i, 598.
51 Porter, *Henry Cooke,* p. 4.
52 Carleton, *Life,* i, 199.
53 *Belfast News-Letter,* 27 April 1795.
54 Carleton, *Traits and stories,* ii, 160–256.
55 Mason, *Statistical account,* i, 598.
56 Porter, *Henry Cooke,* p. 4.
57 *First report,* appendix, pp. 810–11.

6

An Underground Gentry?
Catholic Middlemen in Eighteenth-Century Ireland

KEVIN WHELAN

INTRODUCTION

Was eighteenth-century Ireland a typical colony, or was it simply a representative *ancien régime* society? Such a question can be answered only by looking carefully at a wide range of economic, political, social, and cultural relationships within the island.[1] While the political and economic history of the period is now reasonably well established, its social and cultural history is still in an embryonic phase. There has been little effort to apply in an Irish context the range of questions and methods used by French scholars in exploring the contours of eighteenth-century social and cultural formations. With the honourable exception of work by Cullen, Bartlett, and Connolly, this is still largely untilled ground.[2] There is no specific study of *mentalité*, for example. This essay attempts to recover the *mentalité* of one particular group in eighteenth-century Irish life—the descendants of the old Catholic landowning families, reduced to the level of middlemen and farmers. As the de facto leaders of Catholic society, and in a situation where vertical attachments persisted after their economic power had vanished, such families played a pivotal brokerage role in the articulation of popular culture. The continuing valency of the question of landownership in these special conditions is explored, as are its implications for the political crisis of the 1790s.

1 THE ORIGINS OF THE MIDDLEMAN SYSTEM

The origins of the middleman (or head-tenant) system are simple: in the turbulent 1690s and the cash-starved early decades of the eighteenth century many landlords sought to stabilise their rentals by attracting resident, substantial, improving Protestant head-tenants, who could guarantee cash rent payments and were to be held responsible (through lease covenants) for the development of their holdings.[3] In a way the middleman system was not unlike the chain of command in a military structure, as, for example, in the Cromwellian army; the officer–soldier relationship could easily be replicated in the landlord–middleman one, especially in a situation where large-scale demobilisation had occurred. The actual work of landscape modification therefore devolved on middlemen— delineation of tenancy boundaries, creation of enclosures, making of permanent hedges and ditches, clearance of scrubland, liming, draining, construction of substantial stone-walled and slated dwellings, and planting of orchards and deciduous trees. Besides performing this exemplary role, head-tenants were also to be responsible for the recruitment and organisation of subtenants.

While some middlemen were on perpetuity leases (leases for lives renewable forever) which made them de facto owners, most were on leases for three lives. Landlords favoured leases for lives rather than fixed terms because the element of uncertainty prevented tenants from deliberately exhausting the land in the last years of the lease, and because leases fell in individually and episodically, thereby spreading the administrative costs and income generation while preventing combinations against the landlord in cases of upward adjustment of rent. Leases for lives also conferred voting rights, always an important species of landlord property. The downside of these arrangements was that the irregular expiration of leases made large-scale landlord interventions difficult or protracted. Overall, however, granted the emphatic political bias towards Protestantism, this policy was weighted in favour of immigrant tenants at the expense of native ones. Josiah Bateman, agent on the Boyle (later Devonshire) estate in the 1730s, described the result of this policy on the evolution of this estate:

> This is a fine English colony, which the late Richard Boyle took such pains and cost to plant here by bringing with him families out of England and encour- aging those of English extraction, whose industry he liked, for their improve- ments, and would not set a lease to a native because they are quite the reverse to improvement.[4]

This bias against non-Protestant tenants for perceived laziness was widely shared. A Cork agent in 1710 described an unimproved townland as being 'like a papist's farm, without bounds made up or a bush on the same'.[5]

'Improvements', as implemented by these Protestant head-tenants, had a symbolic as well as a utilitarian purpose. They would articulate in the landscape the visible signs of a stable and civilising Protestant society. In particular, there would be a self-conscious assertion of values superior to those of the indigenous population. Architecturally, for example, this would be reflected by the use of slate rather than thatch, brick and stone rather than mud, isolated as opposed to clustered dwellings, and formal rather than vernacular architectural styles. In this case style would be substance, the medium, the message.

One can identify a sequence of cases in which middlemen would dominate on estates. In areas where there was no resident landlord (as in many remote or environmentally disadvantaged districts), or in areas of absenteeism, middlemen could assume the dominant social and cultural role. Similarly, if estates were mortgaged or owned by merchants and lawyers, and used simply as forms of investment capital (as frequently happened in proximity to cities), the middlemen retained control on the ground. If estates were diminutive (as happened in Normanised areas where the old morcellated landownership matrix acted as the framework for the new), landlords lacked status, and the role of influential middlemen was again accentuated.

While landlords tended to have a preference for Protestant head-tenants, many cases can be identified where the middlemen were Catholics recruited from the ranks of the dispossessed landowners. The new landlords opted for them as a stabilising force, guaranteed of local acceptability and able to smooth the transition from the old to the new régime. Catholic middlemen occurred where the old landlords survived, where the small size of estates militated against large-scale reorganisation, or where it was impossible to recruit solvent immigrants. The survival of Catholic or crypto-Catholic landlords was especially significant in nurturing Catholic middlemen. It is now increasingly evident that such survival was greater in extent than previously assumed.[6] The inaccurate and flawed formulation of the Protestant Ascendancy has by linguistic sleight of hand caused Catholic landlords to disappear from our conception of eighteenth-century Ireland.

Simm's figure of 5 percent Catholic ownership of land in 1776 has frequently been cited to 'prove' that such survival was of minimal importance.[7] Yet, to judge from the number of claimants under the Articles of Limerick, there were as many as 350 landed Catholic families in Ireland in the early eighteenth century.[8] Additionally, it can no longer be safely assumed that 'converts' were a loss to the Catholic interest. Hemmed in by legal restrictions, Catholics quietly discovered loopholes and felt few moral qualms about sqeezing through them. Ignatius Gahagan, a 'convert' from Catholicism in 1757, made the point succinctly: 'I would rather at any time entrust God with my soul than the laws of Ireland with my lands'.[9] In these circumstances the convert laws were soon being expertly manipulated. In 1752 a commentator noted that 'the acts relating to purchases made or leases taken by papists are so eluded by perjuries, trusts in Protestant names, and other contrivances that they are of little significance'.[10]

Collusive discoveries for merely legal reasons became the accepted method of evading the penal laws on property. Plotting the relationship between eighteenth-century 'conversions' and 'discoveries' demonstrates a synchronicity of the two curves which is astonishing. Behind the black letter of the law a subversive strategy had been devised, implemented, and routinised by a group of lawyers specialising in convert business. By the mid-eighteenth century, conversion/discovery proceedings were a fairly normal brand of conveyancing.[11] Thus 'conversions' from Catholic to Protestant cannot be taken as an erosion of the Catholic position; rather, in many cases they strengthened it. If one includes 'convert' estates, the figure for 'Catholic' ownership of land reaches about 20 percent. Almost one-fifth of the island therefore remained in relatively undisturbed ownership; even more importantly, these undisturbed estates were concentrated heavily in certain regions—notably the Pale and the Galway-Clare-Mayo area.

The tantalising theme as to how a non-colonised Ireland might have evolved can be partially studied on these estates. Some conclusions seem clear. These estates nurtured (as in Scotland) proliferating kin-based lineages which controlled the strategic leaseholds. A symptomatic example is the Kavanagh of Borris estate in south Carlow.[12] Because it remained in Catholic hands, this estate attracted no planters (indeed, in the 1660 poll-tax Borris was the only town in south Leinster with no New English presence).[13] Even more strikingly, the head-tenants on the estate remained Catholic in toto, with many being recruited from junior branches of the Kavanaghs. In 1747 there were five principal Kavanagh middlemen who held almost a quarter of the estate at very low rents (Ballybeg, Marlay, Ballynattin, Ballinacoola, Turra, Drummond, Rocksavage, Ballybur, and St Mullins). Other Catholic families—Rossitters, Blackneys, Cloneys, Corcorans—dominated the remaining leases and had in turn an overwhelmingly Catholic subtenantry.

Just as the McMurrough Kavanaghs sheltered minor branches of their family, so too did the Clanricardes in Galway protect junior branches, and the Ormondes in Kilkenny and Tipperary had Catholic Butlers sheltering under their aegis.[14] Dispossessed Catholic proprietors were easily accommodated as middlemen on these Catholic estates, and they could also be incorporated on Protestant-owned estates. In County Dublin, for example, over sixty of the old landowning class can be traced in the hearth-money records of the 1660s still living on their ancestral lands.[15] In south Wexford, a classic region of small estates inherited directly from the medieval landowning system, one can trace twenty-six former landowning families in the role of middlemen in the eighteenth century. If this transition from landowner to middleman is plotted spatially, a striking degree of continuity is manifested.[16]

The pattern is one of lateral translation, an internal low-key dislocation. In this transition from towerhouse to farmhouse, and from small landowner to middleman, social and cultural conservatism was ensured. This is reflected across a whole series of parameters—the survival of farm villages and of vernacular housing styles, the retention of pre-Reformation traditions in the eighteenth century (the singing of Christmas carols, the carrying of wooden crosses in funeral processions, mumming), and the survival of the Yola dialect. At a political level these gentlemen farmers of County Wexford saw themselves and were seen by their communities as an underground gentry, with more authentic roots than the Protestant gentry around them. In this sense these men shared the world view of their Munster counterparts, described by Robert Southwell in 1682 as those who 'expect to be regarded as unfortunate gentlemen, who yesterday lost an estate and were to be restored tomorrow'.[17]

Of equal significance to this widely held feeling was the willingness of others to respect them, thus cushioning their decline and allowing these families to maintain something of their traditional status and leadership role. In 1738 Madden commented specifically on this as an Irish trait, 'our nation, above all others, . . . being the most addicted to follow their great lords and gentlemen of distinction of any in the Christian world'.[18] That role could be expressed in a number of ways. Culturally, these middlemen families set the tone as the apex of the surviving social structure. Especially in remote areas or on the estates of absentee landlords, these old families retained effective cultural control of their communities. The Kerry-Cork borderland provides a good example. The irate letters of Richard Hedges, a new settler in Macroom, in the early eighteenth century link topography ('all mountains, bogs, and rocks') to the population composition ('entirely inhabited by Irish') and the lack of Protestants ('from Dunmanway to Kanturk, which is 40 miles of a barbarous country, there is not an English gentleman of note that lives there, except Wm. Brown, minister of Macromp'). The end product was the uninterrupted sway of the old families:

> I think it is my duty to let ye Govt. know in what an ill state ye publick peace in this p[ar]t of ye Co. of Kerry and some neighbouring parts of ye Co. of Cork is, by means of some heads of Irish clans who not only carry arms and harbour unregistered non-jurist popish priests in defiance of ye laws of the late proclamation, but have gained ye ascendant over ye civil power by their insolence and principles, so that the ordinary course of ye law cannot be put in force against them without hazard to ye lives of such as go about to do it, there being very few Protestants and they overawed by ye multitude of papists.[19]

Looked at by those internal to the culture, however, it seemed natural for displaced Catholic gentry families to retain their status as 'heads of Irish clans'. As late as 1747 fifteen Cork Catholic gentlemen supported the future Catholic bishop of Cloyne's nomination by refuting the charge of obscurity of origins against his family:

> They have never degenerated by following any vile or mechanical profession, but have always lived in a decent and creditable manner in the farming way, as all other Roman Catholic gentlemen in this kingdom are generally obliged to do ever since the Cromwellian and revolution forfeitures of Irish estates.[20]

These attitudes persisted into the late eighteenth century. On the Lansdowne estate in Kerry the agent Joseph Taylor reported in 1775 that 'there are some whose family in former days governed absolutely and who seem to wish still to govern in opposition to my lord's rights'.[21] Charles Vallancey was struck in 1778 by the fact that 'the bond of vassalage is not yet dissolved among them'.[22] The social pretensions of the Sullivan middlemen families on the Lansdowne estate in the late eighteenth century impressed the French traveller Coquebert de Montbret: 'The Sullivans are full of personal vanity. They have their children taught English, which they speak with great purity, and they also speak Latin. They dress well and affect an air of good breeding and affluence that is quite astonishing.'[23]

Contempt for the *arriviste* Cromwellian landlords—a gentry by conquest, not by blood—was embedded in the world view of the families descended from the old proprietors. The convert George O'Malley of Snugborough was proud to note in 1776 that he was 'the direct lineal descendant of the ancient family of the O'Malleys of Bellclaire in the said kingdom, who were for many centuries sovereign princes there of a larger fertile territory that to the present time carries their name'. He then contrasted his lineage with that of 'the upstart Cromwellian race that infest the country'.[24] Such sentiments were echoed two years later by Rickard O'Connell (of the normally impeccably circumspect Derrynane family); O'Connell, an officer in the Irish Brigade, referred to his desire to 'make the rascally spawn of damned Cromwell curse the hour of his birth'.[25] Such sentiments also percolated into the general consciousness. A Dublin tanner was imprisoned in 1714 for sympathising with Jacobites arrested for recruiting: 'Who would blame them for endeavouring to get estates if they could, for that fellows that came over in leathern breeches and wooden shoes now rides in their coaches?'[26]

Faced with the continuous presence of these barely submerged sentiments, Protestant commentators could only deplore the false premises upon which these pretensions rested. Castigating the impact of the Gaelic poems and genealogies which sustained the claims of the old landed class, one Protestant commentator made use of the memorable image of the 'pucán' to make the point:

> In the north of Ireland the Irish have a custom in the winter when milk is scarce to kill the calf and preserve the skin, and stuffing it with straw and set it upon four wooden feet, which they call a puckaun, and the cow will be as fond of it as she was of the living calf. She will low after it and lick it and give her milk down. . . . These writings will have the operation of this puckaun, for wanting the land to which they relate, they are but stuffed with straw, yet they will low after them and lick them over and over in their thoughts and to teach their children to read by them instead of horn books. And if any venom be there, they will give it down at the sign of these writings.[27]

In the 1730s Arthur Dobbs observed that the old native proprietors still 'always pretend a claim to their ancient properties'.[28] If these claims were accompanied

by a flamboyant lifestyle, they were seen as a political affront. Protestant commentators were quick to warn these men about their behaviour. Richard Cox's
charge to the Cork grand jury in 1740 put the point succinctly to the county's
Catholics: 'Patience, resignation, and humility become men daily exposed to the
legal power of their adversaries. These virtues would better recommend them to
pardon and impunity than pride, stubborn[n]ess, and insolence.'[29] Thus Protestant nerves tended to tingle at any suggestion that these pretensions might be
encouraged. In 1736, for example, Lord Clancarthy, a British naval officer and
governor of Newfoundland in the years 1733–5, sought to persuade the British
cabinet to revoke a bill of attainder against his father, which had involved lands
now worth £60,000 per annum. Archbishop Hugh Boulter of the Irish privy
council immediately warned the prime minister, Newcastle, that any acquiescence in Clancarthy's suit would 'be a great blow to the Protestant interest here
and will very much shake the security Protestants think they now have of the
enjoyment of their estates. . . . I think the affair of the first magnitude to the
Protestant interest here.'[30]

2   THE LIFESTYLE OF THE MIDDLEMEN

In a frequently cited diatribe the Catholic Lord Kenmare accounted for the
unimproved condition of his estate in 1755 by reference to the cultural characteristics of his own middlemen:

> This is in a great measure owing to the pride, drunkenness, and sloth of the
> middling sort among the Irish. Every one of them thinks himself too great for
> any industry except taking farms. When they happen to get them, they screw
> enormous rents from some beggarly dairyman and spend their whole time in
> the alehouses of the next village. If they have sons, they are all to be priests,
> physicians, or French officers; if daughters, they are bred up to no kind of
> industry but become encumbrances on their parents and the public, and this
> sloth and beggary are transmitted from generation to generation.[31]

Kenmare's views were far from singular. Joseph Taylor, the agent on the neighbouring Lansdowne estate, reported in 1773 in similar terms:

> It is really shocking . . . to see how these poor wretches spend their time—par-
> ents sauntering about the roads doing nothing, and their sons and daughters
> going to a dancing school at three shillings a quarter when they might be
> spinning or carding, digging, or plowing or sowing.[32]

As an almost constant refrain, Taylor isolated 'pride, insolence, and idleness' as
the distinguishing characteristics of the Kerry middlemen of the old stock. Other

commentators were equally censorious, as was Arthur Young in his celebrated depiction of the lifestyle of the Munster middlemen:

> This is the class of little country gentlemen, tenants who drink their claret by means of profit rents, jobbers in farms, bucks, young fellows with round hats edged with gold, who hunt in the day, get drunk in the evening, and fight the next morning. These are the men amongst whom drinking, wrangling, quarreling, fighting, ravishing, etc., are found as in their native soil.[33]

Young's pen-picture is a remarkable echo of the contemporaneous *Caoineadh Airt Uí Laoghaire*, in which Art is celebrated as a flamboyant custodian of the old Gaelic tradition, eliciting respect and fear in equal measure; he wears a silver-hilted sword, riding boots to the knee, a gold-banded Caroline hat edged with lace, gloves, a brooch, a cambric shirt, and an immaculate suit.[34]

Negative comments on these pretensions were widespread by the 1780s. In 1788, *Finn's Leinster Journal* bemoaned 'two legacies bequeathed to us by our Milesian forefathers—pride of ancestry and contempt of commerce. Family pride in this country betrays its shabby and fantastic form here and there in the character of a petty despot surrounded by a wretched peasantry, racked and oppressed for the support of his vanity—a tenantry whom he considers his vassals.' Because of the 'contempt of commerce', 'money is wasted on learning to fence, dance, ride, drink, hunt, and wench'.[35]

Nevertheless, other accounts demonstrate the continuing valency of the old titles and the social respectability attached to them. Once one starts looking for it, evidence of this type of sentiment crops up in abundance. At Callan, Co. Kilkenny, in 1748 a visitor was struck 'by the respect paid to a man on a little horse and was told that he was a man of an ancient race and derived his birth from some of the most noted clans in the county. Even when the patrimony of such men was gone, the old Irish gave him the title of his ancestors, make him and his lady (if he has one) little presents, cultivating his spot of ground, not suffering him to do the least work to degrade his airy title.'[36] From the same county Thomas Russell, the United Irishman, reported on the strong feelings excited by the visit of his grandmother, an O'Clear, to Ballyraggett:

> In my father's time the recollections of these matters were so fresh that he remembers when riding before his mother through Ballyraggett, which had been the estate of her family, all the poor people coming out of their cabins clapping their hands and crying out her name.[37]

Near Ballyshannon in 1752, Bishop Pococke met an O'Donnell, supposedly descended from the earl of Tyrconnell, who, 'although he has only leases, yet he is the head of the Roman Catholics in this county and has a great interest'.[38] The frequency with which newspaper obituaries referred to the old titles also indicates their continuing validity:

1770: Died Donagh O'Brien of Ballyvaghan in County Tipperary, esquire, the last of the ancient family of the Mac O'Brien in said county.[39]

1774: At Athy, died James Purcell, commonly called Baron Purcell of Loughmoe.[40]

1790: Died near Blarney, Owen McCarthy, esq., commonly called Master-na-Mora.[41]

1793: At Coolavin, County Sligo, died Miles McDermott, esq., commonly called the Prince of Coolavin.[42]

Faulkner's Dublin Journal of 29 February 1752 provided a classic example:

> Lately died in the barony of Iveragh and County of Kerry, Daniel Buee McCarthy, esq., of a very ancient family. . . . For these seventy years past, when in company he drank plentifully of rum and brandy, which he called 'naked truth'. His custom was to walk eight or ten miles on a winter's morning over mountains with greyhounds and finders, and [he] seldom failed to bring home a brace of hares. He was an honest gentleman and inherited the social virtues of the ancient Milesians.[43]

Such families enjoyed immense social prestige, especially in areas distant from Dublin, where the tendency persisted to regard personal and territorial claims as more legitimate than impersonal state ones. The example of Donal Mahony of Dunloe in County Kerry in 1717 demonstrates this:

> The said Daniel Mahony for these seven or eight years past contrived a way to make himself great and dreadful in this county; wheresoever he or those under him had any disgust or animosity, his tenants, which are very numerous, about 4,000 persons and all papists, rises out [*sic*] in great numbers by night, smocked and black in their faces, and give an onset in the nature of fairesses [i.e., fairies].[44]

O'Mahony held amost 300 ploughlands on lease, paid £1,500 per annum in rent, and was agent of the Kenmare property. Other Kerry middlemen held sizeable leaseholds at this stage. Combined with a distinguished ancestry, these conferred considerable social prestige. The Bonane O'Sullivans, for example, held 4,666 acres and had been in possession for fourteen generations; the Mac Fínín Dubh (a 400-year-old title) held 3,111 acres, and the Lynes of Kilmakilloge held 2,900 acres.[45] If necessary, as in the case of O'Mahony, such families could muster formidable 'clans'. In 1740 a hostile Cork observer noted how this power was used by a middleman of this type: 'He has a popish clan that must swagger and must be protected, and whoever does not stick his colours to this clan and its patron, the tyrant prime minister, must sink'.[46] In the 1750s that 'clanning' practice (perhaps a precursor of the faction fight) was still being deprecated by Lord

Kenmare,[47] and in the 1770s the agent of the Shelburne estate, Joseph Taylor, had to run the gauntlet against the O'Sullivan families in Tuosist, Creeveen, and Bonane. His possee was obliged in 1774 'to retire from the superior number of people in arms brought against them by the O'Sul[l]ivans of Tuosista, against whom there is no standing without an army of soldiers . . . ; these Sullivans are a desperate and dangerous gang, so connected and related that there is no breaking them without a military force'.[48] In Taylor's opinion these Kerry middlemen were 'still as uncivilised as in the days of Oliver [Cromwell] and must be handled in the same way. I don't think there is such another set of ungovernable, clamorous, left-handed people in the universe.'[49]

A single incident in Tipperary in 1780 demonstrates that these old allegiances of family and locality died hard. At Killaneve near the Silvermines a family of McNamaras retained possession of the holding by force, with the strong support of local people, long after their lease had expired: 'The MacNamaras are young men who have been looked upon among the mountaineers as a kind of half-gentry [buckeens], and brought up in idleness, have followed dissolute courses'.[50] This influence could be exerted unchecked in regions of absenteeism. In 1811, Anthony O'Flaherty held the whole of the Blake estate at Renvyle in Connemara and was 'the acknowledged chief':

A middleman, possessing an income of £1,500 per annum and surrounded by a numerous and untutored peasantry, utterly unconscious of any other claims on the land, must have undoubtedly been a person of consequence in this county. . . . His authority had an additional sanction from claiming to be a lineal descendant of the old kings of the west, the O'Flaherty of centuries long since gone by.[51]

From Connemara in 1794 a letter of Richard St George Mansergh St George describes the O'Malley smuggling enterprise:

Martin O'Malley, a tenant of [Richard] Martin's, is a notorious smuggler, at one time owner or principally concerned in five vessels. He is in a state of defence on a peninsula in Connemara difficult of access from the land by a morass, Great Man's Bay on one side, Costello on the other. He has, I understand, forty stand of arms in his house and has, it is said, committed many illicit acts besides smuggling. He has great influence in that country and may be considered a chief of outlaws, which he attaches to him by presents of rum liquors, distributing on holydays casks of spirits among them, and is much esteemed for his hospitality and munificence. He rents about £900 a year under Mr Martin's father. . . . Martin O'Malley is connected with most of the merchants in Galway whose trade is smuggling.[52]

The residual respect enjoyed by such families was not just a dead letter. The Freneys of County Kilkenny, now middlemen at Tullagher, continued to regulate clothing (an external marker of social pretensions) by inspecting the mass-goers each Sunday and ripping any items that they found offensive.[53] These families were avidly sought as sponsors by local families—supplying both prestige and patronage and perhaps facilitating access to jobs, subleases, conacre tenancies, or cottier holdings. They were also used to settle local disputes, to act as lubricants if the local social or economic cogs were clogging up. Informal arbitration could sometimes blossom into a professional role as estate agent: a classic example is Peter Walsh on the Bessborough estate in south Kilkenny. The same mentality was present in the evolution of the Rí (king) concept in the west of Ireland. The Rí regulated internal customary practices and also represented the community to the outside world. Frequently, the Rí was the scion of an ancient landed family, as with Edward Joyce at Leenane, Edward O'Malley on Clare Island, or Pádraig Ó Flaitheartha of Cill Mhuirbhigh on Aran in the early nineteenth century.

These families also performed a leading role in the local, familiar moral economy. Wakefield noted in 1812 that they 'possess a very peculiar influence over the common people which is not enjoyed by Protestants of the same rank'.[54] Violet Martin, discussing the Galway method of social control, observed that 'it was give and take, with the personal element always warm in it; as a system, it was probably quite uneconomic, but the hand of affection held it together, and the tradition of centuries was at its back'.[55] These attitudes could surface in various guises. The English land agent Samuel Nelmes had a tough time on the Lansdowne estate in Kerry and was universally disliked, 'his disposition being rather too hot and overbearing among a people who consider themselves as gentry, tho' indeed they have no right to it'.[56] In a revealing couplet Eoghan Rua Ó Súilleabháin observed:

Ní ins an ainnise is measa linn bheith síos go deo, ach an tarcaisne a leanas sin. (It is not being sunk in misery all the time that is worst, but the scorn that accompanies it.)[57]

A crucial aspect of the evolution of the Catholic *mentalité* in the eighteenth century was the uneasy relationship between authority and alienation. Given the sectarian nature of the eighteenth-century Irish state, there was a space—a critical distance—between Catholics and the law. Into that interstitial space was inserted an ambivalent attitude, which allowed for often adroit manipulation or distortion at the very highest level. Right across the board one could trace manifestations of this attitude—forcible possessions, smuggling, treatment of wrecks, anti-tithe combinations, abductions, illegal distillation, food riots, resistance to distraint, faction fighting, duelling. This personalised, localised, and demotic sense of the law frequently exercised legal and administrative commentators: Chief Baron Willes in 1760 considered it 'to be the greatest evil of this kingdom—a disobedience and resistance to the law. I don't mean breaches of particular laws [such] as theft, etc., but a resistance with armed force to the civil process and magistrates, and the taking or keeping of possession by armed force. There is scarce a day but I have complaints of this kind in my court.'[58] A more sympathetic observer, Robert Bell, noticed this characteristic in the 1780s: 'Their independence consisted neither in tranquillity nor competence, but generally displayed itself in a sort of hostile resistance to superiors, attempting acts of injustice or endeavouring to enforce the executions of the laws'.[59] The ability to deflect or bypass the letter of the law also transferred itself down the social spectrum: it linked with an alternative code of law, customary or moral in character but nonetheless legitimised and implementable. This alternative law frequently stood antecedent and antagonistic to the king's writ per se. As a statement from Donegal in 1831 expressed it, 'we are bound to obey the law of the land; but we find that in practice, especially among unlettered people, there is a law which is paramount to it; it is the law of nature, which the very worm when trodded upon acknowledges and which disposes men to resent suffering when it exceeds the power of endurance'.[60]

3 CULTURAL LIFE

The respect paid to the old families had as its reciprocal the dispensing of patronage. The bonds of affection were tightened by the intimate immersion of these families in the popular culture of their communities, essentially as patrons. In the early eighteenth century Denis O'Conor, head of the family descended from the last high king of Ireland, maintained an Irish master, fencing master, and dancing master, while patronising the harpers, Catholic clergy, and 'reduced gentlemen' of his neighbourhood. Turlough Carolan, for example, was a frequent visitor to the house. On Christmas eve in 1723 he is described as 'taking his harp in a fit of rapturous affection for the family of Belanagare' and 'singing extempore the fall of the Milesian race, the hospitality of old Denis O'Conor, and his grandness of soul'.[61] As late as the 1770s Arthur Young, commenting on the special place of the O'Conors in local affections, wrote that 'the common people pay him the greatest respect and send him presents of cattle, etc., upon various occasions. They consider him as the prince of a people involved in one common ruin.'[62] The O'Conors themselves were equally conscious of their role as custodians of the culture. A 1786 newspaper report noted that the O'Conor 'always appeared contented with the degree of deference and respect from his neighbours and acquaintances, which they voluntarily paid him (as knowing him to be a representative of the royal Connacian race)'.[63]

A concomitant was immersion in popular culture—an immersion that remained strong until the last quarter of the eighteenth century. Witness the patronage of music and poetry, the profuse hospitality and heavy drinking, and the enthusiastic espousal of hunting, horse-racing, hurling, and cock-fighting. This could give an almost consciously archaic feel to the lifestyle, memorably evoked in this description of an Iar Chonnacht middleman's house near Maamtrasna in the Joyce country in the 1750s:

> There were two long cabins thatched opposite to one another. In one was the kitchen and apartments for the family. The other was his entertaining room, neatly strewed according to the Irish fashion with rushes, and at the upper end of the room was a kind of platform raised above the ground with boards and two or 3 blankets, on each [of] which was the lodging for strangers and visitors. A bottle of brandy was the wet before dinner, and the entertainment was half a sheep boiled at top, half a sheep roasted at bottom, broiled fish on one side, a great wooden bowl of potatoes on the other, and an heap[ed] plate of salt in the middle. After dinner [there was] some pretty good claret and an enormous wooden bowl of brandy punch, which, according to the old as well as the modern Irish hospitality, the guests were pressed to take their full share of; neither did his hospitality allow him to forget their servants and boatmen, but gave a bottle of brandy between every two of them. Towards evening, when the chief began to grow mellow, he called in his favourite girl to sing, which she did very well and was a neat, handsome, jolly girl. Before he called her in, he stipulated with his guests that they were welcome to any liberties with her from the girdle upwards, but he would not permit any underhand doings. A bagpiper likewise attended, and towards evening an old Irish bard came in, who for their entertainment made verses in rhyme on any subject they gave him, and sung several songs on the virtue of and great prowess of the ancestors of this chief.

In the morning the exhausted guests finally managed to slip away, but the chief 'happening to be awake and finding them gone, immediately mounted a horse barebacked and pursued them. But they had just reached the boat and put off from the shore as he came up; he poured upon them vollies of execrations as uncivil scoundrels and milksops.'[64]

In 1732, Mary Delany had visited a thatched cabin in County Galway belonging to 'a gentleman of fifteen hundred pounds a year'. She was startled by the bareness of the house, but its owner 'keeps a man cook and has given entertainment of twenty dishes of meat! The people of this country don't seem solicitous of having good dwellings or more furniture than is absolutely necessary—hardly so much, but they make it up in eating and drinking.'[65] A similar emphasis was evoked eighty years later, in the 1811 account of the O'Flaherty middleman house at Renvyle. Their 'big house' was a thatched cabin 60- x 20-, only one storey high to all appearances, containing an eating parlour, a sitting-room 20- x 16-, two reception rooms with two small bedchambers off each, and also a loft. There were at least two dozen people present at dinner, including two priests, clansmen, and relatives. The 'profusion of hospitable board', 'bright turf fire', 'dulcet tones of the bagpipes', and 'wine and spirits' were all described as part of the dinner ceremony.[66]

Looking back nostalgically from the radically different nineteenth-century position, Michael Whitty captured the closeness of his big-farmer father to popular culture in the mid-eighteenth century, at Nicharee in Duncormick parish in Wexford:

> My father was a substantial farmer and lived in the low thatched house which his great grandsire had erected about a century before in a little valley which is at the right-hand side of the road that runs from Wexford to Bannow. . . . At chapel he occupied the most prominent form [wooden seat] at the left-hand side of the altar, and his name headed the priest's list whenever a charitable collection was made. Such a man was looked up to by his neighbours with somewhat of reverence, and he was not a little formal in all his proceedings. But above all, he prided himself in following the hospitable example of his father . . . , brewing at home; the black and white puddings which lined the capacious chimney showed that the pig had been for some time in salt, the bullock slaughtered at Christmas, the [brick] oven, the hemlock which polished the pewter dishes, the gritty sand spread over the parlour floor [—all were part of the lifestyle]. . . . There was midnight mass in the little, low, thatched chapel at Rathangan, with its humble roof, a wooden cross stuck on the gable end, little painted altar, the crucifix, the holy-water pots, and the fourteen stations. The old Christmas carols were sung here. . . . After mass the house was filled with friends, followers, and neighbours, who ate brown barley bread, bacon and gritty, roast beef, boiled beef, ducks, chickens, pullets, and turkeys. . . . The mummers were the main point of attraction at Christmas, when their first performance always took place in a field adjoining the chapel, composed of twelve decent young men dressed in gay ribbons and silk handkerchiefs, in snow white shirts, going through their artful evolutions. Their company was an honour which was conferred only on the select few. My father's house was the first they usually visited, and on this occasion the friends and relatives of the family were invited to enjoy the dance and the amusement, and it was then the truly substantial black oak table groaned with the weight of the feast, whiskey punch and rich home-brewed ale thrived in goblets brimming full, sparkling even through the opacity of earthen bowls. The twelve days of Christmas were devoted to mumming, hurling, and dancing, every door stood open, and every table was covered to abundance.[67]

A description of a wedding in 1764 in the barony of Forth in the same county presents a comparable picture:

> They first find a large waste cabin, malthouse, or barn, where they place tables, benches, etc., with wads of straw in several different parts of it. After the couple are joined by the priest's hand and a ring is exchanged, and every person present has heartily smacked the bride, they make a collection for the priest,

and for the piper, and last for the itinerant beggars who have all assembled to
make merry with the happy pair on the joyful occasion. This ceremony over,
they seat themselves to dinner, the bride at the upper end of the table, the
priest at the lower, the bridesmen, bride's maids, etc., all seated in proper order,
with the bridegroom as an attendant or butler, who does not presume to sit at
table but takes a bit, now and then, behind backs. They all eat and drink very
heartily, especially the priest, who does the honours of the table and diligently
helps himself to the titbits—the two legs and wings of the goose, the biggest
one of the puddings, etc. After dinner the bride is handed from the table by
the head bridesman, who has the favour of dancing with her; then there is an
apple thrown up, and whoever recovers it is favoured with dancing second.
When they have danced and drank a great deal, the bridesmen form a party
to carry off the bride, which they commonly accomplish. There is immediately
a hue and cry after them, in which most part of the night is spent. The
bridesmen never do her the least injury; it is only a kind of old custom or
formality used among them.[68]

Laurence Whyte's poem 'The parting cup, or the humours of Deoghedorus'
describes the lifestyle of these types of families in County Westmeath in about
1710. His preface describes the poem as 'setting forth the great hospitality and
good entertainment formerly met with in Irish families, many of who[m] did not
assume to be above the rank of common farmers, whilst some others, who were
second brothers or the descendants of the nobility and gentry, being for the most
part little acquainted with any other kind of industry, turned farmers also and
lived very hospitably; these retained the title of gentlemen and were esteemed as
such at least whilst they could maintain it'. The subscribers' list to Whyte's
Original poems (1740) is a veritable directory of the Catholic gentry of the Pale
area, illustrating the appeal that this type of poetry had in that milieu.[69]

Noticeable in these accounts is how the Gaelic stress on profuse hospitality as
a marker of gentility survived into the eighteenth century. A 1788 account of the
Kavanagh middlemen's lifestyle in south Carlow makes the same point:

The hospitable tables of the inhabitants are furnished with the utmost plenty
and elegance. Their principal joy consists in entertaining those who visit them.
As soon as any company comes to their houses, word is sent to most of their
relations, who join and make the sweetest concord in the world. After two or
three days spent in innocent pleasure, you are all invited to another gentleman's, with the same agreeable round of mirth and so on till you have gone
through the whole race. The day of parting is the only day of grief or
discontent. This is the end and manner of what is called coshering, so much
mistaken by several authors.[70]

The social pressures on these old landed families to be hospitable was intense.

George Ryan of Inch in County Tipperary, inheriting the encumbered ancestral estate in the 1780s, eventually retreated to Toulouse in France where he could live quietly and frugally, without the ruinous expenses of ostentatious hospitality expected of him in his native Tipperary.[71]

These Catholic middlemen families were also brokers across a series of parameters—political, cultural, social, and economic. They frequently faced simultaneously into both local and cosmopolitan life, into archaic and modern modes, were at ease in different cultural streams, and articulated alternate universes. An example is provided by the Sweetman family.[72] Displaced from their ancestral estate at Castle Eve in Kilkenny, the family had moved to the Catholic Leigh of Rosegarland estate in Wexford. The Sweetmans' house at Newbawn is a visual representation of this polyvalent world expressed in architectural terms. The house which they built there in the 1690s still survives—a fine two-storeyed, five-bayed structure of imposing dimensions. It is an instructive example of the blend of traditional and formal in architectural styles: the traditional elements include the thatched roof, the mud and coarse-rubble walls, the iron window bars, and the central chimney; the formal elements include the symmetrical facade, the Gibbsian doorcase, and the sashed windows. The house embodied exactly the social position of the Sweetman family, partaking of both the gentry and common traditions. Alongside the house is a massive cobbled farmyard or bawn surrounded by an array of diverse farm buildings. The whole complex is located centrally in the townland and is approached by curving lanes. The family bridged two worlds and acted as brokers on a number of levels—cultural, social, and political. The Sweetmans were the hubs and hinges on which Catholic society revolved, the solid backbone of the emerging Catholic nation in the late eighteenth and early nineteenth centuries.

An equivalent role was played by them in the Catholic church. These families supplied the senior clergy, the financial support, and the chapel sites, and they underpinned the educational system. A symptomatic example is the way in which Catholic chapels were so frequently located on the edges of their leaseholds.[73] The Sweetmans' prominence in the local community is reflected in the fact that the Catholic chapel of Newbawn was sited on their farm, a nucleus around which the chapel village of Newbawn subsequently developed. In the chapel the Sweetmans had their own reserved gallery, and a special tea room was built by them in the chapel yard where the different branches of the family assembled after Sunday mass to maintain family cohesiveness.[74] Thus the families saw themselves as patrons of the church, a role accentuated by the heavily domestic and local character of the institutional church under the impact of the penal laws. Bishop Sweetman's pronouncement in 1771 throws an oblique shaft of light on the acknowledged social dominance of these families in the local church: 'No pastor or ecclesiastic whatsoever must presume to keep a flock or congregation waiting for any person whatsoever; at least, this compliment must not be paid to anyone oftener than three times in one year'.[75]

As I have illustrated elsewhere, these families were the bedrocks of the Catholic church in Ireland.[76] Bishop Moylan, reporting to Rome on the diocese of Cork and Ross in 1785, was worried by the potentially negative impact on the church of the progressive undermining of these middlemen families: 'In these dioceses up to recently, Catholics held the greater portion of the land on terms that were reasonably fair, so that there was available to them the wherewithal to exercise their hospitality, for which they were renowned, and to generously support their pastors'. Now, when leases expired, they were either ejected or forced to pay increased rents, so that 'there scarcely was left to them the means by which they could provide for their families the most meagre subsistence'.[77]

4 THE RISE OF THE CATHOLIC BIG FARMER

One can contrast the *mentalité* of those Catholic farming families derived from the displaced gentry with that of the strong farmers who had advanced socially from the small-farm ranks in the expansionist economy of the eighteenth century. In a sense both took their values with them, and the Irish big-farm class therefore formed an arresting amalgam of downwardly mobile and upwardly mobile groups, each of them taking their old world view with them into their new situations.[78]

Tighe's admirable *Statistical observations relative to the county of Kilkenny* (1802) provides a classic description of one such rising family—the Aylwards' dairying empire in the Walsh mountains in the late eighteenth century:

This family consist[s] at present of five branches who hold among them over 2,000 acres, including Knockmeilin [Knockmoylan], Ballybrishan, and other large townlands. Their houses are small and near each other and till lately were little better than those of the poorest farmers, but they have not slated them to guard against malicious burnings [by Whiteboys] or robbers. The women of the family constantly marry in it and for this purpose are obliged to buy dispensations at a high price, and if a widow marries a stranger, she loses all except what she brought with her. For one farm of 900 acres they paid a few years ago a heavy fine amounting to more than 2,500 guineas for a new lease of three lives or 31 years, and £600 a year rent. This money was given in hard gold which lay by them, and this is the mode in which the profits of such farms are applied. They slaughter their pigs generally at home and eat the offal, which is the only animal food they usually make use of, living principally on potatoes and some griddle bread. Their incomes are probably not less than £600 or £700 a year.[79]

In contrast to the ostentatious, flamboyant lifestyle of the displaced gentry, frugality, hard work, and reticence were bywords for these families. Even the most successful, like the Aylwards, enjoying a gentry-like income, were very slow to engage in conspicuous consumption, and communities dominated by this type of farmer, as in south Kilkenny, remained very conservative. Atkinson was surprised in 1815 to find prosperous Kilkenny farmers speaking only Irish. In particular, he commented on the 'extensive pig breeders and dairymen of the Walsh mountains who cannot speak a single sentence of plain English'. He also noted how their clothes differed from those of the more modernised districts to the north and east, with the frieze coat still universally popular.[80] When John O'Donovan of Slieverue visited Thomas Larcom for the first time in 1828, Larcom was struck by O'Donovan's 'peasant garb'—his frieze *cóta mór*.[81] In 1732, John Loveday had observed that in Kilkenny most of the men wore a dark frieze of Irish manufacture, and that 'the men affect Spaniard-like to walk ye streets with their great coats thrown over their shoulders by way of a cloak'.[82] It was only in the 1830s, according to Graves, that the local people abandoned their blue frieze coats and mantle in favour of factory-produced textiles.[83]

A similar reticence, conservatism, and lack of conspicuous consumption applied to the housing of these strong farmers. Until the 1780s estate maps show a surprisingly high percentage, often 90 to 95 percent, of farmers living in 'cabins'—in eighteenth-century parlance, small, mud-walled, clay-floored, thatched, single-storeyed houses. That predeliction partially reflected a cultural preference; Amhlaoibh Ó Suilleabháin in 1831 was lyrical in his praise of the vernacular house: 'Snug is a low, sheltered cabin on which the thatch is laid on thick, and in which are food and fire. No house is so comfortable as a thatched, mud-walled cabin, with a solid door, small windows, a big fire, and plenty of provisions.'[84] The preference may also have reflected a typically cautious, low-profile *mentalité* among Catholics. Bishop Ryan of Wexford in 1812 contrasted the limited number of Protestants as opposed to their highly visible public expression:

> They appear more numerous than they really are because they have power and can make a show; we are without it and make none. Look to the chapels on Sundays and look to the churches. They have law on their side and can speak out; we have it against us and must be silent.[85]

For these rising families a coherent family strategy was crucial, one which followed primogeniture and the successful dispersal of surplus children. Only a prudent management of family resources and alliances could achieve these twin aims. The traditional farm-family strategy depended, then, on a dual allegiance--to the ancestors of the past and to the inheritors of the future. Family continuity was crucial: the individual farm holder was merely the baton carrier in the relay race of family destiny. To succeed in this relay race, the acquisition, retention, and transmission of leases was vital. Indeed, the most striking achievement of these strong farm families was precisely their ability to insert primogeniture as a controlling principle of family organisation into the very heart of landlordism— the leasing system. A favourable landlord was essential. In 1729, Robert Keating of Knockagh in Tipperary bequeathed 'to my Lord Cahir's eldest son a young grey mare, now grazing on the lands of Cnocknefalling, as a token of my love to him and his father'.[86] In leasing at least, flattery paid; by 1767 the Keatings held over 3,000 acres on lease.[87]

The acquisition of leases was helped by a number of eighteenth-century developments: the widening distinction between farmer and labourer, the tendency to bypass middlemen and lease directly to the sitting tenant, and the less privileged position of Protestants, increasingly forced to play on a level tenurial pitch. In the background help also came from the menacing (landlord) or comforting (farmer) phenomenon of customary law (enforced by intimidatory and exemplary violence), which again reinforced the sitting tenant's position. Above all, the expanding eighteenth-century economy distributed wealth to leaseholders. The long period of price rises between 1740 and 1810 effectively laid the basis of a comfortable farming class. Dispersal of surplus family members meant that the original leasehold remained intact. The ensuing mobility broadened the kinship network and cultural horizons of the family, frequently distributing surplus sons to the church, trade, or the professions. The astonishing dominance of the Cork dairying industry or the Wexford malting trade by Catholic families from this background has to be understood in the context of this kinship process.

The marriage patterns of these families were carefully controlled to nurture family interests. The central feature was its endogamous character—like marrying like—frequently within a reasonably narrow spatial ambit. Over time the group of strong farm families in particular areas tended to become a self-perpetuating caste because of repeated intermarriage. Family discipline was maintained by recourse to wills, dowries, and marriage settlements. A typical clause in wills regulated daughters' marriage behaviour. In 1829, John Browne of Big Barn in County Wexford made his will in which he bequeathed 'to my daughter Ann £250 sterling and to my daughter Margaret £250 sterling. Should any of my daughters aforesaid transgress before marriage or marry contrary to the consultation of the Reverend James Brown, my son, she or they shall be cut off to one shilling.'[88]

Given close parental control, the paramount obligations of kin, and the obsession with the maintenance of property interests, the arranged match was a sine qua non. Women became the pawns of an elaborate chess game: favoured gambits were cousin marriages, double marriages, and marriages across a series of generations. This endogamous, carefully structured marriage network held the constellation of family interests together, creating a web of reciprocities and obligations evolving out of the soft intimacies of kin but embedded in a hard legal carapace of wills, marriage settlements, dowries, and trusteeships. If disputes arose, the ubiquitous priest in the family was called upon to act as arbitrator. Caution was the watchword for these acquisitive families. According to his son, the Tipperary farmer James Scully's 'principal object was that of acquiring wealth, his next that of preserving it. His views on public subjects were dependent on these objects.'[89] By 1796, pursuing this strategy, Scully had accumulated a leasehold interest of 15,000 acres.[90] James Downes, a Wexford strong farmer pressed on all sides about the disposal of £3,000 which he had on his hands in 1801, stated his own preference: 'If I can, I will lay it out in land for my children'.[91]

The emphasis on tight control of family resources was necessitated by the desire to place other family members off the home farm. That placement demanded resources, especially for education, the key to a successful career. In the eighteenth century these families sustained the so-called hedge-school system, usually by a system of patronage-cum-tutelage. That education paved the way for openings in trade, the church, or abroad. The Whittys of Nicharee in the 1790s offer a paradigmatic example: 'My father, like other Catholics of means, determined one of his sons for the church and, not to say it prophanely [*sic*], he imported a profound teacher, learned in Greek and Latin, from the then classic region of Ireland, Munster'.[92] In the late eighteenth century it was these families who sustained the great Catholic teaching orders for boys and girls, which spread rapidly under their patronage in the Catholic big-farm region of east Munster and south Leinster. Reflecting the symbiosis, the Presentation and Mercy nuns and the Christian Brothers, like the diocesan clergy, were overwhelmingly recruited from these same families.[93]

Given their wealth and increasingly assured position, these families often blended in a surprisingly inconspicuous way into the background. Their typically understated farmhouses could escape an unobservant eye. The hurrying traveller, passing rapidly through the roadside raggle-taggle of miserable cabins, was overwhelmed by images of poverty; he failed to notice the discreet but comfortable world of the strong farmer, embedded in the centre of their farms and insulated from the perimeter of poverty around them. The seat behind the coachman was therefore a biased one in pre-famine Ireland. It is in this broad sense, perhaps, that one should interpret the concept of the 'hidden Ireland'. Corkery's twin insistence on approaching it only from the evidence of Gaelic poetry and on locating it largely in west Munster is misleading. The 'hidden Ireland' of the eighteenth century was not incarnated in the *cos-mhuintir*—the proliferating, poverty-striken base of the social pyramid, nor in the flamboyant but restricted world of the Munster middlemen; the custodians of tradition were the comfortable, Catholic, strong-farm class (a Norman-Gaelic hybrid) of south Leinster and east Munster, who provided stability and continuity.[94]

The social cleavages of Ireland were immersed in a deceptively homogenous landscape, owing to the lack of conspicuous consumption. Patrick Knight described this milieu well from Ballycroy in County Mayo:

> In 1813 I slept in a man's house who had 100 head of black cattle and 200 sheep, and there was not a single chair or stool in his home but one three-legged one, no bed but rushes, no vessel for boiling their meals but one, the madder [*mether*] which was handed around indiscriminately to all who sat around the potato basket (myself among the rest), placed up on the pot for a table; yet this man was said to be very rich, besides the stock named above.[95]

Caesar Otway, reporting from the Joyce Country in 1839, echoed the same point: 'I was also informed that there was much ignorance and contented destitution of all that a better informed people would call comforts, so that a man when he became wealthy did not by any means exhibit it in his living, his house, or his furniture'.[96] An Irish proverb expressed this *mentalité* very succinctly: 'Da mbéadh prataí is móin againn, bhéadh an saol ar a thóin againn'. Viewed from this perspective, Arthur Young's cantankerous grumble in the 1770s appears to be a simple misreading of the Irish social landscape: 'I have in different parts of the kingdom seen farms just fallen in after leases of three lives, of the duration of fifty, sixty, and even seventy years, in which the residence of the principal tenant was not to be distinguished from the cottared fields surrounding it'.[97]

The Rev. J. Burrows, an English clergyman touring Ireland in 1773, was equally baffled by the 'unaccountable circumstances'. Although 'you see a very large extent of country covered with corn, your eye cannot discover one farmhouse or one rick of last year's produce, either of hay or corn. When you ask where the tenants live of such demesnes, you are shown a hovel or two of a cabin, which seem incapable of containing a thousan[d]th part of the produce!' Equally bewildered was Thomas Creswick, who returned from a visit to Ireland in 1837 puzzled at having seen 'no sturdy yeoman distinguished from his labourers both by the respectability of his dress and the air of command with which he looks around him'.[98]

One should not infer from all this, however, that the rise of the Catholic big farmer had occurred without incurring substantial social costs. Irish society evolved from a seventeenth-century situation where social differences among native occupiers were limited, to a situation where the farmer/labourer split became decisive, especially in the more developed regions. By 1841 in County Cork, for example, there was a 7:3 ratio of labourers to farmers,[99] the product of a more complex farming structure which sharpened the social divide between the two groups. The hiving off of farmers and labourers into separate settlement forms was an eighteenth-century phenomenon. On the mid-seventeenth-century Down survey maps, the cabin cluster around the towerhouse is a settlement expression of a society where the classes shared a site. As capitalist penetration prised these elements apart, the labourers were dispersed to the edges of the farms, which performed a fly-catcher function. This created a cottier necklace around the perimeter of tillage farms, with the social dichotomy mirrored in the micro-segregation. Bell described the process in 1804:

> The master never fed a labourer of this description [i.e., a cottier]. It was, on the contrary, a chief object with him to keep such a person as far away from his dwelling as possible. He therefore allowed him to occupy, at some remote corner of his farm, a miserable hut, a mere shell formed of mud or sods, without loft, apartment, or partition and sometimes without any other covering than that of straws, without any other chimney than the door.[100]

In other words, there was a long-run social cost to the rapid commercialisation of Irish agriculture in the eighteenth century. The old partnership (village) and small-farm (gneever) communities were squeezed out, and the proliferation of agricultural labourers was accompanied by a narrrowing of their diet towards a monotonous and dangerous dependence on the potato.

Early nineteenth-century commentators contrasted the older middleman system with the new type which had emerged during the Napoleonic boom. From Wexford a clerical commentator claimed that 'the middlemen of the present day are themselves but low farmers, a set of harpies who spread misery and oppression on the unhappy creatures who are compelled to live under them', while a Cork observer stigmatised them in 1816 as 'a multitude of upstart gentry without manners or education, oppressive to the poor'.[101] The older gentry-derived middleman family had a well-developed distaste for these 'new' men. The post-Cromwellian Book II of *Páirlimint Cloinne Tomáis* mocks the vulgarity and social affectations of upwardly mobile labourers and cottiers, who are not exhibiting sufficient deference to the descendants of the old nobility: 'Is eagóir go mbiodh mac bodaigh nó lóiminigh ar aonnós le mac duine uasail nó deaghathar'.[102] Nicholas Plunkett of the Fingall family, in his Jacobite tract 'The improvement of Ireland', makes the same point:

> I could wish that there were established a solid distinction between the gentry and those who really are not so. . . . I speak this because of an observation made by certain persons how in these late times insolency has crept into the minds of people very mean in their descent but endowed with wealth, some with more, some with less, acquired by industry, whether just or unjust. 'Tis true all honest industry should be encouraged, and may they wear the effects of it since they have won it. Yet let them not turn the same to the abuse or undervalue of such persons to whom there is a respect due for gentility sake, tho' they should not prove so wealthy as these new men. Wealth is no lasting companion to nobility.[103]

Irish poets also peddled this line of argument. Witness Art MacCumhaigh's two satires on the Callaghans of Culloville in Armagh, a typical rising Catholic family investing in milling and leases but dismissed by the poet as 'bodaigh na heorna' (churls of the corn). *Saevo indignatio* also marks his poem on Arthur McKeown[104] and Peadar Ó Doirnín's 'Tarlach Cóir Ó hÁmaill'.[105] Eibhlín Dubh Ní Chonaill, in her caoineadh for her husband Art Ó Laoghaire, regretted the passing of the traditional humility of the cos-mhuintir in the presence of her husband:

> mar a n'umhlóidh romhat mna is fir
> ma tá a mbéosa féin acu
> 's is baolach liomsa ná fuil anois.[106]

5 CATHOLICS, PROTESTANTS, AND THE DECLINE OF THE MIDDLEMAN SYSTEM

The restrained lifestyles of Catholic farmers certainly contributed to their low profile in the first half of the eighteenth century. But this non-assertive, non-conspicuous-consumption attitude had beneficial side effects. With fewer outgoings and a greater capacity to endure material privation, Catholic farmers were usually able to outbid their Protestant counterparts for leaseholds. As early as 1717, Archbishop King in Dublin was already noticing that in competition for leases 'the papists, who live in a miserable and sordid manner, will always outbid a Protestant'.[107] They were thus undercutting Protestants and contributing to the higher Protestant (especially Presbyterian) emigration rates in the 1720s, above all in Ulster. King blamed landlord cupidity for countenancing this, claiming that they had no practical interest in eradicating Catholicism; instead, they 'take care to cherish and support it, alleging that papists make the best tenants, as indeed they pay more rent and are greater slaves to their landlords than Protestants would ever be'.[108] Landlords and their agents had been quick to spot the contrasting lifestyles and differential rent-paying ability. On the Fitzwilliam estate in 1728, William Hume reported:

> An Irish papist is much abler to pay rent for a farm than a Protestant of equal ability with the Roman, by reason that a Roman and his whole family can live upon potatoes and buttermilk the whole year through for to make a rent, which the Protestants cannot do, for the Protestants must have beef and bread and much better clothes than the Romans. The chief tenants have built houses far too big for their farms, with coach[h]ouses, stables, gardens, and pleasure gardens. These tenants run to a vast height of pride. No tenant would drink a drop of ale at any public meeting except good claret, sack, or port. Their wives and daughters have coffee, tea, or chocolate.[109]

From County Cork in the 1740s came essentially similar observations: 'The

Protestant inhabitant must indeed be allowed to keep in his house sometimes bread and small beer and to eat meat once a week, which may occasion an abatement in a rental and be a stumbling block in the way of narrow-hearted men'. This commentator succinctly expressed the result of the differential in lifestyles: 'There is a Protestant price and a popish price for land'.[110]

Four implications followed from this situation. First, Catholic willingness to pay higher rents reflected an unwillingness to move away from their ancestral territories, where extended kin groups had longstanding claims to identifiable land. The higher rent was therefore an expression of rootedness. Second, while Catholics could compensate for the higher rent by a frugal lifestyle, they could also compensate by underinvesting in improvements, since allegedly 'papists will contentedly live in sooty cabins, will destroy improvements, and never will make any new [ones], except to mend a gap with a bush or stone'.[111] Such observations eventually became a deeply embedded set of cultural stereotypes in eighteenth-century Ireland. In 1798 one of the many explanations of the causes of the rebellion reiterated it in classic form:

> Hence [from popery] arises the long observable want of industry, good hu-
> mour, cheerfulness, or cleanliness among the Irish papists; the uncultivated
> state of their farms, their unwillingness to plant trees or quicked fences, build
> brick or stone houses, or improve ground, and the peculiar pleasure they find
> in demolishing other men's improvements.[112]

Third, landlords willing to support the Protestant interest had therefore to explicitly proffer preferential treatment in rental arrangements—a preference noticeable in the frequency with which estates were advertised to be set to Protestant tenants only.[113] Fourth, landlord rentals were inflated by this Catholic willingness to trade excessive rents (and their concomitant, reduced living standards) against retaining a foothold on family farms. It is in relation to circumstances like these that we can begin to reconcile Samuel Madden's 'irrec-oncilable contradiction' in 1738: 'To hear a nation bawling out misery and beggar[y] and to see such numbers of her wise and good children fluttering about the world in splendour and magnificence seems at first sight an irreconcilable contradiction'.[114]

This 'letting of lands to papists who will pay any rents' was a constant refrain in eighteenth-century Protestant Ireland, resurfacing again in Steelboy, Break-of-Day, and Orange propaganda.[115] Almost a century later, these observations had become stereotypes. From Magilligan in Derry it was observed that Catholics were able to outbid Protestants because they were 'inured to scanty fare and manifold hardships'.[116] From Wexford a landlord reported in 1812 that 'Catholic tenants are better than Protestants; they are more industrious, live harder, and pay a greater rent'.[117]

Inevitably, differential leasing policies gave rise to segregation in areas of heavy immigration. McAfee's pioneering probe into the colonisation of the Maghera region in south Derry in the seventeenth and eighteenth centuries shows lucidly how the native and planter populations were gradually filtered into separate areas via the leasing mechanism. These patterns usually had an inbuilt topographic dimension, with the Protestant tenants being steered to the better lands and the Catholic population being gradually directed to the marginal lands.[118] Across Ulster such a pattern is clearly visible, but it is also observable elsewhere. As early as 1728 the agent on the massive Fitzwilliam estate in Wicklow had already recognised that Catholic willingness to undergo material privation, to a greater degree than Protestants, made them the preferred tenants for upland farms, where there was little chance of generating profits sufficient for even a modest degree of conspicuous consumption. In describing the mountain townlands of Toorboy and Ballyguile, the agent observed that 'this farm is fit to be inhabited by the Romans, who will be much abler to pay a rent than Protestants, it being a mountainy farm which produces no corn, and the Romans are entirely maintained by potatoes upon that farm'.[119]

We should be wary, however, of ascribing too much intentionality to these processes. There was never a specific programme of segregation but rather a series of independent perceptions and processes whose long-run interaction created a segregated effect. Differential bargaining power and ease of access to decision-makers was reflected in the leasing system, which in turn structured segregation. Because of the frequent juxtaposition of good and poor land in Ireland, it was easy for a leasing system operating within these perceptual parameters to direct Catholics to townlands which were boggy and hilly, and Protestants to the richer lowlands. Throughout Ulster and in other heavily planted areas like Wicklow and north Wexford, it was usual for 'Catholic' townlands to be found upslope of 'Protestant' ones.[120]

This Catholic advantage was of pivotal significance when the middleman system was undermined in the late eighteenth and early nineteenth centuries. Inevitably, the assault on the middleman system fell disproportionately on the Protestant sub-gentry, whose favoured status had previously been assured by long leases at low rents. The removal of this middleman layer strengthened the Catholic farming interest, because it was occurring practically simultaneously with the dismantling of the penal laws. Catholic farmers were in general more frugal and therefore more solvent and could now avail of long leases, as landlords became more pragmatic in the letting of their estates. Especially in the southern two-thirds of the country, the Protestant middle interest contracted, squeezed in the pre-famine period between landlords adopting a purely mercenary approach and a rising Catholic farming class with lower outgoings. To this factor one could also add the anxieties caused by the instability of the 1790s, which had literally unsettled Protestants. Jane Barber from outside Enniscorthy observed the bad effect which an early introduction to the yeomanry and a military

life had had on her brothers, who afterwards were totally unable to settle on their
farms:

> And [they] continued the same careless, easy life till they became quite unable
> to pay their rents. They then emigrated to America, and on the very ground
> which thirty years ago was in the possession of old Protestant families, there
> now lives the descendants of those rebels who may be said to have been the
> origin of all this evil.[121]

Andrew Meadows, writing from Wexford town in 1822, backed up this claim,
following it with a prophetic warning: 'Since 1798 great numbers [of Protestants]
have emigrated, which has thinned the ranks of our once-numerous yeomanry,
and I say it with great regret that in a few years hence, a Protestant yeomanry in
the county will not be found; the gentry, as a certain consequence, must follow
them'.[122] The pressure on Protestants in retaining leases is reflected in the
threatening notices against Catholics who bid for leases, such as those posted in
the Blackwater and Oulart areas of Wexford in the aftermath of the rebellion.[123]
The altered position of Protestants was a profound psychological shock for them,
a shock accelerated in the 1820s and 1830s when Catholicism seemed to be
increasingly assuming a crudely triumphalist face. As an agonised Protestant
observed to the French traveller de Tocqueville, 'They want to put us in the
position of a conquered people, in which we long held them. That is what we are
not able to endure.'[124]

The elimination of the (predominantly) Protestant middlemen as economic
and political anachronisms strengthened the role of the (predominantly) Catholic
tenant farmers, and in retrospect this can be seen as a major step on the road to
'peasant proprietorship'. It was also part of a process of simplification of the social
structure, a process accelerated later by the post-famine decline of the cottier
class and the legislative euthanasia of the gentry. The consequences of these
changes are described in a letter of the second earl of Rosse in 1822:

> The lower orders are much more formidable now than they ever were on this
> island, from their great increase in numbers, from fewer gentlemen residing,
> from the extinction of the great farmers who were Protestants and the
> descendants of the English. . . . Forty years ago the land of Ireland was let in
> farms of 500 or 1,000 or 1,500 acres; now landlords, finding that they can get
> higher rents and have more voters, let them to Catholics in portions of 20, 30,
> or 40 acres, and these, as they multiply fast again, subdivide them among their
> sons and daughters as they marry. Therefore, the old modes of preserving
> order and enforcing obedience to law will not do now.[125]

This assessment echoed the sentiments of the Offaly agent James Brownrigg,
writing from Edenderry in 1815 about the demise of the Protestant head-tenant:

The misfortune is that the landlords in general don't understand this matter, and that their agents think they are bound to let the land to the highest bidder, and that in doing so, they are doing their landlords the utmost justice, when in fact they are ruining their estates and the country by dispossessing the real yeomanry of the lands and letting them to the mere beggars of the country . . . , thereby over-spreading the whole country with a miserable, discontented, and ungovernable peasantry . . . , having few persons of any respectability living amongst them to repress crime and to make the laws to be respected.[126]

William Armstrong, a disgruntled Armagh middleman on the Trinity College estate, made essentially the same points in his letter to the bursar in 1850, when he heard that he was about to lose his lease:

The lands have been held by my family since originally granted by the crown. By my ancestors these lands, then a wilderness, were brought into a state of cultivation. . . . If the resident gentry be banished from your estates, who, permit me to ask you, will be left to impart knowledge to your tenantry or provide civilisation amongst them?[127]

Miller has estimated that in the pre-famine period almost half a million Protestants emigrated from Ireland, especially from the midlands and south Leinster.[128] Canada, and Ontario in particular, was the main destination, and protracted, intense chain migration occurred. The decimation of the southern middle interest was crucially predicated on the dissolution of the system of the middlemen. Their functions had been eroded by the professionalisation of estate administration (through surveyors, agents, engineers, architects, valuers, and not least the police), which usurped their previous functions. They were now seen as economically parasitic in an expanding rather than a sluggish economy. Landlords also developed a heightened sense of seriousness in the early nineteenth century, in part politically induced ('property has its duties as well as its rights'), and they also became less willing to underwrite a Protestant cultural ethos if it hurt them economically. The disappearance of middlemen invariably led to reduced opportunities for servants and labourers, and poor Protestants could no longer rely on an unfailing source of patronage. They too left. Simultaneously, the collapse of proto-industrialisation and especially of small-town industries exposed many more poor Protestants who had been involved in these activities. The collapse of Dublin's surviving textile industries in the 1820s, when British and Irish tariffs were equalised, had a disastrous effect on Dublin's popular Protestant base. Thus there were economic and social motives to encourage emigration, as well as the loss of political confidence in the face of resurgent Catholic influence.

Middlemen had softened the potentially abrasive interface of landlord and tenant, interposing 'a necessary barrier' or a 'valuable mediation' in their own words, between authority and alienation.[129] While much agrarian agitation in the eighteenth century had an anti-big-farmer/middleman agenda, ignoring the landlords, the nineteenth century saw a sharpening anti-landlord profile because they now dealt directly with the vast bulk of the population and were no longer shielded by an intermediate screen. The elimination of the Protestant middleman interest removed an influential buffer between Catholic tenant and Protestant landlord, strengthened the Catholic interest, and homogenised the population in a way which allowed it to be more effectively penetrated by mass-mobilisation techniques, such as those perfected in the O'Connellite campaigns. It also meant that there were no rivals to the Catholic farmers, who were increasingly the political arbiters and organisers at a local level. The removal of middlemen, then, while serving short-term economic interests, had negative long-term social, cultural, and political effects on landlordism.

6 THE POLITICAL ROLE OF THE MIDDLEMAN

The group of Catholic middlemen families was obsessed, almost to the point of neurosis, with ancestry, family background, and the Cromwellian rupture. Given their tendency to settle locally, and given the rapid proliferation of such families in the expansionary conditions of the eighteenth century, one can easily identify the mechanism by which this displacement mentality percolated down the generations in a widening stream and also diffused across a wide stratum of Catholic society.[130] This consciousness, spread by generational and spatial shifts, was widely present by the late eighteenth century, potently so in the case of middlemen families. Miles Byrne of Monaseed described how his father often 'told me of the persecutions and robberies that both his family and my mother's had endured under the invaders; how often had he shown me the lands that belonged to our ancestors, now in the hands of the sanguinary followers of Cromwell'.[131] John O'Keefe, the dramatist, described a childhood visit to Knockdrim near Edenderry, 'where my father, with pride not unmixed with dejection, led me over tracts of fine land, once the property of his ancestors. My mother had much the same remark to make of her family losses in the county of Wexford.'[132]

It was within this milieu that Irish Jacobitism flourished. Jacobitism was Janus-headed, its obsessive backwards glance towards monarchical rupture balanced by a forward-looking emphasis on restoration. The power of its voice in Gaelic Ireland, the aisling (allegory), lay not in its elegiac cadences and dream-world mistiness but in its prophetic intent, which could easily shade into a radical rhetoric of the reversal of the 'ins' and 'outs' of Irish society--English/Irish, Protestant/Catholic, Hanoverian/Jacobite.[133] This obviously had resonances for the land question as well, with an insistent case being made for the legitimacy of the aspirations of the old landed élite. Such aspirations did not stay fenced within the polite precincts of poetry. A remarkable manuscript volume in the National Library contains a carefully bound and meticulous transcript of 1733 of every deed and indenture dealing with the 'ancient inheritance of the Waddings of Ballycogly' in Wexford. This volume was passed to his son by Thomas Wadding in Tenerife, with a rousing letter of admonition to guard it carefully in anticipation of a Stuart restoration, when the 'Cromelian rebbles' would be displaced and the Waddings restored to their rightful position, 'although we enjoy nothing at present but the bare title, having lost all for our loyalty and Catholic religion (to the glory of our family)'.[134]

Irish Jacobitism therefore provided indigenous ideological ingredients for the subversion of landed titles in advance of the imported radical recipe from France. Accordingly, the political role of the old élite was surveyed continuously and suspiciously. Landlords were wary of the degree of independence exhibited by middlemen who were doing well. After an economic upturn in the early 1750s in west Ulster the agent of the Abercorn estate reported to his landlord that 'many who lately were half-starving appear now like gentlemen and cannot be spoke to'.[135] Joseph Taylor, the Lansdowne agent, considered the local middlemen in the 1770s to be 'the old Milesian breed, who are full of laws and wrangles',[136] while Walter Kavanagh of Borris regretted having granted long leases in the last quarter of the eighteenth century on the grounds that it made his tenants 'too independent'.[137] This had obvious political connotations. Miles Byrne commented on the role of these Catholic middlemen families in Wexford:

> Among those who took part in the insurrection of 1798 there were a great number of Catholic gentlemen, holding land as farmers but descended from those who had been deprived of their property in land at the time of the Reformation and under Cromwell and above all under William III, merely because they were Catholics.[138]

Denis Browne was perturbed in 1807 at the prospects of one of these middlemen, Edward Garvey, being allowed to return to County Mayo: 'In Connaught the return of such a man as Mr Garvey is particularly dangerous in its example, when the resident farmers are mostly of the class, description, and religion of Mr Garvey, where there are few resident gentry to control or interfere with the influence of the middlemen over the peasantry'.[139]

Almost inevitably, such families assumed political roles; a striking feature is how this inherited leadership role could be maintained across a whole series of movements. In cases like the Sweetman, Downes, and Kavanagh families in County Wexford, a political leadership role can be traced from a Jacobite phase through the Catholic Committee and into the United Irishmen, and from there into the O'Connellite, anti-tithe, and Young Ireland campaigns. These families called the shots locally, lent prestige and social solidity, orchestrated crowds, petitions, and voters, interpreted the national political process at a local level, and acted as local tribunes of the people. In many senses they were the penetration point of Catholic politicisation, from whom a radiating effect emanated, deepening the social profile of the politicised group and thus facilitating the transition from élite to popular politics.[140]

One of the most fascinating aspects of the eighteenth century was the way in which the new radicalism grafted itself onto older stocks of resentment, growing out of a heightened sense of identity, consciousness of exclusion, and antipathy to the public political culture. In families like the Byrnes of Ballymanus in Wicklow or the O'Laoghaires and O'Sullivans in Cork, this fusion produced an attitude of aggressive truculence. A typical example occurred in 1784. Count John O'Rourke, born 'in 1735 in the parish of Oghteragh in Breffny', had gone abroad to serve in the French and Prussian armies. In 1784, in the aftermath of the Catholic relief acts which ushered in an 'enlightened age', O'Rourke submitted an extraordinary petition to the king, seeking restitution of some 57,200 acres in Leitrim (in fact, the total area of the county) taken from his family 'by the usurper Oliver Cromwell'. The family had been forced until now 'to submit in silence', but as grandson, he now felt it right to claim assistance 'to support in some degree the honour of his birth and the dignity of his family'. O'Rourke's pamphlet was accompanied by detailed genealogies (supplied by the O'Cornin family, 'hereditary antiquarians and genealogists to the family').[141]

Two decades later, George O'Malley of the Connemara smuggling family discussed his attitude to law and order in the early nineteenth century:

> I grant that society requires law and order to hold its bonds firmly together, and I also hold that this law and order should be respected, but I don't believe that there should be one law for the rich and another for the poor man. When a man is robbed of his properties and title held by his ancestors for no other reason than worshipping the Maker under a certain form of religion, there's nothing Christian in that . . . ; they rob the poor first and make them fight after.[142]

Such latent sentiments could easily be politicised, as happened in the 1790s. The Catholic leader John Keogh summarised Catholic resentments: 'Our grievance is that many men beneath us in birth, education, morals, and fortune are allowed to trample upon us'.[143] The leadership role of these Catholic families had pronounced regional aspects. The aloofness of Ulster from national Catholic politics in the 1760–1830 period can be ascribed to the absence of such families there. By the mid-eighteenth century there was no landed Catholic interest to provide a shield and a seedbed for these families, equivalent to the Ormond, Clanricarde, or Kenmare role in the south. The extent of immigration in seventeenth-century Ulster had been such that there was simply no room for the survival of the old landowners as head tenants. This differential experience is well expressed in a letter from John Dogherty in Inishowen to Morgan O'Connell in 1765:

The original Irish are very happy in your part of the country; the wicked brood of black-hearted heretics have got no foothold there as yet. . . . Here are few except hewers of wood and drawers of water. In short, we are in the most abject slavery in this barony of Inishowen, and not a foot of land to be renewed to any as prime tenant to our landlord, the earl of Donegal, that is of the old stamp.[144]

Deprived of the profits of a substantial leasehold interest, Catholics were subsequently unable to finance their penetration of the more lucrative branches of the linen industry. Thus the highest social roles to which Ulster Catholics aspired were publican, shopkeeper, cattle dealer, butcher, or schoolteacher. Edward Wakefield in 1812 made the wider observation: 'The Protestant gentry of the north, in estimating the character of Roman Catholics, are frequently disposed to form a general opinion from the habits and manners of the wealthier class in Ulster, whose occupations seldom rise higher than that of a grocer or retailer of spirits'.[145]

The inherited leadership cadre of the Catholic community elsewhere simply did not exist in Ulster, where the Catholic experience was radically different, and where deprivation and degradation were much in evidence. The Catholic *mentalité* in Ulster was therefore totally different from its southern and western counterparts. Nonetheless, where even a handful of such families survived, as on the Downshire estate, they could play an important role in stiffening the backbone of the local Catholic community. The Downshire agent blamed the 'insolence' of the cottiers on the estate in 1799 and their 'refractory disposition' on 'the contumacious example of the McArdells, Magenises, and Byrnes (the descendants of the old proprietors) instilling into the minds of a numerous banditti of cottiers under them that you are only entitled to a chiefry upon the lands and cannot dispossess them'.[146] Charles Teeling defined the Defender leader John Magenis principally in terms of his ancestry: 'Magenis was of an old and respectable Irish family, the lineal descendant of the ancient lords of Iveagh. The blood of his ancestors ran pure in his veins, and purer never flowed from a generous heart.'[147] Anxious to stress his respect for such individuals, Teeling added that he had 'always been attached to the ancient names of my country, and when associated with natural achievement, they are doubly objects of my respect'.[148]

7 REACTIONS

There was a curious paradox in the relationship between landlord and tenant in Ireland. At one level there was the apparently unrivalled power of the landlord which so startled Arthur Young: 'It must strike the most careless traveller to see whole strings of cars whipt into a ditch by a gentleman's footman to make way for his carriage'.[149] But at the same time gentry coming from England to Ireland were struck by the independence of the tenantry's private lives from landlord scrutiny or control. Mrs Elizabeth Smith of Baltiboys commented in 1840: 'There was nothing struck me so remarkably when I first came here as the tenants marrying their children, setting them up in different trades, etc., without ever saying one word about it to their landlord. It went through their whole conduct— we were to them only the receivers of a much grudged rent.'[150] Given the evidence of a 'dispossession mentality' in Ireland, and given the continuing vitality, and competition for hearts and minds, of an alternative underground gentry, it is not surprising that the official gentry of the country felt uneasy. Even apparently innocuous wake games could carry a subversive subtext. 'Sir Soipín' (the Knight of Straw), as described by J.C. Walker in 1789, contrasted an Irish landlord representing an ancient family in the neighbourhood with an English landlord, 'the Knight of Straw', so called from his diagnostic sugán headdress.[151] The humorous barbed dialogue between the two offered obvious opportunities for satire and for historical and political commentary in which the 'Irish' landlord always had the upper hand.

The insecurity elicited by living in the penumbra of an alternative gentry around them can frequently be felt under the superficial calm of eighteenth-century landlord life. Anxiety can be seen, for example, in the frequency with which visitors to the country were regaled with stories bearing on it. Thus, when Baron Edward Willes visited County Clare in 1761, he was entertained by the local M.P. Francis Burton, who told him about Charles O'Brien, sixth Viscount Clare (1699–1761), whose family had lost their estate as Jacobites. Burton had met O'Brien in Paris and discovered that he still 'claims a great part of the county of Clare as his patrimony . . . , that he knew all the gentlemen and the estates of the county and their private affairs as well as if he had lived among them . . . , that he had an exact rentroll of all his own estates, that he kept a register of every part that was sold and to whom and for what'.[152]

Travelling in Ireland in the 1770s, Arthur Young picked up similar stories from the dinner tables of the landed gentry:

> The lineal descendants of the old families are now to be found all over the kingdom, working as cottiers on the lands which were once their own. In such great revolutions of property the ruined proprietors have usually been extirpated or banished. In Ireland the case was otherwise, and it is a fact that in most parts of the kingdom the descendants of the old landowners regularly transmit by testamentary deed the memorial of their right to those estates which once belonged to their families.[153]

Examples of this scenario do exist. In the late eighteenth century the Dalton heir to the estate of Kildalton (renamed Bessborough) was living as a cooper in

Carrick-on-Suir. The Ponsonbys' agent, Peter Walsh of Belline, visited him in his old age, offering him £400 to relinquish all claims to the estate, but was peremptorily refused.[154] In the Ballina area a common toast in the eighteenth century was 'Súil Uí Dhubhda le Ard na Riach' (O'Dowd's expectation of Ardnaree)—a reference to the O'Dowd family's hopes of resuming their ancestral property in the event of a successful Jacobite coup.[155]

Landlord obsessions with these threats to their legitimacy may also have been stimulated by the ongoing debate on the validity of leases for lives renewable forever (perpetuity tenancies), a debate culminating in the 1780 Tenantry Act, a major victory for such tenants, confirming their legal status. Under the penal laws leases of this type, if enacted before 1704, were not subject to discovery proceedings, and many Catholic families retained a sub-gentry status by virtue of such leases.[156] The Hay family of Bellinkeele in Wexford is a good example.[157] In the 1770s landlords were keen to undermine such leases, pegged at artificially low levels and therefore redistributing income from landlords to leaseholders. Part of the landlord campaign focused on the political threat posed by these families, and in Munster in particular Young was privy to this type of exaggerated commentary. In Cork he was told that 'all the poor people are Roman Catholic, and among them are the descendants of the old families who once possessed the country, of which they still preserve the full memory, in so much that a gentleman's labourer will regularly leave to his son by will his master's estate'.[158]

It is noticeable that it was in Munster that the four great *cause célèbres* of conflict between old and new families erupted—the Cotter execution in 1720, the Sullivan-Puxley conflict in the 1750s, the Nicholas Sheehy judicial murder in 1766, and the Art Ó Laoghaire-Abraham Morris saga in 1773.[159] Cork and Tipperary were two of the leading Irish counties for recruitment into the French army in the eighteenth century; this may in part explain why the aisling figured so prominently in the poetic tradition of Munster, with the songs being used as part of recruiting campaigns. It may also help to explain why the adoption of the traditional Stuart colour (white) by the agrarian redresser movements of the 1760s instantly conferred a political colouration on Munster Protestants' attempts to understand the phenomenon, and on their hardline political response, in which Jacobite plots and collusive Catholic gentry figured prominently.[160] And this happened despite the fact that the Whiteboys and Rightboys (whose campaigns equally targeted Catholic landlords and middlemen) never included a reversal of the land settlement among their aims.[161] Yet as late as 1770, Shelburne, seeking the establishment of a garrison at Nedeen (Kenmare), described the inhabitants in conventional Jacobite terms: 'Roman Catholics of fierce and uncultivated manners, accustomed to hate and despise civil government, and from many of them having been in the French and Spanish services and other circumstances, inured to arms'.[162]

This consistent sense of irrelevance, of having their legitimacy only grudgingly conceded, of being an embattled minority rather than the nation of Ireland, haunted the landlord psyche in the post-1798 period when their position seemed ever more precarious in a newly volatile, politicised, sectarianised, and strife-torn island. But at times of stress, even in the eighteenth century, the spectre of being merely a colonial élite could also haunt them. In the aftermath of the first Catholic relief acts in the early 1780s, there was considerable Protestant anxiety at the spate of Catholic families seeking reversal of outlawries or recognition of Jacobite titles—including Fingal, Gormanston, Dunsany, and Kenmare.[163]

Even so apparently innocuous a map as Charles O'Conor's of the location of the old Irish clans caused a flutter.[164] Originally published in 1770, its reissue (by Patrick Wogan, also printer to the Catholic Committee) in 1792 at a sensitive time for Irish Protestants caused Patrick Duigenan to associate it with Catholic claims on the confiscated estates: 'They have accurate maps of them. They have lately published in Dublin a map of this kingdom cantoned out among the old proprietors.'[165] Westmorland, the lord lieutenant, was also troubled by the map, reporting to Pitt in February 1792, 'I have sent you a map of Ireland describing the estates of the ancient possessors before the forfeitures. The circulation of this has given fresh alarm to the Protestant possessors of these forfeited lands.'[166] William Todd Jones replied to these charges in *A letter to the societies of United Irishmen of the town of Belfast* (Dublin, 1792):

> "But there is a map!" whispers some English prelate to some English chaplain, aide de camp, or private secretary. . . . "Oh, sir, there is a *map* would singe your eyebrows but to smell the fiery fragment . . . ; you would bless yourself to peruse the hideous barbaric names with which it abounds. . . . Published, sir, by that dangerous Catholic O'Connor [*sic*] for the sole purpose of reminding herdsmen and ditchers what great folks were their grandams. Yes, sir, *a map*, with the charming popish pedigrees as long as the Birdcage Walk, and at their root the old sanguinary Irishmen themselves, lying extended each upon his own Milesian seignory."

Todd Jones then deflates the hysteria surrounding the map by a detailed description of what it *actually* shows, as opposed to what its critics *supposed* it to show:

> It is a fragment of taste—an obscure and imperfect delineation; a map for a poring antiquary, an abstract chronological curiosity, a map without boundaries of barony, townland, or parish, composed of names for the greater part unannexed to any description of territory but the naked counties, without pedigrees, branches of families, Christian names, or any possible clew to direct particular descendants of houses to trace or bring evidence of their claims or of their origins.[167]

Charles O'Conor's map was also referred to in an anti-United Irishmen doggerel published in the spring of 1798, in which the map is used to put words in the mouth of the United Irish organiser as he tries to persuade a generic 'Paddy' to join the organisation:

'Tis hard indeed and harder still but our good rulers have their will
That many families should be reduced to lowest poverty
Perhaps to beg upon the lands once wrested from their father's hands
Now held by those who will not know them and hardly charity bestow them
This is a truth, Paddy, you know it, and —'s map does fully show it
There you may see, tho' we're derided, how Ireland's lands are all divided
Marked with the names of the old proprietors, which in pretence they were
    rioters
Were forfeited, were seized, were given, to any scoundrel under heaven.[168]

In political terms this insecurity expressed itself in a fear that any tampering with the constitution would undermine the landed class. As Fitzgibbon pointed out in 1789, 'the act by which most of us hold our estates was an act of violence . . . , an act subverting the first principles of the common law in England and Ireland . . . , the Act of Settlement'.[169] Meddling with the constitutional status quo would, in the words of the attorney-general in 1782, 'loose the bonds of society and leave the whole island to be grappled for by the descendants of the old proprietors'.[170] Sir Edward Newenham observed in the same year that 'they have an old claim on our estates'.[171] In such a climate of opinion even genealogy was suspect as a pursuit. The Chevalier O'Gorman, for example, was suspected in 1786 of 'collecting accounts of Irish estates of which the Roman Catholics were dispossessed in the time of Cromwell and of the revolution'.[172] The Irish lord lieutenant, Rutland, assured London that O'Gorman's 'conduct has been regularly watched and his correspondence intercepted'.[173] In the same year a French privateer captured the ship carrying the Cromwellian Down survey maps to England. Since it was the administrative basis of forfeitures, there was great official disquiet that 'a work so valuable is in foreign hands'.[174]

The activities of a professional pedigree-monger like O'Gorman were necessary for those Catholics wishing to pursue a military career at an official level in the continental armies, which insisted on proof of noble descent as an entrance requirement.[175] This created a market for pedigrees, real or embroidered. The degree to which Irish Catholic families with reduced patrimonies looked to officer service abroad to retain status was one of the principal reasons why genealogy retained such a central role in their lives. The French diplomat Coquebert de Montbret was astonished to find on visiting Ireland that even famous French army families like Dillon and Lally were mere tenant farmers on Richard Kirwan's estate at Cregg in Galway, while the Mullallys were simply 'peasants'.[176] Nonetheless, the combination of pedigree-mongering and Jacobite connections elicited establishment suspicions about the long-term goals of these families.

These paranoid attitudes were also fed by a much publicised incident in

County Roscommon in January 1786. According to newspaper reports, Roderick O'Connor, claiming to be a descendant of 'Cahal Crubdarg' of the old royal family of Connacht, had peremptorily resumed control of a 20,000-acre estate (formerly in O'Connor hands but now owned by the Burkes) in defiance of legal title and supported by 2,000 followers. The *Dublin Evening Post* reported that his father had had in his possession the ancient crown of the Irish kings but had been forced by penury to part with it.[177] The incident caused a sensation, being loudly debated in parliament and even monitored by the Vatican.[178] The controversy forced a Catholic response. The Catholic gentlemen of Roscommon, headed by his brother, repudiated O'Connor's claims to the estate and dismissed his supporters as 'an ignorant rabble actuated by intoxication'. This was quickly followed by a general address from the Catholics of Ireland to the lord lieutenant, Rutland, disclaiming any hint of a claim to the forfeited estates:

> We also look upon all claims or pretences of claims to any lands or estates, on account of their having been in former ages in the possession of our ancestors, if unsupported by the laws and statutes now in being of this realm, as unjust and highly subversive of that good order and government which it is not only our duty but our intent to support.[179]

This address mollified Rutland.[180] O'Connor himself was quietly acquitted at the September assizes in Roscommon, having been guilty only of the common ploy of retaining possession of a leasehold after the expiry date, hoping by so doing to apply pressure on the landlord to renew the lease.[181] The exaggerated response provides a revealing insight into the insecurity of the landed class. From then on, the Catholic Committee had continuously to reiterate its renunciation of 'all interest in, and title to, all forfeited lands resulting from any rights of our ancestors or any claims, title, or interest therein'.[182] Curiously, the concept of resumption of ancient estates was put into general circulation by the very frequency (and publicity) of these denials and by the continuous harping on it by Musgrave, Duigenan, and Ogle. In the early 1790s it received additional valency from being linked as well to the restoration of 'popery' as signalled by the repeal of the penal laws. Defenders and United Irishmen were both believed to harbour the aim of overturning the Glorious Revolution. Baron Yelverton's charge to the County Antrim grand jury in June 1797 spelled out clearly the common conservative perception of the aims of the United Irishmen, who had allegedly 'marked out properties to be confiscated and the uses to which the produce of these confiscations are to be applied. . . . Your servants and dependents should wade thro' your blood into the possession of your estates.'[183]

An incident in County Meath in April 1797 showed the depth of fear produced by these preoccupations. Benjamin Chapman, the local M.P., reported the incident to Shelburne:

The house of one O'Flynn was searched for arms during the assizes; he was charged to be a captain of the Defenders, but instead of arms there was found a large parcel of his family's ancient title deeds before the rebellion of 1641 to the estates of Killyan, now belonging to Mr Loftus, in whose employ O'Flynn was at this time. This matter is much magnified by some zealots.[184]

Anti-United Irish and anti-Defender rhetoric was obsessed with this issue of the ancient estates. A typical passage appeared in the 1795 tract, *An Irishman's letter to the people called Defenders*:

Your seducers tell you that you shall recover the forfeited estates. If you mean to keep possession of them, your object is open war, and you must first subdue the armed forces of both countries. If you mean to give them to the persons you call their owners, you must in like manner support their possession; consider also that a great number of these forfeited estates are now in the possession of Catholics who will unite with the civil and military powers against you.[185]

By contrast, the United Irishmen were insistent that confiscation would not be general but selective, targeted only at church land and at those who actively fought against the revolution. The Donaghadee United Irishmen resolved in 1797 that 'there are a great many inimical and will no doubt prove hostile to the cause of liberty; their estates or property shall be confiscated and converted to the national benefit'.[186] Miles Byrne, the Wexford United Irishman, made essentially the same observations. He noted that 'the church property becoming immediately the property of the state, and the estates of all those who should emigrate or remain in the English army fighting against their country, being confiscated, the revenue arising from these funds would have been employed to provide for and defray all the expenses necessary for the defence and independence of the country'.[187] Only the most advanced of United Irish thinkers, like Arthur O'Connor, were prepared to go further. O'Connor argued in *The state of Ireland* in the spring of 1798 that the whole legal basis of property had become 'a barbarous mass of complexity, chicane, and fraud', and that it therefore needed reform. To achieve this, he argued, 'we must look to those laws of primogeniture, entails, and settlements which have been set up to secure and perpetuate the despotism of the few and to ensure and perpetuate the exclusion of the many'.[188]

Such perceptions could lead to a radical social perspective in which the idea of a landed gentry itself became problematic. O'Connor attacked the gentry for their lack of humanity arising from excessive wealth, and described them as 'men who have made themselves slaves to the meanest and most contemptible wants, desires, and habits—miserable if their bed is too hard or too soft, their pillow too high or too low, their dinner too much done or too little, regardless of how many millions corruption and tyranny have left without beds to lie on or food to allay the gnawings of ravenous famine'.[189] This Painite-Jacobin streak could also mix with millenarian sentiment to produce a levelling challenge to the landowning class. Witness the handbill circulating in Dublin in 1796, 'The cry of the poor for bread':

> Oh, lords of manors and other men of landed property, as you have monopo-lised to yourselves the land, its vegetation, and its game, the fish of the rivers, and the fowls of heaven . . . , in the present condition of things can the labourer who cultivates your land with the sweat of his brow, the working manufacturer, or the mechanic support himself, a wife, and five or six children? How much comfort do you extort from their misery, by places, offices, and pensions, and consume in idleness, dissipation, riot, and luxury?[190]

Two thousand copies of this handbill had been produced by the Philanthropic Society in Dublin, under the auspices of John Burk, William Lawler, and Le Blanc, to be 'pasted up on corners', sold, or distributed 'to people on the street on purpose to enrage them against government'.[191] A typical millenarian tract, *Christ in triumph coming to judgement*, published in Strabane in 1795, contained similar sentiments embodied in the metaphor of the last judgment: 'The courts of kings, the seats and palaces of noblemen, the banqueting houses of the luxurious, the full barns of farmers, the cottages of husbandmen, and the stalls under which beggars lie, will be as one and come to nothing'.[192] In the aftermath of the failure of the rebellion the revamped United Irish organisation in Dublin city, dominated by these social radicals, made a very explicit attack on landed property in their *Poor man's catechism*:

> *Q*. How would you alter the property in land, preserving the country from anarchy?

> *A*. By dividing the ancient estates among the descendants of those Irish families who were pillaged by English invaders, giving to every person without exception a competent share to enable him or her to get a comfortable livelihood, this provision not to extend to any person who impeded the deliverance of the country by cowardice or treachery, the remainder to be sold by public cant and the money applied to paying off the debts contracted by the former confederacy, and for rewarding the citizens who fought for their country, and providing for their wives and mothers, and giving education to their children and infant relations.[193]

Thus in the changed atmosphere of the 1790s specifically Irish concerns were linking up with a wider international movement to produce a threat to the landed gentry. The gentry responded by interpreting the radical challenge as simply a war of 'poverty against property', devoid of serious ideological substance.[194] But they were haunted by the threat of insidious undermining from within by their servants and dependents. In the immediate aftermath of the rebellion horror stories circulated of perfidy of this type. Musgrave dwelled on the case of the Minchin family of Grange in County Dublin; on the night that the rebellion started, a party of rebels headed by their gardener Curran and gatekeeper McDonogh marched down the avenue, where Curran declared that he would 'take possession of the house and demesne as his own'.[195] Similarly, John Kelly of Killann was reported by Musgrave as having 'made a will by which he left Captain Blacker's estate to a relation in case he should be killed in the rebellion'.[196] In the Ballymena area an anecdote about a local mendicant, Jack McDowell, went into circulation after 1798. On Ballymena being taken, this man headed straight for Sir Robert Adair's demesne, observing, ' "First come, first served." This place is the Adairs' no more, it is the property of Mr Jack McDowell forever."[197] The fears which lay behind these stories were expertly represented by Maria Edgeworth's *Castle Rackrent*, a parodic masterpiece in which the landed class is subverted by the aboriginal owners. The central character Thady Quirke was based on John Langan, the steward at Edgeworthstown.[198]

The official unease about forfeitures can also be seen in the secretive archival practices concerning the records of the forfeiture proceedings of the Cromwellian and Williamite periods. In 1802, for example, when the English genealogist George Beltz sought access to the outlawry lists of these periods, he was initially informed that an inspection warrant could be issued only by the attorney-general in consultation with the lord chancellor, and was then refused the warrant. The stated cause was 'the errors in the judgments upon outlawries which were the basis of these forfeitures, and the fear of renewing ancient animosities in families and disturbing the grants of the crown'.[199] As late as 1822 the Ulster king-of-arms, Sir William Betham, reprobated the indiscretion of the Irish Record Commissioners in publishing seventeenth-century inquisitions which would 'foment discontent among the descendants of the attainted proprietors'.[200]

That same impatient insecurity was still there in 1842 when a disgruntled Munster Protestant chastised the Ordnance Survey officials because they had 'persons sent from this office engaged in taking down the pedigree of some beggar or tinker and establishing him [as] the lineal descendant of some Irish chief whose ancient estate they most carefully mark out by boundaries, and they have actually in several instances, as I have seen by their letters, nominated some desperate characters as the rightful heirs to these territories'.[201] These complaints were stimulated by the type of comment presented, for example, in the Ordnance Survey memoir of Enniskillen parish:

> The name of Maguire predominates in the town of Enniskillen. Though most of them move in rather an humble sphere, they take no small share of pride in tracing back their ancient lineage to the early lords of Fermanagh. Mr Thomas Maguire, ironmonger (according to his own reckoning) is the nearest heir to

the forfeited title and estates of the last Lord Maguire, who was beheaded in London in the year 1644, and to the present day entertains strong hopes of their inheritance.[202]

Such preoccupations were also fed to visiting English politicians by the conservative Dublin Castle establishment. Lord Westmorland reported back in 1793 to Dundas that 'the lower orders of old Irish consider themselves as plundered and kept out of their property by the English settlers and on every occasion are ready for riot and reverse'.[203] John Fitzgibbon, earl of Clare, was particularly prone to use these arguments, as in a 1795 speech when he declared that 'Great Britain can never conciliate the descendants of the old Irish to her interests upon any other terms than by restoring to them the possessions and the religion of their ancestors in full splendour and dominion'.[204] He was able to use his own convert background to dramatise this for effect, as in this reported conversation with Laurence Parsons:

My father was a popish recusant. He became a Protestant and was called to the bar, but he continued to live on terms of friendship with his Roman Catholic relations and early friends, and he knew the Catholics well. He has repeatedly told me that if ever they had the opportunity, they would overturn the established government and church and resume the Protestant estates.[205]

In an earlier debate in 1787, when proposing hardline measures, Fitzgibbon had also focused on the pernicious influence of the old families whom he saw at the centre of the Rightboy disturbances, and whom he ironically termed 'the gentry': 'The gentry for whose perusal I particularly intended the clause are that ruinous set of men called middlemen, who stand between the inheritor and occupier of the land, to the injury of both, and who, I know, for their own base purposes abetted outrage'.[206]

Accordingly, the activities of such families were closely monitored in the 1790s. At the Roscommon assizes in August 1795, Arthur Wolfe was delighted to have secured a 'conviction of consequence'—that of James Sheridan, 'the son of a farmer of some wealth and connection, who has been a great inciter of this sedition [Defenderism] and a great leader of the seditious. . . . He is what is called a buckeen; his sisters appeared in handsome riding dresses with hats and feathers. . . . If examples of this type could reach the rich, this would be a very effectual one.'[207]

8 POPULAR CULTURE

In the first half of the eighteenth century Catholic middlemen had been centrally involved in popular culture and lost no social caste from it. Jonah Barrington identified them as 'half-mounted gentlemen' and described how they 'exercised hereditarily the authority of keeping the ground clear at horse-racing, hurling, and all public meetings'.[208] Laurence Whyte's poem 'The parting cup' had emphasised how, in the early decades of the eighteenth century, these families were immersed in local life:

> They seldom did refuse a summons/to play at football or at commons
> To pitch the bar or throw a sledge,/to vault or take a ditch or hedge
> At leisure hours to unfold a riddle,/or play the bagpipes, harp, or fiddle.[209]

By the late eighteenth century these common ties which had elided social distinction in the informal intimacy of collective engagement in popular culture had snapped, to be replaced by a more formal, distant relationship. The provision of pews and even private galleries in Catholic chapels for the local élite was a graphic representation of the transition. Already by the 1770s it was considered that those who had not disengaged themselves were losing social caste. By 1786, Roderick O'Connor, at the centre of controversy, could be dismissed peremptorily as a nonentity because he was 'a man rather of a mean disposition and rustic education, frequenting hurling greens and football matches, intermingling with the populace at fairs and patrons, drinking to excess spiritous liquors'.[210] O'Connor belonged to that Connacht class described by Maxwell as 'proprietors of little properties called fodeeins [Irish: fóidín], who continued the names and barbarisms of their progenitors. Without industry, without education, they arrogated a certain place in society and idly imitated the wealthier in their vices.' By the early nineteenth century they had 'fortunately disappeared'.[211]

Arthur Young's famous attack on middlemen mingled annoyance at their profit rents with distaste for their lifestyle. His analysis quickly became conventional, and newspaper accounts continually harped on it. In 1787, *Finn's Leinster Journal* reported:

> Trade is too vile an employment, too grovelling an item for youth, if raised but one step above the surface of beggary. The exalted pursuits of cock-fighting, horse-racing, and debauching female innocence are only worthy of their attention. Upon a farm of £200 or £300 a year it is not at all uncommon to see six or seven gentlemen reared. At length, the little patrimony is divided among them, and just as much falls to the share of each as will enable him to subsist without annual labour, to wear a laced waistcoat, once a year to kill a wretched horse with hard riding, to get intoxicated every night with whiskey punch, to be insolent to his superiors and the scourge of them below him.

In 1788 the newspaper returned to the attack:[212]

> What is called hospitality swallows up everything, eating, drinking, and rural sports fills up [*sic*] the whole time of our Irish country gentlemen. The

principal point of ambition is to outdo his neighbours in hospitable profusion. He retires to support his pseudo-dignity by cock-fighting, card-playing, scheming, and skulking among his circle of acquaintances, bullying and cheating every tradesman, running away with an heiress, falls into the road-eating train of some harum-scarum fox-hunter, and dies as he lives, despised by that rank to which he vainly aspired.[213]

By 1793, when Samuel Crumpe wrote his prize-winning *An essay on the best means of providing employment for the people* for the Dublin Society, the attack on middlemen had become a strictly conventional set-piece:

The yell of a pack of starving beagles is more pleasing to their ears than the song of the ploughman. The sight of their fellow sportsmen, drenched to insensibility in whiskey, more pleasing to their eyes than luxurious crops and well-cultivated fields. They are the class amongst whom what remains of the ferocious spirit of drinking which formerly disgraced this kingdom is still to be found.[214]

The transformation of popular culture also stemmed from increasing divisions within the Catholic community. The early penal period had created a strong communal bond. A Cork commentator noted of Catholics in 1740 that 'they are an united band and take care of each other as if one family',[215] while Edward Wakefield observed in 1812 that 'the persecuted and proscribed form of a compact body, distinct from their oppressors, and the union which common misery produces, is firm and lasting'.[216] By the 1760s that solidarity was fracturing under the insistent pressure of economic change, widening class differentiation, and increased hostilities. The great redresser movements, the Whiteboys and the Rightboys, sought a return to the days when their moral economy blunted the impact of the real one. By mid-century the acquisitive strong farmer was increasingly seen as a mere landgrabber or landshark by those he displaced, and therefore he could easily become a legitimate target for exemplary violence. In 1778, 400 inhabitants of Kilcullen, Co. Kildare, marched in solemn procession to the execution by hanging of an effigy of a local land jobber.[217] No wonder that by 1812 it was noted that wealthy Catholics were 'afraid of the populace', and that farmers had moved to slate their potentially vulnerable thatched roofs.[218]

In the most land-hungry region of Europe, and the one in which the stigma of being landless was the most fiercely resented, the strengthening big-farm interest had good reason to feel uneasy, as its members accumulated the grudges and spites of others along with their leases and acres. The 'midnight legislators' could always call, especially, as they pointed out in a vivid phrase, because 'we will know you the darkest nights when you will not know us the brightest day'.[219] Or as one Whitefoot leader commented in 1833, 'The law does nothing for us. We must save outselves. . . . Emancipation has done nothing for us. Mr O'Connell and the rich Catholics go to parliament. We are starving to death just the same.'[220]

The kind of cultural, social, and spatial distancing illustrated here may have been heralded too by sharpening economic antagonisms. The accelerating social divide was part of a modernising process which eventually killed the archaic middleman world. As early as 1738, though perhaps with a strong element of wish fulfillment, Madden observed that Catholics who made money 'were running fast into the neatness and plenty of the English way of living'.[221] But that transition out of the old, local, domestic world really occurred on a large scale between 1760 and 1840. One can see this change in a number of key transitions. It was at this stage that the 'cabin' was relinquished in favour of the two-storeyed slated farmhouse, and that the new house was carefully distanced from the cottiers' cabins. The house also became mimetic of more formal fashions, signalled by the presence of an avenue, decorative trees and gardens, and a miniature demesne. The newer social pretensions were symbolised by the assigning of a name to the farm, usually the townland one—like 'Johnstown House' or 'Ballymore House'. Wealthy farmers were now sandwiched between a 'mister' in front of the name and an 'esq.' at the back. The transition was also reflected linguistically (the decisive break to English-speaking accelerated during this period); politically (for the first time farmers began to play a major role in national politics); and culturally (diet, leisure patterns, clothes, and furniture all began to change in response to new expectations). We are heading towards the nineteenth-century defining characteristics of the strong farmer: 'a priest in the parish, a pump in the yard, a piano in the parlour, and bulled his own cows'.[222]

Above all, these changes were reflected in the attitude to popular culture. Throughout Europe in the late eighteenth century élite groups began to distance themselves from popular culture. In Ireland the sharpening political divides sundered the links, especially in the late eighteenth and early nineteenth centuries. The old allegiances—to calendar custom, hurling, cock-fighting, horse-racing, hunting, patterns, wakes, traditional music, dancing and poetry, public drinking, abduction—fade and wither in the face of this modernising thrust. In a way, once the Catholic big-farm families had disengaged themselves from this culture (oral, local, archaic, and pre-modern), it inevitably withered and died or degenerated into disorder and riots without the social discipline and patronage to regulate and replicate itself. Right across the board in the late eighteenth century one can trace the sinking social centre of gravity of participation in popular culture; hurling and abductions are too well-documented examples.[223]

The withdrawal from and subsequent assault on vernacular religion was part of the same process, mainly inspired by the Catholic clergy, themselves recruited from exactly the same class which was then abandoning its older mores.[224] Of numerous possible examples, the newly respectable voice of Irish strong-farm culture can be heard in Fr Mathew Horgan, parish priest of Blarney, whose denunciations of wakes literally led him to new heights of vituperation:

Irish wakes, I say, are synonymous with everything profligate, wicked, waste-ful, and disgraceful to a Christian people, and every lover of religion, morality, and good order should cooperate to abolish such a foul stain in the Irish character. As I was well aware of the difficulty of rooting out old customs and prejudices, I earnestly proceeded to the task for the good of the people whose governor I am. I cursed in the chapel those who allowed wakes and those who frequented them, knowing their business there was neither sorrow or sympa-thy but to have a glorious night's fun in eating, drinking, and smoking nasty tobacco, and I found that those who frequented wakes, like executions, become hardened villains who could not be trustworthy. I have so well succeeded that the people are grateful and unanimous in their suppression. For this I had a facility which few others could boast of; in the building of my round tower I left a vault of 10 feet in diameter in the base, to which, as soon as a coffin is procured, the body is conveyed to remain there for a time.[225]

Compare this behaviour with the traditional caoin uttered by the people of Kilmackilloge in Kerry on the death of the Mac Fínín Dhubh in 1809, as recounted by Lady Louise Lansdowne:

The moment our boat reached the land, all the inhabitants of the bay, who had assembled themselves on some high ground near the shore, began to howl and lament McFinnin and continued to bewail him the whole time we staid and till our boat was well out of sight. The howl is a most wild and melancholy sound and impresses me with the idea of real sorrow in the people, and as we heard it at Kilmacalogue [sic] echoed by the rocks and softened by the distance, nothing could be more striking and affecting.[226]

9 CONCLUSIONS: BURKE, DEFENDERS, O'CONNELL

The most intriguing contribution to the debate on the Catholic question in Ireland in the late eighteenth century came from Edmund Burke, and it is intriguing precisely because Burke took on board the Jacobite argument that the authentic Irish gentry were indeed the Catholics. Burke pleaded eloquently for Irish Catholics as a local application of his defence of the integrity of traditional society.[227] Extending his espousal of family and local loyalties against abstract claims, Burke argued that Irish Catholics represented those rooted communities whose presence alone sustained the *ancien régime*. Catholic traditions, beliefs, and habits were so ingrained in the fabric of Irish culture that a political system which failed to recognise them would inevitably lack the crucial bonding force that gave political systems their endurance—the affection of the people who lived under them. In the Irish system these well-founded Catholic claims were reduced or denied by a narrow ruling group whose claims to supremacy were based solely on religious persuasion. That ruling group of Irish Protestants was not a rooted, respected aristocracy but merely a plebeian and parvenu ascendancy, a bogus facsimile whose scornful, narrowly based pursuit of power and privilege achieved only resentment and loathing. Like the French Jacobins, they violated the customary affections and rooted relations which made society cohesive and stable.[228] Burke believed that only by admitting Catholics fully into the political nation could Ireland be tranquillised, as their innately deferential and monarchical tendencies would then be expressed in support of the status quo, and they would no longer be prey to factious Dissenters or Jacobin United Irishmen.

Burke's scathing critique of the Irish Protestant gentry stemmed in large part from his bruising encounter in the 1760s with Munster Protestants determined to implicate the Catholic gentry, sub-gentry, and leading merchants in Whiteboy activity. Burke's efforts on behalf of his kinsmen, especially the Nagles, convinced him of the reactionary, vindictive, and squalid character of their antagonists-- gentry families like the Maudes, Bagwells, Kings, Boyles, Beresfords, and Hewetsons. He never lost his scalding sense of partisan indignation derived from this close encounter with 'red hot' Munster Protestantism.

In an inchoate way Burke's high-flown rhetoric mirrored the views of the Defenders, the Ulster-based Catholic secret society which had evolved in the 1780s and 1790s, and which in many ways strongly represented grassroots Catholic political opinion. Like Burke, and unlike the United Irishmen, the Defenders wished not to repudiate but to embrace history. Like Burke, they saw Catholics as the authentic aboriginal inhabitants of the island. Time's arrow was not for them the United Irishmen's untroubled progressive projectile; the Defenders wished to flex time, to bend it back to a pre-plantation idyll. Their potent sense of dispossession expressed itself in hopes of reversing the land settlement, overturning the church establishment, and avenging their seventeenth-century setbacks: 'They can never forget that they have been the proprietors of this country . . . ; they look upon or talk of the English settlers as not of their nation'. They wished 'to plant the true religion that was lost since the Reformation'. They were encouraged 'by the hope of being what they called uppermost'.[229] A consciousness of dispossession, latent or overt, was widely diffused at the popular level. Robert Bell described this attitude in the 1780s:

> Ignorant and obscure as they were, many families among them used to trace their pedigrees back to a very remote period; they knew the rank and estates which their ancestors once held in the country, and they felt no small degree of pride at the recollection that noble blood still flowed in their veins. These families could ascertain every spot of ground which was said to have belonged

to their forefathers and of which they looked on the modern possessors as so many usurpers. Their gross understandings were satisfied with learning by tradition that the lands had once belonged to their ancestors, who had been driven out by powerful invaders, and they never lost sight of the prospect of being one day reinstated in them.[230]

Their solution to Ireland's ills was to reverse their seventeenth-century setbacks by overturning the church establishment, the land settlement, and the social hierarchy which rested on their defeats. Thus, like Burke, they were fundamentally historicists, looking to the past for explanations of their traditional grievances—tithes, taxes, rents, wages, and living conditions. Their millenarianism could also be interpreted in this way: apocalyptic change would be equally subversive of time, again eliding the present. Their levelling tendencies—'the cobbler and the Caesar made level'—were derived from a historically-based sense of social injustice, applicable to the obvious disparities in eighteenth-century Irish life: 'We have lived long enough upon potatoes and salt; it is our turn now to eat beef and mutton'.[231]

Unlike Burke, the Defenders saw in the French Revolution a possibility of casting off old oppressions, of reverting to a version of the status quo ante. It was easy for them to give a sectarian gloss to their readings of Irish history, especially in the cockpit atmosphere of Ulster. Thus the Defenders could also practice the politics of the grudge, develop an adversarial sense of collective awareness, and unify themselves through their common hostilities. The Defenders signalled the democratisation of the political culture of Catholics, the transition from Jacobite to Jacobin, and a break with the century-old Catholic strategy of deferential supplication. The events of the 1780s and 1790s gave the Defenders a heightened sense of nationality. Groping towards a cultural nationalist statement, the Defenders lacked the vocabulary to express it. Appealing to history for authenticity and legitimacy, Defenderism collided with the classic Enlightenment project of the United Irishmen. But it was the Burkean-Defender paradigm that would flourish in the nineteenth century, as the Enlightenment politics of the United Irishmen lost impetus and definition under the challenge of romanticism, nationalism, and sectarianism.

In the Irish context these forces fused into cultural nationalism, which valorised the past, the customary, the particularist, at the expense of the new, the cosmopolitan, the universal. It acknowledged the primacy and potency of a particularist past and argued that a nation could only be assembled organically, not artificially by the law or the state. In Ireland cultural nationalism inevitably intersected with Catholicism, which could represent itself as the traditional and customary religion of Irishmen, the 'national' religion of Irishmen, and the principal repository of a sense of a distinctive Irish nationhood. The O'Connellite campaign was to empower this reading of Irish history, and in this sense O'Connell built on Burke and the Defenders, not on the United Irishmen.[232] In such a formulation there was little role or need for the Protestant gentry, whose subsequent legislative euthanasia merely confirmed the writing on the demesne walls. Thus, despite the fact that it remained a profoundly agrarian society in many ways, Ireland was the first European country to shed its landed gentry.[233] In this sense the seemingly stable seventeenth-century settlement proved in the long term to be quite brittle. The ultimate winners were the big-farm class; their resistance and stability derived substantially from their self-image as an old landowning class, displaced in the seventeenth-century upheavals. This sense of identity gave the Irish big-farm class a character different from that in other European societies. It also created an ambiguous position for the Irish gentry of that time. As Arthur Browne memorably phrased it in a 1787 debate, 'Elsewhere landed title was purchase, in Ireland it was forfeiture. The old proprietor kept alive the memory of his claim. Property in Ireland resembled the thin soil of volcanic countries spread lightly over subterranean fires.'[234] These ambiguities make it difficult to slot Ireland simply into an *ancien régime* model and force considerations of colonial contexts.

NOTES

1 S. Connolly, *Religion, law, and power: the making of Protestant Ireland, 1660–1760* (Oxford, 1992). For an alternative viewpoint, see T. Bartlett, ' "A people made rather for copies than originals": the Anglo-Irish, 1760–1800' in *Int. Hist. Rev.*, xii (1990), pp. 11–25; idem, 'The rise and fall of the Protestant nation, 1690–1800' in *Éire-Ireland*, xxvi (1991), pp. 7–18.

2 L. Cullen, *The emergence of modern Ireland, 1600–1900* (London, 1981); T. Bartlett, 'An end to moral economy: the Irish militia disturbances of 1793' in *Past & Present*, no. 99 (1983), pp. 41–64; Connolly, *Religion, law, and power*. For a general discussion of the literature on *mentalité*, see R. Darnton, *The kiss of Lamourette: reflections in cultural history* (London, 1990).

3 D. Dickson, 'Middlemen' in T. Bartlett and D. Hayton (ed.), *Penal era and golden age* (Belfast, 1979), pp. 162–85; L. Cullen, 'Catholic social classes under the penal laws' in T. Power and K. Whelan (ed.), *Endurance and emergence: Catholics in Ireland in the eighteenth century* (Dublin, 1990), pp. 57–84.

4 J. Bateman, *A just and true relation of Josiah Bateman's concerns under the Rt. Hon. Richard, earl of Burlington, ever since the year 1713* (n.p., n.d. [*ca.* 1734?]), p. 8.

5 Cited in J.H. Andrews, *Plantation acres* (Belfast, 1985), p. 84.

6 L. Cullen, 'Catholics under the penal laws' in *Eighteenth-Century Ireland*, i (1986), pp. 23–36.

7 J.G. Simms, *The Williamite confiscation in Ireland, 1690–1703* (London, 1956), pp. 193–6.

8 *N.H.I.*, iv, 16.

9 Obituary in *Monthly Magazine*, July 1797, p. 70; E. O'Byrne (ed.), *The convert rolls* (Dublin, 1981), p. 115.

10 *Dialogue between a Protestant and a papist* (Dublin, 1752), p. 10.

11 T. Power, 'Converts' in Power and Whelan, *Endurance and emergence*, pp. 101–28; W. Osborough, 'Catholics, land, and the popery acts of Anne', ibid., pp. 21–56.

12 Kavanagh estate papers, N.L.I. mic. 7,155; G.O., MS 471; P.R.O.N.I., T.3331.

13 *Census Ire., 1659*, p. 358.

14 For the Butlers, see K. Whelan, 'The Catholic church in County Tipperary, 1700–1900' in

W. Nolan (ed.), *Tipperary: history and society* (Dublin, 1985), pp. 215-55. For the Clan-rickardes, see P. Melvin, 'The composition of the Galway gentry' in *Ir. Geneal.*, vii (1986), pp. 81–96.

15 W. Smyth, 'Exploring the social and cultural topographies of sixteenth- and seventeenth-cen-tury County Dublin' in F. Aalen and K. Whelan (ed.), *Dublin city and county: from prehistory to present* (Dublin, 1992), p. 173.

16 K. Whelan, 'The Catholic community in eighteenth-century County Wexford' in Power and Whelan, *Endurance and emergence*, pp. 137–44.

17 Cited in Dickson, 'Middlemen', p. 172.

18 S. Madden, *Reflections and resolutions proper to the gentlemen of Ireland* (Dublin, 1738), p. 104.

19 R. Hedges (Ross Castle) to ––-, 8 June 1714 (Nat. Archives, MS 757).

20 Petition of fifteen gentlemen of County Cork, 3 June 1747, cited in D. Dickson, 'An economic history of the Cork region in the eighteenth century' (Ph.D. dissertation, T.C.D., 1977), pp. 144–5. James Lyons, reporting to Rome in August 1763 about a candidate for episcopal advancement in Dublin, observed: 'He is in the first place a man of low birth, and that is something which does not pass unnoticed in this country' (*Collect. Hib.*, xi (1968), p. 104).

21 J. Taylor to Wall, 21 February 1775, cited in G. Lyne, 'Landlord-tenant relations on the Shelburne estate in Kenmare, Bonane, and Tuosist, 1770–1785' in *Kerry Arch. Hist. Soc. Jn.*, xii (1979), pp. 47–8.

22 Cited in J. Andrews, 'Charles Vallancey and the map of Ireland' in *Geog. Jn.*, cxxxii (1996), p. 59.

23 S. Ní Chinnéide (ed.), 'A new view of eighteenth-century life in Kerry' in *Kerry Arch. Hist. Soc. Jn.*, vi (1973), p. 93.

24 G. O'Malley, 'The present state of the name and fameyly of O'Malley in Ireland in yr. of Our Lord 1776' in O. O'Malley, 'O'Malleys between 1651 and 1725' in *Galway Arch. Hist. Jn.*, xxv (1952), pp. 32–46.

25 R. O'Connell to M. Leyne, 20 August 1779, in M. O'Connell, *The last colonel of the Irish Brigade* (London, 1892), pp. 223–4.

26 Cited in J. Brady, *Catholics and Catholicism in the eighteenth-century press* (Maynooth, 1965), p. 311.

27 Cited in Bagwell, *Stuarts*, iii, 32–5.

28 A. Dobbs, *An essay on the trade and improvement of Ireland* (Dublin, 1731).

29 R. Cox, *A charge to the grand jury of County Cork* (Cork, 1740), p. 7.

30 Cited in E. Johnston, *Ireland in the eighteenth century* (Dublin, 1972), p. 230.

31 E. MacLysaght (ed.), *The Kenmare manuscripts* (Dublin, 1942), p. 230.

32 J. Taylor to Shelburne, 5 July 1773, in [Sixth] marquis of Lansdowne, *Glanerought and the Petty-Fitzmaurices* (Oxford, 1937), p. 75.

33 Young, *Tour in Ire.*, ii, app. p. 13. See also ibid., 'On the tenantry of Ireland', pp. 17–25.

34 S. Ó Tuama (ed.), *Caoineadh Airt Uí Laoghaire* (Dublin, 1963). Compare the description by Denis McCarthy of Nedeen ('a reduced gentleman') of his clothes when wealthy: he 'used to wear broadcloath and ruffles and three-leged wig with fringe of gold and Brussel's lace cravat and fine beaver with gold lace and cockade' (Lansdowne, *Glanerought*, p. 90).

35 *F.L.J.*, 29 November–1 December 1788.

36 Cited by R. Lightboum in 'Eighteenth- and nineteenth-century visitors to Kilkenny' in *Old Kilk. Rev.*, iii, no. 1 (1983), pp. 6–7.

37 C. Woods (ed.), *Journals and memoirs of Thomas Russell, 1791–95* (Dublin, 1991).

38 G. Stokes (ed.), *Pococke's tour in Ireland in 1752* (Dublin, 1891), pp. 71–2. For examples in Carlow and Kilkenny cited by the Catholic bishop of Ossory in the 1830s, see E. Larkin (ed.), *Alexis de Tocqueville's journey in Ireland, July–August 1835* (Dublin, 1990), p. 63.

39 *F.L.J.*, 22–25 August 1770.

40 *F.L.J.*, 30 November–2 December 1774. Purcell's will added an unusual clause: 'My body shall be preceded to the grave by twelve of the best performers on the small pipes which can

conveniently be had, to whom I will give one crown each for their trouble in playing my favourite tune of Granuail'.

41 *F.L.J.*, 8–11 December 1790.

42 *F.L.J.*, 26–30 January 1793.

43 *Faulkner's Dublin Journal*, 29 February 1752.

44 M. Hickson, *Selections from old Kerry records* (London, 1874), p. 158. O'Mahony held the barony of Dunkerron and Iveragh under a grand lease of 1697 from the Petty family, a leasehold of *ca.* 20,000 acres. He was also a tenant on the Evans, Pritty, and Stopford estates in Kerry and Cork (Lansdowne, *Glanerought*, p. 53).

45 G. Lyne, 'Dr Dermot Lyne: an Irish Catholic landholder in Cork and Kerry under the penal laws' in *Kerry Arch. Hist. Soc. Jn.*, viii (1975), pp. 54–7; idem, 'The Mac Fínín Dubh O'Sullivans of Tuosist and Bearehaven', ibid., ix (1976), pp. 32–67; idem, 'Land tenure in Kenmare and Tuosist, 1696–1716', ibid., x (1977), pp. 19–54.

46 *Seasonable advice to Protestants containing some means of reviving and strengthening the Protestant interest* (2nd ed., Cork, 1745), p. 23.

47 MacLysaght, *Kenmare manuscripts*, pp. 183, 187, 190.

48 Lansdowne, *Glanerought*, p. 166. John Lyne of Cashelkealty was similarly described as being 'so surrounded by a clan that he fears nothing'.

49 Ibid.

50 *F.L.J.*, 12–15 July 1780. See also the long account in the collection of news cuttings, N.M.I. 6–1935, under 14 July 1780.

51 [H. Blake], *Letters from the Irish highlands* (2nd ed., London, 1825), pp. 12–13. For a report of deliberate wrecking by this family at Inishboffin in 1741, see Brady, *Catholics*, p. 63.

52 R. St. George Mansergh St. George to Dublin Castle, 17 March 1794 (Nat. Archives, R.P., 620/21/18).

53 J. Burtchaell and D. Dowling, 'Social and economic conflict in County Kilkenny, 1600–1800' in W. Nolan and K. Whelan (ed.), *Kilkenny: history and society* (Dublin, 1990), p. 257.

54 C. Ó Danachair, 'An Rí, the king: an example of traditional social organisation' in *R.S.A.I. Jn.*, iii (1981), pp. 14–28; Wakefield, *Ire.*, ii, 544–5. For an account of Ned Joyce and Edward O'Malley, see [Blake], *Letters*, pp. 41, 106. For Ó Flaitheartha, see T. Robinson, *Stones of Aran* (Dublin, 1986), p. 6. For a contrast to Wakefield, see Charles O Hara's comment in 1772 on the Sligo gentry as 'mostly the descendants of adventurers who have rather the spirit of domination handed down to them' (N.L.I., MS 20,397).

55 Edith Somerville and Martin Ross, *Irish memories* (London, 1917), p. 4. For similar comments, see R. Bell, *A description of the conditions and manners as well as the moral and political character, education, etc., of the peasantry of Ireland such as they were between the years 1780 and 1790* (London, 1804), p. 7, and Wakefield, *Ire.*, ii, 545. ('A Roman Catholic gentleman of fortune has thus a paternal character and is looked up to with affection by the population of a very extensive district. Towards the Protestant landlords there is no such feeling; their influence is limited to their own immediate tenants.')

56 J. Taylor to Shelburne, 9 November 1773, cited in Lyne, 'Kenmare, Bonane, and Tuosist, 1770–1785', p. 50.

57 S. Ó Tuama and T. Kinsella (ed.), *An Duanaire: poems of the dispossessed* (Dublin, 1990), p. 29.

58 J. Kelly (ed.), *The letters of Lord Chief Baron Edward Willes, 1757–1762* (Aberystwyth, 1990), p. 29.

59 Bell, *Description*, p. 1.

60 *Londonderry Jn.*, 25 January 1831.

61 C. O'Conor, *Memoirs of the life and writings of the late Charles O'Conor of Belanagare* (Dublin, 1796), p. 162.

62 Young, *Tour in Ire.*, i, 185.

63 *Dublin Evening Post*, 4 February 1786.

64 Kelly, *Willes*, pp. 90–1.

65 A. Day (ed.), *Letters from Georgian Ireland: the correspondence of Mary Delaney, 1731–1768* (Belfast, 1991), p. 124.

66 [Blake], *Letters*, pp. 14–15.

67 [M. Whitty], article in Walsh scrapbook, N.L.I., MS 14,040 (unpaginated).

68 A. Griffith, 'An account of the barony of Forth' in *Dublin Magazine* (1765), p. 505. For a remarkably similar account *ca.* 1780, see Bell, *Description*, pp. 18–19.

69 L. Whyte, *Original poems on various subjects* (Dublin, 1740), preface, p. vii.

70 *The compleat Irish traveller* (London, 1788), i, 78–9.

71 J. Condon, 'Don Jorge Rian of Inch, County Tipperary, 1748–1805' in *Ir. Ancestor*, xvii, no. 1 (1986), pp. 5–10.

72 J. Mannion, 'A transatlantic merchant fishery: Richard Welsh of New Ross and the Sweetmans of Newbawn in Newfoundland, 1734–1862' in K. Whelan (ed.), *Wexford: history and society* (Dublin, 1987), pp. 373–421. For another example, see E. Ó Néill, *Gleann an Óir* (Dublin, 1988), a case-study of the O'Neill family of south Tipperary and south Kilkenny. The thrust of this book is summarised in K. Whelan, 'Gaelic survivals' in *Ir. Review*, vii (1989), pp. 139–43.

73 K. Whelan, 'The Catholic parish, the Catholic chapel, and village development in Ireland' in *Ir. Geog.*, xvi (1983), pp. 1–15.

74 *Wexford People*, 21 August 1909.

75 W. Grattan Flood (ed.), 'The diocesan manuscripts of Ferns during the rule of Bishop Sweetman, 1745–1786' in *Archiv. Hib.*, iii (1914), p. 117. For rows over precedence in Catholic chapels among these old families, see Lansdowne, *Glanerought*, p. 68; [P. Kennedy], *Evenings in the Duffry* (Dublin, 1869), pp. 299–312.

76 K. Whelan, 'The regional impact of Irish Catholicism, 1700–1850' in W. Smyth and K. Whelan (ed.), *Common ground: essays on the historical geography of Ireland* (Cork, 1988), pp. 253–77.

77 K. O'Shea (ed.), 'Bishop Moylan's *Relatio status*, 1785' in *Kerry Arch. Hist. Soc. Jn.*, vii (1974), pp. 24–5.

78 Cullen, 'Catholic social classes', pp. 57–84.

79 W. Tighe, *Statistical observations relative to the county of Kilkenny* (Dublin, 1802), pp. 382–6. For equivalent comments on the Walsh farm at Earlsrath, see ibid., p. 387.

80 A. Atkinson, *The Irish tourist* (Dublin, 1815), pp. 471–2.

81 J. Andrews, *A paper landscape: the Ordnance Survey in nineteenth-century Ireland* (Oxford, 1975), p. 223.

82 J. Loveday (ed.), *Diary of a tour in 1732 through parts of England, Wales, Ireland, and Scotland made by John Loveday of Caversham* (Edinburgh, 1890), p. 58.

83 J. Graves and J. Prim, *The history, architecture, and antiquities of the cathedral church of St. Canice, Kilkenny* (Dublin, 1885), p. 137.

84 M. McGrath (ed.), *Cinnlae Amhlaoibh Uí Shuilleabháin* (4 vols, London, 1928–34), iii, 15 (my translation).

85 Wakefield, *Ire.*, ii, 628.

86 Will of Robert Keating, 1729, in *Ir. Geneal.*, iv (1938), p. 125.

87 K. Whelan, 'Catholic mobilisation, 1750–1850' in P. Bergeron and L. Cullen (ed.), *Culture et pratiques politiques en France et en Irlande XVIe–XVIIe siècle* (Paris, 1991), pp. 235–58.

88 B. Browne and K. Whelan, 'The Browne families of County Wexford' in Whelan, *Wexford*, p. 478.

89 Cited in J. O'Donoghue, 'The Scullys of Kilfeakle: Catholic middlemen of the 1770s' in *Tipp. Hist. Jn.*, ii (1989), pp. 38–51.

90 N.L.I., MS 27,577.

91 J. Downes (Adamstown) to J. Colclough (Tintern Abbey), 2 November 1801, N.L.I., MS 29,766 (25).

92 M. Whitty to R.R. Madden, 14 May 1868, in *The Past*, vii (1964), pp. 127–30.

93 Whelan, 'Catholic community', pp. 159–64; J. O'Shea, *Priests, politics, and society in post-famine Ireland: a study of County Tipperary, 1850–1891* (Dublin, 1983), pp. 326–60.

94 L. Cullen, *The hidden Ireland: reassessment of a concept* (Gigginstown, 1988); T. Jones Hughes, 'The large farm in nineteenth-century Ireland' in A. Gailey and D. Ó hÓgáin (ed.), *Gold under the furze* (Dublin, 1982), pp. 92–100; K. Whelan, 'Society and settlement in eighteenth-century Ireland' in G. Dawe and J. Foster (ed.), *The poet's place* (Belfast, 1991), pp. 45–62.

95 P. Knight, *Erris in the Irish highlands* (Dublin, 1836), p. 104.

96 C. Otway, *A tour in Connaught comprising sketches of Clonmacnoise, Joyce Country, and Achill* (Dublin, 1839), p. 252.

97 Young, *Tour in Ire.*, i, 126.

98 J. Burrows, 'A tour in Ireland in 1773' (P.R.O.N.I., T. 3551, p. 99).

99 *Census Ire., 1841*, County Cork.

100 Bell, *Description*, pp. 8–9. Compare this account with Madden's in 1738: 'rather huts than houses, and those of our cottiers are built like bird's nests of dirt wrought together and a few sticks and some straw, and like those, are generally removed once a year' (Madden, *Reflections*, p. 35).

101 W. Eastwood, 'An account of the parish of Tacumshane' in Shaw Mason, *Parochial survey*, iii, 426; W. Parker, *Observations on the intended amendment of the Irish grand jury laws* (Cork, 1816), p. 134.

102 N. Williams (ed.), *Páirlimint Cloinne Tomáis* (Dublin, 1981), p. 55. See also the passage on pp. 60–1.

103 P. Kelly (ed.), 'The improvement of Ireland' in *Anal. Hib.*, xxxv (1992), pp. 83–4.

104 T. Ó Fiaich (ed.), *Art Mac Cumhaigh: dánta* (Dublin, 1973), pp. 102–5.

105 B. Ó Buachalla (ed.), *Peadar Ó Doirnín: amhráin* (Dublin, 1969), p. 55.

106 Ó Tuama, *Caoineadh*, p. 62.

107 Archbp William King to archbp of Canterbury, 2 June 1717 (Pearse Street Library, Gilbert MS 28, p. 327).

108 Cited in Connolly, *Religion, law, and power*, p. 306.

109 W. Hume, 'Remarks on my Lord Rockingham's Irish estate, 1729/30' (Fitzwilliam MSS, N.L.I., MS 6054, p. 16).

110 *Seasonable advice*, pp. 19, 21.

111 Ibid., p. 19.

112 *To the Protestant inhabitants of Great Britain and Ireland* (Dublin, 1798), p. 12. See also his observation: 'Arts, sciences, manufactures, schools, colleges, and a civilized manner of living, improvements in the cultivation of land, architecture, and trade of all descriptions have been attempted to be forced by the English on the sulky, sanguinary barbarians [Irish Catholics] without effect' (p. 7). See S.P.O., R.P., 620/39/10.

113 For examples, see *Belfast Newsletter*, 17 July 1750; 9 September, 21 October, 13 December 1763; 27, 31 May, 19, 23 August 1768; 16 February, 6 March, 27 April 1770; 11–15 October 1776.

114 Madden, *Reflections*, p. 7.

115 H. Senior, *Orangeism in Ireland and Britain, 1795–1836* (London, 1966); Froude, *Ire.*, i, 659; ii, 132–3.

116 G. Sampson, *A memoir explanatory of the chart and survey of the county of Londonderry, Ireland* (London, 1814), i, 336–7.

117 Z. Cornock, Cromwellsfort, Co. Wexford, cited in Wakefield, *Ire.*, i, 410.

118 W. McAfee, 'The colonisation of the Maghera region of south Derry during the seventeenth and eighteenth centuries' in *Ulster Folklife*, xxiii (1977), pp. 70–91.

119 Hume, 'Rockingham's estate', p. 19. For essentially similar observations, see also ibid., pp. 20–1, 23, 25, 26–7, 44, 47, 70, 109.

120 I would like to thank W.H. Crawford for his observations on these points.

121 J. Barber, 'Memoir of my experiences in 1798' (typescript in N.L.I., p. 9).

122 A. Meadows to Dublin Castle, 8 May 1822 (Nat. Archives, S.O.C. 2509/11).

123 E. Hay, *History of the insurrection in the county of Wexford in the year of 1798* (Dublin, 1803), p. 204.

124 Larkin, *De Tocqueville's journey*, p. 63.

125 2nd earl of Rosse to Lord Redesdale, 30 March 1822 (P.R.O.N.I., T. 3030/13/1).

126 J. Brownrigg to Lord Downshire, 31 August 1815, cited in W. Maguire, *The Downshire estates in Ireland, 1801–45* (Oxford, 1972), pp. 262–4.

127 W. Armstrong to bursar, T.C.D., 10 May 1850, cited in R. McCarthy, 'The estates of Trinity College, Dublin, in the nineteenth century' (Ph.D. dissertation, T.C.D., 1982), p. 196.

128 K. Miller, 'The erosion of the Protestant middle class in southern Ireland during the pre-famine era' (unpublished paper), p. 1.

129 T. Rawson, *Statistical survey of the county of Kildare* (Dublin, 1807), p. 54; W. Stokes, *Observations on the population and resources of Ireland* (Dublin, 1821), p. 31.

130 Browne and Whelan, 'Browne families', pp. 467–89.

131 Miles Byrne, *Memoirs* (2 vols, Paris, 1863), i, 3.

132 J. O'Keefe, *Recollections of the life of John O'Keefe written by himself* (2 vols, London, 1826), i, 8–9.

133 B. Ó Buachalla, 'Irish Jacobite poetry' in *Ir. Review*, xii (1992), pp. 40–9; idem, 'Jacobitism and nationalism: the Irish literary evidence' (paper presented to the conference 'Nations and nationalisms in the eighteenth century', U.C.D., 1992: idem, '*Parliament na mBan:* the making of an Irish Jacobite' (lecture at U.C.D., 26 February 1992).

134 'The ancient inheritance of the Waddings of Ballycogley' (N.L.I., MS 5193, ff 154–9).

135 J. Colhoun to Abercorn, 10 April 1752 (P.R.O.N.I., T. 2541).

136 Lansdowne, *Glanerought*, p. 165.

137 Wakefield, *Ire.*, i, 248.

138 Byrne, *Memoirs*, i, 253.

139 Cited in T. Garvey, 'The case of Edward Garvey of Rosmindle' in *Cathair na Mart*, vi (1986), p. 69.

140 Whelan, 'Catholic community', pp 155–9.

141 J. O'Rourke, *The case of Count O'Rourke presented to his majesty in June 1784* (London, 1784). See copy in N.L.I., MS 52/K/4B.

142 G. O'Malley, Autobiography (N.L.I. mic. 208, p. 543).

143 Cited in T. Bartlett, *The fall and rise of the Irish nation: the Catholic question, 1690–1830* (Dublin, 1992), p. 288. For two examples of this attitude in the 1790s, see [J. Quigley], *The life of the Rev. James Coigley* (London, 1798); E. Sweetman, *Speech delivered to the freeholders of County Wexford* (Dublin, 1792).

144 J. Dougherty (Inishowen) to M. O'Connell (Derrynane), 22 March 1765 (N.L.I. Reports on private collections, no. 361).

145 Wakefield, *Ire.*, ii, 745. See also his comment about Ulster Catholics that 'they are a miserable people, without an aristocracy to which they can fly, either for example or protection, and who drag out a wretched existence in penury' (ibid., p. 649).

146 T. Lane to Downshire, 12 October 1799 (P.R.O.N.I., D.607/6/200).

147 C. Teeling, *Personal narrative of the Irish rebellion of 1798* (Dublin, 1828), p. 115.

148 Ibid., pp. 103–5 (referring to a descendant of Patrick Sarsfield who kept a public house near Slane in County Meath).

149 Young, *Tour in Ire.*, ii, 54. See also Bell, *Description*, pp. 31–3.

150 D. Thompson (ed.), *The Irish journals of Elizabeth Smith, 1840–1850* (Oxford, 1980), p. 6.

151 J. Walker, 'An historical essay on the Irish stage' in *R.I.A. Trans.* (1785–9), pp. 75–6. See also H. Morris, 'Irish wake games' in *Béaloideas*, viii (1938), p. 123; *Anthologica Hibernica* (December 1794); *Cinnlae Amhlaoibh*, iii, 39.

152 Kelly, *Willes*, p. 79.

153 Young, *Tour in Ire.*, ii, 133.

154 Carrigan MSS, St. Kieran's College, Kilkenny (N.L.I. mic. 903).

155 S. Fenton, *It all happened: reminiscences* (Dublin, 1948), p. 171.

156 K. Nicholls, 'Catholics and the popery laws' (unpublished paper), p. 2.

157 Hay MSS (in the possession of William Sweetman, Whitemills, Co. Wexford).

158 Young, *Tour in Ire.*, i, 249.

159 Willes referred to the 'red hot' Protestants of Tipperary in the 1760s (Kelly, *Willes*, p. 46), while Foster Archer commented in 1801: 'There is not in Ireland a county where the names of Englishman and Protestant are more hated than in the county of Cork. They are synonymous in their phrase and the object of their deep and bigotted hatred' (P. Lysaght, 'Rev. Foster Archer's visit to Limerick and Clare, 1801' in *N. Munster Antiq. Jn.*, xviii [1976], p. 53).

160 See especially W. Burke, *History of Clonmel* (Waterford, 1907), pp. 393, 404–5, for lists of those targetted. These incidents also left an indelible impression on Edmund Burke. See L. Cullen, 'Burke, Ireland, and revolution' in *Eighteenth-Century Life*, xvi (1992), pp. 21–42.

161 J. Donnelly, 'Irish agrarian rebellion: the Whiteboys of 1769–76' in *R.I.A. Proc.*, clxxxiii (1983), pp. 293–331.

162 Lansdowne, *Glanerought*, p. 62. See also Froude, *Ire.*, iii, 106, for similar comments by Townshend in 1770.

163 Bartlett, *Fall and rise*, pp 111–12.

164 C. O'Conor, *Ortelius improved* (Dublin, 1770). For its reissue in 1792, see *Hib. Jn.*, 15 February 1792. For the context, see J. Andrews, 'The cartographer as antiquarian in pre-Ordnance Survey Ireland' in C. Thomas (ed.), *Rural landscape and communities* (Dublin, 1986), pp 31–63.

165 Musgrave, *Memoirs*, app., p. 110.

166 Westmorland to Pitt, 18 February 1792 (P.R.O.N.I., T.3319/12).

167 W. Todd Jones, *A letter to the societies of United Irishmen of the town of Belfast* (Dublin, 1792), pp. 21–2.

168 *The United Irishmen: a tale founded on facts* (Dublin, 1798), pp. 5–6. For other references to the map, see Wakefield, *Ire.*, ii, 644–5; H. Townsend, *Statistical survey of County Cork* (Dublin, 1810), p. 78.

169 Froude, *Ire.*, ii, 553.

170 Ibid., iii, 386.

171 *Charlemont* MSS, i, 48.

172 *Rutland* MSS, iii, 281.

173 Ibid., p. 285.

174 Ibid.

175 A. Ravina, *Burguesia extranjera y comercio Atlantico: la empresa comercial Irlandesa en Canarias, 1703–1771* (Tenerife, 1985).

176 S. Ní Chinnéide (ed.), 'A journey from Mullingar to Loughrea in 1791' in *Old Athlone Soc. Jn.*, ii (1978), p. 18.

177 *D.E.P.*, 24 January, 4, 9, 18, 25 February 1786.

178 *Rutland* MSS, iii, 279–81. A. Zondari, archbp of Adana, to Cardinall Buon-Compagni, 28 January, 7, 21 March 1786, in *Collect. Hib.*, xi (1968), pp. 73–4.

179 Address of Roman Catholics of County Roscommon to lord lieutenant, in *D.E.P.*, 28 February 1786.

180 *Rutland MSS*, iii, 284.

181 *F.L.J.*, 30 September–4 October 1786. For another account of the O'Connor incident, see Bell, *Description*, pp. 27–8. For a truly extraordinary account of the O'Connor family, see S. Gibbon, *The recollections of Skeffington Gibbon from 1796 to the present year 1829, being an epitome of the lives and characters of the nobility and gentry of Roscommon, the genealogy of those who are descended from the kings of Connaught, and a memoir of the late Madame O'Conor Dun* (Dublin, 1829).

182 R. Edwards (ed.), 'The minute book of the Catholic Committee, 1773–1792' in *Archiv. Hib.*, ix (1942), pp. 157–8. As late as 1826 the Catholic hierarchy still felt it necessary to declare:

'The Catholics of Ireland, far from claiming any right or title to forfeited lands resulting from any right, title, or interest which their ancestors may have had therein, declare upon oath that they will defend to the utmost of their power the settlement and arrangement of property in this country, as established by the laws now in being' (J. Doyle, *An essay on the Catholic claims* [Dublin, 1826], p. 310).

183 *Yelverton's charge to the Antrim grand jury of Carrickfergus, 17 June 1797* (printed broadsheet in R.I.A., Day MS 12/10/13, p. 75).

184 B. Chapman to Shelburne, 25 April 1797 (Shelburne MS, Ann Arbor, Michigan). In a later letter dated 20 May 1797, Chapman made the remarkable comment: 'I should not omit to argue with all this kingdom in acknowledging the legitimate fairness of your lordship's great estates here. My family thought proper to get rid of that imputation in the County Kerry estate belonging to Lord Desmond; we sold to Lord Cork in the reign of James the 1st.'

185 *An Irishman's letter to the people called Defenders* (Dublin, 1795), p. 4.

186 *Report from the committee of secrecy . . . of the House of Commons of Ireland* (2nd ed., London, 1798), p. 28.

187 Byrne, *Memoirs*, i, 4.

188 A. O'Connor, *The state of Ireland* (London, 1798), p. 17.

189 Ibid., p. 104.

190 *The cry of the poor for bread* (Dublin, 1795), broadsheet copy in Nat. Archives, R.P. 620/18/14. For another printed Philanthropic handbill, see T. Bartlett, 'Defenders and Defenderism in 1795' in *I.H.S.*, xxiv, no. 95 (May 1985), p. 390.

191 Information of Thomas Kennedy concerning Dublin Defenders, 15 March 1796 (Nat. Archives, R.P. 620/23/59).

192 *Christ in triumph coming to judgement* (Strabane, 1795), p. 31 (copy in Nat. Archives, R.P. 620/29/8).

193 *The Union doctrine or poor man's catechism* (Dublin, 1798) (copy in Nat. Archives, R.P. 620/43/1, reproduced in Musgrave, *Memoirs* (2nd ed., Dublin, 1801), pp. 166–70, where he notes that it was published and circulated since the rebellion had been put down).

194 Judge R. Day's charge to the grand jury of County Westmeath, 12 April 1798 (R.I.A., MS 12/W/11, p. 39. Compare General Thomas Knox's comment to Pelham, 14 May 1797, that 'the present is a contest of the poor against the rich' (B.L., Add. MS 33104, f. 59).

195 Musgrave, *Memoirs*, p. 224.

196 Ibid., app., p. 160.

197 *Old Ballymena: a history of Ballymena during the 1798 rebellion* (Ballymena, 1857), p. 36.

198 T. Dunne, 'Edgeworthstown in fact and fiction, 1760–1840' in R. Gillespie and G. Moran (ed.) *Longford: essays in county history* (Dublin, 1991), pp. 95–122.

199 See the sequence of letters in G. Lyne, 'George Frederick Beltz, Lancaster herald, and his quest in Ireland in 1802 for the ancestry of Sir Richard Joseph Sullivan, part II' in *Ir. Geneal.*, vi, no. 4 (1983), pp. 491–4; part III, ibid., no. 5 (1985), p. 642.

200 Cited in R. McDowell, *The Irish administration, 1801–1914* (London, 1964), p. 272.

201 Cited in Andrews, *Paper landscape*, p. 167.

202 P. MacWilliam and A. Day (ed.), *Ordnance Survey memoir for County Fermanagh* (Belfast, 1991), p. 75.

203 Westmorland to Dundas, 24 May 1793 (H.O. 100/43/319–20).

204 Froude, *Ire.*, iii, 116.

205 Rosse to Redesdale, 9 May 1822 (P.R.O.N.I., T.3030/13).

206 *Proceedings of the Irish parliament in 1787* (Dublin, 1787), under 19 February 1787.

207 A. Wolfe to E. Cooke, 27 August 1795 (Nat. Archives, R.P. 620/22/136).

208 J. Barrington, *Personal sketches of his own time* (2 vols, Dublin, 1828), i, 150.

209 Whyte, *Original poems*, p. 72.

210 *D.E.P.*, 9 February 1786.

211 W.H. Maxwell, *Wild sports of the west* (London, 1832), pp. 375–6.

212 *F.L.J.*, 8–11 August 1787.

213 *F.L.J.*, 26–29 November 1788.

214 S. Crumpe, *An essay on the best means of providing employment for the people* (Dublin, 1793), pp. 431–2.

215 *Seasonable advice*, p. 32. Compare Edmund Burke's advice to his Cork Catholic relatives that they stick together (*Burke corr.*, i, 289).

216 Wakefield, *Ire.*, ii, 645.

217 *F.L.J.*, 25–28 February 1778.

218 Wakefield, *Ire.*, ii, 743: Tighe, *Kilkenny*, p. 385.

219 N.L.I., Drogheda papers, MS 9749.

220 Larkin, *De Tocqueville's journey*, p. 41.

221 Madden, *Reflections*, p. 103.

222 I am grateful to Caoimhín Ó Danachair for this elegant County Limerick definition of a strong farmer.

223 For hurling, see L. O'Cathnia, *Scéal na hIománá* (Dublin, 1981). For abductions, see M. Weiner, *Matters of felony* (London, 1967). See also *F.L.J.*, 21 April, 28 August 1779; 2 February 1780.

224 S. Connolly, *Priests and people in pre-famine Ireland, 1780–1845* (Dublin, 1982); E. Larkin, *The historical dimensions of Irish Catholicism* (Washington, D.C., 1984).

225 R.I.A., MS 12/M/11, p. 395.

226 Lansdowne, *Glanerought*, p. 171.

227 S. Deane, 'Edmund Burke, 1791–1797' in S. Deane (ed.), *The Field Day anthology of Irish writing* (3 vols, Derry, 1991), ii, 807–9; C. Cruise O'Brien, *The great melody: a thematic biography of Edmund Burke* (London, 1992), esp. pp. 3–57; Cullen, 'Burke, Ireland, and revolution'; idem, 'Catholics of the Blackwater Valley, 1730–1780' (lecture at T.C.D., 1991).

228 Compare Burke with Skeffington Gibbon's comments on those who celebrated the 1688 settlement in Ireland: 'I do not wonder at the progeny of those wolves and tigers idolizing those detestable and sanguinary times, as it rescued many of their ancestors from the worst and most abject stations in life and placed them and their posterity in the mansions and wide domains of the ancient nobles of the kingdom (Gibbon, *Recollections*, pp. 153–4).

229 Bartlett, 'Defenders and Defenderism', pp. 376, 390.

230 Bell, *Description*, p. 27.

231 Bartlett, 'Defenders and Defenderism', p. 385.

232 K. Whelan, 'The United Irishmen, the Enlightenment, and popular culture' in D. Dickson, D. Keogh, and K. Whelan (ed.), *The United Irishmen: republicanism, radicalism, and rebellion* (Dublin, 1993).

233 C. Ó Gráda, *Ireland: a new economic history, 1780–1939* (Oxford, 1994), p. 257.

234 Cited in Froude, *Ire.*, iii, 523.

7

The 'Merry Wake'

GEARÓID Ó CRUALAOICH

Writing on the ecclesiastical organisation of Ireland in the mid-eighteenth century, J.L. McCracken notes that Roman Catholic bishops 'had to contend with the ignorance and superstition of their flocks and the excesses which attended traditional gatherings'.[1] Pilgrimages, pattern-festivities, and wakes are identified as phenomena specially incurring ecclesiastical disapproval because they manifested in officially unacceptable ways a religious sensibility on the part of the rural masses that derives as much from a Celtic or pagan cosmological tradition as from a Christian one. This native or ancestral religious sensibility, at once alternative to and co-existent with orthodox Christian values, beliefs, and ritual, should not be seen, in the eighteenth and nineteenth centuries, as an ever feebler and more marginalised vestige of archaic Irish culture. The evidence suggests that as a part of the world view and life style of the majority, non-élite population which experienced both immense demographic growth and radical socioeconomic transformation in the period in question, ancestral Irish religious belief and practice responded to and reflected prevailing social and historical circumstances in a way that made them in that age very much a 'going concern'. That the 'excessive' mortuary ritual characteristic of the rural Irish population in the early modern period should have proved resistant to official ecclesiastical exhortation and command until the early decades of the twentieth century suggests that the ritual in question was highly significant in the symbolic culture of the population that practised it. It also suggests that the ritual was functionally significant in relation to the structure and organisation of social relationships in the Irish eighteenth- and nineteenth-century worlds. It is a part of the aim of this essay to suggest that the merry wake was in fact a central social mechanism for the articulation of resistance—or at least reaction—on the part of the Irish peasantry to new forms of civil and clerical control in Irish society in early modern and modern times.

Seán Ó Súilleabháin's study of the games played at wakes includes a transcription of some of the edicts whereby Roman Catholic ecclesiastical authorities attempted to suppress the 'excesses' of the merry wake over a period of at least three hundred years.[2] The changing nature of the terms in which these edicts were expressed is evidence of the dynamic nature of the wake as a social institution. This evidence bears out my view that the practices of the wake and funeral in Irish popular culture that gave offence to eighteenth- and nineteenth-century Catholic church authorities are very far from being vestigial remnants clinging to the fringes of orthodoxy.

The earliest edict noted by Ó Súilleabháin was issued by the Synod of Armagh in 1614. We should note that the primary complaint of that synod in relation to contemporary popular mortuary rites was that the common people were, inappropriately it is claimed, imitating their social and financial betters in both the matter of wearing black clothing to express their grief and in the provision of a feast to those attending the wake and the funeral. These things were objectionable in the eyes of the bishops because the expenditure of money which they entailed was thought excessive and was said to impoverish the succeeding generation of the family indulging in it.[3] While the custom of dressing in fashionable and expensive black mourning clothes does not seem to have persisted into the eighteenth and nineteenth centuries among the common people, the question of the costs of the wake and funeral feasts remained an issue. The amateur antiquarian and folklorist Thomas Crofton Croker reported more than two hundred years later that it was usual for the peasantry to provide shroud and burial dress for themselves many years before they were wanted and not to resort to wearing any of these articles in life 'despite wretchedness and rags'.[4] He also claimed that it was not unusual 'to see even the tombstone in readiness and leaning against the cabin wall'.[5] If the practice of holding a feast involving conspicuous consumption by family, neighbours, and friends of the deceased began to establish itself in the ranks of the common people in the early modern period, as the evidence from the Synod of Armagh suggests, then such a practice was certainly firmly established by the time Crofton Croker described the popular culture of the south of Ireland in the early 1820s. He depicted the peasantry as 'looking forward to their death as a gala given by them', and even in the case of the 'destitute and friendless', seeking to 'hoard for the expenses of their wake and funeral'.[6]

A second ground on which the Synod of Armagh spoke out against customary wake practice in the early seventeenth century was that wakes were an occasion for the performance of 'obscene songs and suggestive games' that would be inappropriate even in legitimately merry contexts.[7] This is a charge that is constantly repeated across three hundred years, with the Maynooth Synod of 1927 still specifically outlawing the practice of engaging in immodest behaviour in the presence of the corpse.[8] Here again I believe that the symbolic significance and the important social function of such practices must be emphasised.

The problem of excessive expenditure on wake feasting and the problem of merriment, gaming, and misbehaviour are again alluded to in Statute 20 of the Synod of Tuam in 1660. Here it was suggested that such money as was involved would be better spent as mass offerings for the clergy or given as alms. In this statute censure was also expressed against those females who engaged in excessive keening and lamentation at wakes, something which had already been deplored a generation earlier in Statute 3 of the Tuam Synod of 1631. Merriment in the forms of music and dance were also deplored in 1660 in the edicts of the Synod of Armagh, where excommunication was prescribed for those indulging in such musical merriment, just as it was for those indulging in the provision or consumption of poitín ('*aqua composita*') during matchmaking.[9] Such direct, specific, and punitive opposition to the characteristic practices of the merry wake was repeated in the edicts of synods and in the pastoral letters of bishops through the later seventeenth and all of the eighteenth centuries in various parts of Ireland—Armagh, Meath, Dublin, Leighlin, Cashel and Emly, Waterford and Lismore, and so on.[10] Nevertheless, we find recorded from the diocese of Cashel and Emly for the years around 1800 a pastoral letter, which the archbishop there directed to be read each year before Christmas in every chapel of the archdiocese, and in which he solemnly warned his flock against the shameful and obscene behaviours at wakes which, he reported, are 'growing in strength daily', to the disadvantage of the faith.[11] Specifically identified as being most shameful and injurious were those games in which the officers and offices of the church were mimed and mocked—especially the sacrament of marriage. Those guilty of partaking in such games were to be excommunicated and to be required to undergo heavy penalties before being readmitted to the sacraments, including having to obtain written absolution from the archbishop himself or from the vicar general of the diocese. Such solemn prohibition from the wakehouse of the mimicry of the sacraments, especially marriage, and of sexual gratification in the festive access of young women and men to each other was kept up by hierarchy and clergy in official pronouncements throughout the nineteenth century. In places—Dublin in 1831, Monaghan in 1832, Ardagh in 1834—virtual curfew was imposed on young people, especially the unmarried, in an attempt to combat what the church considered the shameful and irreligious behaviours in which those attending the wakehouse indulged.[12]

Besides their opposition to the merriment and games of the wakehouse, clerical hostility to the activities of keening women at both wakes and funerals was a further continuous element in the response of the ecclesiastical authorities to manifestations of popular ancestral religious feeling from the seventeenth century to the beginning of the twentieth. Ó Súilleabháin lists edicts against the practice of employing the services of keening women at wakes and funerals from Tuam (1631), Armagh (1660), Dublin (1670), Armagh (1670), Meath (1686), Kildare and Leighlin (1748), and Cashel and Emly (1800). He quotes oral traditions from the nineteenth century in the same sense.[13] Thus the two characteristic elements of mortuary ritual in the ancestral common culture of the Irish rural population in early modern times that were most severely opposed by the officers of orthodox Roman Christianity were (a) ritual public mourning and (b) merriment and licence, especially of a sexual nature. These are of course the two elements of mortuary passage rites that van Gennep identified on a comparative basis as being the universally present elements of funerary ritual in traditional cultures. While there is no mention of Ireland or Irish mortuary tradition in van Gennep's work, the rituals of the Irish merry wake and funeral are nevertheless consonant with his theories, not least in respect to his comment regarding the situation where, as in Ireland, more than one cosmological system informs the world view of a population: 'Funeral rites are further complicated when within a single people there are several contradictory or different conceptions of the afterworld which may become intermingled with one another, so that their confusion is reflected in the rites'.[14]

In the merry wake and funeral of eighteenth- and nineteenth-century popular Irish culture an ostensibly Christian ritual marking the translation of the soul of the deceased to the Christian afterlife was very strongly marked by a vivid native and localised apprehension of the otherworld and of death that drew on a cosmology and a religious sensibility deriving from a native, or pagan, or Celtic world view alternative to the Christian one. Such ambiguity of world view in the popular culture of early modern and modern Ireland was a central characteristic of the products and manifestations of the culture—ritual, literature, and political life. The merry wake was an institution embodying that ambiguity in a specially marked way.

A general sampling of the practices and beliefs surrounding death and burial in the popular culture of rural Ireland in the later nineteenth century, as reflected in the archival materials accumulated by the Irish Folklore Commission field-workers in the early and middle years of the twentieth century, will, I hope, support what has been so far claimed for the symbolic and social significance of the merry wake and provide a basis for further interpretation.* For reasons of space I confine the data presented here to those of informants from two counties only, Galway and Cork. I am aware of the extensive discussion required as to the representativeness of this selection of material in the context of the considerable regional and historical variation to be found throughout the archival folklore evidence of wake ritual. The data selected derive, for the most part, from fieldwork carried out in the 1930s with elderly informants. Typically, we find there material recorded in, say, 1935 from someone aged about seventy-five who was allegedly relating what he or she recalled of what parents or grandparents related of their own young days. Thus the material can easily take us back to the middle of the last century, to a time when the merry wake was still practised or enacted in both counties in the case of certain communities or families. There is of course very little direct contemporary insider evidence for the functioning and significance of the Irish merry wake at the time when it appears to have flourished

* Permission from Professor Bo Almquist to consult, copy, and take extracts from the Irish Folklore Commission MSS now in the custody of the Department of Irish Folklore, University College, Dublin, is gratefully acknowledged.

at non-élite levels during the later eighteenth and early nineteenth centuries.** The evidence we do have from Folklore Commission informants in the 1930s is a mixture of personal memory and recalled anecdote, with little possibility of cross-checking or other verification, and it has been subject to a variety of collecting and editing variables. Nevertheless, it yields authentic data for examination.

The County Cork data used here is from at least seven communities ranging from Beara and Bantry in the west to Araglen and Kilworth in the east; from Glandore on the south coast to Charleville near the Limerick border to the north, and including mid-county communities in the baronies of West Muskerry and Kinalmeaky. The County Galway data used is from both the western coastal communities of Cois Fhairrge and Connemara, viz., the parishes of Knock, Ros Muc, Carna, Baile na Cille, etc., and from such inland communities as Menlough, Moycullen, Craughwell, and Kiltartan. The data are, for the sake of coherence, presented in the ethnographic present tense under a succession of headings: (1) death and the moment of dying; (2) the laying out of the corpse; (3) keening and keening women; (4) the consumption of food, drink, tobacco, and snuff; (5) tricks, games, and play; and (6) funeral and burial.

1 DEATH AND THE MOMENT OF DYING

(a) *County Cork* Certain things are a sure sign that a death is imminent in the community. Among these are the crowing of a cock by night or throughout the day, the hearing by night of the death-tick in a wall or in an old timber bed, the absence of a shadow thrown on the wall by a person lighting a lamp indoors at Halloween, the presence of grey crows about the house, the hearing of the 'banshee', the supernatural female death messenger, in the vicinity of the household, and meeting with a fairy or ghostly funeral on the road by night.

Death itself is looked on as a punishment for sin. Violent or sudden death is held in great awe since it is a sign of 'bad living' leading to a 'bad end'. The death of the young person or child is taken as a sign that they were 'too good' for this sinful world. The will of God is in operation behind all death, and an easy death after a long life is seen as a reward for good living.

'Unnatural' deaths result in the dead person being 'in the fairies', and certain 'forbidden' acts bring the danger of this type of death. Such acts are, for instance, interfering with 'the good people's' property (forts, sgeachs, thorns) or removing or altering old passages or laneways and so causing annoyance and disturbance to 'the good people'. Such acts lead to ill-health and ultimately to death.

** Among fictional accounts of wake ritual in nineteenth-century Anglo-Irish literature the story 'Larry McFarland's wake' included by William Carleton in his *Traits and stories of the Irish peasantry* (1830) is perhaps the most prominent.

Before a person dies, the 'habit' must be in the house, and the dying individual must be allowed to touch it. They say that there is half a claim from this side and half a claim from the other side on a dying person, and that when the person lays his or her hand on the habit, they are 'more reconciled to go'. Near the moment of death those in the house light the blessed candle and read and recite the litany of the dead. Once death has taken place, the corpse should be left undisturbed for a certain period of time in order to allow the deceased to get safely to heaven and to communicate with God regarding the state of his or her soul.

It is believed that the souls of relatives dying far way come back to visit the old place one last time before taking flight to God. Such a visitation is signalled by a loud knocking in the middle of the night. It is believed that people, and especially the elderly, come back to the place which they frequented in this life. Consequently, the old man's walking stick is, after his death, left beside his bed every night for a half-year, and his pipe, filled with tobacco, is left on the shelf above the bed. The deceased old woman's tea-caddy is for a similar reason left in the clevy (poll an fhalla) for a long time.

Word spreads quickly of a death in a townland. Work stops in the fields and implements are abandoned 'as a mark of respect'. Work remains halted until after the burial. Within the deceased's house the clock is stopped as soon as death occurs, and mirrors are covered. A sanction of prolonged critical gossip ensures that this is done. No dance or festive gathering takes place for a year in a townland where a death has occurred.

Immediately after a death is announced, neighbours start to congregate at the corpse house, especially the elderly and the female; the younger men will mostly come there at nightfall. Two neighbours go with a family member to procure a coffin and wake provisions—food, drink, tobacco, and snuff. Nobody would dare to go on this errand alone, even in broad daylight.

It is wrong and dangerous to go to or come from a wake alone, since the souls of the deceased and of other ancestors are likely to be encountered in the vicinity of the corpse house, and there is safety in numbers. Between midnight and daybreak especially, the spirits of the dead and the fairies are likely to be very active about the corpse house. At daybreak some of the people at the wake start to go home, but some must stay until other neighbours arrive because a corpse house must never be left without company. The custom of bringing the body to the chapel for the second night of the wake is opposed by many people on the grounds that this involves two 'funerals', and that it is displeasing to the deceased to be brought in and out of the chapel in quick succession.

Fairy keening or lamentation is frequently heard in the vicinity of the corpse house, and such a thing occurs in particular families. This fairy crying is not regarded as terrifying since it is proper that respect be shown to the dead from 'the other side' as well. Sometimes a dead relative of the deceased will come back to the wake—a dead sister, perhaps, and there are stories of fairy women coming into the wake to tell the household where they should bury a 'stranger' (for instance, an itinerant farm labourer or a traveller) who is being waked among them.

(b) *County Galway* Sometimes a death is foreseen in the sighting of a fairy funeral party bearing a cróchar ('stretcher') on which is carried the coffin of the one about to die.

A hard bed of oat straw or rushes is laid on the floor next to the dying person's bed, and the dying one is lifted off the down mattress and placed on the hard 'bed' to provide him or her with an easier death. A down mattress or a feather bed (especially of hen's plumage) will delay a dying person's demise and give them a hard death.

Those present at the bedside of a dying person will pray 'Aves and Ár nAthairs (Our Fathers)' in turn while passing around a tied bundle of twelve lighted candles. The one with the bundle holds it in over the deathbed for a short time while reciting the prayers, and then hands it on. A person who can recite the litany of the dead is summoned to pray it over the dying person.

No one is allowed to take fire out of a house where a person is dying, not even in the form of a light lit in the house, i.e., a lamp or pipe.

Once death has occurred in a dwelling-house, it is referred to—until the burial has taken place—as a corpse house by day and as a wake house by night. At nightfall members of the local community continue to converge on the wake house until quite late at night. The 'dirt', i.e., the sweepings of the floor of a wake house, must never be thrown out until the corpse is gone from the house.

Two people at least, and certainly never one alone, must always 'go' for the boards to make a coffin and for the wake provisions. Nothing else may be bought on such a trip—'nothing for the living'. If anything other than wake provisions has been bought, then some misfortune will occur; e.g., the horse will fall or bolt on the way home.

It is not right to go to or come from a wake on one's own. A pregnant woman should not attend a wake and should certainly not be present in a wake house while a corpse is being coffined. Persons going to or just returned from a wake or a funeral must put a pinch of salt into their mouths, their pockets, and perhaps into the fire too as a way of protecting themselves from the fairy host. It is not right to welcome anyone to a wake house or to a funeral. The hand of a visitor is silently shaken, and if a welcome is uttered in mistake, then that welcome is left unanswered.

No one goes home alone from a wake for fear they would meet the deceased on the way. The dead person is believed to be 'in the fairies', especially if he or she died 'without the priest'. Fairy keening is heard after the death of certain people, for instance, children and young people, and when it is heard, it is taken as a sign that these people did not die ordinary deaths but were taken by the fairies and are now in a different life. There is a certain village from which in the course of ten years twenty-one husbands were taken into the fairies from twenty-one village families.

2 THE LAYING OUT OF THE CORPSE

(a) *County Cork*   After a certain period of time has elapsed during which the corpse has been left undisturbed, it is washed and dressed and laid out by some local female who specialises in this work. On no account must any member of the family of the deceased handle the corpse or touch it while it is being thus readied for the wake. A male neighbour is got to shave a male corpse if this is considered necessary. When washed, the corpse is dressed and laid out on the kitchen table or perhaps on a bed where the corpse house is large enough to have sizable bedrooms. The face of the corpse should always look to the east.

The corpse is dressed in either the deceased's best clothes (the last worn to mass) or else in a black or brown 'habit', a dress-like garment often associated with lay membership of a religious order. A rosary is twined around the deceased's hands, which are folded and joined on his or her breast, and a prayer book may be placed on the breast or under the deceased's chin.

Some corpses are not dressed in a habit because of the belief that the person whose corpse wears a habit will not meet with his or her 'own' relatives or ancestors in the next life.

While the feet of a corpse are usually fastened together during the wake either with a cord or a sock-pin (where socks are put on the feet), there is a great fear of coffining the corpse with such foot-fastening still in place. Were such fastening to be left undone, it would prove to be a severe impediment to the deceased's activities in the next life of the otherworld. Also for this reason no pin or clip is left in the habit or other corpse garment, even though a number of these have been used in the dressing and laying-out procedure. The woman who lays out the corpse must undo the room when the corpse is taken away. The tented linen sheets that stand or hang about the corpse during the wake must be taken down before the body is coffined. These sheets, together with every scrap stripped off the table or bed on which the corpse was waked, must be bundled up into a heap in the centre of the room while the corpse is being coffined. The person who brings the loan of clothes or sheets to the wake house has to be the person who takes these back again to wherever they came from. In the case of loaned sheets the woman who washed the corpse must afterwards wet the four corners of the bundled sheets before they can be sent away again.

These 'waking sheets' are five in number. They are kept at one house in every ploughland and may never be used for anything else. One of them goes under the corpse on the wake bed or on the kitchen table; one goes overhead, fastened to the ceiling; one goes to one side of the corpse and one each goes to its head and feet, with these also being fastened to the ceiling so that the corpse lies within a sort of linen tent.

Brass candlesticks are kept for wakes at the same house as the sheets. Five candles are lit in them and kept lighted for a corpse dressed in a shroud or habit. Three candles are lit and kept lighted in the case of a corpse dressed in its own clothes.

The pillows and bolster on which the corpse rested, the mattress of the bed, and even the kitchen table on which the corpse was waked must be turned over after the corpse is coffined. The two sides of the deceased's family will compete with each other to be the first to do these turnings in an attempt to turn away from themselves the next succeeding death that is to occur. The length of time to such next succeeding death can be gauged by the relative stiffness or limpness of the deceased's corpse during the wake. A limp corpse is regarded as a sure sign of impending further death in the family.

The little stumps of the first candles lit during the wake are kept in the house for a very long time and used as a leigheas (cure) for both people and animals. The water in which the corpse was washed is also regarded as having a 'cure' in it and is kept for this purpose by some people, who will rub it on sores subsequently, saying at the same time, 'In the name of the Father and of the Son and of the Holy Ghost'. Where it is not kept in this way, it is at least carefully retained until the end of the wake and then, when the funeral leaves the house, 'thrown after the corpse' in the direction in which the coffin has moved off. To throw out the corpse water before the corpse has been buried is regarded as a very dangerous thing to do, and such instances have been followed by a lot of trouble and misfortune for a long time afterwards.

(b) *County Galway* It is not right to say a prayer for the soul of the deceased until the body is laid out os cionn cláir (literally, 'on top of a board'). Immediately after death occurs, two or three persons are picked to lay out the corpse. The first task is to wash it. The oldest woman in the townland is properly the one to wash the corpse and wrap it in a white sheet on the table, with a pillow under its head and perhaps a sod of turf under its chin to complement the marbh-fháisg ('the binding of the hands, feet, and chin of a corpse'). The two big toes are tied together until the body goes cold.

If the deceased was the 'man or woman of the house', i.e., the male or female head of household, then they have to be laid out in the kitchen. Invariably, the feet of every corpse must lie to the east. Those who have washed and laid out the corpse are the ones who eventually coffin it. Whoever puts up the cábán ('tent') of white sheets around and above the corpse is the one who has to take it down again.

A male corpse is dressed in home-made stockings, a *báinín* (homespun white-flannel) vest and white-flannel drawers. A female corpse wears a homemade white- or red-flannel 'coat', a grey-flannel jacket, and a little shawl on the head.

The corpse of a young girl wears a dark dress with a white shawl on the shoulders. The aiséadach ('gravecloth') made from five yards of 'union cloth' is put on the corpse before coffining. It has a hole cut for the head of the corpse at its mid point and is put on so that half is under and half over the corpse. The sides of the aiséadach are cut off in three-cornered sections to be kept as a leigheas ('cure') against lumps and swellings. The triangular sections are most often made up by the old woman who has washed and laid out the corpse. The hand of the corpse at a wake is rubbed over a wound, lump, or ulcer as a 'cure'. People are brought up to the corpse for this purpose at various stages of the wake in order to have the deceased's hand rubbed over the affected part.

Any clothes or cloths hanging on the walls of a house in which a person dies are taken down and left in a bundle in a corner of the house until the funeral is over. The deceased's own clothes and bedclothes are washed and hung out on bushes after the burial. Any neighbour who wishes to rid his own or a relative's family of illness can cut an ascallán ('a four-cornered section') out of the clothes and take and use this as something having a leigheas ('cure') in it.

3 KEENING AND KEENING WOMEN

(a) *County Cork*   It is not right for any member of the family to touch the corpse or go near it to express grief until it is laid out properly. Then the whole family assembles around the corpse and cries over it, talking to it and calling back the deceased. Later, when the corpse is coffined and just before the lid is put on, every member of the family must again come and cry over the corpse and kiss it. The final family crying is done outside the house just before the coffin moves off. When the family have finished their initial crying over the corpse, the neighbours cry over it in turn as they arrive at the wake house during the course of the night. The special 'keeners' also cry over the corpse from time to time during the wake. These are old women who are especially good at crying and composing extempore verses in praise of the deceased, for which they are rewarded with drink and money. They are like poets in the wake house, and their performance makes people very 'lonesome'. It also elates the whole assembly when they 'open up' in the middle of the night after the rosary has been said. Such 'keeners' were summoned from miles away to come and perform at wakes, and it is disrespectful to the deceased not to arrange to have keening at the wake and funeral.

The keening women walk with the coffin during the funeral or ride with it in the horse-cart, often sitting on the coffin itself, if the journey to the graveyard is a long one.

(b) *County Galway*   When the corpse is first laid out, the household members come together over it and 'keen'. When other 'family' arrive, they do likewise and are joined at these times by the available household members. A final, very loud keening by members of the deceased's family takes place on the day of the funeral, when, after coffining, the deceased is taken out of the house and placed for a short while on two or four chairs in the sráid ('roadway') outside the house.

Apart from the family, the keen is also performed by old women with shawls on their heads who stand around the corpse, cry over it, and praise the deceased in verse. Tension is generated by the attempts of such keeners to outdo one another. Sometimes the keening old women will 'turn on each other', attacking each other in verse and heaping up verbal abuse. This gives rise to great amusement and merriment at the wake.

There is twice as much keening when it is a young woman or a young man who has died, and in such cases especially (though it is the common practice anyway), the keen is kept up on the day of the funeral all the way to the graveyard. The keeners will walk with the coffin, regardless of whether it is shouldered or horse-drawn on a cart. When the latter is the case, then one old keening woman walks in front, two others sit with the coffin on the cart, and the remaining women keeners walk alongside the cart, while holding onto the cart by one hand and keeping up the keen.

4 THE CONSUMPTION OF FOOD, DRINK, TOBACCO, AND SNUFF

(a) *County Cork* No one leaves the wake house without receiving and eating some kind of a meal. Local girls help to provide this, just as local men are the ones who provide and tend to the fire which is kept blazing throughout the wake. The company at the wake is fed several times during the night, and there can be no shortage of food or drink, since special supplies will have been acquired immediately following the death. Tea, it is said, is a great thing to dispel loneliness and sadness. Tea is made throughout the day for those coming in and out, and again throughout the night for those assembled inside. It is expected that there will be large quantities of food and drink available to the assembly for consumption during the wake.

There must also be plenty of tobacco and snuff and chalk pipes supplied to everyone so that they can all have a smoke. These chalk pipes will be given out to the men either already filled with tobacco or together with a saucerful of cut tobacco from which each fills up his pipe. Similarly, saucerfuls of snuff are sent around among the women. Everyone at the wake, male and female, young and old, is expected to take tobacco or snuff in this fashion, and on starting to either smoke or sniff it, to say, 'Beannacht Dé le hanamann na marbh/The Lord have mercy on the dead'. The consumption of tobacco and snuff continues throughout the wake and involves people who may otherwise be non-smokers and non-consumers of snuff. The preparation of the chalk pipes, the cut tobacco, and the plates of snuff is an important part of preparations for a wake, and together with the tending of the fire, is the responsibility of male neighbours of the deceased.

This smoking occurs not only during the wake but also as part of the funeral. Baskets or boxes of filled pipes will have been placed on walls or bushes in the vicinity of the corpse house for use by those attending the funeral. A little before the funeral leaves the house, a man goes on ahead with a basket of chalk pipes on his arm. As he meets people who are still on their way to the wake house, or either coming to or waiting to meet the funeral on the way, he gives each of them a filled pipe. Pipes remaining unused after the wake and funeral are left in a basket on the grave, and anyone at all is welcome to take one.

Whiskey or poitín is also supplied to those attending a wake. A small amount is usually distributed to all, men and women alike, towards the middle of the night, and the keening women will get drinks of whiskey as they perform. On the day of the funeral, while the corpse is being coffined, the men in attendance are given a drink, and there is a custom that the man giving out this drink spills a little of it into the coffin. It is believed that because of excessive drinking at wakes the priests made a rule that the corpse should be brought to the chapel for the second night of the wake.

(b) *County Galway*   Large quantities of tobacco are consumed during the wake and funeral. For funeral consumption a supply of cut tobacco is carried from the wake house in a stocking and distributed to those at the funeral and in the graveyard. There are detailed rules known to all concerning the provision of tobacco, pipes, and snuff to those at the wake, and it falls to the male neighbours of the bereaved household to arrange the provision and distribution of these. A bodhrán ('winnowing-pan *cum* musical instrument') is the usual container for the filled clay pipes. There are ten bodhrán-fuls of clay pipes at every wake. Two or three men who have previously cut the tobacco fill the pipes and give them to all arriving at the wake house. There is an obligation on every person arriving at a wake to take a pipeful (whether or not they usually smoke), to light and draw on the pipe, and to pray for the dead. A bodhrán-ful of chalk pipes is left on the ditch by every road leading to the wake house on the day of the funeral so that everyone attending the funeral can take a pipe for themselves. One version of the origin of tobacco at wakes is that tobacco was the plant that grew over the tomb when Christ had risen; another that Mary, the mother of Christ, smoked the first pipe when in distraught fashion she was mourning her son's passion and death.

Poorer families can afford to supply food and drink at a wake only to those from outside the neighbourhood who have travelled a distance to be in the assembly, or to those who stay up all night with them in the wake house. The middling and strong farming families, on the other hand, can supply a glass of whiskey to everyone who comes to the wake, and in the case of the better-off, whiskey as well as tobacco are given out in the graveyard on the day of the funeral.

5 GAMES, TRICKS, AND PLAY

(a) *County Cork* When people are waked on the kitchen table, there is great sport at wakes, with flutes, music, and dancing. Sometimes there will be mummers present during the night, with everyone dressed up in different clothes. A wake can be like a wedding, with all the fun and laughter. If there is no one to keep the 'fine boys' in check—say, at the wake of an old woman who has few relatives and who is 'no loss'—then they get up to a great deal of 'devilment' as the night passes, tying to their chairs people who doze off to sleep or to the hen-coop on which they are stretched, or shaving, in their sleep, bearded old men who have dozed off near the fire.

Once the rosary has been said after nightfall at a wake, then horseplay and rough tricks can be expected. 'Croosting' occurs with no objection or interference from the family of an elderly deceased person. This involves the pelting of various individuals at the wake with little pieces of turf brought along specially in their pockets by the 'fine boys' to create mischief. Those 'prime lads' have great fun annoying some cranky man, knocking the clay pipe out of his mouth, for instance, by firing a cadhrán ('piece of hard turf') at him unawares. The general horseplay of this type can amount to 'the devil's own kip-of-the-reel'—all sport and blackguarding and every fellow trying to be better (i.e., more outrageous) than the next.

It is known for the corpse to be secretly roped by tricksters during the wake so that it can be hoisted into an upright position in the middle of the night, striking terror and panic into the assembly, especially the women, who then attempt to flee the house. Sometimes the people of the house are extremely angry at this, and there is very nearly 'a real fight'. At other times a family will not mind, as such behaviour is half-expected, and if given a chance, they would play the same tricks themselves. There is generally some old man in each district who is well known for organising and directing such 'devilment' at wakes, and the 'prime boys' will send up to five miles for such a person to come to a local wake so as to indulge in sport and tricks.

Some of these gaming activities are organised set pieces. The young men will start to erect a pyramid of themselves and ask some innocent or inexperienced fellow to top it off for them, telling him to catch the cross-beam of the roof for a moment and then all running away so as to leave him hanging. Occasionally, a not-so-innocent individual will allow himself to be duped like this but will extract revenge by suddenly flinging down ashes or soot into the eyes of those gazing up.

Sometimes an unsuspecting individual will be pounced on and made to crouch in the centre of the floor as an anvil. Two or three others will start sledging him with their fists. The cry will be taken up, 'Buail é, buail é, buail é trína chéile, buail é, buail é, buail é go léir' ('Beat him, beat him, beat him all over, beat him, beat him, beat him entire'), and perhaps ten or twelve fellows in all will be pounding him. Someone will suddenly shout, 'Tá sé ag dóigheadh' ('He is burning'), whereupon the 'anvil' will be picked up and rushed either to a bucket of water or outside to a mud puddle to be doused. Another version of this game involves having a patient, lying on the floor, visited and examined by all the 'doctors' at the wake and thus subjected to rough handling. In this game too the victim sometimes turns the tables by suddenly throwing a concealed fistful of ashes or soot in the face of his visitor.

On one occasion a group of five or six 'lads' going to a wake could not decide which of them should lead their party into the wake house to go and stand over the corpse and cry a little, as it was customary for everyone attending a wake to do. They drew lots for the honour and it fell to a 'hardy boyo'. As they went in the door of the house, one of them struck their leader a terrible blow on the earhole with his fist so that his crying over the corpse was remarkably authentic. The others had to back out of the door again because of their need to burst out laughing.

'Brogue about' is regarded as the best and most popular game of all. For this all the men sit around on the kitchen floor in a circle with their legs pulled up to them. An old shoe is passed around the circle under the raised knees, and someone is prevailed on to stand in the middle of the circle and to try to intercept the shoe in its passage. As he turns to scan the circle of knees, he may be struck with a crack of the shoe on the poll while his back is turned to whomever happens to have it. If a 'slow fellow' is sitting in the middle, he may be a very long time looking for the shoe and will have to endure a great deal of punishment. In general, this is regarded as a 'great' game.

(b) *County Galway* It is the custom for some piece of clothing belonging to each individual at a wake to be collected into a shawl and brought to the centre of the room. Each item is held up in turn and its owner identified. Unless the owner can perform with either a story or a song, the item of clothing is first threatened with a lighted candle and is finally burned with the candle flame so that a hole is left in it, should its owner absolutely refuse to perform.

It sometimes happens that people assembled in a house for storytelling or recreational purposes organise a false wake so as to provide themselves with entertainment of greater scope and intensity. A stranger in the community, usually a beggar man or woman, can be prevailed on to act the part of the corpse, and word will be sent out to neighbours and friends to gather at the house. Special provision of food and drink will be made, and the merriment will last through the whole night until morning.

The boisterousness of the horseplay and gaming at wakes is well illustrated in the account of a Galway informant, who says that once, in about 1868, not having previously seen 'Cleas na mBullán' ('The bull-calf game'), he was pressed into playing the part of a bull-calf along with several other young men. In the course of the game, which mimicked buying and selling, the 'calves' were hemmed in and pressed against the wall of the kitchen with such vigour that the wall collapsed onto three or four children who were in bed in the room on the other side of it. All at the wake ran out of the house in terror, expecting that there would be three or four extra corpses at this wake now. But the children were brought out unharmed, and the crowd returned to resume the wake, except for four or five boatmen from Connemara, who, having fled in terror like the rest, never stopped until they boarded their boats and made off from the land.

Boisterous behaviour at wakes begins when people—always men in these accounts—begin to fire small objects at each other and at certain targeted persons at the wake in order to cause merriment and disruption. Pieces of hard turf are used in this way, as are bits broken off the ten-inch shanks of the chalk pipes that are being smoked on all sides—pipes known as 'Lord ha' mercies' from the response required on being presented with one on arrival at the wake house. These bits of chalk clay are extremely hard and sharp-edged, and the way in which they are fired hard is extremely dangerous, especially to people's eyes.

Once they have prayed at the side of the corpse, parties of young men arriving at a wake by night will straightaway fall to playing such group games as 'Hurry the brogue', 'Hunt the slipper', and 'Who has the marble'. To be caught out in these games means to suffer the lash of a stick on the hand or a blow on the head. Regarding the most commonly played game of all, called 'Faic' (another name for 'Hurry the brogue'), it is said that at the wake of an elderly deceased it was commonly the case that the roughness and horseplay was such as almost to dislodge the corpse from the table on which it lay. Legend tells of a local rogue who actually stole the corpse from a wake house where the only people present were a handful of elderly people who had all fallen asleep. He later won a reward of £5 from the priest of the parish for 'finding' the corpse again.

6 FUNERAL AND BURIAL

(a) *County Cork* When coffined, the deceased is brought out of the house feet-first, and the coffin is placed for a little while on two or four chairs in the open air. The family engage in their last crying over the deceased before the funeral moves off. When it does so, the chairs on which the coffin last rested will be knocked over, together with other chairs and seating brought out of the house after the coffin itself. All of these, together with the table inside the house on which the corpse was laid out and which will have been knocked over at the time of coffining the corpse, will be allowed to remain in the fallen position until after the burial has taken place.

Four male relatives of the deceased, if possible with the same surname, should be the ones who 'go under' the coffin when it comes out of the house, when it goes into the chapel, again when it leaves the chapel (that is, when the corpse is brought to the chapel at all), and finally, when it enters the graveyard.

There are memories of bodies being buried uncoffined, carried to the graveyard either on a stretcher or else in a coffin merely borrowed for the occasion and later returned to its owner; this was the 'hinge' coffin, so called from the hinged-end board that swung open to allow the body to slide out into the grave.

The coffin is preferably shouldered all the way to the graveyard, especially if the deceased was well liked. Relays of men 'go under' the coffin as required. If the journey to the graveyard is very long, then after a mile or so, the coffin can be placed in a horse-cart and drawn the rest of the way to the gate of the graveyard, where it is again shouldered by close relatives.

The funeral procession takes the longest traditional route to the graveyard, with no shortcut whatsoever, in accordance with the customary injunction, 'an timpeall chun an teampaill' ('the long way round to the churchyard'). Once brought into the graveyard on the shoulders of four close relatives, the coffin is carried all around the perimeter path in a sunwise (deiseal) direction before being brought to the grave. At the graveside, before the earth is piled on top of the coffin, the screws on the lid are either loosened or withdrawn altogether and placed on the lid in the form of a cross. This is done to ensure that deceased persons have cead a gcos ('footroom', 'liberty') in the other world.

It is reported as 'usual enough' not to have any priest in the funeral procession or at the grave, though in some places it has become the custom for two priests to attend every funeral. When no priest is present, the funeral will halt at any crossroads, the coffin will be let down, and the people will all gather around it. Someone will then recite the *De profundis* and other prayers for the soul of the deceased.

A 'bog sod' should be carried at the end of every funeral. This is a 'blanket' of turf or top sod, about eight feet by four, which is cut in a local bog or field and rolled in one piece onto a stick and tied with rope. This 'blanket' is unrolled after the burial and laid carefully in one piece over the filled grave.

The grave itself should always be aligned on an east-west axis and should be opened or dug, not by any relative of the deceased, but by a 'gravedigger' or else by a neighbour not having the same surname as the deceased. The grave is usually 'reddened' (i.e., opened by removing the top sod and turning the earth) on the day after the death occurs. On no account, however, can a grave be 'reddened' on a Monday, so that the grave of someone dying on Sunday is either opened that same day or else on the following Tuesday. A grave is usually opened by two men working together. When it is made, the two who made it cross their shovels over it, and these are left in position until the burial time as a protection against interference with the grave by spirits or fairies. For both people making a grave and people at a burial it is wrong to clean boots or shoes afterwards on graveyard grass and wrong to spit while in the graveyard.

Some people will open a grave but will on no account close it again themselves, even it if has been opened in error. Having been opened, a grave must receive something before being closed again, even if it is only half-opened. If nothing is put into a grave, even a partly opened one, before closing it again, then it is sure to claim one of the family whose grave it is within a very short time.

Just as all those meeting a funeral— even a fairy funeral— on the road should turn and travel 'trí choischéim na trocaire' ('the three merciful steps') with it, so those closest to the deceased, and to the grave at burial, should throw in three shovelfuls or three fistfuls of earth onto the coffin before the business of closing the grave begins in earnest. The noise of these first few shovelfuls of earth thudding onto the coffin causes the bereaved family to cry again in unison, a cry taken up once more and for the final time by any keening women present.

When a person has died and been buried, his or her clothes are given away to someone else to wear as something that will benefit the soul of the deceased. The deceased's best suit of clothes, for instance, will be given 'in the name of God' to his best friend to wear to mass on the next three Sundays. These clothes may not be altered in size to suit the recipient, and after the three Sundays on which they are worn to mass, they are often kept hanging up in the recipient's house until they melt away in moth-holes, just as it is believed that the body of the deceased melts and withers away in similar fashion in the grave.

(b) *County Galway* Certain rules apply to bringing a coffin into and out of a house. It must be brought in through a southern door and out again through the same (or through a back door), as normal practice. When, however, a 'stranger' is being buried from a house, his or her coffin goes out a northern door so as to take the bad luck and the harm of death with it out of the house and out of the family. An attempt is often made by a man's own family to enforce this same rule of 'stranger brings and takes bad luck' in the case of the death of a new wife, as in childbirth, for instance. In such cases the woman's death is regarded as being due to 'ill-luck' and as ultimately attributable to fairy intervention. The woman's own family may oppose this practice, and the result is often dissension and fighting.

Once brought out of the house, the coffin is put down on two or more chairs to rest briefly. When the coffin is taken up again, to be placed on a stretcher or hearse, these chairs are tumbled upside down.

There are accounts of corpses buried without coffins in the 1880s. These were brought to the graveyard in a hinged coffin, from the opened side of which they were slid into the grave. One hinged coffin is said to have served all the townlands connected to the one burial ground. On the coast the coffin, shouldered by four men to the graveyard, rests on two oars and is covered with a white sheet which is knotted and pinned in its corners and afterwards brought home again.

Four men of the same surname as the deceased should shoulder the coffin out of the house and later from the gate of the burial ground to the graveside. No two brothers should ever be among the bearers for fear that the death of one of them within the year will result. Everyone 'going under' the coffin in a funeral should do so three times in all to avoid subsequent bad luck. Bad luck or the fairies themselves will reside in any spot where a coffined corpse rested during a funeral procession, and so the coffin is never 'let down' anywhere between the house and the graveyard. Funerals stop, however, at places where a roadside cairn of stones marks the spot where another, previous death has taken place. Prayers are said at such stops and small stones added to the cairn.

Anyone meeting a funeral on the road should turn and accompany it for three steps, and not to do so is to show lack of respect for the deceased and lack of sympathy in the bereavement.

Where a horse is used to draw a coffin in a funeral going a long distance, people never like to use a mare that is in foal for this purpose. Nobody on the way to or from a funeral should make any purchase, as this will surely lead to misfortune. 'Bail O Dhia' ('God bless the work') is never said to someone at work making a coffin or a grave. Those who dig a grave should be the ones to fill it in again. Anyone with any contact with a grave should wash their hands on returning home, even if their hands are 'crystal-clean'. The loy and the shovel are left crossed over the open grave from the digging of it until the arrival of the coffin at the graveside. No grave will be dug on a Monday if the top sod has not already been removed on the previous day, since it is very bad luck to turn the sod on a Monday.

Every family has its own grave into which the generations go, except that no grave can be reopened until seven half-years have passed since the last interment. If a second death occurs sooner than that, then a new grave must be dug next to the old. When, after at least seven half-years, an old grave is opened, the old boards and any bones found are taken up and replaced on top of the new coffin, which must always go to the bottom of the grave. Conflict has been known to arise in the case of elderly brothers, one of whom is married and makes clear his intention of burying his deceased wife in his parents' grave. The unmarried brother in this instance runs the risk of being excluded from his parents' grave should his own death occur within the seven half-years required before the grave may be opened a second time. Potential conflict is also present in the instance where the family of a young woman who dies early in marriage will want to 'bring her home' to the family grave. The reason given for her family's wanting this is that the bereaved husband is likely to marry again, and that his first wife really has no business being buried in his family grave.

At the graveside the pins of the sheet that covered the coffin during the funeral journey are thrown into the open grave. A bottle of 'holy' (i.e., blessed) water brought from the chapel will also be put into the grave. People at the graveside, along with the family and relatives of the deceased, catch up three handfuls of earth each and fling them down onto the coffin at the bottom of the grave. A man from County Clare introduced the practice of putting a scraith ('sod') down on the coffin before the grave is filled so as to reduce the stark sound of earth and stones falling onto the coffin.

Finally, before people move away from the graveyard and the funeral ends, 'close mourners', i.e., a spouse, parent, child, or sibling of the deceased, may be taken by the arms and swung by neighbours three times over the filled grave. This is done in order to 'take away' the close mourners' grief for the deceased.

7 COMMENTARY

The above material, taken as a whole, makes clear that the merry wake and funeral, the characteristic mortuary ritual of Irish popular custom, involve a centering of the life of the community into a traditional assembly with both sacred and social significance. A structural principle of traditional cosmology in Ireland has always been the centering of community life into occasional sacred assemblies that 'serve to renew social order as well as to acknowledge and venerate supernatural forces'.[15] The ancient royal assemblies at burial sites, for example, Tailtiu, Carmun, etc., which featured horse-racing, board games, and athletic contests, are early examples of such centerings occurring as events of an annual or triennial community calendar. The merry wake and funeral are a later and more proletarian manifestation of the same structural principle, occurring not in calendrical sequences but in accordance with the arrival of crisis points in the life cycles of individual members of the community. Assembly custom is especially prominent in the Irish cultural tradition, at both learned and popular levels, at Samhain/ Halloween, when the otherworld is closest to the human social order and when otherworld powers, ancestral and fairy, present the greatest danger to human life. Play and performance in assembly, whether in the royal banqueting hall or around the peasant fireside, have always had at Samhain prophylactic significance in relation to the threat of otherworld contact. The merry wake can be seen as a kind of movable Samhain assembly, playing its protective and expressive role at the liminal interface of life and death in the community and constituting a prominent part of the means by which the community effects the re-establishment of social order in the face of the disruptive power of death, which requires the deceased to pass into an afterlife ambiguously ancestral/fairy and Christian. If the 'old man' or 'borekeen',*** who is said to have been well known in each district as an organiser and director of the pranks and games of the wake assembly, is the agent of that socially cathartic chaos out of which a renewed social order can emerge,[16]

*** The term 'borekeen' as used by John Prim (1852) may be assumed to be a transliteration of a diminutive form of the Irish bórachán, 'a bow-legged person', 'a person with crooked feet'. This term is applied to the 'joker' in card-playing, and its use in relation to the 'joker' or master of revels at wakes is an extension of this meaning.

Figure 1

OTHER WORLD

Individual transition/incorporation

'Bean chaointe'   SACRED
                          WAKE ----------- ASSEMBLY
                                  SOCIAL   'Borekeen'

Communal reversal/regeneration

HUMAN SOCIAL REALM

then the keening woman, the bean chaointe, is the agent of the transition to the next life of the individual whose corpse lies at the heart of the wake assembly, and whose passing is ritually mourned all the way to the grave in the highly charged performance of the female practitioners of the caoin.

The structural outline of what occurs in the merry wake is suggested in schematic form in Figure 1. The role of the bean chaointe as the female agent of the mournful transition of the deceased individual to the afterlife of an ambiguously Christian/fairy otherworld should be viewed in relation to other female roles which in Irish cultural tradition also associate the female with the sovereignty of the supernatural in human affairs. At the supernatural level itself there is the preeminent figure of the sovereignty queen, the intimate spouse and divine legimatrix of the rightful ruler,[17] but also a terrifying figure of war and death,[18] who alternates between the poles of this fundamental hag/spouse opposition in Irish ancestral cosmology and mythology. The 'banshee', who in Irish tradition is the supernatural messenger portending death to the family and community about to be bereaved,[19] and who is heard crying and keening in the vicinity of the wake-house-to-be, is a reflex in popular culture of the aristocratic figures of the great sovereignty queens associated in medieval Gaelic literature with royal and ruling lineages. I suggest that we view the bean chaointe at the wake as a flesh-and-blood reflex of the supernatural female sovereign who rules over the otherworld and into whose domain the deceased is now to be translated. In this light the bean chaointe is the (human) structural adjunct of the 'banshee', and the bean bhán, the female corpse-washer, is another being who must be seen as having symbolic and structural status that insulates her against the common plight of other mortals at risk of pollution and misfortune by virtue of their contact with death and the corpse of the deceased.

The figure of the male 'borekeen', the trickster-master of ceremonies at the merry wake, is free of such supernatural associations. Rather, his role is that of the social order itself personified. In the person of the 'borekeen' and of his willing helpers and henchmen (the 'hardy boys' and 'prime lads'), the community displays its vitality and continuity in the face of mortally threatening contact with the supernatural realm. In this regard especially, the merry wake became a focus in eighteenth- and nineteenth-century Irish popular culture for the carnivalesque element of social life, which was increasingly denied expression in those other domains subject to those wielding new civil and clerical forms of social control, as the forces of modernisation impinged economically and politically on the Irish peasant population. In the imitative and mocking games played at wakes,[20] the matter of culture and the matter of history mingle in ways which articulated in traditional symbolic language both a commentary on and a resistance to social forces threatening the continuance of old ways and old mentalities. This was not, of course, a unique development and was akin to similar articulations in peasant communities elsewhere.[21]

The degree to which such wake rowdiness and playacting was offensive to contemporary Christian religious sensibility is well illustrated by the remarks of the County Kilkenny antiquarian John Prim, who wrote in 1852:

These wake games are never performed in the houses of persons who felt really afflicted by the bereavement which they might be supposed to have endured in the demise of a member of their family. They are reserved for the deaths of old people who had survived the ordinary span of life, or young children who cannot be looked upon as an irreparable loss. They are placed under the conduct of some peasant of the district who excelled in rustic wit and humour, and this person, under the title of 'borekeen', may be termed the hierophant of the observances, whose orders are carried into force by subordinate officers, all arrayed in fantastic habiliments. The 'game' usually first performed is termed 'Bout' and is joined in by men and women, who all acted a very obscene part which cannot be described. The next scene generally is termed 'Making the ship', with its several parts of 'laying the keel', forming the 'stem and stern', and erecting 'the mast', the latter of which is done by a female using a gesture and expression proving beyond doubt that it is a relic of pagan rites. The 'Bull and the cow' is another game strongly indicative of a pagan origin, from circumstances too indelicate to be particularised. The game called 'Hold the light', in which a man is blindfolded and flogged, has been looked upon as a profane travestie of the passion of our Lord; and religion might also be considered as brought into contempt by another of the series, in which a person caricaturing a priest and wearing a rosary composed of small potatoes strung together, enters into conflict with the 'borekeen' and is put down and expelled from the room by direction of the latter. If the former games be deemed remnants of pagan rites and of ante-Christian origin, these latter may be looked upon as anti-Christian, and devised with a view of making religion ridiculous at a time when the masses had a lingering predilection for paganism. 'Turning the spit' and 'Selling the pig' are the names of two other of those games; in that called 'Drawing the ship out of the mud' the men engaged actually presented themselves before the rest of the assembly, females as well as males, in a state of nudity, whilst in another game the female performers attired themselves in men's clothes and conducted themselves in a very strange manner. Brief as are these particulars, they will give sufficient idea of the obscene and demoralising tendency of the wake orgies and show the necessity which existed for their total suppression.[22]

We can assume a corresponding outrage on the part of the practitioners of the civil professions—doctors, lawyers, merchants—whose activities and image were mercilessly pilloried in the games described so thoroughly in Ó Súilleabháin's account. Ó Súilleabháin, of course, makes it clear that there was a marked regional distribution in the practice of indulging in games at wakes, and he asserts that the excesses and improprieties of the merry wakes of the other three provinces were unknown in the funerary traditions of south-west Munster, his native region.[23] He offers no explanation for this marked regionalism in the content of the prophylactic-assembly performance that constitutes the licensed revelry of Irish traditional mortuary rites. It would appear, however, that there is a correspondence between the distribution of carnival-type games at wakes and other indicators (in the market place or at the holy-well pattern) of the acculturation in Ireland during early modern times of European-derived popular pastimes and recreations. The way in which such carnivalesque games and performances, redolent of the street culture of early modern Europe, became quite specifically focused on the Irish wake house, whose traditional performances were hitherto of a more verbal nature (storytelling riddling, etc.), is a matter needing further research. What is clear, however, is that all such performance at wakes of story, song, trick, game, or mime is a manifestation at group level of a social solidarity and continuity that contrast with the matter of the deceased's transition and incorporation into an otherworld—a matter that is, at the level of the individual, the other and equal concern of the wake and funeral ritual and those participating in it.

The extent to which ancestral, otherworld incorporation is a joint primary function of the wake has perhaps not been sufficiently emphasised in previous commentary on the significance of the merry wake. In the wake and funeral as Christian ritual, however unorthodox, the function of delivering the soul of the deceased into the afterlife of the communion of saints in the Christian heaven is clear. The perception, however, that any non-Christian meanings in the ancestral rites of wake and funeral were simply vestiges of archaic and primitive custom has not done justice to the way in which structures and values of ancestral cosmology (i.e., concerning the location of and access to the otherworld) could still inform the world view and lifestyle of Irish peasant communities until at least the mid-nineteenth century.

Ó Súilleabháin does refer to mortuary rites in contemporary traditional societies elsewhere, but his own understanding of the theoretical and functional significance of the merry wake—mourning and merriment—extends no further than to say, following the ideas of the Scandinavian scholar Christiansen whom he openly acknowledges, that the merry wake was a vestigial survival in Irish tradition of a set of rites from ancient pre-Christian times designed to effect two things: (a) to protect the community by means of a communal feast against the anger of the deceased at dying and to pacify the deceased by having him or her as the guest of honour at the valedictory assembly; and (b) to heal in a ceremonial fashion the wound in the social fabric which the deceased's departure has occasioned.[24]

In his treatment of the native supernatural S.J. Connolly accepts the Ó Súilleabháin-Christiansen explanations for the origin and significance of the practices of the merry wake, and he adds a further pair of assertions connected with what he calls 'the important psychological function' of the merry wake. It attests, he claims, the vitality of community even in the presence of death, and the continuity of social life in the face of the sudden social rupture of an individual's demise.[25]

I consider this explanatory theory of the merry wake to be too general and too static, if not actually ahistorical. Certainly, it is hampered by one major flaw from the outset. It is claimed that the merry wake existed to assuage the anger of the deceased individual, to heal the social wound of death, and to manifest the continuing vitality of social life in the face of sudden rupture. Why, then, is it the ethnographic reality that merriment, vitality, and excess were minimal, if not entirely absent, at precisely those wakes where anger, social wounding, and sudden rupture were likely to have been at their most acute, as in the sudden and calamitous death of young, healthy adults (by accident or misfortune, including female death in childbirth), or in the kind of death traditionally attributed to fairy abduction and so well exemplified in the Donegal legends collected by Ó hEochaidh.[26]

In the case of such deaths our evidence suggests that the wake at least was a subdued affair, with too much genuine grief to allow for the levity and revelry of the full-blown merry assembly. The funeral, on the other hand, in the case of deaths attributed to fairy abduction—certainly, when the death was that of a young married woman—appears to have been regularly marked by interfamily rivalry. This tallies with Richard Jenkins's idea that explanations of death as fairy abduction are tied to the incorporation process in Irish tradition.[27] Clearly, a young wife dying in childbirth and subsequently regarded as the victim of fairy abduction had not been fully or finally incorporated into her husband's family life. Thus her own family were especially concerned to bury her body in their own graveyard with their own ancestors as the nearest they could come to reincorporation and recovery from the otherworld of the sí. There was even a known way, reported in the oral narrative tradition of Coolea in the Cork barony of West Muskerry, whereby the changeling corpse could be disposed of so as to restore the abducted deceased to her human family again. This involved opening the coffin three times on each of three bridges over which the funeral procession passed on its way to the woman's ancestral graveyard. On the third bridge, if the bereaved family were certain that the body was not that of their kinswoman but rather a changeling who lay in the coffin, then they should fling the corpse out into the running stream and their own kinswoman would be at home before they arrived there![28] Beliefs such as those articulated in this legend lay behind the ritualised struggle to carry off the corpse to the graveyard of one's own side during funerals, a practice which was widely reported.

Deaths of the sort attributed in Irish traditional culture to fairy abduction were regarded as 'untimely' in contrast with the 'timely' deaths at advanced ages of elderly community members who had lived a full life and whose demise was understood as the will of God. This distinction between timely and untimely death determined the extent to which merriment coincided with mourning in each specific instance of individual demise, and thus it determined the overall character of the ritual occasion within which various lesser rituals occurred.

Basically, what is at issue in the distinction between timely and untimely death in Irish tradition is the recognition of two separate cosmological mechanisms or agencies of death, the one ancestral or Celtic, the other Christian. A distinction between the 'natural' and the 'magical' is also involved here, with untimely death, attributed to the agency of the powers and personages of the contingent ancestral/Celtic otherworld, being regarded as 'magical', while timely death, attributed to the agency of the Christian divinity and his ordinances, is held to be 'natural'. Thus an elderly deceased, deemed to have lived out an entire life-span and to have enjoyed the full range of human fulfillment in the course of that life, was thought to have undergone a natural death that was timely and offered no very sudden or serious challenge to the social order. On the other hand, unforeseen or accidental sudden death, especially in those who were young or in the fullness of life, was judged as untimely and attributed to the magical agency of the fairies. Fairy abduction was thus commonly said to have been the cause of such sudden or accidental deaths as those of the young mother who died in childbirth, the young man who, collecting firing, fell over a cliff-edge, the cowherd who perished on the home mountain, the fisherman drowned in calm weather, or the child who grew sickly and then wasted away.

The fairy abduction that explained such untimely deaths was considered not only a grievous rupture of the social order but also a serious challenge to the whole social realm and its continuing vitality. Revelry and merriment were subdued in the waking of the untimely dead by comparison with the behaviours exhibited during the wakes of the elderly and timely deceased (see Figure 2 below).

Figure 2

UNTIMELY DEATH

Explanation	Agency	Response	Emphasis	Performer
Magical	Fairy interference	Restrained	Incorporation	Bean chaointe
Natural (Religious)	God's will	Unrestrained	Dissolution	Borekeen

TIMELY DEATH

This reduction of emphasis on the function of the 'borekeen'—mirroring the way in which untimely death was perceived as seriously impairing society's 'natural' ability to restore social order in the face of 'natural' death—placed increased emphasis on the function of the bean chaointe, whose role was chiefly concerned with effecting the transition of the deceased to the afterlife and with ensuring his or her incorporation with the family ancestors, as these were perceived to co-exist dualistically, both in a Christian heaven and in the fairy realm. Such special concern with the proper incorporation of the deceased was justified in the sense that fairy abduction, the attributed cause of the deaths in question, had disrupted and impaired the process of incorporation in both the social realm of this life and the afterlife of the otherworld. As previously noted, Richard Jenkins has suggested that explanations of death as fairy abduction were tied to the process of kinship-group incorporation in Irish tradition.[29] Faulty incorporation denied the individual access to the benefits of membership in his or her kin group in both this life and the next. This is particularly relevant to the case of the deaths of young married women. Clearly, such victims of fairy interference in human affairs were not fully or finally incorporated into the husband's family, and their incorporation into an appropriate ancestor group in the otherworld was now problematic because of their abduction. The extensive archive of oral tradition collected by the fieldworkers of the Irish Folklore Commission from 1935 on suggests that in such cases a struggle or contest frequently took place between the original family of the deceased and the family of her husband, with each side seeking to bury the body in their own ancestral graveyard with their own ancestors.

A revealing late eighteenth-century account exists of one such struggle that took place at a funeral in Killarney and was witnessed by a French traveller, the Chevalier de Latocnaye. Even though he described the events of the funeral rather than the wake, de Latocnaye captured essential features of the effectively unified mortuary ritual of the popular Irish culture of his day:

> I was witness here, a few days after, of a somewhat strange scene. Hearing the funeral bell, I went out to observe the procedure. It was the funeral of a poor woman who was being carried to her last resting-place, the coffin surrounded by a prodigious number of females who wept and chanted their '*hu lu lu*' in chorus, the men looking on rather indifferently. When the funeral arrived at the head of the 'T', that is, at the end of the principal street of the town, a singular dispute occurred between the husband and the brother of the deceased. One of the parting ways led to the abbey of Muckross, where it was the custom for the family of the husband to bury their dead; the other led to Aghadoe, where are buried the family of the brother. The latter assumed the right to direct the funeral toward Aghadoe, while the husband wished to go in the other direction to Muckross. The friends of the two parties took hold in turn of the remains of the poor woman, each wishing them to be carried to the side they favoured; but each finding themselves unable to succeed, by common accord they deposited the bier on the street and commenced a vigorous fight to determine by blows of sticks to which side the remains should be carried. I was at the time with the minister of the parish, Mr Herbert, who is also a justice of the peace. With great courage he threw himself into the middle of the fight, seized the collars of the two principal combatants, and after some explanation he decided that the husband had the right to decide where his wife should be buried. He allowed the husband then to go without letting go hold of the brother-in-law, and the funeral moved in the direction of Muckross. I remarked that neither fight nor controversy which followed arrested the cries of the wailing women, who continued to beat their breasts, tear their hair, and cry '*hu lu lu*' as if neither fight nor controversy proceeded.[30]

The chevalier and the clergyman *cum* legal officer thought that they had witnessed a senseless outrage, a breakdown of law and order bordering on the obscene. To the anonymous actors in the event, however, its meaning was very different. In terms of both robust assembly and ritual mourning, honour and respect had been shown publicly to the individual deceased and to both sides of her family. Her radical transition to a new order was mirrored and marked in the public drama of the transfer of her mortal remains, a drama that also represented the reestablishment of a renewed social order in the aftermath of her demise. De Latocnaye found it especially remarkable that the keening should have continued throughout the fracas. But this was of the very essence of the merry wake and funeral that they should simultaneously serve a dual function, mourning a transition and also resolving and removing social tension. He was also surprised when, as he said, 'the peasants showed the greatest respect to the magistrate and submitted promptly to his decision'. They did so presumably because this was not a real battle and because they had already shown in their mounting of such a public ritual—in this case in the actual physical presence of their legal masters and social betters—their claim to independence of a resented civil authority and their allegiance to ancestral ways.

In the eighteenth and early nineteenth centuries the merry wake and funeral together constituted a central institution of popular Irish rural culture which had both great symbolic and behavioural significance in people's lives. This institution articulated for them, in powerful ways which they long continued to value highly, their collective response to their life experience. It performed this function as a sophisticated amalgamation of the symbolic resources of both the magico-religious and the socio-political universes of discourse. Along with other aspects of the popular culture of pre-famine Irish tradition, it succumbed to the immense transformation of the society of the 'lower Irish' that overtook Ireland and Irish popular culture in the mid-nineteenth century.

NOTES

1 J.L. McCracken, 'The ecclesiastical structure, 1714–60' in T.W. Moody and W.E. Vaughan (ed.), *A new history of Ireland*, vol. iv: *Eighteenth-century Ireland, 1691–1800* (Oxford, 1986), pp. 98–9.
2 Seán Ó Súilleabháin, *Irish wake amusements* (Cork, 1967). This work was originally published in Irish in Dublin in 1961.
3 Ibid., pp. 146–7.
4 Thomas Crofton Croker, *Researches in the south of Ireland illustrative of the scenery, architectural remains, and the manners and superstitions of the peasantry, with an appendix containing a private narrative of the rebellion of 1798* (London, 1824), pp. 166–7.
5 Ibid., p. 167
6 Ibid., p. 166.
7 Ó Súilleabháin, *Ir. wake amusements*, p. 146.
8 Ibid., p. 154.
9 Ibid., p. 147.
10 Ibid., pp. 146–54.
11 Ibid., p. 150.
12 Ibid., pp. 152–3.
13 Ibid., pp. 138–41.
14 Arnold van Gennep, *The rites of passage*, trans. Monika B. Vizedom and Gabrielle L. Caffee (Chicago, 1960), p. 146.
15 Liam de Paor, *Portrait of Ireland* (Bray, 1985), pp. 145–55.
16 J.G.A. Prim, 'Olden popular pastimes in Kilkenny' in *R.S.A.I. Jn.*, ii (1852–3), pp. 333–4.
17 R.A. Breathnach, 'The lady and the king: a theme of Irish literature' in *Studies*, xlii (1953), pp. 321–36.
18 Máire Breathnach, 'The sovereignty goddess as goddess of death' in *Zeitschrift für Celtische Philologie*, xxxix (1982), pp. 243–60.
19 Patricia Lysaght, *The banshee: the Irish supernatural death-messenger* (Dublin, 1986).

20 Ó Súilleabháin, *Ir. wake amusements*, chaps. 4–5.
21 See Peter McPhee, 'Popular culture, symbolism, and rural radicalism in nineteenth-century France' in *Journal of Peasant Studies*, v, no. 2 (1978), pp. 238–53; Norman Simms, 'Ned Ludd's mummers play' in *Folklore*, lxxxix, no. 2 (1978), pp. 166–78.
22 Prim, 'Olden popular pastimes', pp. 333–4.
23 Ó Súilleabháin, *Ir. wake amusements*, p. 161.
24 Ibid., pp. 171–2.
25 S.J. Connolly, *Priests and people in pre-famine Ireland, 1780–1845* (Dublin, 1982), p. 152.
26 Seán Ó hEochaidh *et al.*, *Síscéalta ó Thír Chonaill/Fairy legends from Donegal* (Dublin, 1977).
27 Richard P. Jenkins, 'Witches and fairies: supernatural aggression and deviance among the Irish peasantry' in *Ulster Folklife*, xxii (1977), pp. 33–56.
28 Donncha Ó Cróinin (ed.), *Seanachas Amhlaoibh í Luínse* (Dublin, 1980).
29 See n. 27 above.
30 De Latocnaye, *A Frenchman's walk through Ireland, 1796–7*, trans. John Stevenson (reprint ed., Belfast, 1984; originally published 1917), pp. 105–6.

8

The Pattern

DIARMUID Ó GIOLLÁIN

The feast day of a parish's patron saint was in former times a remarkable spectacle. It was celebrated at a sacred site connected with the saint, usually including a well, often the ruins of a church or monastery, and other features. The festivities, known as a 'pattern' from a pronunciation of the word 'patron', included religious devotions at the holy site followed by amusements of an often riotous nature. The boisterous pattern is well documented in the writings of various representatives of church and state, antiquarians and curious travellers, and, to a certain extent, in the abundant material of the folklore archives. This essay will mainly utilise the former set of sources in order to investigate the meaning of the pattern in its prime as well as its decline and renewal.

1   ST GOBNAIT'S WELL, DUNQUIN, CO. KERRY

This well is situated at a point overlooking the sea in the townland of Ferritersquarter (An Cheathrú). A modern stone image of the saint and a slab with an inscribed cross stand over the well, which is dry in summer. Some distance above the well, to the side, are two cairns, and above those is a large outcrop called Cill Ghobnait (cill, a church), on the side of which stands a small weather-beaten stone cross.

On 11 February 1989—the feast of St Gobnait, the patron of Dunquin—and again the following year, the present writer had the opportunity of observing the pilgrimage to the well and of hearing a detailed report of the local tradition about it from Mrs Cáit 'Bab' Feiritéar, a celebrated storyteller, and Dr Seosamh Ó Dálaigh, a former teacher and full-time field collector for the Irish Folklore Commission, both natives of the district.

The day began with a mass in the local church, after which people began to come in small numbers to the pilgrimage site. On arrival each pilgrim knelt before the cross on Cill Ghobnait, made the sign of the cross, and silently prayed:

Chughatsa a thánasa, a Ghobnait naofa,
Faoi mar a bheannaigh Muire dhuit beannaím féin duit.
Chughatsa a thána ag gearán mo scéil leat
Agus ag iarraidh mo shláinte ar son Dé ort.

('To you I come, O holy Gobnait. As Mary greeted you, so I greet you. To you I come complaining about my circumstances and asking you, for God's sake, to grant me my health.') Nine circuits were then made of Cill Ghobnait, after which the pilgrim clambered up to the cross, made seven 'rounds' of it, knelt down and prayed (the rosary is sometimes said at this point), and then kissed the cross. The next stage brought the pilgrim down to the well to make seven circuits of it, during each of which a decade of the rosary was said. Next, he or she took three drinks of water from the well, prayed, and before departing, left a token of some kind; in Mrs Feiritéar's youth this usually took the form of tassels from a shawl (since St Gobnait reputedly sewed tassels on her own shawl), or buttons, or beads from a rosary. Nowadays a coin is usually left, and a number of silver and bronze coins of small denominations can be seen in and around the water. Those who leave an offering are said to have three requests granted. The final part of the ritual took place at the two cairns. The pilgrim made five circuits of one cairn and added five stones to it, and four circuits of the other, leaving four stones. The prayers were then completed and the pilgrimage was finished.

Local tradition has it that the pattern on St Gobnait's Day was formerly a riotous occasion with fun and games, drunkenness, and fighting, until a man was killed. The local parish priest then prohibited the celebration of the patron day as a holiday, though the people continued to make the pilgrimage. He removed the cross from Cill Ghobnait, intending to bring it on his horse to Cill Mhaol-céadair, but on his way home with it three local men came before him and tried to reclaim it. The priest succeeded in keeping it but cursed the three men (and a local legend explains how the curses were effected). He locked the cross in his shed, but when he went to inspect it afterwards, it had disappeared and was subsequently found to have been magically transported back to its proper place.

The priest has been identified as Tomás de Staic (Thomas Stack), who died in 1803. The incident of the cross is apparently referred to in the *Ordnance Survey Namebooks*, in the entry under 'Kilmalkedar'. Reportedly, the cross was part of the pattern there but was 'removed by the Ferriters to Dunquin, where it is still kept at Killgobbinet'.[1] From 1906 to 1924 Tadhg Ó Grífin was parish priest,[2] and he declared St Gobnait's Day a holiday again. He asked the old people of the community to show him how to make the pilgrimage, which has been publicly observed ever since then; apparently, it had become moribund.

St Gobnait's Day heralds the beginning of spring and the time of sowing. It was a holiday for the people of Dunquin parish. No work was done on that day. Tradition holds that whoever went from Dunquin to the neighbouring parish to help in the sowing on that day had an accident. A boy or a man from Dunquin who worked on the day developed a sore foot and was invalided for life.[3] Cill Ghobnait is supposedly the site of the saint's first foundation. She came to Dunquin searching for nine white deer as a mystical sign to her. She discovered three, but found nine at Ballyvourney in west Cork, and there she remained. She visited Dunquin. She was a beautiful woman but was very shy and avoided the public road in order not to meet anyone. She resolved never to marry. She used to be seen near Cill Ghobnait putting tassels on her shawl. She died there. The well dedicated to her is particularly efficacious in curing eye diseases, but cures for throat ailments are also mentioned in connection with it.[4]

The pilgrimage to St Gobnait's Well is typical of the pattern as it is today. It differs from others, of course, in its date, in incidentals connected to the saint's life, in the type of ailment whose cure is sought during the pilgrimage (which is frequently explained through an event in the saint's life), and in the nature of the site. In the essentials it is typical, and in the ritual it descends from the pattern which we know from the various accounts of it taken down in its heyday. Thus the pious side of the pattern has changed little over time.

2 SOME EARLIER ACCOUNTS OF THE PATTERN

A French visitor, de Latocnaye, who travelled in Ireland in 1796 and 1797, visited a holy well and noted that even the local Protestants visited it when all other remedies had failed. Acknowledging the pious part of the pattern, he observed that 'the greater part of these peasants, however, come in a rather careless spirit, seemingly more with a desire to meet their friends than to perform penitences'.[5] He questioned one of them, who admitted coming 'to do what the others do and to see the women'. Latocnaye mentioned the arranging of marriages at patterns and the fruitless prohibition of patterns by the local bishop.[6]

The amateur antiquarian and folklorist Thomas Crofton Croker attended a pattern at Gougane Barra, Co. Cork, on St John's Eve, 1813.[7] He saw large crowds on the shore of the lake there and a great multitude in and around the chapels on the island (accessible by causeway), those inside mostly on their knees, some with arms uplifted, praying aloud, others quietly counting the beads of their rosaries, or using a small pebble, or cutting notches on a stick or cudgel for the same purpose of indicating the number of prayers to be repeated. A rusty piece of iron was passed from one pilgrim to the next and placed on the head three times, accompanied by a prayer. He noticed a man, apparently belonging to a mendicant order, scratching the wall of the well with small pieces of slate, following the imprint of a cross which was nearly two inches deep. The pieces of slate were sold to pilgrims afterwards as relics. Crowded inside the door of the well were seven or eight people, some with their arms, others with their legs in the water, exhibiting their sores and other ailments. These pilgrims were quickly replaced by others. Outside, little glass bottles of well water were sold and applied to an infected bodily part or drunk on the spot. Women waited with naked infants for the opportunity to dip them in the waters of the well.

On the shores of the lake were booths and tents selling whiskey, porter, bread, and salmon. In most tents was a piper, and young people danced, the women choosing their partner. After the dance the young men rewarded the musician with a coin. The tents were very crowded, often with twenty or thirty people in each, drinking heavily and singing rebellious songs which were greeted with yells of approval. By evening most people were drunk, 'cudgels are brandished, the shrieks of women and the piercing cry of children thrill painfully upon the ear in the riot and uproar of the scene'. Crofton Croker remarked, 'All become actors — none spectators. . . '.[8] People were still visiting the well at midnight, while 'the dancing, drinking, roaring, and singing' continued all night. Bonfires, lit early in the evening to commemorate St John, greatly impressed him. He sympathised with the simple devotion of the common people, 'but drunken men and the most depraved women mingled with those whose ideas of piety brought them to this spot; and a confused uproar of prayers and oaths, of sanctity and blasphemy sounded in the same instant on the ear'.[9]

Of particular interest were the small prayers he noted on sale at the pattern. The one that he quoted was headed, 'Taken from the writings of Irish clergymen. Copy of a prayer to be said at the well of St John's.' The text included the following words, to be repeated: '. . . I hope to render myself worthy of the favor I mean to ask, to avoid drunkenness and licentiousness, and hope to find favor in thy sight'. It concluded with an admonition from its compiler: 'You must be careful to avoid all excess in drinking, dancing in tents, for it is impossible [that] characters can find favor in the sight of God, such as these'.[10] Crofton Croker noted the common loss of life at patterns owing to faction-fighting. As a result, the pattern of Gougane was banned by Dr John Murphy, the bishop of Cork, in 1818. The description ended with reference to 'the disgraceful riot of the patron, a meeting that seems established only to profane all that is impressive, simple, and pious'.[11]

The Protestant controversialist Caesar Otway also gave an account of the Gougane pattern, published in 1827. He estimated from a written scheme of prayer at the site that each pilgrim should say a total of 936 Paters, Aves, and Credos. He described coming upon seven or eight men and women around a fire in one of the vaults on the sacred site where the 'stations' were performed during the pattern; all were laughing very loudly: 'I asked Cornelis what they were doing there. "Oh, sir, they are only laughing and chatting like happy pardoned Chris-thens, after performing the rounds." '[12]

To these two accounts of Gougane Barra one can add that recorded in 1942 from a noted storyteller, the tailor Tadhg Ó Buachalla (born in 1863), but referring to some time in the nineteenth century. The pilgrimage to Gougane could be made at any time between St John's Day and the last Sunday of September. The various districts of its hinterland often had their own special day for attending, but the presence of rival groups at the same time led to conflict:

A multitude of people used to come here on St John's Day and the night before.

Trouble developed between the Uíbh Laoghaire people and the people of Bonane (which is in the parish of Kilgarvan), and they set upon each other. The parish priest then stopped the people of this parish [i.e., Uíbh Laoghaire]: he would not let them go to Gougane on St John's Day or the night before, in case they would have a fight with the Kerrymen. Since then the local people here do not go on St John's Day; they wait until autumn.[13]

To explain the pattern the gifted novelist William Carleton, writing in the 1830s, stressed the love of fun as 'the essential principle in the Irish character', and that no event, 'no matter how solemn or how sorrowful it may be', was allowed to occur without it. He instanced the sincere and severe piety of the pilgrim to the holy well who shortly afterwards could be found in a tent, dancing 'with an ecstatic vehemence'.[14] The Rev. Philip Dixon Hardy, a Protestant cleric of extreme views, published a polemical pamphlet on holy wells in 1836 in order to present to the public the 'superstitious and degrading practices' associated with them and thereby to show 'that they are really the prolific sources of much of the IRRELIGION, IMMORALITY, and VICE which at present prevail to such an awful extent through so many portions of our highly favoured land'.[15] In the pamphlet is an account of the midsummer pattern at Struel, Co. Down.[16] The ceremonies began there on the Sunday before and ended on the Sunday following midsummer, though few pilgrims stayed longer than half the week, with the latter half being considered as the holier, particularly the last day called 'big Sunday'. Pilgrims arrived in Downpatrick, took holy soil from St Patrick's grave there, and went to mass. They then proceeded to Struel, a short distance away, where they climbed a 150-foot-high hill on their knees, some carrying a large stone balanced on their backs while holding their hands on the backs of their necks (if they were atoning for a grievous sin). They ran down the hill and repeated the exercise three, seven, nine, or twelve times or more. Following this, each person sat in St Patrick's 'chair', an unusually-shaped rock, and was turned in it three times by the superintendent of the 'chair', who was rewarded with a penny. The pilgrims then moved to some cairns, crawling or running, and added a stone to the heap (the cairns were in groups of seven or twelve). The next part of the procedure entailed visiting 'the body well', the large holy well, but first touching a flagstone in the outside wall around the well. Those who paid a certain sum visited the larger well, where there was room to undress inside its enclosure. Otherwise, they went to 'the limb well', but first stripped in the adjoining fields. They then bathed together naked, regardless of sex, washed their eyes, and went on to another well, from which they drank.

At this point the pious ritual was complete and the pilgrims proceeded to the next part of the festival: 'The employments of the day seem to be considered as the labours of virtue, those of the evening are her rewards. . .'.[17] Tents were erected in the surrounding fields, and it was in and around these that people amused themselves:

They spend the whole night quaffing the soul-inspiring beverage and indulging in various gratifications to which the time and place are favourable; for it
is understood that while the jubilee continues, and as long as the happy
multitude remain on the sacred ground, they cannot contract new guilt.[18]

The famous English novelist W.M. Thackeray described the pattern at the
mountain of Croagh Patrick, Co. Mayo, during his tour of Ireland in 1842. He
noted that it began on a Sunday and that the local priests going up to the mountain
forbade music and dancing. Thousands of people climbed the mountain (2,518
feet high) in their bare feet. The first 'station' consisted of a cairn or heap of stones
around which the pilgrim walked seven times, casting a stone and saying a prayer
before and after each stone. The second station was on the summit and consisted
of a great stone altar, to which pilgrims crawled on their knees, said fifteen
prayers, then circled the mountaintop fifteen times and said fifteen more prayers.
The third station was near the bottom of the mountain and consisted of three
cairns. The pilgrims went seven times around these collectively, then seven times
around each individually, saying a prayer before and after each circuit. The
penitents finished this 'frightful exhibition, suffering severe pain, wounded and
bleeding in the knees and feet, and some of the women shrieking with the pain
of their wounds'. About fifty tents were pitched at the foot of the mountain, where
the people congregated, and food and drink were sold from booths and stalls
erected by merchants from the nearby towns. It was a particularly bad day: 'The
pleasures of the poor people—for after the business on the mountain came the
dancing and love-making at its foot—was [sic] woefully spoiled by the rain, which
rendered dancing on the grass impossible, nor were the tents big enough for that
exercise'.[19]

3   THE HOLY WELL LEGENDS

This part of the tradition has survived along with the pious ritual. Since it has
been admirably described by Caoimhín Ó Danachair, it will be dealt with here
only in brief.[20] Legends are a recognised genre of oral narrative. Here they are
primarily concerned with the holy well itself and with the saint, and they help to
legitimate the devotion. Origin legends are set *in illo tempore,* that mythical time
which is relived in the festival, and are the ultimate authority on the sanctity of
the sacred site. The other legends may be called belief legends following the usage
of scholars in oral narrative. They provide the proof of supernatural power in the
form of concrete empirical accounts and at the same time tacitly counsel people
on how to deal appropriately with that power.

Origin legends tell how the saint caused the well to spring up: he was thirsty
and touched the ground with his staff, or his or her tears fell on the spot. In some

cases an existing well was sanctified by the saint, for example, by his being bathed in it as a child. Hollows or other marks near the well were the prints of the saint's hands, knees, or feet, or the paws of hooves of a favourite animal. Sometimes the virtue of the well was revealed by a miracle performed there, such as a wonderful cure. Particularly common are legends which deal with the theme of respect for the well. Profaning it, for instance, by washing clothes or watering horses in it, led to its drying up, or to its appearing in a different place, or to its losing the power to heal and protect.

The malefactor suffered bad luck. The same respect was required for the water itself and for the observance of the patron day as a holiday. The consequences of disrespect are the theme of many legends. A number of legends deal with miraculous cures caused by the well or with the water or pebbles from the well protecting people from harm. Apparitions, too, are a common theme—of the saint to bless the pilgrims to the well or to warn those intending to profane it. There are legends of treasures buried at holy wells guarded by monstrous animals. A common belief was that a fish lived in the holy well, most usually a trout or salmon. The fish symbolised the virtue of the well. To see it meant that the pilgrim's prayer would be answered. Legends tell of water, taken in innocence by a stranger and which did not boil, being found to contain the sacred trout, which was then returned to the well. No punishment followed the innocent deed.

The following are a few brief examples of holy-well legends. Tobar na mBan Naomh, 'The well of the holy women', in Teelin, Co. Donegal, was visited on 23 June. The holy women were three sisters who were reared beside the well and who blessed it after they had become nuns. Their names were Ciall, Tuigse, and Náire (Sense, Understanding, and Modesty). Fishermen passing the well on the way out to the open sea in their boats lowered their sails and took off their caps in honour of these saints and asked for their help and blessing.[21]

St Colmcille, under pursuit, is said to have leaped from a hill at Tobar na Súl, 'The well of the eyes', to the rock where his footprints are still to be seen.[22] A hunted priest, in the time of religious persecution, made for Tobar na nAingeal, 'The well of the angels', and began the ritual in honour of the angels. A thick fog descended and made him invisible to his pursuers.[23]

At St Conall's Well on Inniskeel Island, Co. Donegal, the saint's day falls on 22 May, and between that day and 12 September the pilgrimage was made. For that purpose the 'Bearnan Conall', a relic of the saint, was brought to the island. The relic was traditionally in the possession of a certain family and from them it passed to another family, the Breslins, who sold it in the 1870s or 1880s. The cattle and sheep which Breslin bought with the proceeds of the sale all died. It was believed that St Conall visited the island every year on the first of June.[24]

Of St Patrick's Well in Kellistown, Co. Carlow, it was told that a poor cottier in need of firewood went to the well to cut down one of the trees growing beside it. Twice he saw his cottage on fire, but when he ran home, each time he found that it was only an illusion. The third time he succeeded in felling the tree, but his home was burnt to the ground.[25]

THE MEANING AND FUNCTION OF THE PATTERN

It has been noted that there was a traditional relationship between a saint and a particular territory, and that saints' shrines represented not just boundaries between this world and the otherworld, but between one settled territory and the other, or between cultivated and uncultivated land. The saint, then, was a sort of *genius loci* who was linked ceremonially with the annual cycle through feasts celebrated at critical points in the agricultural year.[26] The saint's cult, of course, represented vestiges of previous religions in the location of its shrine (at a holy well, for instance) and in its calendrical position (at midsummer, for example). The location of the cult is significant. The cult of saints' relics arose in the middle ages in the graveyards outside the walls of cities and 'gave greater prominence to areas that had been treated as antithetical to the public life of the living city'.[27] Writing about French holy wells, Brigitte Caulier remarks that it is easy to understand how the cults should prosper on the *limes* when the town was the centre of a rigorous ecclesiastical control.[28] Writing of archaic societies, Mircea Eliade describes how the supreme divinities 'are constantly pushed to the periphery of religious life where they are almost ignored; other sacred forces, nearer to man, more accessible to his daily experience, more useful to him, fill the leading role'.[29] The creation of religious sanctuaries is a response to a local need which is fulfilled from local spiritual resources. The post-Tridentine Catholic reform, with its reinforcement of the role of the clergy and the normalisation of expressions of cult, led to a rash of visions and apparitions among the common people of the personnages forgotten by the official movement.[30] The essence of the pilgrimage is direct contact of the faithful with the sacred. It involves the avoidance of the clerical intermediary and official church liturgy in a sort of democratisation of the sacred, to the advantage of lay people and particularly of women, who are usually recipients of the vision on which certain pilgrimages are based, and may also be the depositories of traditional devotional formulae.[31]

In traditional Irish society the sacred was located in countless sites close to man. These included thirty or forty thousand forts or raths, popularly known as 'fairy forts', where the fairies, the otherworldly beings who existed in the closest proximity to human society, had their abode. Sacred trees ('lone bushes'), dolmens, and stone circles were also associated with the fairies. The holy wells of Ireland numbered at least three thousand,[32] and there were numerous other sites with long Christian associations, such as ruined churches and ancient burial grounds. All of these were very much local sites of the sacred, from the holy wells dedicated usually to local patrons, to the sites associated with the fairies, who often had their own identified local rulers, such as Áine in County Donegal, Donn Fírinne at Cnoc Fírinne in County Limerick, and Clíodna in some other parts of Munster. These local sacred sites were always more numerous than the sites of modern official religion. Seán Connolly has shown how in the first part of the last century Catholic chapels were still lacking in many parts of Ireland, with mass being said in private houses or outdoors. The pre-famine chapel was often only a mass-house, used for that purpose only on Sundays and holy days; the host was not kept permanently there, baptisms and marriages were not celebrated there, and it might be used on weekdays as a schoolhouse or even as a threshing floor.[33]

Misfortune had a local cause and was addressed by recourse to local powers. Illness of humans or animals, or their untimely deaths, bad harvests, poor catches, or general ill-luck were attributed to the action of an enemy (using the evil eye or sorcery), to the breaking of a taboo (a child's club foot was 'caused' by its mother entering a graveyard while pregnant), or to the anger of a spirit (avenging itself for the desecration of a holy well or fairy fort). Misfortune was reversed in various ways: by placating otherworldly powers with offerings (at holy wells or forts), or by undoing the harm which provoked their ill-will (such as demolishing the house built on a fairy path), or by using human intermediaries called 'fairy doctors' or 'wise women' who could diagnose the problem and recommend the cure (how to restore the child abducted by the fairies or how to protect oneself against harm, for example, by carrying a black-hafted knife or a pebble from a holy well).

The holy-well rituals have come down to us as part of the cult of a local patron saint, but it should not be forgotten that this has been superimposed on the age-old cult of water: neolithic and Roman offerings, for example, have been found at some holy wells in France.[34] Water existed before land; according to *Genesis*, it was the primordial element from which forms were created. Similarly, in the myth of a deluge which renews a sinful humanity, or in the sacred bath such as the Christian rite of baptism or the bathing of pilgrims, or the ritual washing of their afflicted members, the immersion in water annuls the old form of the sickly body or the sinful soul and renews it in health and purity. Water is a symbol of life, fertilising all creation.[35] In many countries there are springs with powers to cure barrenness in women, such as St Éanna's Well in Aran.[36] The sacred trout has been rationalised as a memory of the fish which monks kept in wells and streams near their monasteries,[37] but fish and other water animals, including sea monsters, are widely known as sacred symbols 'because they stand for *absolute reality,* concentrated in water'.[38]

It is common enough that traditional therapeutic sanctuaries should involve complex devotional circuits in their rituals (church, chapel, well, cross, sacred stones, votive niches), and even the larger European sanctuaries may have a series of complementary sacred places which are visited as well.[39] The circumambulations, at times barefoot or on the knees, are not just a penance but also a measure

of the place, a delimitation of the sacred which needs precise boundaries in order
to maintain a sacral consistency.[40] But a complex series of circumambulations to
a sacred centre also suggests a labyrinth, a means of defending a sacred space
from the uninitiated. As Eliade wrote, 'it represented . . . access to the sacred, to
immortality, to absolute reality, by means of initiation'.[41] The sacred site is a
centre, the intersection of the different cosmic spheres of heaven and earth, and
must be difficult of access. It is also a microcosm, which is why cosmic unity is
symbolically represented in it.

The number of circumambulations to be made around each station of the site
has a cosmological significance, though this may not be clearly understood in the
local tradition. Donatien Laurent's study of the sexennial Troménie pilgrimage
in Brittany argues convincingly that the topography of the site and the number
of circumambulations are connected to ancient Celtic calendrical conceptions,
indeed that the ideal annual course of the sun is mapped onto the site by the
pilgrimage.[42] The circuits are always made sun-wise. Ternary circumambulations
are generally connected with Christian symbols; three appears to signify the
divine and going beyond the corporeal duality of man.[43] The quaternary circumambulation may relate to the points of the compass or to the four seasons of the
year, signifying a cosmic unity, the four quarters making up the whole. In the
same way five can indicate the four quarters ranged around a fifth point, the
centre. Seven, the number of days in the week, is another way of expressing
completeness. Nine figures very prominently in Celtic tradition and, like five,
symbolised the whole. It has been suggested that the Celtic peoples considered
the week to consist of nine nights.[44]

It has been argued that traditional societies have no real historical consciousness; their history is a sacred history which is preserved and transmitted through
myths and rituals. History, then, is the work of supernatural beings and mythical
heroes whose deeds were performed at the beginning of time. Human activities
imitate these primeval models which are the archetypes for all significant actions.
By so connecting the events of everyday life to sacred deeds, they are transferred
to mythical time and become significant.[45] Mythical time, then, is 'cyclic, recurring, and born of the merging of two time dimensions, the great primaeval time
and the present moment'.[46]

Sacred history in this way often provides a charter for present-day behaviour
or an explanation for various phenomena. The Travellers ('Tinkers') are ill-
treated and lead a harsh existence because they were cursed for making the nails
with which Christ was crucified. The plaice has a crooked mouth because it
sneered at St Patrick. The wren is hunted on St Stephen's Day because it helped
to drive in Christ's nails with its beak or because it betrayed the Irish to the
Vikings.[47]

The sacred calendar must be understood as the periodic reactualisation of the
creative acts performed by divine beings at the beginning of time. The festival is

the ritual reenactment of a deed effected *in illo tempore*. It abolishes profane time and reinstitutes the mythical time which preceded it. It annuls old forms, even temporally, and regenerates them. It makes possible a personal renewal for those who immerse themselves in this sacred time-out-of-time. Dixon Hardy, quoted above, mentioned the belief of the crowds at the pattern that 'as long as [they] remain on sacred ground, they cannot contract new guilt'. The belief that the waters of the holy well are at their maximum efficacy at a particular time, apparently on the saint's day, suggests that this sacred moment is the reactualisation of the patron's original consecration of the well. The appearance of the saint himself at the well dedicated to him during the period of the rounds at it, noted above from Inniskeel Island, supports this assertion. In France there are wells which appear or heal only on the sanctified day.[48]

The pattern is always associated with a particular calendrical festival, and it should be seen as part of the ritual complex associated with that festival, which may take many forms, of which the pattern is but one. Máire MacNeill's exhaustive study of Lughnasa, the Celtic festival of the beginning of harvest, is illuminating in this regard. She showed the cosmological unity of a wide variety of patterns, fairs, or festive assemblies at lakes and rivers, at wells, or on heights. Of the traditions of nearly eighty holy wells which she examined, faction-fighting is a common feature: 'We learn most about it at Mám Éan between the Joyce Country and Conamara, at Arderin on Slieve Bloom, which divides Leix from Offaly, at Caher Roe's Den on the Blackstairs between Carlow and Wexford. At these three places the opposing parties were from opposite sides of the mountain range. . . .'[49] Referring to the common traditions of fairy groups from two different regions fighting for the crops, she suggested that the faction-fighting represented such a battle on the mortal plane:

> Apparently, it sufficed if the custom was duly observed, i.e., it was the observance, not the victory, which was important. Fortunately, we have Inglis's eye-witness account of Mám Éan in 1834. According to him, the fight lasted 'perhaps ten minutes', it was fought with sticks . . . which descended oftener on other sticks than on opponents, 'five or six were disabled', and we may be sure not seriously or Inglis would have said so, and he saw some who had been opposed to each other shake hands and kiss, apparently as good friends as before.[50]

This account seems to be borne out by a local song which she quoted, in which the narrator avers that he has done nothing more shameful than striking a blow of a stick on Mám Éan pattern day, 'mar isé bhí gnásúil ariamh sa tír' ('because that was always the local custom').[51] She saw faction-fighting as possibly descending from a ritual battle 'between parties representing the forces of fertility and blight, or perhaps from a real rivalry inspired by the concept that the prosperity of the year might go to the victorious side'.[52] In many cultures contests and fights are known in connection with spring and harvest festivals, sometimes taking the form of ritual battles between representatives of winter and spring or summer.[53] It is worth looking at the Gougane Barra faction fight at midsummer in that light; it should be compared with the Breton *pardon* of Saint-Servais, celebrated on the same day:

> it was traditionally the meeting-place of sixteen or seventeen thousand pilgrims from Cornouaille, Trégor, and Vannetais, come to invoke the saint to protect their seeds. The ceremonies always finished with a formidable row between Cornouaillais and Vannetais, with cudgel blows . . . in order to take possession of the banner and the statue of the saint, to the great terror of the clergy. The joint intervention of civil and diocesan authorities put an end to one of the great Breton 'panegyrics'.[54]

It was not uncommon for a person to travel long distances to a noted pattern. As Caulier points out, 'the necessity of exteriority is essential to all pilgrimages, for which it is necessary to touch or go beyond the symbolic limit of quotidian space'.[55] Anton Erkoeka divides the sanctuaries to which the Basques have recourse into three: first, the very local and accessible ones which could be reached in a short excursion within the same day; second, those of provincial fame or well known in several provinces, and specialising in particular ailments, for which it was necessary to visit a distant shrine; and finally, those of international fame such as Lourdes or Garabandal,[56] whose cult tends to be of more recent origin. Dixon Hardy mentioned people from as far away as Scotland and England coming to Struel Wells. He instanced John Lalley, who had walked barefoot from County Galway to Struel to do penance for a man whose spirit had appeared to him, and who depended solely on charity. Lalley began the pattern ritual at six o'clock each morning and did not break his fast until seven in the evening. He could not leave the pattern, where he had already spent ten days, for some time afterwards because his feet were so bruised and his knees ulcerated from making his rounds.[57]

The distinguished anthropologist Victor Turner used the term 'liminality' to refer to any condition which is outside of, or on the margins of, ordinary life, a condition which is potentially sacred.[58] Pilgrimage, as a journey to a place which is sacred and peripheral at a time outside of ordinary profane time, is a particularly liminal occasion. It liberates the individual from mundane structure (since the pilgrim must disengage from everyday life) and reduces all to the same status in the 'movement from a mundane center to a sacred periphery which suddenly, transiently becomes central for the individual'.[59] The ritual humiliation and the ordeals, the removal of signs of status and the equalisation of rank bring about 'communitas or social anti-structure', characterised by the liberation of the individual from general norms and distinctions in an unmediated, unrestrained communion and comradeship with others which is direct, spontaneous, and egalitarian.[60] In hierarchical social structures calendrical rituals have periodically affirmed communitas with its equalising of statuses or status reversal.[61] The old self, as it were, dies and a new self is reborn. The everyday self, of course, comes back to life after the pilgrimage, but it has been renewed through being physically cured or spiritually transformed.[62]

This sense of communitas produced by the festival makes the individual feel indissolubly a part of a biological collectivity outside of all temporal organisation, whether social, economic, or political, 'a member of the people's mass body', argues Mikhail Bakhtin.[63] This is the biological humanity which is constantly being born and dies, and that is why festive forms emphasise 'the material bodily principle': the profusion of food and drink as well as sexual images encourage the regeneration of the mass human body, the triumph of material abundance, growth, and renewal. The beatings and fighting symbolically hasten the death of the old self. The games of cards and dice and the wheel of fortune[64] could be interpreted as 'a condensed formula of life and of the historic process: fortune, misfortune, gain and loss, crowning and uncrowning'.[65] Thus the people enjoy the utopian realm of community, freedom, equality, and abundance and become aware of their sensual bodily unity. They enjoy the festivities with a degree of moral and social freedom rarely experienced. All are participants (as Bakhtin notes, 'carnival . . . does not acknowledge any distinction between actors and spectators'[66]). The festive affirms for them their immortal character and proves the relativity of authority.

These carnivalesque images of death, birth, and sensuality belonged to the culture of the market-place, as Bakhtin calls it, of which the popular, unofficial side of the religious festival was a part. Medieval man led two lives, an official, serious one full of fear, dogmatism, and piety and under strict hierarchical control, and an unofficial and free one, that of the carnival and the market-place, full of license, laughter, familiarity, and mockery of everything sacred. Laughter was as universal as seriousness; it was 'the world's second truth'. The concrete reality was understood only by exploring the festive side to everything serious. This unofficial folk culture had its own territory, the market-place, and its own time, the festival, which was a temporary suspension of the prohibitions and hierarchical order of the official system, which lost its power to inspire fear only during this short period. The temporary suspension of social rank created a special intimacy of communication, annulling social distance and norms of etiquette and decency. These free and familiar contacts were deeply felt; people were reborn for new relations based purely on a common humanity: 'The utopian ideal and the realistic merged in this carnival experience, unique of its kind'.[67] The official feasts of the middle ages, whether ecclesiastical, feudal, or sponsored by the state, sanctioned the existing world order. They asserted the status quo, hierarchical ranks, and the existing moral and political values. It was to their 'monolithical seriousness' that the folk culture was opposed.[68]

Eade and Sallnow, setting themselves against Turner's model, have emphasised that pilgrimage is 'above all an arena for competing religious and secular discourses, for both the official co-optation and the non-official recovery of religious meanings, for conflict between orthodoxies, sects, and confessional groups, for drives towards consensus and communitas, *and* for counter-movements towards separateness and division'.[69] They argue that a shrine's power rests in its character 'almost as a religious void, a ritual space capable of accommodating diverse meanings and practices', though of course there will be attempts to impose a single discourse. This is what allows a shrine to have a universalistic character: 'its capacity to absorb and reflect a multiplicity of religious discourses, to be able to offer a variety of clients what each of them desires'.[70]

5   THE DECLINE OF THE PATTERN

Beginning in the seventeenth century the privileges of the market-place began to be restricted, according to Bakhtin, as the state encroached upon festival life. The sphere of laughter became more and more narrowed and lost its universal quality; it gradually turned into 'a mere holiday mood'.[71] Already in the seventeenth century we find clerical condemnations of the pattern, with the prohibition of dancing, flute-playing, riotous processions, and other abuses at holy wells by the Synod of Tuam (1660).[72] But the church was in no position to enforce such prohibitions at that time. An act passed in 1703 prescribed severe penalties for those who participated in pilgrimages to holy wells. By the middle of the eighteenth century the Catholic clergy, or at least the hierarchy, appeared to be rallying against patterns: attempts were made to prevent the letting of land for erecting tents and booths; exhortations were made and penalties imposed; patterns were prohibited and excommunication was threatened against participants.[73]

The common participation of the lower clergy in the pattern made it more difficult to suppress. Dixon Hardy was outraged by this practice. Writing in the 1830s, he instanced priests imposing the rites of the pattern as a penance, or recommending them for indulgences or for the relief of souls in purgatory, with the blessing of Archbishop Daniel Murray, whose words he quoted. He also referred to a Catholic catechism to show that it too supported the pattern.[74] Official clerical disapproval for a long time had little impact, though we can see evidence of attempts at control in the written scheme of prayers at Gougane Barra observed by Otway, or in the admonitions of the printed prayers noted by Crofton Croker. John Carr, visiting Ireland in the first decade of the nineteenth century, noted that 'in the year 1780 the priests discontinued their attendance, but the patrons . . . still continued the same, and to this day attract all the country for ten or twenty miles around'.[75] The 'body well' at Struel, with its enclosure behind which the paying pilgrim could undress, is evidence of the intrusion of bourgeois moral standards.

In 1818 Dr John Murphy, the Catholic bishop of Cork, prohibited the pattern of Gougane Barra. Otway was told by his informant Cornelis that the parish priest at the bishop's command had thrown all but one of the crucifixes from the eight vaults of the ruined chapel into the lake. The last crucifix had been saved by the local people, unknown to the priest, and it was shown to Otway when being used in the rounds. Asked why the pattern had been stopped, Cornelis replied: 'Ah, sir, they tould lies about it; besides, they say the bishop and his clargy were afraid of the Protestants'.[76]

In the 1930s Edward O'Toole investigated the holy wells of County Carlow. He located fifty-six of them (some were still visited for cures) and uncovered documentary as well as oral traditional information about them, including the time when the patterns associated with them began to decline. Thus St Patrick's Well in Rathvilly was no longer visited in the 1930s, and O'Toole quotes a source from 1839 when stations at the well were already a thing of the past, as was the case again with the pattern at St Brigid's Well, Ballon Hill. A pattern was held at St Brigid's Well in Clonegall 'previous to the ugly, wicked year of '98'. Another at St Brigid's Well, Rostyduff, continued until the beginning of the nineteenth century. That at St Laserian's Well in Old Leighlin was banned by the parish priest in 1812 and already by 1839 had few visitors. The pattern dedicated to the same saint at Lorum was no longer held by 1833. Around 1788 the pattern at St Bernard's Well at Rampere was discontinued. That at St Martin's Well at Cronelea lasted until the 1830s. At St Mogue's Well, Clonmore, the pattern came to an end in the first decade of the nineteenth century. That at Sunday's Well, Kineagh, was brought to an end around 1825. Around 1798 that at Tubber Cranavan had already been discontinued. In 1838 the pattern at Tobersnil was no longer remembered by the local people.[77] Though there is evidence of patterns being suppressed by the Catholic clergy in the 1860s or even much later,[78] it is clear that by the end of the eighteenth and the beginning of the nineteenth centuries the decline was well in train.

The pre-modern (and hence pre-national) community was small in scale and governed largely by face-to-face relationships. It

> was in a certain sense a mechanical bloc of social groups, often of different race: within the circle of political-military compression . . . the subaltern groups had a life of their own, institutions of their own, etc., and sometimes these institutions had state functions. . . . The modern state substitutes for the mechanical bloc of social groups their subordination to the active hegemony of the directive and dominant group, hence abolishes certain autonomies, which nevertheless are reborn in other forms as parties, trade unions, cultural associations.[79]

Integration into capitalist relations and coordinated state administration extended the scale of human interaction. The territory of the state became more homogeneous horizontally, as it were, but more heterogeneous vertically (leading to the beginning of class politics). The person was forced into an individual relationship with the state, encouraged to participate in civil society, and disciplined by the new institutions of school, workshop, barracks, prison, asylum, and so forth. Modernity led to new forms of collective identity which transcended the local, of which the nation has been by far the most important. The modern nation, as Orvar Löfgren pointed out, is populated by modern individuals 'who first had to be freed from traditional collective identities in order to be nationalised into the new collective of the nation'.[80]

Ernest Gellner saw the modern age in terms of an age of universal high culture.[81] In other words, access to a particular cultural code is a prerequisite for participation (and the only possibility of building a better life) in the modern state. Since modernity involves the collapse of the traditional social order and world view and a forcible incorporation into the life of the state, the individual has little realistic alternative but to participate. Gramsci distinguished two realms within the state. Political society consists of the state machinery of the law, the army, the administration, and other services whose task is coercion and intervention. Civil society is the domain of voluntary participation, of consent and free will, and consists of private institutions such as the communications media, political parties, and trade unions.[82] He viewed history as a process whereby a social class attains a position of dominance economically as well as morally and intellectually. It acquires the consent of the majority to the general direction which it imposes on society by compromise and by being able to represent the interests of other groups as well as its own. As Gramsci observed, 'A social group can and indeed must already exercise "leadership" before winning governmental power (this, indeed, is one of the principal conditions for winning such power)'.[83] Civil society is crucial to this leadership; it is the terrain where leadership is won and where new collective identities are formed. Hence the nature of the new national community will depend on the group which 'imagines' it and mobilises it.[84]

The decline of traditional Irish culture was an inevitable consequence of modernity. Whether some elements could be rescued in order to contribute to a new national culture was a question of political strategy. The decline of the pattern involved both coercion and consent. The consent was forthcoming when modern values began to be internalised by the people. A peculiar twist to the Irish situation was the power of cultural authority held by the Protestant elite, which persisted long after the loss of its monopoly of political power. Naturally enough, this cultural prestige was held in the greatest awe by the social class nearest to them. Sir William Wilde quoted (around 1850) a letter he had received from a Catholic friend of his:

The tone of society in Ireland is becoming more and more '*Protestant*' every year; the literature is a Protestant one, and even the priests are becoming more Protestant in their conversation and manners. They have condemned all the holy wells and resorts of pilgrims, with the single exception of Lough Derg, and of this they are ashamed: for whenever a Protestant goes upon the island, the ceremonies are stopped![85]

The Catholic church in many ways is paradigmatic of the Irish experience of modernity. Its reorganisation gave it a privileged role in forming a new collective identity since it had a head start over other institutions of civil society, and since the ethnic divide was conventionally understood in denominational terms (as it was understood in linguistic terms in, say, Finland or Estonia). Since the middle ages there has been a constant battle against 'abuses' in pilgrimages; the church has sought to integrate into its own system those sacred forces whose origin is foreign to it.[86] (What complicated the matter in Ireland was that until the nineteenth century Catholicism itself was an 'abuse'.) In the modern era this battle has to a certain extent been won. Local sanctuaries have been marginalised in favour of a few large sanctuaries; the majority of patterns died out. The Blessed Virgin more and more takes pride of place, and in a form closer to dogmatic theology. In those places of pilgrimage which continue to flourish, the official liturgy has become central under a rigorous ecclesiastical control, which has quickly been asserted on the occasion of visions or apparitions which may lead to new pilgrimage centres.[87] 'The institution does not reject charisma: it tends to feed on it by bringing it down to dimensions which it can accept.'[88]

6 REVIVING THE PATTERN

Visits to sacred sites often survived the suppression of the pattern. Sometimes they were revived much later. O'Toole, writing in 1933, gave some examples of this. He observed of St Patrick's Well in Rathvilly, where patterns had apparently ceased in the middle of the eighteenth century, though individual pilgrims were still visiting it in the 1930s: 'At present it is in a rather neglected condition, but a movement has been set on foot to have it renovated, and considerable funds have been secured for that purpose'.[89]

A farmer who was cured of a serious complaint at St Laserian's Well in Old Leighlin vowed to renovate it but died before he could fulfill his vow. A neighbour, a farmer and captain of the local Gaelic Athletic Association football team, determined to make good the dead man's wish. He organised a football tournament in order to raise funds, and a committee was set up with the cooperation of the local parish priest. Eventually, a considerable sum was realised, and 'in due course the well and cross were enclosed and solemnly blessed by the late Most

Rev. Dr Foley in 1914'.[90] Patterns had ceased at the well almost a century earlier, though it was still visited. The organised pattern was not reinstituted, but in the 1930s high mass was celebrated in the local church on St Laserian's Day, after which people visited the well, prayed, and drank from it. The local schoolchildren were given a holiday.

In the case of Lady's Well, Tullow, the pattern had died out at the beginning of the nineteenth century, but in the late 1920s the religious principal of the local school made enquiries and had a search made for the well: 'He got the people of the town interested in the matter, and sufficient funds were subscribed to enable him to have the well suitably and tastefully enclosed, and a statue of the Blessed Virgin erected over it'.[91]

The pilgrimage to Croagh Patrick appeared to be on the point of dying out by the closing decades of the nineteenth century. In 1903, however, Dr John Healy became the new archbishop of Tuam, the diocese in which the mountain lies. He built a new oratory on the summit so that mass could be said there rather than in the ancient ruin of Temple Patrick:

> Annually on the last Sunday of July the archbishop and other dignitaries of the church climbed the hill and celebrated mass on the summit before crowds which increased each year. His successors in the see of Tuam have continued to patronise and support the pilgrimage. Now in the middle of the twentieth century thousands attend it; special trains are run for it from Dublin and other Irish cities. . . . Although it draws its main support from Connacht and the hierarchy of the province of Tuam, it is assuming the character of a national devotion.[92]

It is significant that it was on the initiative of members of national organisations —those individuals who mediated between the state and the local community— that this revival took place, and it was part of a national discourse: consider the cultural and political climate of contemporary Ireland. In Brittany there are many examples of the promotion of local pilgrimages or of their restoration, normally on the initiative of the clergy, during the second half of the nineteenth century. These coincided with a renewed affirmation of a devalued Breton culture, visible in studies of Breton hagiography and the 'Celtomania' of historians and archaeologists.[93] It is a question of the nationalisation of religion and the legitimation of its modern form at the local level; on a broader level the nation-state works in exactly the same way. Continuity is established in form, even if less so in content: one thinks of the doctrine of culture 'national in form, socialist in content' in the communist world.

Holy wells are now marginal to the religious experience of Irish people. Modern Marian shrines such as Knock, Lourdes, and more recently Medjugorje are now more central and represent the progressive globalisation of religion. Nevertheless, as the 'moving statue' Marian phenomena of 1985 testify, there is a powerful and irrepressibly popular stratum in the field of religion which the institution always rushes to control as soon as it becomes manifest:

> There is a continuous and necessarily uneven and unequal struggle by the dominant culture constantly to disorganise and reorganise popular culture; to enclose and confine its definitions and forms within a more inclusive range of dominant forms. There are points of resistance; there are also moments of supersession. This is the dialectic of cultural struggle. In our times it goes on continuously in the complex lines of resistance and acceptance, refusal and capitulation, which make the field of culture a sort of constant battlefield.[94]

NOTES

1 See under Kilmalkedar parish, *Ordnance Survey Namebooks*, Book 1028, p. 28.
2 Mícheál Ó Mainín, 'Na Sagairt agus a mbeatha i bParóiste an Fheirtéaraigh' in Mícheál Ó Ciosáin (ed.), *Céad Bliain, 1871–1971* (Ballyferriter, 1973), pp. 19–20, 33.
3 Caoimhín Ó Danachair, 'The holy wells of Corkaguiney, Co. Kerry' in *R.S.A.I. Jn.*, xc (1960), p. 73.
4 Besides the sources cited earlier, I have also consulted I.F.C., MS 1823, p. 72; MS S418, pp. 104–5 (Dept. of Irish Folklore, U.C.D.).
5 De Latocnaye, *A Frenchman's walk through Ireland, 1796–7*, trans. John Stevenson (Belfast, 1917), p. 110.
6 Ibid.
7 Thomas Crofton Croker, *Researches in the south of Ireland* (reprint ed., Dublin, 1981), pp. 277–83.
8 Ibid., p. 281.
9 Ibid., p. 280.
10 Ibid., p. 279.
11 Ibid., p. 283.
12 Caesar Otway, *Sketches in Ireland descriptive of interesting and hitherto unnoticed districts in the north and south* (Dublin, 1827), pp. 307, 309.
13 Aindrias Ó Muimhneacháin (ed.), *Seanchas an táilliúra* (Dublin, 1978), pp. 69–70 (my translation).
14 William Carleton, *Traits and stories of the Irish peasantry* (2 vols, New York, 1862), i, p. xxiv.
15 Philip Dixon Hardy, *The holy wells of Ireland . . .* (Dublin, 1836), p. iii.
16 Ibid., pp. 38–42.
17 Ibid., p. 39.
18 Ibid.
19 W.M. Thackeray, *The Irish sketch book, 1842* (reprint ed., Belfast and Dover, New Hampshire, 1985), pp. 236–40.
20 Caoimhín Ó Danachair, 'Holy well legends in Ireland' in *Saga och Sed* (1960), pp. 35–43.
21 Énrí Ó Muirgheasa, 'The holy wells of Donegal' in *Béaloideas*, vi, no. 2 (1936), pp. 148–9.
22 Ibid., p. 155.
23 Ibid.
24 Ibid., p. 151.
25 Edward O'Toole, 'The holy wells of County Carlow' in *Béaloideas*, iv, no. 1 (1933), pp. 5–6.
26 Victor and Edith Turner, *Image and pilgrimage in Christian culture* (New York, 1978), pp. 206–7.
27 Peter Brown, *The cult of the saints* (London, 1981), pp. 3–4.

28 Brigitte Caulier, *L'eau et le sacré* (Paris, 1990), p. 23.
29 Mircea Eliade, *Patterns in comparative religion* (London, 1958), p. 43.
30 Pierre Boglioni, 'Pèlerinages et religion populaire: notes d'anthropologie et d'histoire' in Pierre Boglioni and Benoît Lacroix, *Les Pèlerinages au Québec* (Québec, 1981), pp. 6–7.
31 Ibid., pp. 9–10.
32 This figure is quoted by Charles Plummer, *Vitae sanctorum Hiberniae* (Oxford, 1910), i, p. cxlix.
33 S.J. Connolly, *Priests and people in pre-famine Ireland, 1780–1845* (Dublin and New York, 1982), pp. 94, 96–7.
34 Eliade, *Patterns*, p. 200.
35 Ibid., pp. 188–212.
36 W.G. Wood-Martin, *Traces of the elder faiths of Ireland . . .* (2 vols, London and New York, 1902), ii, 99.
37 Rev. John Healy, *The holy wells in Ireland*. I have been unable to find a date or place of publication for this pamphlet.
38 Eliade, *Patterns*, p. 193.
39 Boglioni, 'Pèlerinages', p. 14.
40 Ibid., pp. 15, 17.
41 Eliade, *Patterns*, p. 381.
42 Donatien Laurent, 'Le juste milieu: réflexion sur un rituel de circumambulation millénaire: la troménie de Locronan' in *Tradition et histoire dans la culture populaire* (Doc. d'Ethn. Rég. no. 11, C.A.R.E., 1990), pp. 255–92. I am very grateful to Dr Sylvie Muller for this reference.
43 Caulier, *L'eau*, p. 104.
44 Alwyn Rees and Brinley Rees, *Celtic heritage* (London, 1961), chap. 9 and *passim*.
45 Mircea Eliade, *The myth of the eternal return* (Princeton, 1971), pp. xiii-xiv, 5.
46 Lauri Honko, 'Kalevala—myth or history?' in Bo Almqvist, Séamas Ó Catháin, and Pádraig Ó Héalaí (ed.), *The heroic process* (Dublin, 1987), pp. 59–65.
47 Diarmuid Ó Giolláin, 'Myth and history: exotic foreigners in folk-belief' in *Temenos*, no. 23 (1987), pp. 59–65.
48 Caulier, *L'eau*, p. 34.
49 Máire MacNeill, *The festival of Lughnasa* (Dublin, 1982), p. 424.
50 Ibid., p. 425.
51 Ibid.
52 Ibid., p. 380.
53 Eliade, *Patterns*, pp. 319–21.
54 Michel Lagrée, *Religions et cultures en Bretagne, 1850-1950* (Paris, 1992), p. 299 (my translation). I am grateful to Dr Neil Buttimer for the reference to this book.
55 Caulier, *L'eau*, p. 23 (my translation).
56 Anton Erkoreka, 'Patologías por las que se recurre a santuarios en el País Vasco' in C. Álvarez Santaló, Maria Jesús Buxó, and S. Rodríguez Becerra (ed.), *La religiosidad popular, III: hermandades, romerías, y santuarios* (Barcelona, 1989), pp. 340–2.
57 Dixon Hardy, *Holy wells*, pp. 40–2.
58 Victor Turner, *Dramas, fields, and metaphors* (Ithaca and London, 1974), pp. 46–7.
59 Turner and Turner, *Image and pilgrimage*, pp. 206–7.
60 Ibid., p. 250.
61 Turner, *Dramas*, p. 53.
62 Lauri Honko, 'Theories concerning the ritual process' in Lauri Honko (ed.), *Science of religion studies in methodology* (The Hague, Paris, and New York, 1979), p. 388; Turner, *Dramas*, p. 197.

63 Mikhail Bakhtin, *Rabelais and his world* (Bloomington, Indiana, 1984), *passim*.
64 These were noted at St Declan's pattern at Ardmore, for example. See Dixon Hardy, *Holy wells*, pp. 40–2.

65 Bakhtin, *Rabelais*, pp. 78–9.
66 Ibid., p. 7.
67 Ibid., p. 10.
68 Ibid., *passim*.
69 John Eade and Michael J. Sallnow (ed.), 'Introduction' to *Contesting the sacred: the anthropology of Christian pilgrimage* (London and New York, 1991), p. 2.
70 Ibid., p. 15.
71 Bakhtin, *Rabelais*, p. 33.
72 Kevin Danaher, *The year in Ireland* (Cork, 1972), p. 181.
73 Connolly, *Priests and people*, pp. 140–1.
74 Dixon Hardy, *Holy wells*, pp. 59–60.
75 John Carr, *The stranger in Ireland, or a tour in the southern and western parts of that country in the year 1805* (London, 1806), p. 255.
76 Otway, *Sketches*, p. 313.
77 O'Toole, 'Holy wells', pp. 3–23, and pt ii of the same article in *Béaloideas*, iv, no. 2 (1933), pp. 107–30.
78 Connolly, *Priests and people*, p. 146.
79 Antonio Gramsci, *Selections from prison notebooks*, ed. and trans. by Quintin Hoare and Geoffrey Nowell Smith (London, 1971), p. 54.
80 Orvar Löfgren, 'The cultural grammar of nation-building' in Pertti J. Anttonen and Reimund Kvideland (ed.), *Nordic frontiers: recent issues in the study of modern traditional culture in the Nordic countries* (Turku, 1993), p. 221.
81 See Ernest Gellner, *Nations and nationalism* (Oxford, 1983), pp. 35–8.
82 Tony Bennett, Graham Martin, Colin Mercer, and Janet Woolacott (ed.), *Culture, ideology, and social process* (London, 1981), pp. 214, 216.
83 Gramsci, *Prison notebooks*, p. 57 n.; see also Bennett *et al.*, *Culture*, pp. 197–9.
84 The reference here, of course, is to Benedict Anderson's *Imagined communities* (London and New York, 1983). He sees 'the convergence of capitalism and print technology' as performing a crucial integrating function (p. 46).
85 Sir William Wilde, *Irish popular superstitions* (reprint ed., Dublin, 1979), p. 17.
86 Boglioni, 'Pèlerinages', p. 12.
87 Ibid., pp. 12–13.
88 Ibid., p. 11 (my translation).
89 O'Toole, 'Holy wells', pt i, p. 5.
90 Ibid., pp. 15–16.
91 Ibid., pt ii, p. 111.
92 MacNeill, *Lughnasa*, p. 80. Lagrée points out that modern means of transport speed up 'the rotation of the faithful', and in that sense 'the train is the enemy of the "abuses" and "disorders" traditionally inseparable from the pilgrimage . . .' (*Religions et cultures*, p. 305, [my translation]).
93 Lagrée, *Religions et cultures*, pp. 299–301.
94 Stuart Hall, 'Notes on deconstructing "the popular" ' in Raphael Samuel (ed.), *People's history and socialist theory* (London and Boston, 1981), p. 233.

9

The Lost World of Andrew Johnston: Sectarianism, Social Conflict, and Cultural Change in Southern Ireland during the Pre-Famine Era

KERBY A. MILLER

Since the Reformation sectarianism has been deeply rooted in both Protestant and Catholic Irish cultures, expressed in songs and folklore as well as in politics and violence. However, whereas religious prejudices may always be latent in Irish popular culture, it is arguable that often their most violent manifestations occur when each of the two religious communities is itself sharply divided by socio-economic and cultural antagonisms, and when Catholic and Protestant leaders therefore have special need to mobilise their respective followers against the 'traditional' enemy. In the early nineteenth century, for example, an ambitious Catholic middle class and an anxious Protestant ascendancy were locked not only in political conflict with each other but also, less overtly but no less significantly, in social conflicts with their own inferiors. In the pre-famine decades both the Catholic bourgeoisie and the Protestant landlord class sought to rationalise Irish agriculture, increase profits, and impose a free-market ethos on their poorer co-religionists. Both Catholic peasants and at least some members of the rural Protestant middle and lower classes resisted the blandishments of liberalism— the former through the violence of the agrarian secret societies, the latter in anguished letters to Tory newspapers—for both regarded the spirit of the market-place as inimical not only to their economic survival but also to archaic beliefs in an organic, paternalistic, and hierarchical society. Thus to deflect popular resentment within their own communities, as well as to challenge their rivals more effectively, Catholic and Protestant leaders alike employed political and religious symbols to marshal their co-religionists into all-class alliances and crusades for sectarian advantage. Faced with economic depression, overpopula-tion, and fierce competition for land and employment, most ordinary Catholics and Protestants faced the options of enlisting in those crusades or emigrating abroad—of supporting their own socio-economic exploiters or sailing to North America. As a result, both the triumph of liberal capitalism and the consequent sectarian and political struggles shaped a modern Ireland which became both profoundly bourgeois and deeply divided. For better or worse, in the process a way of life—an older world of different values and relationships—was lost forever. The trials and betrayals of Andrew Johnston, an insignificant but perhaps not an ignoble figure in the maelstrom of Irish history, illustrate how that process occurred.

During the twentieth century violent conflict between Irish Catholics and Protestants has been confined almost exclusively to Northern Ireland. But in the last quarter of the eighteenth century and the first half of the nineteenth, sectarian outrages frequently occurred throughout the island. Indeed, to judge from thousands of Irish petitions to the British Colonial Office, a desire to escape from violence was second only to the goal of economic independence in explaining why an estimated 500,000 Irish Protestants (with an approximately equal number of Catholics) emigrated during the pre-famine decades (1815–44). The same motive impelled significant numbers of Protestants and Catholics to migrate within Ireland, seeking safety in areas dominated by their co-religionists. Although the Protestant proportion of the future Northern Ireland was not appreciably diminished by emigration, and was probably enhanced by internal migration, the effects of these population movements on the much smaller Protestant communities in the counties of southern Ireland were very significant. The hemorrhage of southern Irish Protestants both resulted from and greatly contributed to the rise of middle-class Catholic political and economic ascendancy in those counties, and also contributed to a weakening of landlord control and British authority which eventually proved fatal to both.

For example, in 1834 County Longford contained 10,337 Protestant inhabitants, almost all members of the established Church of Ireland, about 9.1 percent of the county's population. But between 1834 and 1861 Longford's Protestant population fell by 33 percent, only slightly less than the 37 percent Catholic decline despite the much more severe impact of the great famine of 1845–51 on the county's predominantly Catholic lower classes of peasants and labourers. Prior to the famine one major cause of Protestant decline was the attrition of Protestant middlemen—head tenants who leased several hundred acres or more, most of which they sublet to a multitude of under-tenants. Once prominent members of County Longford society, Protestant middlemen were not only pillars of Protestant ascendancy, but also—in their roles as sublettors, investors, employers, and magistrates—they served as vital mainstays for the humbler ranks of Protestant small farmers, shopkeepers, artisans, and labourers. Consequently, their disappearance during the pre-famine decades eroded the infrastructure of Protestant society and ultimately weakened landlord and British power. This essay will investigate the causes of the middlemen's decline in County Longford by focusing on the fate of the Andrew Johnston family, whose remarkable letters to their emigrant children are preserved in the Huntington Library in California.[1]

Andrew Johnston, his wife, sister-in-law, and twelve children (five of whom emigrated in the 1830s) lived in the town of Ballymahon, located on the River Inny, in the parishes of Shrule and Noughaval in south Longford. In 1841 Ballymahon had 1,229 inhabitants, about 90 percent of whom were Catholics, the remainder parishioners of the local Church of Ireland. Although consisting primarily of only one main street, Ballymahon was blessed with a combined courthouse and markethouse, where markets were held every Thursday; large flour and corn mills; four annual fairs, one of which—the May cattle fair—was considered second only to the great Ballinasloe fair in regional importance; two schools; a dispensary; and a constabulary barracks. The town was also the residence of the Catholic bishop of Ardagh. The countryside surrounding Bally-mahon was fertile and considered ideal for grazing, although prior to the famine the land was still devoted primarily to tillage, especially to conacre, owing to its dense population of peasants and labourers. Ballymahon had a nearby dock on the Royal Canal, which provided cheap transport to Dublin, and it was sur-rounded by an unusually large number of gentlemen's 'big houses' and demesne lands. The proprietor of two of those houses, Ballymulvey and Moigh House, was William Molyneux Shuldham, who owned all of Ballymahon and most of the adjacent parishes—in all about 2,600 acres, later valued at nearly £2,700 per year.[2]

Andrew Johnston was a younger, non-inheriting son of a small proprietor, Peyton Johnston, from mid-Longford. From at least 1804 onwards, Andrew Johnston was a head tenant and middleman on the Shuldham estate. By the late 1820s and early 1830s Johnston was leasing about 30 percent of the Shuldham property—over 800 statute acres with an annual value of nearly £500—usually on leases running for three lives or thirty-one years. Sixty of these acres were in Ballymulvey townland, immediately adjacent to Ballymahon, and in the town itself Johnston rented eight more acres, divided into four lots, on which were located the town markethouse, his flour and corn mills, a flax-dressing concern, and his own residence—the latter situated in the shadow of his landlord's town house, Inny View, and just across the narrow bridge which spanned the river and separated Johnston's house and mills from the bulk of the town. On paper at least, Johnston's holdings made him one of Ballymahon's most affluent and influential citizens. In 1837 Johnston was fifty-six years old; during the preceding decades he had served as a vestryman, churchwarden, and tithe assessor in the local Anglican church; in 1821 he had registered to vote as a £50 freeholder (in 1832 as a £20 freeholder); and he and his family participated on equal terms in the social life of the lesser gentry of the south Longford-Westmeath border region. As will be seen later, Johnston also enjoyed one other species of property, also leased from Shuldham, which brought him unusual income, power, and ultimate disaster.[3]

The great crisis in Andrew Johnston's life began on Thursday, 21 September 1837. That evening about seven o'clock, one of his employees, a somewhat simple-minded and often inebriated Protestant named John Frayne, got into a fight with a young Catholic, a candidate for the priesthood named Thomas Ferrall, while the two men were crossing Ballymahon bridge in front of the Johnston residence. Andrew Johnston and his eldest son John moved to intervene, as did a sizable number of Ferrall's friends. The result was a small but fatal riot. Before the constabulary arrived to restore order, Johnston and his son were badly beaten, and Ferrall was mortally wounded when stabbed twice in his side. As a result of the testimony of several witnesses, including the accusation of the dying Thomas Ferrall, Andrew and John Johnston were arrested. The coroner's inquest was held over the next two days, and the coroner's jury concluded that Ferrall had been murdered--stabbed to death by John Johnston, aided by his father. Accordingly, the two men were arraigned for trial at the March 1838 assizes on the charge of murder, although both were soon released on bail. Their trial was later postponed until the July assizes, and the charge was reduced from murder to manslaughter. Prior to the trial, in late November 1837, Andrew Johnston barely escaped assassination when four bullets fired by unknown assailants struck the gig in which he was riding while inspecting his farms.

The Johnstons' trial was held at Longford town on 16 July 1838 before Judge Edward Pennefather. At the conclusion of the testimony the judge instructed the jury to acquit Andrew Johnston since the blows he had struck during the riot obviously had not been fatal. He then charged the jury that 'with respect to John Johnston they must be satisfied that the blows as stated, inflicted by him [on Thomas Ferrall], were in the defence of his father's life, at that time endangered, before such stabs could be justified' and the defendant acquitted; 'if they had a doubt,' he concluded, 'they should give the prisoners the benefit of it, for the criminal law requires every charge to be fully proven'. After briefly retiring, the jury acquitted both prisoners. Shortly afterward, however, Andrew Johnston relinquished or sold the interest in all his holdings, packed up his family and goods, and left Ballymahon and County Longford forever.[4]

It is impossible to determine what really transpired during the riot of 21 September 1837, for the specific issue of the Johnstons' guilt or innocence was entirely submerged in bitter political and sectarian interests which have coloured all the surviving evidence. The riot, the coroner's inquest, and the Johnstons' trial were covered extensively by the three provincial newspapers which served County Longford. According to the O'Connellite journal, the *Athlone Sentinel*, the affair was 'THE BALLYMAHON MURDER'—committed in cold blood by John Johnston. But the Tory newspapers, the *Athlone Conservative Advocate* and the *Westmeath Guardian and Longford News-Letter*, called Thomas Ferrall's death 'justifiable homicide' and hailed the Johnstons as 'innocent men, whose only crime has been the defence of their lives from the fury of . . . priest-ridden and furious mobs'. The Conservative weeklies, the constabulary reports, and the Johnstons' own letters claimed that the coroner's inquest was conducted unfairly, in an atmosphere of public excitement and intimidation; that the Johnstons were prevented from calling a single witness on their behalf; that the Catholic witnesses lied under oath; and that the coroner's jury which charged the Johnstons with murder was packed with ten Catholics against two Protestants. For their part local Catholics accused the magistrates of Orange bias when they released the Johnstons on bail, and the O'Connellite *Athlone Sentinel* ignored the subsequent attempt on Andrew Johnston's life, whereas the Tory papers featured it prominently.[5]

At the trial itself the prosecution witnesses claimed that the Johnstons had been the aggressors on Ballymahon bridge and that Andrew Johnston had beaten Ferrall senseless with a poker before John Johnston stabbed him with a dagger in front of sober, peaceful, and horrified Catholic bystanders. By contrast the defence witnesses testified that the Johnstons had carried no weapons; that before they could even touch Ferrall they had been set upon and badly beaten by a mob of drunken Catholics who had emerged from an adjacent public house; and that John Johnston had already fled into another house before Ferrall received his mortal injuries—presumably inflicted accidentally by other members of the crowd who were attempting to stab the Johnstons. (It is fruitless to attempt a reconciliation of such totally contradictory evidence, although it may be significant that Andrew Johnston's private account of the affair, conveyed in letters to his emigrant sons, largely corroborated the story later told by his defence witnesses.) Needless to say, the *Athlone Sentinel's* editor was disgusted with the Johnstons' ultimate acquittal by a jury allegedly containing nine Protestants and only three Catholics, while the *Westmeath Guardian* and other Conservative journals rejoiced at the Johnstons' narrow escape from 'popish persecution'.[6]

Of course, the Ballymahon riot was merely one of many 'outrages' which occurred in pre-famine Ireland, especially during the anti-tithe campaigns of the 1830s. Moreover, violence seems to have been unusually prevalent in County Longford. As early as 1793 Ballymahon itself was the venue of a major anti-militia riot, and in 1798 the final, horrific scenes of the United Irish rising were played out at Granard and Ballinamuck: the atrocities then committed by both Catholic insurgents and Protestant yeomen and militia created lasting hatreds. Because of a combination of circumstances—economic depression, tension over land use between commercial and subsistence cultivators, high population density, and the presence of a significant Protestant minority—Longford was wracked with agrarian and sectarian conflict during the pre-famine decades. From 1806 through the mid-1840s local secret agrarian societies were almost continuously active, and according to police reports, the Ribbonmen were unusually strong among the county's lower middle- and labouring-class Catholics, especially among townsmen and workers on the Royal Canal.[7]

Most important, beginning with the Catholic emancipation crisis of the late 1820s, political activity by the county's middle-class lay Catholics and clergy served to legitimate or at least to corroborate violent expressions of popular grievances against the Longford ascendancy. By the early 1830s Longford's Catholics were effectively mobilised in support of the perennial Liberal candidates for parliament, Luke White and his brother, Colonel Henry White, while the Conservatives rallied Protestant voters behind the ultra-Tory Anthony Lefroy, Viscount Forbes, and after Forbes's death in 1836, behind Charles Fox. Unhappily, the county witnessed almost constant political strife during the 1830s, for there were no fewer than six general or by-elections in the decade, and nearly all were extremely close contests since the restrictive £10 freehold franchise heavily favoured the more affluent Protestant minority. As mentioned earlier, the Catholic bishop of Ardagh, Dr William Higgins, resided in Ballymahon: he and many of his priests were ardent supporters of O'Connell, and their sermons and political activities helped to make south Longford a centre of pro-Liberal and anti-tithe agitation. For their part the county's Conservatives relied heavily on the Anglican clergy and the resurgent Orange Order to mobilise Protestant voters; during the 1830s Longford contained at least nine Orange Lodges, with an alleged total of 5,000 members. According to their critics, the local Tories also utilised the magistracy, the constabulary, and the prerogatives of landlordism to intimidate or punish enfranchised Catholics. Indeed, it appears that several of the wealthiest landlords, especially Lord Lorton, systematically cleared Catholic tenants from their estates and replaced them with Protestants. The result was further bitterness and a convergence of political protests and agrarian violence which culminated in the so-called Ballinamuck land war of 1835-9. Despite these Tory efforts, the Protestant cause in Longford was ultimately a losing one. Liberal election victories in 1832 and 1836 were thwarted by successful Tory petitions to parliament, but the last election of the decade in the summer of 1837 witnessed a great Liberal-Catholic triumph: Longford sent both Whites to parliament, and at Dublin Castle the newly-appointed Whig administration began what the defeated Tories called the 'Mulgravisation' of County Longford's magistracy and constabulary. As Andrew Johnston's sister-in-law despaired in early 1837, 'nothing is now given to Protestants but left to the mercy of papists, who are ruling them with a rod of iron'. As her comment suggests, by 1837 County Longford was bitterly polarised.[8]

Much evidence indicates that nearly all Longford's Protestants feared for their lives and fortunes in the 1830s—and especially after the Whites' 1837 victory—at the hands of what the *Westmeath Guardian* called a 'brutal and unintelligent' and now unrestrained 'peasantry'. Indeed, early in September 1837, a week prior to the Ballymahon riot, a mob of Catholics attacked a Protestant farmer and his labourers near Ballymahon, and a few months later a member of the Irish Constabulary, an Ulster Protestant, was murdered near Longford town. Nevertheless, although this climate of agitation and animosity provided the general context of the Ballymahon riot, it does not explain why Andrew Johnston and the Tory press believed that he and his family had been singled out as *specific* targets of 'popish persecution'. To be sure, Johnston consistently voted Tory, but so did nearly all Longford Protestants, and neither his letters nor the local newspapers suggest that he was prominent or even especially interested in either politics or the Orange Order. Likewise, the O'Connellite *Athlone Sentinel* failed to levy the usual charges that Johnston was a rack-renter or an 'exterminator', and what little evidence survives suggests that his relationships with his own Catholic subtenants and labourers were remarkably good. Moreover, in 1829—at the very height of the Catholic emancipation crisis—Johnston had founded in Ballymahon a Masonic Lodge which welcomed and contained many Catholic as well as Protestant members, perhaps in an attempt to create a social bridge between the otherwise divided religious communities in the region. Thus, in order to understand the popular animosity towards Johnston, it is necessary to examine more closely both his own position in Ballymahon and the dynamics of Catholic agitation in south Longford.[9]

Andrew Johnston not only leased 800 acres of farmland from the Shuldham estate, but he also leased the local mills and, more important, the right to levy and collect the 'tolls of markets' and the 'customs of fairs' held in Ballymahon. Since the weekly market was reportedly 'well-attended', and since the cattle fairs of the town were of considerable regional significance, Johnston's monopoly of the 'tolls and customs' brought him substantial profits. The *Westmeath Guardian* alleged that the tolls and customs amounted to £600 annually, and Johnston claimed that he made 'upwards of £200 a year' from them. Truly, Johnston was a 'middleman' in more than the usual sense of the term, for the leasing of both the local mills and the tolls and customs placed him in an economically strategic and intermediate position between the Catholic farmers and peasants of the south Longford countryside and the Catholic dealers and shopkeepers of Ballymahon. It was a highly lucrative position, but it was also a fatally vulnerable one.[10]

In pre-famine Ireland generally, Catholic political agitation on the local level was led by representatives of an aspiring bourgeoisie: strong farmers, professionals, shopkeepers, publicans, and priests of middle-class origins. County Longford was no exception, and its conflicts between middle-class Catholics and Protestants may have been especially fierce because in numerical terms the two groups were so evenly balanced. In his doctoral thesis Fergus O'Ferrall identified over thirty of the Liberal activists in and around Ballymahon during the pre-famine decades. For our purposes the most important of these men were Fr Peter Dawson, the administrator of Shrule parish in the years 1835–40 and an ambitious would-be bishop; Owen Maxwell, a grocer, and his brother Thomas Maxwell, a draper; George Corcoran, a physician; and Valentine Dillon, a substantial tenant on the Shuldham estate. Another prominent Liberal was H. Wilson Slator, a member of an affluent Protestant mercantile family, who nominated Luke White for parliament in 1837.[11]

Among such men liberal principles nicely converged not only with their own economic and political interests but also with their lower-class followers' traditional prejudices against both the Sasanaigh and 'parasitical middlemen' (such as the hated 'tithe-farmers'). As a result, it was not difficult for O'Connell's local champions to mobilise popular crusades under the banner of 'Catholic liberalism' against what they called 'artificial monopolies', which denied Catholics both equal political rights and equal opportunities to compete economically with Protestants. Of course, there were certain inconsistencies in Catholic liberalism. Lower-class Catholics in the secret agrarian societies, often engaged in an *intra*-communal class war over conacre rents and wages, knew that many members of the Catholic bourgeoisie were at least as exploitive as their Protestant counterparts. Likewise, the policy of 'exclusive dealing' (later known as 'boycotting'), which Catholic merchants often employed against their Protestant peers, certainly violated the liberal 'free market' ethos. Nevertheless, in a county as polarised along sectarian lines as Longford, a middle-class Catholic campaign against Protestant privilege could command widespread support. Moreover, a crusade against a *specific* Protestant's monopoly of tolls and customs could unite Catholics of all classes in both town and countryside behind middle-class leadership—and thus serve both the broad hegemonic and the personal economic interests of that leadership.[12]

Interestingly, the *Athlone Sentinel* never alluded to the possibility that the Ballymahon riot might have been sparked by middle-class Catholic hostility to or jealousy of Johnston's control of the tolls and customs, though this Liberal newspaper often reported and applauded Catholic assaults on that peculiar monopoly which occurred elsewhere in Ireland. However, according to the Tory press, the Johnstons' own letters, and some of the testimony which emerged at their trial, the riot of 21 September could not be understood except in such a context. According to this evidence, shortly after the Liberal victory in the 1837 election, Ballymahon's Catholic activists determined to punish Johnston, ostensibly for his Tory convictions, by denying him his profits from the tolls and customs. In late August or early September some of the Whites' chief supporters, led by Fr Peter Dawson, erected three public 'cranes' or weighing scales and directed their followers to use these, instead of Johnston's, on market days. This boycott was extremely effective: in a letter to his son, Johnston complained that he 'never rec[eive]d a penny for anything since' that 'vilinous [*sic*] priest Dawson put up' the new cranes. Moreover, the incident which precipitated the Ballymahon riot, the fight between Thomas Ferrall and Johnston's employee John Frayne, seems to have occurred as a direct result of the strain and humiliation consequent on this boycott. Not only did the fight occur at the end of a market day, when popular tensions surrounding the issue were at their height, but Ferrall seems to have been one of Fr Dawson's more active and boastful adherents, while Frayne's major duty (perhaps the only one of which he was capable) was the management of Andrew Johnston's now-deserted crane. Finally, although it is unlikely that the riot—*as it actually occurred*—was premeditated, there were indications in the trial testimony, brought out under examination by the defence counsel, that a public meeting or a popular protest of *some kind* against Johnston's monopoly had been planned for that very evening.[13]

Of course, Thomas Ferrall's death and the Johnstons' subsequent arrest, trial, and hasty departure from Ballymahon could not have been foreseen. Nevertheless, there is strong circumstantial evidence that local Catholic activists were quick to take advantage of the Johnstons' sudden vulnerability. For example, it may be significant that the presiding magistrate at the coroner's inquest which refused to hear the Johnstons' witnesses and which charged Andrew and John Johnston with murder was none other than Luke White—though surely under ordinary circumstances such a minor affair would not have commanded personal attention from an M.P. and a newly-appointed lord lieutenant of the county. Perhaps more telling, during the inquest itself both Thomas Maxwell and Dr George Corcoran gave especially damning testimony, swearing that Thomas Ferrall, in a dying declaration before the local priest Fr Peter Dawson, had branded John Johnston as his murderer. Corcoran later repeated his testimony at the Johnstons' trial, and although Maxwell did not testify again on that occasion, another witness for the prosecution—James Armstrong, whom even the *Athlone Sentinel* described as 'a wretched, ragged creature'—hinted under cross-examination that Maxwell and others might have rewarded him for his testimony. Indeed, according to Andrew Johnston's sister-in-law, among all of Ballymahon's leading Catholics only Valentine Dillon, a member of the coroner's jury, 'behaved handsomely' during the crisis, perhaps because—of all the Catholic leaders involved—only he was also a member of Andrew Johnston's Masonic Lodge.[14]

At this distance, of course, it is impossible to be as certain as were the Tory newspapers and Johnston's sister-in-law Alicia Welsh that, in her words, 'all this ha[d] been planned'. Nevertheless, Ballymahon's middle-class Catholics certainly benefited in general from the Johnstons' downfall, for no one dared henceforth to lease or enforce Shuldham's tolls and customs, and 'free trade'— largely in Catholic hands—became the order of the day in Ballymahon. In addition, it may have been more than fortuitous that some local Liberal leaders benefited personally from the Johnstons' discomfort and departure. For example, almost immediately, the family of H. Wilson Slator, the Liberal Protestant ally of Luke White, secured Johnston's old lease of the town's corn and flour mills. More significantly, in 1839, in what was surely a sale forced by his distress, Andrew Johnston transferred his lease of Derrynagalliagh, a townland of 320 acres, to Owen Maxwell in a transaction witnessed by Dr George Corcoran. Indeed, within a few years the Catholic Maxwells—scarcely mentioned in the 1826 tithe-applotment lists—seem to have supplanted the Protestant Johnstons in Ballymahon. By the mid-1840s Owen Maxwell was a member of the local poor-law board of guardians and rented at least 24 acres of land within and immediately adjacent to Ballymahon; according to the local historian, by mid-century Owen Maxwell owned or rented 'half the town'. Similarly, his brother Thomas became secretary of the local loan fund, and by 1871 he owned outright nearly 570 acres in south Longford. Clearly, for such men patriotism in the service of Catholic Ireland could be more than spiritually rewarding.[15]

Yet it would be misleading to attribute Andrew Johnston's downfall solely to *Catholic* pressure and to *sectarian* conflict. Johnston's economic position had been deteriorating long before the Ballymahon riot, and, most importantly, the Protestant middle class in Longford and more generally in southern Ireland was being eroded by socio-economic and cultural conflicts *within the Protestant community itself.* In part Andrew Johnston's economic problems reflected the long postwar depression which afflicted Ireland in general and the middleman class in particular. In 1819 the Anglican curate of Shrule parish had described Ballymahon as 'thriving', but twenty years later John O'Donovan observed that 'little business is carried on'. In 1834 Johnston himself wrote that 'it was a fortunate day' when his emigrant sons 'left Ballymahon, as there is nothing to be done in the country'. After the Napoleonic wars domestic industry in the north Leinster counties collapsed while prices for both livestock and tillage products contracted sharply. Still, according to British traveller H.D. Inglis, Longford's burgeoning population and intense competition for land kept rents exceptionally high, and for head tenants like Johnston, whose long leases had been negotiated during the prosperous war years, the results were catastrophic. '[E]very thing the landholder has to dispose of is low' in price, Johnston complained, but 'the landlords [were] not making any [rent] reduction[s]'.[16]

Johnston's letters indicate that he struggled heroically to avoid falling into arrears, but by 1837 what Johnston's wife Eliza called his 'enormous' rents, plus the failure of some ill-judged speculations in grain futures, forced him to advertise his beloved farm, 'Highlands', on the shores of Lough Ree. But Johnston was unable to find a purchaser prior to the Ballymahon riot and his farm's subsequent forced sale. Thus in March 1837, six months before the fatal incident on Ballymahon bridge, his wife admitted that 'wee [*sic*] are at present in a very precarious state as to our affairs'. Certainly, by that summer Johnston was exceptionally vulnerable to any assault on the tolls and customs, which had now become the primary source of his declining income.[17]

Andrew Johnston's economic situation was not unique in southern Ireland, for middlemen specifically—and middle-class Protestants generally—appear to have suffered acutely during the depressed pre-famine decades. For example, the Johnstons' own letters reveal that most of their relatives and acquaintances were living shabbily, in genteel poverty—'struggling . . . to keep up an appearance upon very little'. Some of their kinsmen suffered dramatic declines in status, and Johnston's own niece—heir to his brother's now bankrupt estate—married a gardener's son and worked in Dublin as a servant or, at best, a governess. The

Johnstons' correspondence also suggests that under the impact of economic distress middle-class Protestant society was crumbling from within, just at the moment when solidarity in the face of Catholic assaults was most essential. According to the letters, ties of kinship and mutual assistance were dissolving rapidly in a welter of acrimonious disputes and lawsuits, most of which stemmed from the unwillingness or inability of relatives to honour family settlements and other legal obligations which had been incurred in more prosperous times. Likewise, young Protestants often found it difficult or impossible to secure employment or other assistance from relatives who still possessed some wealth and influence. Thus, despite Andrew Johnston's past generosity to his own and his wife's kinsmen, he was unable to secure similar financial aid when his fortunes faltered in the mid-1830s.[18]

But a more important source of Johnston's troubles—and perhaps the key reason why local Catholics felt by 1837 that they could attack him with impunity--was that Johnston's own landlord had turned against him and was undermining his social status. According to the local Protestant curate, in the late eighteenth and early nineteenth centuries the relationship between Captain John Brady Shuldham and his tenants had been characterised by generous paternalism from above and willing deference from below. The people of south Longford regarded Captain Shuldham with affection, he wrote, for their landlord's 'family had been endeared to them and their ancestors by countless acts of kindness for many generations'. 'If every Irish landlord . . . would follow the example of Captain Shuldham', the curate concluded, 'Ireland would be happy and contented.' During those happier times Andrew Johnston had even named one of his sons Shuldham in his landlord's honour, and he and the captain's other tenants had celebrated Shuldham's victory in a protracted lawsuit as if it had been their own triumph, parading through Ballymahon and illuminating the neighbourhood with bonfires.[19]

Unfortunately, however, Captain John Brady Shuldham died unmarried in 1832, and his Longford estate then passed to his brother William Molyneux Shuldham. Whether for personal, economic, or ideological reasons, the new proprietor displayed a much more instrumental and exploitive attitude towards his estate and its tenants. Indeed, in 1833 Shuldham became a semi-permanent absentee, residing primarily at his new wife's estate at Bellaghy, Co. Antrim, and visiting his Longford properties only occasionally. Meanwhile, he employed a salaried agent to manage his south Longford estate—thus bypassing Andrew Johnston and his other middlemen--and began to press his lessees for rent, to deny lease renewals when old contracts expired, and to evict old tenants for non-payment of arrears. Thus in 1834 the Johnstons complained that since the Shuldhams had left Ballymahon, there was 'no word, no talk of there [sic] return, but writing every day to the agent for money is the[ir] cry'. Moreover, the income raised thereby was invested in County Antrim, not on the Longford properties.

There is 'no order for leases, no order for building, no order for any one thing to improv[e] the tenants since' [Shuldham's departure]. Johnston's wife complained, 'it is folly to live here strug[g]ling to make rent for such a man'. Traveling through south Longford in the same year, Inglis noted the unhappy consequences: Ballymahon and its environs, he wrote, were 'utterly neglected by the proprietor, who grants no leases and acts . . . as if he had no interest in the permanent improvement of his property'. '[B]ad as this town looked when you saw it,' Andrew Johnston wrote to one of his emigrant sons, 'it is fifty times worse now: houses falling out of the face and no sign of loans or any encouragement what ever.'[20]

Johnston himself suffered immediately from Shuldham's new policies, which led to a growing personal estrangement between himself and his proprietor. 'Mr Shuldham is grown more and more every day dark and darker to your father and shows no intention to renew' his leases, wrote Johnston's wife in 1835; 'times are sadly altered [since the days] when a Johnston was supposed to have a first claim on a Shuldham', but now 'every one thinks he [Shuldham] wishes to thro[w] of[f] the old tenants'—that is, the middlemen—and let his lands directly to the Catholic farmers at higher rents and on shorter leases or even annual tenancies. By the spring of 1837 Johnston was desperate to sell the interest in his holdings, for he now knew—as his embittered sister-in-law declared—that he could expect nothing but 'enmity from his landlord . . . , as he is grinding his tenants to the dust'. Indeed, no sooner had the Ballymahon riot and the coroner's inquest occurred than Shuldham served Andrew Johnston with eviction notices for all his tenancies. Neither Johnston's ultimate acquittal nor the intercession of mutual friends and local Tory leaders could dissuade Shuldham from his cruel course, and in the end Johnston left Ballymahon with only 'about £500 to begin the world anew'.[21]

Johnston's fate serves to highlight the contradictory economic and political strategies which landlords in County Longford and elsewhere in Ireland pursued in the pre-famine decades. On the one hand, Irish Protestant leaders had long recognised the relationships between population and power, and their periodic inquiries into the demographic 'progress of popery' clearly demonstrated what they most feared: that ever since the early eighteenth century the Protestant population of southern Ireland had declined in proportional if not absolute terms. In County Longford itself, for example, the Protestant percentage of the population had shrunk from 15 percent in 1731 to 13 percent in 1766 and to merely 9 percent by 1831–4. Primarily, this decline was due to emigration (and to a lesser extent, conversions to Catholicism) among middle- and lower-class Protestants. And according to historian Louis Cullen, the Protestant community's demographic decline was attributable especially to the economic downfall and emigration of Protestant middleman families: 'the accelerating decay of the middleman's world', Cullen wrote, 'greatly weakened the Protestant interest in the [Irish] countryside'; 'the central pockets of rural Protestants fell apart', and Protestant society in southern Ireland began an inexorable decline. In turn, of course, reduced Protestant numbers inevitably meant diminished Tory power and a consequent weakening of support for the union, for the established church, and for landlordism.[22]

Therefore, in hindsight at least, Shuldham's harsh treatment of Andrew Johnston and the other Protestant middlemen on his estate would appear to have been detrimental to his own long-term interests and to those of the entire Protestant ascendancy. Indeed, Johnston's sister-in-law immediately recognised the implications of Shuldham's policies: 'your papa was the person [who] should stand between Shuldham and the people,' she wrote to her nephew in America, 'but that is all over now. He [Shuldham] must fight the battle now himself.' Shuldham's actions were by no means unique, however, and landlord policy generally in the pre-famine period was to clear middlemen from their estates, thus abolishing economic niches that hitherto had sheltered Protestants of middling wealth and rank. Likewise, ordinary Protestant tenant farmers, who might previously have expected preferential treatment from their landlords, also were becoming victims of rent-maximising leasing policies. For example, in 1837 the staunchly Tory *Westmeath Guardian and Longford News-Letter* admitted that the 'gentlemen of the county have . . . taken their lands out of the hands of Protestant tenants' and leased those farms to Catholics willing to pay higher rents. Letters to the same newspaper indicated that many middling and poor Protestants felt bitterly betrayed by their proprietors' new policies, and they asked how Tory landlords expected to maintain their party's political strength if they continued to take advantage of the 'ruinous spirit of competition' for leases which was driving the Protestant yeomanry out of the island. And given the likely conditions of sectarian hiring practices, a loss of Protestant farms would in turn result in a contraction of labouring opportunities for the poorer categories of Protestants. The effect of this negative multiplier would not have stopped there, but would also have extended to shopkeepers, artisans, and others servicing Protestant farmers and labourers.[23]

What we appear to be seeing, therefore, in the case of Andrew Johnston and others is the dissolution of earlier patterns of paternalism and preference in favour of classic liberal, free-market principles of maximising the returns to land-ownership—even at the expense of straining or even destroying the social bonds that extended vertically through Protestant communities. Those bonds, rooted in the original colonial settlements and in pre-modern notions of hierarchy and organic community, had drawn sustenance from shared religious and political affiliations. But in an increasingly commercialised Irish society conflicts of interest across class lines now cut across community solidarity. Thus, just as the Catholic bourgeoisie raised the banners of religion and repeal to mobilise peasants and labourers behind middle-class leadership, so also did many of County

Longford's Protestant landlords and clergy try to compensate for the increasing instrumentality of their class's economic policies by sponsoring the spread of the Orange Order, by financing the evangelical enthusiasm of the New Reformation, and by mobilising the Protestant electorate in the Brunswick Clubs. In addition, a few Protestant proprietors, such as Lady Rosse and Lord Lorton, renewed their ancestors' sectarian leasing policies in order to generate what the *Westmeath Guardian* termed 'a spirit of encouragement . . . to those [Protestants] who for some years past have been too much neglected and driven from these shores to seek protection in foreign lands'.[24]

Through such strategies upper-class Protestants successfully redefined the terms of Protestant solidarity and thereby renegotiated their cultural hegemony over their poorer co-religionists. By themselves, however, such largely symbolic actions could not stem the steady attrition of southern Ireland's Protestant communities. For all its notoriety, 'exclusive leasing' in favour of Protestants was practiced inconsistently and by only a handful of proprietors. Whether resident or absentee, too many landlords were either short-term profiteers or sincere champions of a free-market ethos which challenged the maintenance of an artificial, sectarian market-place. Despite their demands for Protestant loyalty and deference, most landlords pursued economic policies which gave their middle- and working-class co-religionists little option other than emigration. Ironically also, the increasingly visible Orangeism, evangelicalism, and abrasive politics sponsored by Longford's leading Tories only invited Catholic reprisals on more vulnerable middle- and working-class Protestants, which in turn stimulated their further emigration. For example, in the late 1830s the crown solicitor of the county noted that Longford's population had become so religiously and politically polarised that Catholics considered all 'the lower population who are Protestants' to be bitter Orangemen, 'whether they [really] are so or not'. Thus Andrew Johnston testified that the members of the mob which had attacked him on Ballymahon bridge had cried out, '[H]ere he is again, the Orange rascal. [N]ow is our time to mas[s]acre them all'—despite the fact that Johnston's sponsorship of an interdenominational Masonic Lodge strongly indicated his aversion to Orangeism and its bigoted spirit.[25]

Sadly, by the late 1830s Andrew Johnston was an anachronism, whether viewed from the perspective of a Protestant landlord class which preached traditional Toryism yet generally practiced free-market liberalism, or from the perspective of an aspiring Catholic bourgeoisie which waved the banner of anti-monopoly capitalism but used it to cloak sectarian warfare against their Protestant competitors. Even Johnston's own sister-in-law recognised the hopelessness of his position in an era when neither his traditional loyalty to the Shuldhams nor his customary paternalism towards his Catholic under-tenants was any longer rewarded by 'an ungrateful, treacherous people'.[26]

Furthermore, the conflicts within Protestant society were cultural as well as

economic, internalised as well as overt, and in these respects Andrew Johnston
was also a 'middleman', trapped in an increasingly untenable position, whose own
kinfolk mirrored his community's internal tensions. For example, though both
Johnston's and his wife's families originally came from County Cavan, they
represented very distinct epochs of Protestant social history. Johnston's ancestors
had migrated to Longford in the 1740s, when his grandfather married a local
heiress from east Connacht. What can be reconstructed of his family's history
tends to characterise the males as stereotypically eighteenth-century, southern
Irish 'squireens', with the easy-going, hard-drinking, but relatively tolerant
habits which were described nostalgically by Sir Jonah Barrington and critically
by Arthur Young. For example, by the 1830s it appears that Andrew Johnston's
older brother had long since frittered away the family estate in mid-Longford,
perhaps by contracting a second marriage to a Catholic woman less than a third
his age, and Johnston himself frequently joined his Catholic subtenants and
labourers to drink illegally-distilled *poitín* at cockfights and harvest festivals. In
sharp contrast Johnston's wife, Eliza Welsh, had come from Cavan much more
recently, and most of her relatives still lived in south Ulster, where they were
small proprietors, Church of Ireland clergy, enthusiastic evangelicals, and
staunch Orangemen. In short, the Welsh family was resolutely Protestant, bourgeois, and respectable in nineteenth-century terms, and Johnston's wife was
'much fretted about' her husband's behaviour and enjoined her children to avoid
'idleness', 'drink, and high living'. The Johnston correspondence leaves no doubt
that both Eliza and her resident sister Alicia Welsh revered Andrew Johnston, but
it is equally obvious that they regarded him as a champion of a vanishing era,
whose customs and attitudes were disfunctional in an increasingly instrumental
and intolerant age. Thus, while Johnston long resisted the necessity of abandoning Ballymahon, his sister-in-law was more realistic: between their 'heartless
landlord' and 'a rabble of papists', she wrote, there no longer existed a 'middle
ground'. Instead, 'the country is in such a state [that] each now stick to their
party.'[27]

When one's traditional 'party' was no longer led by paternalistic landlords but
instead dominated by rural capitalists of convenient convictions, there were few
options to migration or militant Orangeism. Ironically, as Longford's Protestant
middle class and demographic strength steadily waned, local landlords had to
rely more and more heavily on formal instruments of British power—the magistracy, the constabulary, and ultimately the army—to maintain their authority.
But in the late 1830s that recourse failed during Lord Mulgrave's reform
administration, and even the Tories' return to power in 1841 under Robert Peel
did not signal the return to Orange ascendancy which Alicia Welsh and other
ultra-Protestants had anticipated. Subsequently, some prominent local Tories,
such as Samuel Blackhall and Richard Maxwell Fox, openly deserted their
erstwhile followers and joined the Liberal camp. In such a climate of expediency

it was no wonder that in the years 1841–3, when Johnston and his relatives begged the Tories in Dublin Castle for government appointments, their well-founded claims that they had been 'driven to beggary for [their] exertions in the Conservative cause' went unheeded. Once an obstacle to the economic ambitions of his landlord and his Catholic competitors alike, Johnston—like the archaic world view which he represented—was now merely an embarrassment to his former friends and political spokesmen.[28]

Whatever happened to middle-class, southern Irish Protestant families such as the Johnstons? At least a few converted to Catholicism, as some of Andrew Johnston's poorer relatives seem to have done. A very much larger number emigrated, particularly to British North America, where they could attempt to recreate past securities in a new, yet culturally familiar and politically congenial environment. Finally, an unknown number, perhaps chiefly from border counties like Longford, followed the bitter path which Andrew Johnston took from Ballymahon to the safety of strong Protestant-majority areas in the future Northern Ireland. By 1839 Johnston's economic problems were still considerable, but he was now leasing a farm from the deputy grand master of the Orange Order, on the shores of Lough Erne, in a County Fermanagh parish which was over 85 percent Protestant. Whether Johnston actually found happiness, as opposed to mere physical security, among his co-religionists in the 'black north' is another matter, and his sister-in-law's last letters suggest that he had more trouble dealing with Protestant Ulster's 'clever' business practices than with the waterlogged and weed-choked pastures of his new farm. What is more certain is that Johnston's move to Ulster symbolised the final erosion of any 'middle ground' between Ireland's increasingly polarised worlds of Protestants and Catholics, landlords and peasants. The increasing congruence of religion, politics, and geography prefigured Ireland's ultimate partition into two hostile, sectarian, petty-bourgeois, and culturally-repressive states, neither of which, one suspects, would Andrew Johnston have found very congenial. Likewise, whether Johnston's former subtenants and labourers in south Longford benefited from his downfall and departure is problematic. But as one of the few apologists for the old order lamented, 'if the middleman had been his tenant's master, he was also his . . . protector', and now 'there is no link between the highest and the lowest'. By the eve of the famine, wrote another, more critical observer, the formerly 'large and prosperous, albeit parasitic class' of Protestant middlemen had virtually disappeared, and with its disappearance fell one of the pillars of landlordism, of Protestant society, and of an older, unequal, yet less bitterly sectarian society in Longford and elsewhere in southern Ireland.[29]

NOTES

1 I would like to thank Sharon Fleming and Patricia Miller, whose painstaking transcriptions of
the Johnston letters made this essay possible; Dr Líam Kennedy of the Queen's University,
Belfast, for generous sharing of ideas, office space, and research tasks; Dr Fergus O'Ferrall,
for allowing me to read his masterful doctoral thesis on early nineteenth-century Longford
politics; the Research Council of the University of Missouri-Columbia, the American Council
of Learned Societies, the Huntington Library, and the National Endowment for the Humani-
ties for financing this research; and most of all, Paddy Whelan, Marian Keaney, Fr Owen
Devaney, Jude Flynn, and the other members of the County Longford Historical Society who
made my inquiries into south Longford history both profitable and enjoyable. I would also like
to thank the editors of the *Huntington Library Quarterly* for permission to republish portions
of this essay, which first appeared in vol. 49, no. 4 (Autumn 1986), pp. 295–306, of that journal.
    On population, see W. T. Hamilton (ed.), *Abstract of the first report of the commissioners
appointed to enquire into the state of religious and other instruction in Ireland* (London, 1835), pp.
16–189; and W. E. Vaughan and A.J. Fitzpatrick (ed.), *Irish historical statistics: population,
1821–1971* (Dublin, 1978), p. 51.
On middlemen generally, see David Dickson, 'Middlemen' in Thomas Bartlett and D.W.
Hayton (ed.), *Penal era and golden age: essays in Irish history, 1690–1800* (Belfast, 1979), pp.
162–85; L. M. Cullen, *The emergence of modern Ireland, 1600–1900* (Dublin, 1983 ed.), pp.
99–107, 128–31; and Cormac Ó Gráda, *Ireland: a new economic history, 1780–1939* (Oxford,
1994), pp. 31–3, 125–7.
The Johnston family manuscripts, formally titled the Peyton Johnston MSS, form part of the
Robert Alonzo Brock collection at the Huntington Library, San Marino, California. A typescript of most of the letters has been deposited in the Longford-Westmeath County Library
Headquarters in Mullingar.
2 Information on Ballymahon from *The traveller's new guide through Ireland* (Dublin, 1815), pp.
184–5; William Shaw Mason, *A statistical account or parochial survey of Ireland* (Dublin, 1819),
iii, 337–67; James Johnston, map of 'The town of Ballymahon, 1825' (Longford-Westmeath
County Library); H.D. Inglis, *A tour throughout Ireland in . . . 1834* (London, 1835), i, 338
and *passim;* T. MacManus, 'One hundred years ago', *Longford year book, 1931* (Longford,
1931), pp. 9–13; *Thom's directory of Ireland* (Dublin, 1846), citation courtesy of Paddy Whelan,
Ballymahon; *Report of the commission on public instruction, Ireland* [C 45–6], H.C. 1835, xxxiii,
pp. 62–3; *Parliamentary gazeteer of Ireland* (Dublin, 1844), i, 182; *Return of owners of land of
one acre and upwards in . . . Ireland* (Dublin, 1876), pp. 52–5.
3 James Johnston, map of 'James Dowdall's part of . . . Ballymahon, 1804' (N.L.I., 16F. 15);
Tithe-applotment books, Co. Longford, 1826 (National Archives [Ireland], hereafter cited as
N.A.); James Johnston, map of 'Town of Ballymahon'; Lease of Derrynagalagh, L. Warren
and W. Barton to Andrew Johnston, 2 April 1822 (N.A., 805/475/542, 810); Andrew Johnston
to Peyton Johnston, 15 October 1837 (Peyton Johnston MSS); Shrule parish-vestry minute
book (Representative Church Body Library, Dublin); Lists of freeholders, Co. Longford (Irish
Genealogical Office, Dublin), courtesy of Dr Kevin Whelan.
4 See Johnston family letters of 22 June 1835 (on Frayne), 20 December 1837, and 12 January
1838 (Peyton Johnston MSS); Report of Samuel Alworthy, 22 September 1837 (N.A., State
of the country papers, 1837/19/197); *Athlone Sentinel*, 22, 29 September 1837, 20 July 1838;
Westmeath Guardian and Longford News-Letter, 28 September, 2 November 1837, 8 March,
19 July 1838; *Athlone Conservative Advocate*, 28 September 1837 (all newspapers in the British
Library, London).
5 See note 4 above, and also 'A resident of Longford', 'Insurrectionary state of the county of
Longford', *Dublin University Magazine,* ii (January 1838), pp. 121–3.
6 See the sources cited in note 4.

7 *Parliamentary gazeteer of Ireland,* i, 182; H.A. Richey, *A short history of the Royal Longford Militia, 1793–1893* (Dublin, 1894), pp. 10–12; Sean Murray, 'A short history of County Longford' (MS in Longford-Westmeath County Library), p. 57; J.P. Farrell, *Historical notes and stories of the County Longford* (Dublin, 1886), p. 204; M.R. Beames, *Peasants and power: the Whiteboy movements and their control in pre-famine Ireland* (Dublin, 1983), pp. 43, 85–6, 132; idem, 'The Ribbon societies: lower-class nationalism in pre-famine Ireland' in *Past &Present,* no. 97 (November 1982), pp. 129, 140; Tom Garvin, 'Defenders, Ribbonmen, and others: underground political networks in pre-famine Ireland' in *Past & Present,* no. 96 (August 1982), pp. 133–55, esp. p. 151; Report of Capt. Edward Hill, R.M., 31 January 1842 (P.R.O., C.O. 904/9).

8 Fergus O'Ferrall, 'The struggle for Catholic emancipation in County Longford, 1824–29' in *Teathbha,* no. 1 (October 1978), pp. 259–79; idem, 'The Ballinamuck "land war", 1835–39' in *Teathbha,* no. 2 (March 1983), pp. 104–9; idem, 'The growth of political consciousness in Ireland, 1824–1848' (Ph.D. thesis, University of Dublin, 1978), pp. 485–676; C. Moloney, 'Parliamentary returns, 1830–80: a thesis' (MS in Longford County Library, Longford), no pagination; B.M. Walker (ed.), *Parliamentary election results in Ireland, 1801–1922* (Dublin, 1978), pp. 228–9, 298–9; J.J. MacNamee, *History of the archdiocese of Ardagh* (Dublin, 1954), pp. 458–9; James Monahan, *Records relating to the diocese of Ardagh and Clonmacnois* (Dublin, 1886), pp. 160–68; Donal Kerr, *Peel, priests, and politics: Sir Robert Peel's administration and the Roman Catholic church in Ireland, 1841–46* (Oxford, 1982), p. 8; *Report from the select committee to inquire into the nature . . . of the Orange Lodge associations. . .* , [C 377], H.C. 1835, ix, appendix, *passim*; Grand Orange Lodge, Book of warrants, no date, and Book of new warrants, 1875 (Library, Grand Orange Lodge Headquarters, Belfast); 'Resident of Longford', 'Insurrectionary state', p. 123; Alicia Welsh to Peyton Johnston, 8 February 1837 (Peyton Johnston MSS).

9 *Westmeath Guardian andLongfordNews-Letter,* 24 August, 14, 21 September 1837, 4 January 1838; Masonic Lodge warrant books (Library, Grand Lodge of the Order of Masons, Dublin), with assistance from Paddy Whelan in identifying Ballymahon Lodge members.

10 *Westmeath Guardian and Longford News-Letter*, 19 July 1838; *Parliamentary Gazeteer of Ireland,* i, 182; Andrew Johnston to Peyton Johnston, 20 December 1837 (Peyton Johnston MSS).

11 Tom Garvin, *The evolution of Irish nationalist politics* (Dublin, 1981), pp. 34–52; Fergus O'Ferrall, *Daniel O'Connell* (Dublin, 1981), *passim*; idem, 'Growth of political consciousness', pp. 484–6, 499–501, 518, 530–9, 548–9, 595, 603–5, 675–6, 687–8; on Slator, see *Athlone Sentinel,* 19 August 1837.

12 On Liberal–Catholic ideology, see O'Ferrall, *Daniel O'Connell*; idem, *Catholic emancipation: Daniel O'Connell and the birth of Irish democracy* (Dublin, 1985). The literature on agrarian secret societies is voluminous; see especially Samuel Clark and J.S. Donnelly, Jr. (ed.), *Irish peasants: violence and political unrest, 1780–1914* (Madison, 1983).

13 On Catholic-Liberal protests against tolls and customs elsewhere in Ireland, see *Athlone Sentinel,* 27 April 1838 (Moate), 1 June 1838 (Ballyboy), 24 August 1838 (Nenagh). See also *Westmeath Guardian and Longford News-Letter,* 28 September 1837, 19 July 1838; *Athlone Conservative Advocate,* 21, 28 September 1837; 'Resident of Longford', 'Insurrectionary state', pp. 121–3; Alicia Welsh to Peyton Johnston, 1 October 1837, and Andrew Johnston to same, 15 October 1837 (Peyton Johnston MSS).

14 *Athlone Sentinel,* 29 September 1837; *Westmeath Guardian and Longford News-Letter,* 19 July 1838 (revealingly, James Armstrong's reference to Maxwell was omitted from the *Athlone Sentinel*'s transcription of the trial testimony—one of several curious discrepancies between the two newspapers' reports of the trial); Alicia Welsh and Anna Cox to Peyton Johnston, 28 September–1 October 1837 (Peyton Johnston MSS), on Valentine Dillon. See also Masonic Lodge warrant books, cited in note 9 above.

15 Alicia Welsh to Peyton Johnston, 1 October 1837 (Peyton Johnston MSS); on Shuldham's

tolls and customs and the tenancies of the Slators and Maxwells, see *Valuation of land* [*Griffith's*], *Ballymahon union* (Dublin, 1872), *passim;* Lease of Derrynagalliagh, Andrew Johnston to Owen Maxwell, 5 April 1839 (N.A., 1839/6/219); on Owen Maxwell, I have also relied on O'Ferrall, 'Growth of political consciousness', pp. 587–8, 675, and on information from Paddy Whelan, Ballymahon; on Thomas Maxwell, see *Slator's national commercial directory*, p. 11; *Return of owners of land*, pp. 52–5.

16 Shaw Mason, *Statistical account*, iii, 337; John O'Donovan cited in MacManus, 'One hundred years ago', p. 9; Andrew Johnston to Peyton Johnston, 20 January 1834 (Peyton Johnston MSS); Inglis, *Tour throughout Ire.*, i, 348–53.

17 Eliza Johnston to Peyton Johnston, 27 January 1834, 24 October 1835, 4 October 1836, 20 March 1837. See also Andrew Johnston, 20 January 1834, and Alicia Welsh, 9 May 1837 (Peyton Johnston MSS).

18 Cullen, *Emergence*, pp. 99–107, 128–31; idem, *An economic history of Ireland since 1660* (London, 1976 ed.), pp. 100–33; Eliza Johnston to Peyton Johnston, 19–20 March 1834, 22 June 1835; Alicia Welsh to Peyton Johnston, 22 June 1835, 20 March 1837 (Peyton Johnston MSS). On the plight of Andrew Johnston's neice, see Mary Johnston to Peyton Johnston, 9 January 1835 (Peyton Johnston MSS).

19 Shaw Mason, *Statistical account*, iii, 367.

20 For information on the Shuldham family, see *Burke's landed gentry of Ireland* (London, 1912 ed.), pp. 638–9; research of Paddy Whelan, Ballymahon. See also Eliza Johnston to Peyton Johnston, 27 January 1834; Andrew Johnston to Peyton Johnston, 27 January 1834 (Peyton Johnston MSS); Inglis, *Tour throughout Ire.*, i, 343.

21 Eliza Johnston to Peyton Johnston, 24 October 1835; Alicia Welsh to Peyton Johnston, 9 May, 1 October, 20 December 1837 (Peyton Johnston MSS).

22 Líam Kennedy and K.A. Miller, 'The long retreat: Protestants, economy, and society, 1660–1926' in Raymond Gillespie and Gerard Moran (ed.), *Longford: essays in county history* (Dublin, 1991), pp. 38–40; Cullen, *Emergence*, pp. 106–7, 128–31.

23 Alicia Welsh to Peyton Johnston, 1 October 1837 (Peyton Johnston MSS); *Westmeath Guardian*, 28 September, 2 November 1837, 5 July 1838; Kennedy and Miller, 'Long retreat', pp. 44–5.

24 Kennedy and Miller, 'Long retreat', pp. 44–50; O'Ferrall, 'Ballinamuck "land war" ', pp. 104–9; *Westmeath Guardian*, 28 September 1837.

25 Kennedy and Miller, 'Long retreat', p. 59; Andrew Johnston to Peyton Johnston, 15 October 1837 (Peyton Johnston MSS).

26 Alicia Welsh to Peyton Johnston, 1 October 1837 (Peyton Johnston MSS).

27 The background of the Johnston family was traced to the 1740s in the deeds and wills formerly located in the Registry of Deeds, King's Inn, now in N.A.; in E.S. Gray, 'Some notes on the high sheriffs of Co. Leitrim, 1701–1800' in *Irish genealogist*, i, no. 10 (October 1941), pp. 301–9; and in the research of Paddy Whelan, Ballymahon. On the Welsh family in south Ulster and their evangelical and Orange connections, see J.B. Leslie, *Clogher clergy and parishes* (Belfast, 1928), pp. 101, 268; idem, *Raphoe clergy and parishes* (Enniskillen, 1940), p. 85; *Report of the proceedings of the Grand Orange Lodge of Ireland ... 1851* (Dublin, 1851); *Report of the proceedings of the Grand Orange Lodge of Ireland ... 1852* (Dublin, 1852); *The Grand Orange Lodge of Ireland for the year 1853* (Dublin, 1853), p. 16 (Loyal Orange Lodge Headquarters Library, Belfast). For Eliza Johnston's and Alicia Welsh's bourgeois critique of Andrew Johnston and 'squireen' society in south Longford, see Eliza Johnston to Peyton Johnston, 8 December 1834, 22 June, 24 October 1835; Alicia Welsh, 22 June, 29 October 1835, 8 February 1837 (Peyton Johnston MSS).

28 O'Ferrall, 'Growth of political consciousness', pp. 708–16; Eliza Johnston to Peyton Johnston, 20 June 1841, and Alicia Welsh, 23 September 1841 (Peyton Johnston MSS). See petitions to Dublin Castle on the Johnstons' behalf in N.A., Index to Registered papers, 1842, second division, CSORP, Z15,732, 17 December 1841; 1843, second division, CSORP, Z7426, 31

May 1843; and in Registered papers, second division, 1843, item 2910, 24 February 1843; Z9716, 14 July 1843.

29 See Kennedy and Miller, 'Long retreat', pp. 41–4, on Protestant conversions and out-migration. The Johnstons' new farm was 'St Angelo' in Srahenny townland, Trory parish, and was leased from Edward Archdall of Riversdale. See 'The Johnstons of St Angelo' (typescript in the possession of Mr and Mrs S. Bothwell, 'St Angelo'). On Archdall's Orange associations, see *Report from the select committee to inquire into the nature . . . of the Orange Lodge associations . . .* [C3 77], H.C. 1835, xv, p. 42; *Report of the proceedings of the Grand Orange Lodge . . . 1852.* See also Alicia Welsh to Peyton Johnston, 3 September 1839, 21 September 1841; Eliza Johnston to Peyton Johnston, 20 June 1841 (Peyton Johnston MSS); K.A. Miller, *Emigrants and exiles: Ireland and the Irish exodus to North America* (New York, 1985), pp. 46–9, 210–11.

10

Nationalism without Words: Symbolism and Ritual Behaviour in the Repeal 'Monster Meetings' of 1843–5

GARY OWENS

'In Ireland', wrote the novelist George A. Birmingham in 1912, 'public meetings are absolutely necessary preliminaries to any enterprise. . . . The hard-headed, commercially minded Ulsterman is just as fond of public meetings as the Connacht Celt. He would hold them with drums and full-dress speechifying, even if he were organising a secret society and arranging for a rebellion.'[1] Birmingham's observation reflects an apparent truth about the popular culture of modern Ireland: assembling and parading in large numbers has been a favourite national pastime for at least two centuries. Pattern festivals and fairs, Orange parades and St Patrick's Day marches, fenian funerals, Land League meetings, and commemorative celebrations—the list of crowd-worthy occasions seems endless.

And yet, for all their variety and conspicuousness, we know surprisingly little about them, particularly in the nineteenth century when demonstrations and public assemblies became increasingly familiar forms of political expression.[2] What did the experience of assembling and parading mean to those who took part in them? Can such mass phenomena be read as texts that might tell us something about the popular and political cultures that produced them?

Until recently, historians rarely asked such questions. Parades and mass gatherings were traditionally relegated to the margins of history, and when they were noted at all, it was usually as incidental backdrops to the 'main events' of politics. Thanks in part to the influence of cultural anthropologists, especially Clifford Geertz, Max Gluckman, and Victor Turner, these kinds of public rituals are now considered worthy of analysis in their own right. Historians of France, England, Germany, and the United States have begun to show how festivals and other mass phenomena were, through their use of ritualism and symbolic language, as essential to the political process and to the transmission of ideas as other forms of discourse.[3] The present study examines this theme in its Irish context, taking as its subject the most celebrated political gatherings in Irish history, the so-called repeal 'monster meetings' of 1843–5.

I

In Ireland, as in the rest of Europe, massive crowds and processions became familiar features of political life during the late eighteenth and early nineteenth centuries. They were a prominent part of Daniel O'Connell's campaign for Catholic emancipation in the 1820s and in the parliamentary elections that followed. Over the next decade the Chartist movement in Britain demonstrated how carefully-staged outdoor rallies could be used to build popular support for a political cause. So too, in a different context, had the temperance crusade of Father Theobald Mathew. Starting in 1839, his movement regularly attracted crowds in the tens of thousands. At about the same time O'Connell began to appear before immense repeal gatherings around the country.[4] Huge meetings had become such fixtures in the popular culture of rural Ireland at this time that one observer could write, 'in the country such an event is an epoch which fills a great portion of the peasant's existence; it is the hope of his entire family for months before, and the boast for months after'.[5] It was almost predictable, therefore, that the campaign to rescind the act of union in 1843—the so-called repeal year—would use massive assemblies as part of its tactical repertoire.

Between the spring of 1843 and the autumn of 1845 members of the Repeal Association organised over fifty massive outdoor assemblies, or monster meetings, across the three southern provinces.[6] Their purpose was to show the British government that popular support for self-government was overwhelming. For this reason the calculating of crowd sizes was a matter of crucial importance. Organisers were known to arrange the settings of meetings so that crowds appeared bigger than they were, especially to journalists who viewed them from speakers' platforms.[7] In parliament and the popular press attendance figures became subjects of heated debate.[8] Nationalist newspapers described almost every assembly as numbering in the hundreds of thousands, and in one case, the famous meeting at Tara Hill in August 1843, sympathetic reporters put the total at between 750,000 and 1.5 million. In anti-repeal papers and police reports the crowds were always smaller, sometimes significantly so. Often, the gap between pro- and anti-repeal estimates was so wide that it seemed as if reporters had attended entirely different events. According to the pro-repeal *Freeman's Journal* and the *Nation*, for example, between 250,000 and 300,000 'enthusiastic' people took part in the Castlebar monster meeting in late July 1843. Another paper put the figure at a more modest 150,000. To the anti-repeal *Mayo Constitution*, however, these were 'ridiculous statements . . . made for the purpose of . . . frightening the government'. To prove its point the paper brought a military expert down from Dublin who, after taking careful measurements of the streets and meeting grounds, calculated the size of the assembly at no more than 15,000. Even this was excessive, according to a local stipendiary magistrate who wrote phlegmatically to Dublin Castle: 'the meeting was a thin one and the numbers far short of what was expected. I should think between seven and ten thousand might be about the estimate. Very little excitement seemed to prevail."[9]

Such disparities were more common than not, and this creates an obvious difficulty for anyone who wishes to gauge the size of the monster meetings.[10] Historians have commonly dealt with the problem by dutifully warning their readers that the O'Connellite press exaggerated crowd sizes; they have then disregarded their own warnings and quoted the inflated numbers appearing in nationalist papers as if to suggest that they were not far off the mark.[11] In reality there is no more compelling reason to accept pro-repeal figures than those supplied by anti-repealers, except that citing lower numbers produces less colourful narratives.[12] This is not to suggest that historians should cease to view the monster meetings as impressively large assemblies, but merely to insist that estimates of crowd size need to be scaled down considerably. Even reducing nationalist calculations by as much as 75 percent would mean that about one and a half million people—or approximately one-quarter of the total population of the three southern provinces—attended monster meetings in 1843.[13] This in itself would suggest a high degree of popular participation and would constitute an unparalleled achievement in political mobilisation in the British Isles.

Writers have had less difficulty in describing what took place at these gatherings. Most suggest that the meetings combined an atmosphere of good-natured enthusiasm with solemnity of purpose. Above all, they emphasise the peacefulness and sobriety of the crowds and their rapt attentiveness during O'Connell's speeches. A good example is Edward Bulwer Lytton, who in his epic poem 'St Stephen's', written in 1860, captured the drama of O'Connell speaking before a monster meeting. Dozens of historians have used it to enhance their narratives ever since:

> Once to my sight the giant thus was given,
> Walled by wide air and roofed by boundless heaven;
> Beneath his feet the human ocean lay,
> And wave on wave flowed into space away.
> Methought no clarion could have sent its sound
> E'en to the centre of the hosts around.
> And, as I thought, rose a sonorous swell,
> As from some church tower swings the silvery bell;
> Aloft and clear from airy tide to tide,
> It glided easy as a bird may glide.
> To the last verge of that vast audience sent,
> It played with each wild passion as it went:
> Now stirred the uproar, now the murmurs stilled,
> And sobs or laughter answered as it willed.

> Then did I know what spell of infinite choice
> To rouse or lull has the sweet human voice.[14]

Writing at about the same time, the young W.E.H. Lecky provided a vivid impression of a typical monster meeting:

> They usually took place upon Sunday morning, in the open air, upon some hillside. At daybreak the mighty throng might be seen, broken in detached groups and kneeling on the greensward around their priests, while the incense rose from a hundred rude altars, and the solemn music of the mass . . . seemed to impart a consecration to the cause. O'Connell stood upon a platform surrounded by the ecclesiastical dignitaries and by the more distinguished of his followers. Before him that immense assembly was ranged without disorder or tumult or difficulty . . . and inspired with the most unanimous enthusiasm. There is perhaps no more impressive spectacle than such an assembly, pervaded by such a spirit and moving under the control of a single mind. The silence that prevailed . . . during some portions of his address; the concordant cheer bursting from tens of thousands of voices; the rapid transitions of feeling as the great magician struck alternately each chord of passion . . . were sufficient to carry away the most callous. . . .[15]

Echoes of Lecky and Bulwer Lytton have reverberated in subsequent descriptions of the assemblies. Michael MacDonagh's popular biography of O'Connell (1903) described a typical repeal gathering this way:

> A heart-stirring roar of applause went up on his [O'Connell's] appearance on the platform, and then a stillness, almost overpowering in its intensity, fell upon the vast concourse eager to hear his burning words. The orator's voice went rolling over the crowd, and they shook and trembled as he played upon their feelings, their prejudices, their fears, their joys, their love of country, their devotion to their faith—sobbing in sorrow, shrieking in fury, or laughing with faces relaxed in good humour, according to the varying moods of the magician.[16]

More recent studies relate how people 'shouted, groaned, laughed, scorned, or exulted, according to their cues'.[17] Above all, 'hundreds of thousands came to listen'.[18] In fact, people were reputedly so eager to hear O'Connell that relay speakers had to be stationed among the crowd to repeat his words to those at the rear.[19] Altogether, the meetings were, as Donal McCartney puts it, 'hedge schools in which the masses were educated into the nationalist politics of repeal'.[20]

For nearly a century and a half, therefore, the popular image of monster meetings has remained essentially unchanged. It is one of immense crowds sprawled thickly over many acres and listening intently to the inspirational oratory of the Liberator. There are problems with this image, however, not the least of which is that it does not accord with the observations of many who attended the events. A stipendiary magistrate in County Meath, for example, dashed off a memo to his superiors from Tara Hill while the great meeting was still in progress. As he wrote, people all around him were leaving for home and had been doing so for some time. 'It did appear to me very remarkable', he recounted, 'that *very* shortly after Mr O'Connell arrived, thousands left the grounds without even endeavouring to hear him speak, and I was surprised at observing that almost all the country people assembled appeared quite careless as to whether or not they heard any of the speeches.'[21] It had been the same story in Enniscorthy a few weeks earlier. A *Times* reporter, who was otherwise impressed with the size and demeanour of that gathering, remarked that people began to leave the field in droves shortly after the meeting opened, and were obviously not interested in hearing what O'Connell had to say.[22] In its account of the Galway meeting in June the *Freeman's Journal* claimed that over half the crowd that had cheered or accompanied O'Connell on his triumphal procession through the streets of the city stayed behind rather than attend the speeches that followed. Similar stories were reported from the Ennis and Loughrea meetings.[23]

Many of those who did show up for the speeches apparently paid little attention to what O'Connell said. The nationalist historian Canon John O'Rourke attended the Tara meeting as a youth and later recalled how 'the people cared little for the speeches; they knew they could read them next day in the newspapers, and they seemed, moreover, to feel that listening to speeches was not their chief business there'.[24] Jacob Venedey, a German visitor sympathetic to the repeal cause, witnessed the Athlone monster meeting from a seat near O'Connell on the speakers' platform. During the orations, he conceded, 'it seemed to me as if the great body of the auditory paid as little attention to them as I myself had done'. He observed that in the area beyond the main body of the crowd small knots of people lay on the ground or stood talking among themselves, oblivious to the oratory.[25] The same was true at other assemblies. O'Rourke recalled that contrary to received opinion, the Tara meeting was not a densely packed assembly. Except for a group of no more than 30,000 immediately around the speakers' platform, he commented, most people were spread out over the hill, conversing in detached groups.[26] 'To a person surveying one of these meetings from a [speakers'] platform', observed a journalist who had attended many of them,

> there is an appearance of solidity and denseness [that is] utterly deceptive. For a radius of some twenty yards fronting the platform there is a compact semi-circle of men, as closely packed as they can stand; immediately outside its circumference (which is composed of those persons who, by straining every ear, can catch some of the words of the speaker) the crowd thins away into a talkative, gossiping assemblage of persons who seem quite indifferent to the proceedings, and between whom there is no difficulty in passing in any direction with the greatest facility. The conversation in this portion of the

meeting is quite of a general character. Indeed, the persons composing it seem to attend the demonstration just as they would make a holiday or a fair.[27]

Many people did not listen to the speeches for the simple reason that they could not hear them. No unamplified voice, not even O'Connell's, could have reached more than a fraction of most crowds. Even when meetings were held in relatively small and enclosed spaces such as market squares, it was impossible to hear much of what was said.[28] Suggestions that special 'relay speakers' passed on O'Connell's words as they were spoken to people behind them are without foundation.

It would therefore seem that if the monster meetings were indeed political 'hedge schools', truancy and student apathy were rampant. But should we conclude from such examples of crowd behaviour that the gatherings meant little to those who attended them; that many were indifferent to the proceedings or at best passive audiences for speeches that only a portion of them could grasp? Should we also conclude that active participation was restricted to those who organised or spoke at the events?[29] Such judgments would be warranted if we assume, as many historians have done, that the monster meetings consisted simply of bringing large masses of people together in an open space to hear speeches. In reality the meetings were about far more than inspirational oratory. They were also 'collective ceremonies'[30]—elaborate secular rituals that drew upon the active participation of the majority of those who attended. When eyewitnesses spoke of crowds as 'assisting' at the meetings, they were not being metaphorical.[31] What is more, the ritualistic elements in the repeal gatherings meant that they were necessarily concerned with the construction of meaning in ways that were more symbolic than verbal. As such, they touched far more people than those who were within earshot of O'Connell. By concentrating upon the content of speeches and the responses of listeners—important as these were for the development of political culture—historians have overlooked an extraordinary and in some ways more significant set of activities taking place far away from the speakers' platforms.

II

Every monster meeting was nothing less than a dramatic performance in three acts whose players and audiences shifted with each change of scenery. They commenced with a huge procession of bands in uniform, floats, carriages and carts, trade and fraternal bodies, and thousands of local residents on foot or horseback. Tradesmen wearing coloured sashes and other distinctive clothing bore banners—many of them elaborate allegorical paintings—that identified their craft. Others displayed their skills on floats, or they carried miniature buildings, carriages, ships, or ploughs on poles. Ordinary townsmen and country people often displayed boughs and branches of evergreen, laurel, and oak. Most processions marched out from a town en masse to greet O'Connell and escort him back for the second part of the proceedings: the gathering in a large open space, usually a field, race-course, or fair-ground, where the speeches took place. Crowds gathered around a makeshift speakers' platform that held anywhere from 200 to 1,000 men. Here sat newspaper reporters, local dignitaries, and anyone else who could pay one shilling for the privilege of hearing O'Connell and being seen close to him on the platform. Following the speeches, the crowd dispersed, and a few hours later the third part of the ceremonies began for a more restricted audience. This was an evening banquet for O'Connell and a few hundred paying guests—almost all of them clergymen, landowners, professionals, and shopkeepers—in a large hall or specially built pavilion.

Processions, outdoor oratory, and formal banquets had been familiar features of Irish political culture for some time. Parliamentary election rituals and formal civic occasions usually required the staging of at least one of them.[32] What made them special during the repeal campaign of the 1840s was that all three events were regularly and sequentially combined to form day-long or two-day ceremonies that were built around O'Connell and the idea of repeal. In addition, they were almost always bigger, better planned, more colourful, and more thoroughly reported in the national and British press.

For the majority of those who attended monster meetings, the largest and most popular of the three events was unquestionably the procession. To watch or take part in processions was clearly what drew many people to the meetings in the first place. 'It was generally considered the procession was the chief part of the demonstration', remarked a reporter for the *Freeman's Journal* after the Loughrea meeting. That, he said, was why half the crowd left for home as soon as it finished and did not attend the speeches that followed.[33] Processions lent colour to every public occasion; no great event was considered complete without one. It was not good enough, for example, that O'Connell was cheered wildly as he walked to his Dublin home following his release from Richmond prison in September 1844. It was essential that he be granted his freedom symbolically and in the ceremonial context of a grand parade. Thus on the morning after his release he returned alone to the prison and waited patiently for hours inside its walls as a mammoth procession made its way to him. At the proper moment the prison gates burst open and O'Connell, waving a green cap and an olive branch, emerged to music and thunderous cheers. He then mounted a fancifully designed triumphal chariot which became the centrepiece of the parade that noisily wound its way back to the house he had quietly left that morning.[34]

The obvious appeal of processions lay in the entertainment they provided. Above all, they were good fun.[35] Thus, advertising placards encouraged attendance by emphasising the attractions to be seen in the processions: 'TARA:

Repeal! Repeal! Repeal!' declared a placard that appeared on the streets of Trim in July 1843: 'Trumpeter on Horseback; Harper in Open Carriage, Four Horses . . . Footmen Six Deep . . . Carriages, Cars & Gigs; Horsemen Four Deep!'[36] Processions commonly stretched for miles and took hours to complete. So great was the need to witness them that participants were known to drop out of parades and watch them momentarily from nearby vantage points. Organisers deliberately arranged the routes of some processions to double back upon themselves so that every marcher could observe and thereby identify with the huge spectacle of which he or she was a part.[37] Eyewitness accounts of the tumultuous scenes in towns during parades call to mind Peter Burke's description of carnival celebrations in Renaissance Europe: 'the main streets and squares became stages, the city became a theatre without walls and [with] the inhabitants, the actors and spectators, observing the scene from their balconies'.[38] Roof-tops and even chimneys were crowded, women waved handkerchiefs from windows or cheered from footpaths, and children scattered bouquets of flowers along the way.[39] Jacob Venedey, who had witnessed many royal entries into continental cities, considered those ceremonies to be child's play compared with the rapturous reception that he saw O'Connell receive in Dundalk.[40]

Local trade bodies, fraternal organisations, civic officials, and shopkeepers often spent weeks planning each town's procession. Groups vied with each other to produce spectacular displays. Some of them were variations on traditional themes that had long been part of civic processions. The tailors in Cork, Galway, and Limerick, for example, all represented their trade with tableaux depicting a naked Adam and Eve in the Garden of Eden. Their floats featured two long-haired children wearing flesh-coloured body-stockings and standing beneath a large tree hung with apples; around its trunk coiled a large apple-bearing serpent.[41] Printers' floats in many towns displayed printing presses painted green and decorated with roses, laurel leaves, and banners. As they trundled along the parade route, members of the trade struck off copies of a specially composed ode to O'Connell which was ceremonially read and presented to him at some point in the procession. Hundreds of these sheets were then scattered to the crowd from the float as the parade made its way back through the town to the open-air meeting.[42]

Every procession featured temperance bands, sometimes dozens of them, whose presence, said one paper, was vital because they inspired 'that species of martial peacefulness which keeps men together in one mind'.[43] The journalist T.D. Sullivan belonged to one as a teenager in Bantry. He later recalled how in neighbouring Skibbereen, as part of that town's monster-meeting festivities, he and his fellow musicians were pulled through the streets in a large, 24-oared pinnace that was mounted on wheels and decorated with flags and bunting. Bands in other towns displayed themselves in similar fashion.[44]

At least half a dozen processions featured an allegorical figure whom reporters referred to as 'the ancient harper', a bearded, long-haired, elderly man who apparently travelled from demonstration to demonstration. His striking appearance in the Cork procession in 1845 was a study in Celtic revivalism. Dressed in a long green robe, a yellow tunic, and a decorated conical cap, he sat beneath an oak tree on an elevated platform playing patriotic airs on a harp. At his side were two uniformed pages holding banners with patriotic inscriptions. Behind him stood three figures: one, in armour, wearing a crimson robe and bearing a battle-axe entwined with laurel, represented the earl of Desmond; the others, dressed in green and yellow ('the favourite colours of the ancient Irish') and carrying lances and swords, were his nobility. When this elaborate float drew past O'Connell, the harper unfurled a parchment scroll and read, in Irish, a specially composed ode. One reporter, dazzled by the romantic symbolism of it all, declared this to be the most impressive display he had ever seen, 'representing at once the costume, the music, the chivalry, and the too long neglected . . . language of our country'.[45]

O'Connell himself was often presented to crowds against a backdrop of romantic allegory. His appearance on a bizarre float in the same Cork procession rivalled in ostentation that of the ancient harper. He sat on an elevated chair beneath a large canopy that towered twenty feet above the crowd. Holding the canopy aloft were four female figures representing Justice, Truth, Fortitude, and Prudence. Beneath each of them hung scrolls that bore patriotic mottoes.[46] A painted figure of Erin looked down from a canvas behind O'Connell's chair. Specially designed repeal caps, identical to the one O'Connell wore and suggestive of Phrygian caps of liberty, hung from the four corners of the canopy. An enormous repeal cap and a huge shamrock crowned the top of the vehicle.[47]

Processions often featured dramatic vignettes that carried unambiguous political messages. Stretching above the parade route in Ennis was a large chain joined at the centre by a thin cord. Over it hung a green banner with this inscription: 'The Liberator of Ireland/Will cut asunder/The chains of slavery/We labour under'. When O'Connell's carriage appeared beneath the display, a swordsman standing on a platform cut the cord with a flourish, and as a witness declared, 'the chain was shivered on both sides amidst the shouts and acclamations of thousands that rent the air for some minutes'.[48]

Among the floats that passed in review before O'Connell at the start of the Cork ceremonies in 1845 was that of the coopers, on which two costumed youths stood beneath a tree. One, representing Africa, bore the label 'Free' and held in his hands a length of broken chains. The other, portraying Ireland, was tightly bound and wore around his neck the inscription 'A slave still'. When the float drew before O'Connell's reviewing stand, it stopped and 'Africa' thanked the Liberator for helping him to gain his freedom but reminded him that his companion was still in bondage. Pointing to his fettered companion, he recited Thomas Moore's verse:

Oh, where's the slave so lowly,
Condemned to chains unholy,
Who, could he burst
His bonds accursed,
Would pine beneath them slowly?

When he had finished, 'Ireland' knelt before O'Connell and at the Liberator's command burst his chains. As the float moved off through the city, the boy triumphantly displayed his free arms to cheering onlookers.[49] O'Connell valued this kind of street theatre and from time to time staged his own one-man performances. During mammoth processions through Dublin in 1844 and 1845 he delighted in halting his carriage before the old houses of parliament on College Green, rising from his seat, and pointing dramatically at the building as the crowd around him went wild with joy.[50]

Performances such as these were almost always built around O'Connell. But on at least one occasion participants honoured other heroes who represented a different tradition of nationalism. Before the speeches began at Tara, a procession of trade bodies and bands solemnly marched through the centre of the crowd to the ancient Ráth na Ríogh or royal enclosure. Beneath the rath lay some of the insurgents killed in the battle of Tara in 1798, and they were the focus of the ritual that followed. Twenty-one tradesmen carried flags to the crest of the rath and planted them in a circle around its perimeter. They then knelt in prayer and were immediately joined by thousands around them as a band on the summit of the mound played the 'Dead march in Saul'. Throughout the remainder of the day people crowded around the site to pick and carry away a red plant ('sheep's sorrel') which grew wild there in the belief that its colour derived from the blood of the patriots buried beneath it.[51]

Banners and triumphal arches were ubiquitous features at every monster meeting and served as stationary props for the processions that moved under, around, and through them. Newspapers scrupulously recorded the inscriptions on the dozens of these devices that lined every parade route. The police also took an interest in what the banners said and watched for any that appeared to incite violence. Consequently, organisers of the demonstrations strictly censored their content. The themes were usually predictable and repetitive.[52] Inscriptions stressed non-violence ('The man who commits a crime gives strength to the enemy' or 'Peace and order will conquer'); loyalty to the crown ('God bless our queen and grant wisdom to her ministers'); and group solidarity (''Tis the wild shout of Erin that rings for repeal' and 'We are nine millions'). Other banners emphasised the justice of the cause ('Erin, oh Erin, now bright through thy tears, of a long night of bondage thy spirit appears'), or they expressed a kind of Hibernian jingoism—a familiar banner depicted an Irish wolfhound with the motto, 'Gentle when stroked, fierce when provoked'.

III

Whether one witnessed repeal processions first-hand or read about them later in newspaper accounts, it was impossible to mistake the political messages that these devices and performances contained. For the most part they lacked semiotic and verbal ambiguity, and virtually anyone could decipher them fairly easily. There were other symbolic devices and ritual forms, however, whose meanings were more deeply hidden. They were more multi-vocal in expression and sometimes required specific knowledge to decode them. Demonstrators had ways and means of saying things symbolically to their immediate audiences—sometimes subversive things—that could be unintelligible to anyone ignorant of their cultural context.

A good example was their use of plants. Evergreen, laurel, and other greenery were widely used to decorate meetings and demonstrations throughout the British Isles during the nineteenth century. They were abundant, inexpensive, pleasing to the eye, and adaptable to scores of uses. In Ireland during the repeal campaigns of the 1840s they adorned streets, houses, parade floats, and even people. Days before O'Connell arrived in Ennis in June 1843, men, women, and children could be seen bearing branches and whole trees into town on their shoulders. They planted so many of them along the streets and used so much shrubbery to decorate buildings that by the time O'Connell arrived, the town was said to resemble a green wood.[53]

Above all, Irish people liked to carry plants as they marched in processions. Everyone who took part in a massive cavalcade that escorted the Liberator into Kilkenny in 1841 was said to carry a green bough, 'and a considerable portion, not content with such slight emblems of joy and triumph, had entire young trees waving over their heads'.[54] At a monster meeting in Charleville two years later, the procession that brought O'Connell to town was described as 'a vast mass of humans . . . carrying laurels and boughs of trees in their hands, so as to present the appearance of a moving forest'.[55]

Plants were universally accepted emblems of specific qualities: laurels, for example, represented amity, peace, and regeneration; yew branches signified endurance and constancy. But in Ireland plant symbolism was more complex and multi-vocal than this. Trees and bushes had been worshipped as sacred objects since antiquity, and they continued to be venerated well into modern times.[56] From at least the 1790s they took on distinctive political connotations. The image of the withered tree became a familiar device in the literature of the United Irishmen; it was the dead plant that would bloom again, the lost cause that would one day triumph.[57] During the 1798 rebellion green boughs and sprigs became standard insignia of the insurgents.[58]

These symbolic associations remained part of the Irish folk memory four decades later. They were not the only meanings that green plants called to mind, however. It was unlawful under the party-processions act of 1832 for anyone who took part in public demonstrations in Ireland to 'bear, wear, or have amongst them . . . any banner, emblem, flag, or symbol' that might provoke sectarian animosity. The act effectively banned green flags and political banners from repeal processions.[59] They appeared nonetheless but not in their customary form. When thousands of marchers paraded with green boughs, bushes, and whole trees, they were symbolically brandishing nationalist emblems. Like peasants in other countries who made clever use of everyday materials and colours to symbolise their allegiance to subversive political movements, Irish men and women used the greenery that was everywhere around them to create surrogate national flags.[60] Green boughs and branches became instant banners that conveyed a number of meanings: they signified loyalty to the repeal cause, sympathy with a tradition of patriotic sacrifice, and, above all, a clever evasion of the law.

Processionists made roughly the same statements when they bore aloft loaves of bread on poles as symbols of poverty and, by implication, tokens of British misrule;[61] or when hundreds of them displayed their repeal membership cards on the ends of sticks or white wands or tied them to their hats, coat buttons, or necks by green ribbons.[62] The six-by-nine inch cards depicted around their borders a pantheon of ancient and modern Irish heroes, including Brian Boru, Hugh O'Neill, Owen Roe O'Neill, and Patrick Sarsfield. Forming a shamrock shape above them all were portraits of Henry Grattan, Henry Flood, and— uniting the trinity in slightly larger form than the rest—O'Connell. The head of St Patrick formed the stem of the device, and above it was a smaller shamrock encircled with the motto, 'Remember 1782'. Clustered beneath them all was a pile of broken swords, shields, and guns surmounted by an uncrowned harp set against a sunburst.

These symbol-encrusted cards, each of them bearing the name of its owner, were prized commodities among repeal supporters. Exhibiting them publicly in processions bestowed on those who carried them a sense of pride, singularity, and empowerment. In this regard the cards were invested with talismanic qualities similar to those of a scapular worn by the devout. At the same time they acted as ersatz political banners and betokened a subtle evasion of the law.[63]

Practices such as these, which anthropologists refer to as 'guileful ruses' or 'trickster' (in Irish, cleasaí) behaviour, are common throughout peasant cultures. 'Tricks and ruses', explains John Fiske, 'are the art of the weak that enables them to exploit their understanding of the rules of the system and to turn it to their advantage.' Subordinated people customarily use the cultural weapons that they find around them to engage in a kind of 'semiotic guerilla warfare' against their superiors.[64] Thus the victuallers' company of Cork appeared to present an innocent but eye-catching depiction of their trade in the city's repeal procession of 1845. Their float displayed a large live bull covered in flowers and coloured ribbons and tethered to the sides of a wagon pulled by two draft horses. The sight was remarkable enough, but what gave it meaning was the presence of two uniformed members of the victuallers' company on either side of the beast. One held a large wooden mallet, the other an executioner's axe, and both pretended to be in the act of slaughtering the animal. The allusion was obvious: the ritual destruction of John Bull was being enacted in unforgettable fashion before tens of thousands. Like the use of green boughs, repeal cards, and bread loaves as substitute flags, this *tableau vivant* represented a clever flouting of the law as it made a memorable political statement.[65] It also illustrates James C. Scott's observations about the ways in which subordinate groups employ codes or 'hidden transcripts' to insinuate meanings into rituals that are clear to one audience but opaque to another. The excluded (and usually powerful) audience, he notes, 'may grasp the seditious message in the performance but may find it difficult to react because the sedition is clothed in terms that also can lay claim to perfectly innocent construction'.[66]

But symbolic acts of this kind were not always so innocent. When, for example, tens of thousands exhibited their patriotism with green boughs and bushes, many of them were necessarily drawn to commit acts of vandalism. Most of the plants which they cut down and brought to the demonstrations had to be taken from private lands; in many, if not most instances these were the demesnes and plantations of wealthy landlords. Some landowners allowed people to remove plants from their estates, but others posted guards around their property before monster meetings to keep them from being plundered.[67] In so doing, they were confronting a deeply rooted tradition. In the folk culture of rural Ireland stealing trees and bushes from the lands of rivals or landlords, particularly for festive occasions, was a time-honoured custom. Plants taken in this way were traditionally put on public display or used as centrepieces in ritual festivities.[68] They were treated, in other words, as if they were victory trophies. And that was one of the salient meanings which they assumed when thousands of people carried them in repeal processions or used them to decorate streets and buildings: they were spoils of symbolic battle.

As the monster meetings grew in size, organisers worried that the triumphal display of greenery was needlessly provocative and that stealing plants would lead to violence. Therefore, repeal leaders urged people to attend the gatherings 'unprovided with boughs or a twig that would betoken injury to the plantations of the aristocracy'.[69] Such orders seem to have brought an end to processions that resembled 'moving forests', but they did not altogether stop people from carrying green boughs as trophies or flags; nor did they halt the practice of transforming townscapes with foliage from the surrounding countryside.[70]

The language of processions was not confined to mobile displays and decorations. The very structure of parades—the way that participants arranged themselves in a particular order of march and the routes they followed—constituted a kind of semiotic vocabulary. Public processions were, as Robert Darnton puts it, 'a statement unfurled in the streets', through which a community represented itself to itself and to the outside world.[71] Their structure also constituted a symbolic declaration of political beliefs that underscored the countless other visual and verbal messages that swirled through every stage of a monster meeting. Processions naturally varied in detail from place to place, but they were similar enough in their general morphology that we can construct a rough sketch of what most of them looked like.[72]

Processionists usually assembled in a town square or main street hours before O'Connell arrived, and formed themselves into an order of march. A uniformed band or a body of horsemen typically took the lead, and behind them came the local trade bodies—each with its distinguishing banners, floats, and uniforms—whose order had been determined by drawing lots the day before. Temperance bands from outlying towns separated each group of tradesmen. In larger towns repeal clubs, temperance groups, and fraternal organisations followed behind the trades. Then came the public at large, most of them on foot but many on horseback or in farm carts, accompanied by scores of parish clergy. In the west particularly, peasant women marched in groups or rode behind their menfolk.[73] Their presence was usually the subject of special comment. The success of any meeting was often measured by the proportion of men in attendance: when anti-repealers wished to discredit a meeting, they pointed to the large number of women present; conversely, when nationalist reporters wished to praise a repeal gathering, they emphasised the number of men and horses in attendance as opposed to women and children. In time, however, O'Connellites began to take pride in the large number of women at the meetings. Their participation, they declared, demonstrated the all-inclusiveness of the repeal movement and, be-cause none of them were molested, the respect that Irish men bore for females.[74]

At the appointed time the cortège noisily marched off to meet the Liberator at a prearranged rendezvous a few miles outside the town. Leaving separately, either before or after the main body of the parade, were local dignitaries in carriages: town councillors and aldermen, professionals, leading clergymen, and wealthier shopkeepers. After these groups ceremonially greeted O'Connell, the procession re-formed into a different configuration for the march back through the town to the meeting ground. As before, the trade, temperance, and volunteer bodies led the cavalcade, but they were now joined by the town magistrates and other notables who formed up immediately behind them. O'Connell usually took his place somewhere in the midst of the dignitaries or at their rear. Trailing off behind the Liberator's carriage came the great bulk of the citizenry.

The procession constituted a text that could be read in two ways simultane-ously. First, it presented a caricature of a community's social structure. Beginning with the trade bodies and running upwards through middle-class groups to the civic and clerical hierarchy, it culminated in the imposing figure of O'Connell riding atop a special float or in his carriage pulled by four horses. He formed the symbolic centre of every procession, the peak of a moving status pyramid, before whom marched ascending ranks of labourers, artisans, and representatives of the middle and professional classes, and behind whom followed a relatively unstructured mass of town and country folk. O'Connell was the unifying element in a repeal procession, and that was the second way in which the parade could be read. Invariably, two groups marched out separately from a town to greet the Liberator: trade bodies, townsfolk, and country people on the one hand and local dignitaries on the other. When they returned, it was as a unified body with O'Connell forming their central nucleus and symbolically fusing the components of the community which had hitherto been separated. In this way the procession became a visual metaphor of the way in which O'Connell had unified tenant farmers and the urban middle classes throughout Ireland under the banner of repeal.[75] This striking image acquired deeper meaning, not to mention emotional power, through its close resemblance to familiar ritual forms in the Catholic church. O'Connell's symbolic function was roughly analogous to that of a saint's image or the sacred host carried in a religious procession. In those ceremonies the sacred object is typically accompanied by civic and ecclesiastical officials who are surrounded and followed by members of the community at large. Its purpose in the cortège, as Roberto DaMatta points out, is to unite disparate elements: 'happiness and sadness, the healthy and the sick, the good man and the sinner, and, most significantly, the authorities and the people'.[76] By the same token repeal processions were all-inclusive. They joined rich and poor, young and old, men and women, clergy and laity, town and country, magistrates and people, participants and spectators.[77]

The spaces that repeal demonstrations occupied or marched through were also part of their vocabulary. Organisers deliberately selected a handful of meeting sites for their rich historical associations. The crowds that gathered on sacred spaces such as Tara Hill or the Rock of Cashel drew implicit contrasts between a golden age that had flourished under Ireland's ancient kings and its present condition; in so doing, they suggested the desirability of restoring self-government.[78] Organisers were deliberately provocative when they picked battle sites such as Clontarf or scenes of English treachery like Mullaghmast in County Kildare for meetings. Ordinary processions could also use space in symbolic ways. All crowds, as Elias Canetti observes, metaphorically capture the spaces they occupy. When crowds challenge governmental authority or try to change its policies, their occupation of public places can be especially symbolic.[79] John Berger remarks:

> demonstrators interrupt the regular life of the streets they march through or of the open spaces they fill. They 'cut off' these areas, and not yet having the power to occupy them permanently, they transform them into a temporary stage on which they dramatise the power they still lack. . . . Demonstrations

express political ambitions before the political means necessary to realise them have been created.[80]

Thus, when an enthusiastic journalist described a massive repeal demonstration through the heart of Dublin as 'the taking possession at once and in full of the monster meeting ground of Ireland at large', he expressed more than he probably realised.[81]

Those who organised repeal demonstrations were alert to the symbolic advantages that well-chosen processional routes could offer. The Dublin tradesmen who paraded through the city in July 1843 to a repeal meeting in Donnybrook went not by the most direct route, but one that allowed them to make symbolic political statements along the way. Beginning in the heart of the working-class district in north Dublin, the marchers proceeded along Upper Dorset Street to Capel Street and across Essex Bridge.[82] At the top of Parliament Street, just outside the gates of Dublin Castle, each contingent paused as bands played 'God save the queen' and 'St Patrick's day'. The procession then continued east along Dame Street to the former Parliament House, where each band broke into 'Our old house at home' amid the cheers of marchers and spectators.[83] A year later, the triumphal procession that escorted O'Connell home from Richmond prison symbolically nullified his incarceration by tracing in reverse order the route by which the authorities had brought him there in the first place.[84] In the provinces organisers of monster meetings almost always arranged for the formal speeches to take place on the opposite side of town from where O'Connell arrived so that the procession would pass through the main streets. In smaller places processions intentionally followed a circuitous route or went twice around a town's perimeter in order to prolong the spectacle before moving off to the speeches.[85]

IV

The gatherings which followed the processions—the monster meetings proper— were necessarily different in tone, structure, and purpose. Sometimes they were noticeably smaller. As we have seen, processions evoked a sense of carnival; they communicated ideas visually and symbolically to an audience that was close at hand. They were linear in structure, they necessarily occupied public spaces, and the boundaries between processionists and spectators were often fluid or non-existent. The overall effect was to emphasise group solidarity and corporate oneness.

Most meetings, by contrast, took place on private lands, and space was clearly segmented along general lines of class and gender. A large, raised speakers' platform on one corner of the grounds held a few hundred fee-paying listeners, all of them magistrates, clerics, reporters, or other worthies. As newspaper reports indicate, these men and the crowd standing immediately in front of them engaged in a form of dialogue with the orators, breaking into their speeches with shouts of encouragement, observations, and responses to specific points. The group immediately facing the speakers' platform was sometimes ringed by a cordon of carriages or horsemen, behind whom 'lay on the ground, stood, or walked about the women and the less strong or the less curious'.[86] At some meetings, such as those at Athlone and Tara, middle-class women watched and listened from a separate grandstand nearby or, as at Nenagh, from open carriages drawn up near the speakers' platform. To those in the crowd who were out of earshot, and in most cases they probably constituted the majority, the men making the speeches were themselves symbols. Like the banners around the speakers' platform, the music of the bands, and the massed crowd itself, they were but one part of the entire *mise en scène.*[87]

Only the third and final part of a repeal gathering, the banquets that followed in the evening, allowed everyone who was present a chance to hear O'Connell and others speak. These were the smallest, the most exclusive, and the most structured of the three main events. Attendance was restricted to those who could afford the high admission charge of eight to ten shillings and whose livelihoods did not depend on rising early the next day. This effectively narrowed attendance to the dignitaries who had clustered around O'Connell on the speakers' platform at the mass meeting or ridden close to him in the procession. The assembly, which could range in size from a few hundred to nearly 1,000, was invariably divided into three groups: a few dozen notables who sat on either side of O'Connell at an elevated head table; the main body of men who filled the centre of the hall; and the women who watched their menfolk dine from a special gallery at the rear.

The visual adornments at banquets reflected the middle-class sensibilities of the audience and stood in sharp contrast to the nature of those used in processions. Touches of medievalism and neo-gothic imagery appeared in the form of coats-of-arms (O'Connell's, local gentry's, or bishops') that hung along the walls or canopied chairs-of-honour that resembled thrones.[88] Royal initials and emblems mingled with shamrocks, harps, and the words 'Repeal' or 'O'Connell' spelled out in gaslight above the head table. Touches of theatricality might occur, as at Cork when a replica of a dove 'was made to alight on the head of O'Connell as he took his seat at the table amid peals of applause'.[89]

On the whole, however, banquets were less concerned with visual imagery than with verbal communication aimed at a literate, well-informed audience. Banquets, in fact, like the massive meetings that had preceded them, were really pitched at two audiences. The first consisted of those who were present; the second was comprised of people in other parts of Ireland and in Britain who would later read the speeches in newspapers. Banquets were also the most overtly political of the events that comprised a monster meeting.[90] Toasts to the queen and members of the royal family, 'the people', or 'O'Connell and repeal' were followed by speeches that everyone heard because of the relatively intimate surroundings.[91] Members of the crowd frequently interrupted O'Connell with cheers, shouts, and other loud responses. Banners, some of them in Irish, hung along the walls, each bearing slogans or quotations from repeal speeches. The tone of many of them was more militant than the ones which had appeared along the routes of processions. O'Connell, who was known to tear down combative-sounding street banners at processions (e.g., 'Ireland her own parliament, or the world in a blaze' that appeared on the streets at Tullamore), allowed equally belligerent slogans to remain during banquets ('Sir Robert Peel talks of civil war—Let him try it if he dare', which appeared at the Mullaghmast banquet), presumably on the assumption that middle-class banquet-goers could better resist revolutionary temptation than crowds of common folk.[92]

V

In December 1843 a ballad singer in Dundalk was arrested for publicly singing and selling a composition entitled 'Sheil's nocturnal vision'. The poem, composed by the popular lyricist Richard Sheil, was appropriate to the repeal year because it appeared to describe an imaginary monster meeting.[93] It begins:

> I speak in candour, one night in slumber,
>> My mind did wander to Athlone;
> The centre station of this Irish nation,
>> Where a congregation to me was shown.
> Beyond my counting upon a mountain,
>> Near to a fountain that clearly ran;
> I fell to tremble, I'll not dissemble,
>> As they assembled for the rights of man.

The narrator then relates how the heroic figure of Granuaile, dressed in green and bearing a harp, appeared before the crowd. She urged them to be true to 'the rights of man' and predicted their imminent liberation from English domination. A priest-figure suddenly descended from heaven bearing a mitre, a cross, and a shamrock with which he proceeded to perform a kind of political mass. At its conclusion a mysterious wind wafted the priest away. Then Granuaile, after promising the people that she would return to free them, also flew into the sky.

> Then the population or congregation,
>> In exultation agreed to part;
> Shook hands like brothers and kissed each other,
>> Whilst friendship smothered each Irish heart.
> They separated, all animated,
>> And elevated at what went on;

> And day was breaking, brave Sheil awaken'd,
>   A contemplating on the rights of man.

Other ballads appeared during 1843 that celebrated monster meetings, but none of them did so with the remarkable imagery of 'Sheil's nocturnal vision'.[94] The gathering which it describes is so allegorical and dreamlike, so devoid of references to actual people and events (apart from the reference to its author), that it might be argued that the poem has nothing to do with monster meetings. In reality it has everything to do with them.

The poem recounts in verse what anthropologists refer to as a liminal experience. As described by Arnold Van Gennep and developed by Victor Turner, liminality is that stage in any rite of passage—whether an initiation ceremony, an investiture, or a political demonstration—during which established social rules and structures are suspended. An individual or a group is detached from their normal condition and, in Turner's words, 'passes through a cultural realm that has few or none of the attributes of the past or coming state'.[95] During this stage liminal characters or 'ritual elders' appear who embody the conscience and values of the community at large and who impress these ideals upon the persons undergoing the experience. Out of liminality arises what Turner calls *communitas*, an occasion of 'full, unmediated communication, even communion' between those in the liminal state. It can also be described as the realisation of a social anti-structure or a state of egalitarianism.[96]

'Sheil's nocturnal vision' provides an obvious illustration of this model. Its narrator, suspended between states of consciousness, is taken to the geographic mid-point of Ireland where a large crowd is gathered on a mountainside. Liminal characters appear who, through ritual, speech, song, and symbolism, impress upon them the central values of the Irish people: namely, the 'rights of man' and the Catholic faith. *Communitas* takes place at their departure when the crowd, now 'animated and elevated', agree 'in exultation' to leave, shaking hands and kissing in brotherhood and friendship as they do so.

Here in verse is an archetypal monster meeting, a gathering that displayed in an imaginative and idealised way qualities that were common to O'Connell's repeal assemblies. Monster meetings were, like all crowd situations, liminal phenomena in which familiar constructs of time, space, work, and social relationships were momentarily set aside.[97] Participants experimented with what Turner calls 'the factors of liminality', symbolic forms that inverted, parodied, or challenged the prevailing order. Like many other types of liminal events, these were subversive, 'representing radical critiques of the central structures and proposing utopian alternative models'.[98] As we have seen, processions themselves could depict the image of an all-inclusive and harmonious community united under O'Connell's leadership. This ideal was underscored through thousands of visual devices that often made sly taunts at British rule as they did so. Above all, the simple word 'repeal', displayed on countless banners, placards, and signs and repeated endlessly in speeches and in print, bore a utopian connotation. Just as the ideals suggested by the ambiguous but emotive phrase 'the rights of man' formed the basis of *communitas* at the imaginary monster meeting of 'Sheil's nocturnal vision', so 'repeal' lay at its heart in the mass gatherings of 1843–5.[99] 'Repeal' was the guiding metaphor among a cluster of symbols and ritual acts through which hundreds of thousands of people communicated among themselves.

The repeal monster meetings were a remarkable achievement in mass mobilisation. Never before had so many people come together for a common political purpose over such a wide area and for such a prolonged period. If the meetings failed in their avowed aim to persuade the members of parliament to restore Irish self-government, they almost certainly created a new perception of national politics in the minds of those who witnessed them first-hand. To take part in a monster meeting was to participate actively or, as contemporaries put it, to 'assist' in a dynamic movement that transcended locality and region. Hundreds of thousands of people who were otherwise isolated from the political process were able to imagine themselves as part of a vast national community in a way they had never been able to do before. This perception was rendered all the more vivid because it derived in large part from a repertoire of ritual behaviour and symbolic forms that was at once dramatic, inspiring, and familiar.

* * *

I wish to thank Jim Donnelly, Jacqueline Hill, Anne Kane, Gerry Moran, Maurice O'Connell, Mary Helen Thuente, Kevin Whelan, and Christopher Woods for reading earlier drafts of this essay. Different versions of it were presented at the inaugural conference of the Society for the Study of Nineteenth-Century Ireland at St Patrick's College, Maynooth, in July 1992; at the Third Annual Daniel O'Connell Workshop in Derrynane, Co. Kerry, in October 1992; and at the 1993 meeting of the American Conference for Irish Studies at Villanova University in April 1993.

NOTES

1 George A. Birmingham, *General John Regan* (London, 1912), p. 92. Similarly, E. Estyn Evans observed that 'the Irish countryman enjoys nothing so much as "a gathering" of people. . . . A crowd goes to his head like poteen.' See his *Irish folk ways* (London, 1957), p. 253.

2 Aspects of the subject are touched upon in Thomas Bartlett, *The fall and rise of the Irish nation: the Catholic question, 1690–1820* (Dublin, 1992), pp. 311–20; James Loughlin, 'Constructing the political spectacle: Parnell, the press, and national leadership, 1879–86' in D. George Boyce

and Alan O'Day (ed.), *Parnell in perspective* (London, 1991), pp. 221–41; Pauric Travers, 'Our fenian dead: Glasnevin cemetery and the genesis of the republican funeral' in James Kelly and U. MacGearailt (ed.), *Dublin and Dubliners* (Dublin, 1990), pp. 52–72; C.J. Woods, 'Tone's grave at Bodenstown: memorials and commemorations, 1798–1913' in Dorothea Siegmund-Schultze (ed.), *Irland: Kultur and Gesellschaft VI* (Halle, 1989); Jacqueline Hill, 'National festivals, the state, and "Protestant ascendancy" in Ireland, 1790–1829' in *I.H.S.*, xxiv, no. 93 (May 1984), pp. 30–51; Peter Alter, 'Symbols of Irish nationalism' in *Studia Hibernica*, no. 14 (1974), 104–23.

3 As Lynn Hunt observes, 'political symbols and rituals were not metaphors of power; they were the means and ends of power itself'. See her *Politics, culture, and class in the French revolution* (Berkeley, 1984), p. 54. On this and related themes, see Mona Ozouf, *Festivals and the French revolution*, trans. by Alan Sheridan (Cambridge, Mass., and London, 1988); Charles Rearick, 'Festivals in modern France: the experience of the Third Republic' in *Journal of Contemporary History*, 12 (1977), pp. 435–60; John Brewer, *Party ideology and popular politics at the accession of George III* (Cambridge, 1976); Frank O'Gorman, 'Campaign rituals and ceremonies: the social meaning of elections in England, 1780–1860' in *Past & Present*, no. 135 (May 1992), pp. 79–115; Paul Pickering, 'Class without words: symbolic communication in the Chartist movement' in *Past & Present*, no. 112 (August 1986), pp. 144–62; G.L. Mosse, *The national-isation of the masses: political symbolism and mass movements in Germany from the Napoleonic wars through the Third Reich* (reprint ed., Ithaca, N.Y., and London, 1991; orig. ed., New York, 1975); Peter Shaw, *American patriots and the rituals of revolution* (Cambridge, 1981); Susan G. Davis, *Parades and power: street theatre in nineteenth-century Philadelphia* (Philadelphia, 1986); Mary Ryan, 'The American parade: representations of the nineteenth-century social order' in Lynn Hunt (ed.), *The new cultural history* (Berkeley, 1989), pp. 131–53; and Kathleen Neils Conzen, 'Ethnicity as festive culture: nineteenth-century German America on parade' in Werner Sollors (ed.), *The invention of ethnicity* (New York, 1989) pp. 44–76.

4 Fergus O'Ferrall, *Catholic emancipation: Daniel O'Connell and the birth of Irish democracy* (Dublin, 1985), pp. 192–7; idem, 'The growth of political consciousness in Ireland, 1823–1847: a study of O'Connellite politics and political education' (Ph.D. thesis, T.C.D., 1978), pp. 305–30; K. Theodore Hoppen, *Elections, politics, and society in Ireland, 1832–1885* (Oxford, 1984), pp. 423–35; James Epstein, *The lion of freedom: Feargus O'Connor and the Chartist movement, 1832–42* (London, 1982), pp. 110–23, 286–7; Pickering, 'Class without words', *passim*; Elizabeth Malcolm, *'Ireland sober, Ireland free': drink and temperance in nineteenth-century Ireland* (Dublin, 1986), chap. 3. See also the tantalising evidence of an enormous and well-organised demonstration that was planned for Shinrone, King's County, in 1828, in *Tipperary Vindicator*, 18 January 1845. Coverage of about a dozen massive repeal meetings in 1840–2 can be found in the nationalist press. On the emergence of mass gatherings as a form of political expression in the British Isles, see Charles Tilly, 'Britain creates the social movement' in James E. Cronin and Jonathan Schneer (ed.), *Social conflict and the political order in modern Britain* (London, 1982), pp. 21–51.

5 Thomas Wyse, *Historical sketch of the late Catholic Association of Ireland* (London, 1829), i, 240–1.

6 The term 'monster meeting' originated with a reporter for the *Times* in 1843. Just under forty meetings took place that year; another dozen or so were held in 1845. These fifty-odd gatherings were built around O'Connell and are the focus of this essay. More than a dozen other mammoth gatherings took place which he did not attend. Taken as a whole, the number and location of the events made it possible for almost everyone in Leinster, most parts of Munster and Connaught, and portions of south Ulster to attend at least one of them. Oliver MacDonagh, who has written the best analysis of the monster meetings, suggests that this was the intention of the organisers. See his map showing the sites of the 1843 meetings in *The emancipist: Daniel O'Connell, 1830–47* (London, 1989), p. 225. Organisers conspicuously avoided holding meetings in Ulster that featured O'Connell, apparently out of concern that they would provoke violence.

7 One reporter noted, for example, that an hour or so before the speeches began at the famous gathering on Tara Hill, the meeting ground was not particularly crowded, though '*it bore the appearance of being so when viewed from the platform* [my emphasis], which was placed not in the centre, but at the lowest point of the area [i.e., probably down the slope to the north-west of the *Rath na Ríogh*].' See *Times*, 17 August 1843. This placement is also suggested in the well-known drawing of the Tara meeting in the *Illustrated London News*, 26 August 1843. O'Connell was particularly concerned that space be provided for journalists on the speakers' platform at Tara. See minutes of Repeal Association meeting, *FJ*, 15 August 1843.

8 Evidence of contemporary concern over crowd sizes can be seen in the way that newspapers struggled without success to arrive at an acceptable formula for calculating attendance. Some reporters reckoned attendance figures on the basis of one man per square foot; others used a formula of six or even seven men per square yard. See *Nation*, 12 August 1843; *Pilot*, 18 August 1843; *Times*, 19 July 1843. See also Mark Harrison, *Crowds and history: mass phenomena in English towns, 1790–1835* (Cambridge, 1988), p. 176, on similar efforts to gauge crowd sizes in England.

9 *FJ*, 2 August 1843; *Times*, 2 August 1843; *Nation*, 5 August 1843; *Mayo Constitution* (Castlebar), 4 August 1843; National Archives (Ireland), Chief Secretary's Office Registered Papers, Outrage Reports (hereafter cited as CSORP.OR), 1843, Mayo, 21/15/603, T. Banon to Edward Lucas, 31 July 1843. Stanley Palmer, *Police and protest in England and Ireland, 1780–1850* (Cambridge, 1988), p. 467, gives an estimate of 400,000 for the Castlebar meeting.

10 Some low and high estimates of 1843 meetings culled at random from newspapers and CSORP.OR are as follows: Cashel (30,000–300,000); Clifden (5,000–100,000); Drogheda (14,000–170,000); Ennis (25,000–500,000); Kilkenny (20,000–300,000); Longford (30,000–280,000); and Roscommon (2,000–200,000).

11 Paul Pickering detects a similar tendency among Chartist historians ('Class without words', pp. 146–7). By adding together all the estimates given in the nationalist press, at least two nineteenth-century writers reached the startling conclusion that a total of 7 to 8.6 million people attended the monster meetings—roughly the total population of Ireland at the time. See, for example, C.M. O'Keefe, *The life and times of Daniel O'Connell* (Dublin, 1864), p. 688; D.B. Sullivan, 'O'Connell: the story of his life from the cradle to the grave' in *The O'Connell illustrated centenary record* (Dublin, 1875), p. 15.

12 It is difficult to understand, for example, why historians apparently consider the reporters of the *Nation* and the *Pilot* (who estimated the crowd at Tara at 750,000 and over one million respectively) to be more accurate witnesses than Capt. George Despard, the stipendiary magistrate for County Meath. Despard, who had lived in the area for two decades and whose job entailed attending all public gatherings in the county, was present at Tara and was clearly impressed by what he saw. The crowd was much larger than he expected, and there was a sense of amazement in his report to Dublin Castle on the following day: 'I do not think I overrate it when I say there were nearly 100,000 persons collected, more than two-thirds of whom were able young men' (CSORP.OR, 1843, Meath, 22/16/583, report of Capt. George Despard, 16 August 1843). See also John E.P. Wallis (ed.), *Reports of state trials*, new ser., vol. v, *1843–4* (London, 1893), pp. 268–70. The reporter for the *Times* (17 August 1843) also believed that there were over 100,000 at Tara, not 'approximately one million', as many writers have insisted.

13 The total population of Leinster, Munster, and Connaught in 1841 was just under 5.8 million. See W.E. Vaughan and A.J. Fitzpatrick (ed.), *Irish historical statistics: population, 1821–1971* (Dublin, 1978), pp. 15–16.

14 Edward Bulwer (Lord Lytton), *The new Timon: St Stephen's and the lost tales of Miletus* (London, 1875), p. 187. It is sometimes suggested that Lytton based these lines on observations of the monster meeting held at Clifden, Co. Galway, in 1843. Apparently, however, the only visit that he ever made to Ireland took place in 1834. During that trip he witnessed an event that apparently influenced his famous poem. One evening in Dublin, he was surprised to find the area beneath his hotel balcony 'black with masses of human beings, *waves upon waves of them silently heaving from end to end of it, a real black sea* [emphasis mine]'. They had gathered

there to catch sight of Lytton himself, who, they were told, was an English aristocrat. Lytton ordered a local piper to play for them, after which, he said, 'they dispersed as noiselessly as they had collected'. Here, it would seem, was the experience that informed his poetic description of O'Connell at a monster meeting. See earl of Lytton, *The life of Edward Bulwer, first lord Lytton* (London, 1913), i, 462–3.

15 W.E.H. Lecky, *The leaders of public opinion in Ireland* (London, 1861), pp. 238–9.

16 Michael MacDonagh, *The life of Daniel O'Connell* (London, 1903), p. 309.

17 Oliver MacDonagh, *Emancipist*, p. 230.

18 D.J. Hickey and J.E. Doherty, *A dictionary of Irish history, 1800–1980* (Dublin, 1987), p. 421.

19 See, for example, Raymond Moley, *Daniel O'Connell: nationalism without violence* (New York, 1974), p. 155.

20 Donal McCartney, *The dawning of democracy: Ireland, 1800–1870* (Dublin, 1987), p. 153.

21 CSORP.OR, 1843, Meath, 22/16/583, 22/16/663, Capt. George Despard to Chief Secretary, 15, 16 August 1843. The *Times* (17 August 1843) reported the same crowd behaviour.

22 *Times*, 24 July 1843.

23 *FJ*, 28 June, 12 September 1843. See also *Galway Vindicator*, 28 June 1843; *Galway Standard*, 30 August 1843; CSORP.OR, 1843, Clare, 5/11/639, George Rutland to Inspector General, 16 June 1843.

24 Canon John O'Rourke, *The centenary life of O'Connell* (9th ed., Dublin, 1905), p. 260.

25 J. Venedey, *Ireland and the Irish during the repeal year, 1843* (Dublin, 1844), p. 30. See also *Times*, 21 June 1843.

26 O'Rourke, *O'Connell*, pp. 260–1. On the other hand, some monster meetings were densely packed. Oral evidence concerning a man who attended the Loughrea meeting as a youth suggests that the six- to ten-acre meeting ground was filled to capacity and that part of the crowd had to stand in the shallows of the adjoining lake to hear the speeches (University College, Dublin, Department of Irish Folklore, Irish Folklore Commission, MS 569, pp. 260–1, hereafter cited as U.C.D., I.F.C.).

27 *Times*, 21 October 1845, reporting on the Sligo monster meeting. For similar accounts of crowd structure and behaviour, see CSORP.OR, 1843, Longford, 19/10/165; *Times*, 24 May 1845, reporting on the 1845 Tara meeting.

28 O'Connell once boasted that he could easily be heard by 50,000 people and that his voice could extend 'to the very extreme of a crowd', but this was characteristic hyperbole (*FJ*, 27 May 1843). At Ennis at least half the crowd were reportedly unable to hear a word of the speeches; the same was true at Tullamore, where a more compact crowd occupied every available space in and around the market square (*Limerick Chronicle*, 17 June 1843; *Times*, 19 July 1843).

29 Samuel Clark, for example, comments upon the 'political limitations' of the meetings: 'they did not entail much active participation for many more than the few people who organized them. . . . Despite the presence of all classes in the audience, the meetings had a tone of social exclusiveness about them.' See his *Social origins of the Irish land war* (Princeton, 1979), p. 99. Similarly, James O'Neill concludes that the participation of the peasantry in the Catholic emancipation and repeal campaigns was 'essentially passive'. See his 'Popular culture and peasant rebellion in pre-famine Ireland' (Ph.D. thesis, University of Minnesota, 1984), pp. 373–4.

30 A term that has been defined as 'a dramatic occasion, a complex type of symbolic behaviour that usually has a statable purpose, but one that invariably alludes to more than it says and has many meanings at once'. See Sally F. Moore and Barbara B. Myerhoff, 'Secular ritual: forms and meanings' in Moore and Myerhoff (ed.), *Secular ritual* (Assen and Amsterdam, 1977), p. 5.

31 'No small portion of those who "assisted", as the French say, at the [Waterford] demonstration resided twenty, thirty . . . miles from the place of meeting' (*FJ*, 11 July 1843). The *Pilot* (6 August 1843) took note of the many people who had travelled from England 'to be present and assist' at the Tara monster meeting.

32 Hoppen, *Elections*, pp. 423–35; O'Gorman, 'Campaign rituals', *passim*.

33 *FJ*, 12 September 1843. Similarly, Maurice Johnson notes how processions were indispensible

features of the amnesty meetings of 1869. See his 'The fenian amnesty movement, 1868–1879' (M.A. thesis, St Patrick's College, Maynooth, 1980), pp. 201–2, 232.

34 *FJ*, 6, 7, 9 September 1844; *Times*, *Saunders' News-Letter*, and *Evening Mail*, 9 September 1844. Three years earlier, Chartists had done exactly the same thing to celebrate the release of Feargus O'Connor from York Castle (Pickering, 'Class without words', pp. 156–7).

35 Elizabeth Malcolm, 'Popular recreation in nineteenth-century Ireland' in Oliver MacDonagh *et. al.* (ed.), *Irish culture and nationalism, 1750–1950* (London and Canberra, 1983), p. 49, draws attention to certain similarities between the O'Connellite meetings and the Irish tradition of attending fairs and pattern festivals. Many of the latter, like monster meetings, took place at historic sites; they drew people from a wide area and were a source of recreation and amusement. Such comparisons should not be drawn too closely, however. There were also significant differences between the two kinds of events, chiefly in their planning, complexity, organisation, sponsorship, ritual composition, and (not least) sobriety and peacefulness.

36 CSORP.OR, 1843, Meath, 22/15/995, placard put up in Trim; see also ibid., Louth, 20/10/497.

37 This was done in Dublin and Skibbereen in 1843 and at Cork in 1845. See *FJ*, 4 July 1843; T.D. Sullivan, *Recollections of troubled times in Irish politics* (Dublin, 1905), p. 2; *Cork Examiner* (hereafter cited as *CE*), 9 June 1845. A reporter who was in the Clifden procession described how, as the parade neared the town, 'hundreds of the horsemen in the rear and many of the footmen, anxious to get a view of the entire procession, dashed up the mountain . . . and formed themselves a most interesting feature in the entire panorama' (*FJ*, 20 September 1843). George Mosse comments on similar behaviour in May Day demonstrations in nineteenth-century Vienna (*Nationalisation*, p. 168). See also David Kertzer, *Ritual, politics, and power* (New Haven and London, 1988), pp. 10–11.

38 Peter Burke, *Popular culture in early modern Europe* (New York, 1978), p. 182.

39 *CE*, 12 June 1843; *Times*, 19 July 1843.

40 Venedey, *Ireland during repeal year*, p. 86.

41 *CE*, 22 May 1843; *FJ*, 28 June 1843; *Galway Vindicator*, 28 June 1843; *Limerick Reporter*, 16 June 1843; Venedey, *Ireland during repeal year*, p. 84.

42 *CE*, 22 May 1843; *Galway Vindicator*, 17, 28 June 1843.

43 *Pilot*, 17 May 1843.

44 Sullivan, *Recollections*, pp. 1–2. The *Cork Examiner* (23 June 1843) also gives a description of the boat. See similar examples in Galway and Castlebar (*FJ*, 28 June, 2 August 1843). There is evidence in the oral tradition of large, ocean-going boats having been used in repeal processions (U.C.D., I.F.C., MS S640, p. 99).

45 *CE*, 9 June 1845. The ancient harper is shown in two drawings from the *Illustrated London News* that are frequently reproduced in secondary works. One is the famous illustration of the Tara meeting; the other is of the procession through Dublin at the time of O'Connell's release from Richmond prison in September 1844.

46 That of Justice read, 'Self-government and nothing else'; Fortitude: 'Eight millions—Love of country will overcome everything'; Prudence: 'Agitation—Formerly we conquered by these arms'; Truth: 'English friendship! Carthaginian faith! It is the nature of man to hate whomever he has injured.'

47 *CE*, 9 June 1845; *FJ*, 11 June 1845. On the use of caps of liberty and other symbolic devices in public demonstrations, see James Epstein, 'Understanding the cap of liberty: symbolic practice and social conflict in early nineteenth-century England' in *Past & Present*, no. 122 (February 1989), pp. 75–118.

48 *Limerick Reporter*, 16 June 1843.

49 *CE*, 9 June 1845.

50 *FJ*, 9 September 1844, 31 May 1845.

51 Even the reporter for the *Times* was moved to call the ritual on the rath an 'extraordinary and extravagant scene' (*Times*, 17 August 1843). See also *FJ*, 16 August 1843; O'Rourke, *O'Connell*,

pp. 259–60. This ceremony had been planned weeks beforehand and was apparently instigated by the relatives of men buried beneath the rath. See CSORP.OR, Meath, 22/15/371, Capt. George Despard to Chief Secretary, 29 July 1843.

52 In fact, some banners were carried from demonstration to demonstration. One journalist commented that 'many I recognised as having done duty on former occasions, some having been despatched by the same conveyance that brought me [to the Loughrea monster meeting] from Dublin' (*Times*, 14 September 1843).

53 *Limerick Reporter*, 16 June 1843; *FJ*, 17 June 1843.

54 *FJ*, 27 July 1841.

55 *Limerick Reporter*, 19 May 1843.

56 See A.T. Lucas, 'The sacred trees of Ireland' in *Journal of the Cork Historical and Archaeological Society*, lxviii (1963), pp. 16–54; W.G. Wood-Martin, *Traces of the elder faiths of Ireland* (London, 1902), ii, 152–60.

57 G.D. Zimmermann, *Irish political street ballads and political songs, 1780–1900* (Geneva, 1966), pp. 41–2.

58 Ibid., p. 43. See also Nancy Curtin, 'Symbols and rituals of United Irish mobilisation' in Hugh Gough and David Dickson (ed.), *Ireland and the French revolution* (Dublin, 1990), pp. 76–8; Nicholas Furlong, *Fr John Murphy of Boolavogue, 1753–1798* (Dublin, 1991), p. 131.

59 2 and 3 William IV, c. 118. Only trade banners were allowed to be carried in processions. In a demonstration at Navan in 1845, O'Connell 'tore away with his own hands' a political banner being carried near his carriage. T.D. Sullivan recalled that when O'Connell spotted the green banners which he and his fellow bandsmen had proudly used to decorate their float in the Skibbereen procession, he rose in his carriage and 'with a wave of his hand' shouted, 'Take down those flags; they are not allowed by law!' See *FJ*, 23 May 1845; Sullivan, *Recollections*, p. 2.

60 French peasants, for example, used animal blood, coloured pins, and red shirt buttons to express their sympathy with radicalism. See Peter McPhee, 'Popular culture, symbolism, and rural radicalism in nineteenth-century France' in *Journal of Peasant Studies*, 5 (1977), pp. 246–7.

61 In the Ennis procession each of the thirteen trade bodies carried loaves of bread on poles (*Limerick Reporter*, 16 June 1843; *Galway Vindicator*, 17 June 1843).

62 Reporters were often impressed by this practice. An account of the procession that brought O'Connell into Rathkeale in 1845 noted: 'one striking peculiarity in this vast assemblage . . . was the extraordinary display of repeal cards which were borne high above the heads of the people, in almost every instance on white wands, and which lent a feature of the utmost interest to the gathering' (*Tipperary Vindicator*, 25 October 1845).

63 A pawnbroker from Galway who appeared in the Clifden procession was so proud of his card that he wore in his hat a green-coloured version of it that was three times larger than normal (*State trials*, v, 272). Repeal wardens frequently wrote to the Repeal Association in Dublin asking for the cards. One writer begged that his be sent as soon as possible, 'for I hear they are beautiful. This way I may frame it along with my [repeal warden's] diploma, that they may live after my death when my children will say that their father helpt to bring back the parliament.' See Henry Smyth to 'Mr Clancy', 1 June 1843, N.L.I., MS 13,625 (54). A bound collection of Repeal Association membership cards compiled by T.M. Ray is in the N.L.I. (IR 94108, R#13).

64 John Fiske, *Reading the popular* (London and New York, 1989), pp. 17, 24, and *passim*. See also his *Understanding popular culture* (Boston, 1989), esp. chaps. 1 and 2; M. de Certeau, *The practice of everyday life* (Berkeley, 1984).

65 *CE*, 9 June 1845; *FJ*, 11 June 1845. The figure of John Bull had been familiar in the popular culture of the British Isles for over a century. For a recent comprehensive treatment of the subject, see Miles Taylor, 'John Bull and the iconography of public opinion in England, c.1712–1929' in *Past & Present*, no. 134 (February 1992), pp. 93–128. See also Jeanine Surel,

'John Bull' in Raphael Samuel (ed.), *Patriotism: the making and unmaking of British national identity* (London, 1989), iii, 3–25.

66 James C. Scott, *Domination and the arts of resistance: hidden transcripts* (New Haven, 1990), p. 158 and *passim*. See also his *Weapons of the weak: everyday forms of peasant resistance* (New Haven, 1985).

67 *CE*, 12 June 1843.

68 Lucas, 'Sacred trees', p. 21; Sir William Wilde, *Irish popular superstitions* (reprint ed., Dublin, 1979; orig. ed., 1852), pp. 47–8; Kevin Danaher, *The year in Ireland* (Cork and Dublin, 1972), pp. 89–95; O'Neill, 'Popular culture and peasant rebellion', pp. 144–5.

69 *FJ*, 10 June 1843; *CE*, 12 June 1843. In parts of the country where faction-fighting remained popular, the presence of sticks, switches, and branches would have been needlessly provocative. Ballad-singers were also banned from some meetings (*Tipperary Vindicator*, 27 September 1845).

70 At a procession in Mountmellick in August, for example, someone threw a green branch they were carrying at a group of women who had heckled O'Connell (*FJ*, 15 August 1843). Pro-repeal newspapers sometimes described how streets and houses were decorated with greenery, but as one of them assured its readers, the plants were 'not the produce of plunder' (*FJ*, 12 September 1843, describing the Loughrea meeting).

71 Robert Darnton, 'A bourgeois puts his world in order: the city as a text' in *The great cat massacre and other episodes in French cultural history* (London, 1984), p. 117. See also Ryan, 'American parade', pp. 137–53.

72 Journalists frequently took pains to describe the arrangement of processions. See especially the reports of those in Drogheda, Ennis, Limerick, and Galway in 1843 and Cork in 1843 and 1845 (*FJ*, 7, 17 June 1843; *Limerick Reporter*, 16 June 1843; *Galway Vindicator*, 28 June 1843; *Nation*, 27 May 1843; *CE*, 9 June 1845).

73 These seem to have been rare occasions, however. It was a cause for special comment when a 2,000-strong delegation from Kinsale was led in the Cork procession by a group of 200 'elegantly dressed' women (*CE*, 9 June 1845).

74 *FJ*, 10 October 1843; 2, 23 May 1845.

75 Fergus O'Ferrall, *Daniel O'Connell* (Dublin, 1981), p. 115. For examples of separate contingents merging for marches back through towns, see *FJ*, 6 May, 17, 28 June, 12 September 1843. At Tuam a third group consisting of the archbishop, Lord ffrench, and a local MP went out separately to meet O'Connell (*FJ*, 26 July 1843).

76 Roberto DaMatta, 'Constraint and license: a preliminary study of two Brazilian national rituals' in Moore and Myerhoff, *Secular ritual*, pp. 252–3. See also his 'Carnival in multiple planes' in John J. MacAloon (ed.), *Rite, drama, festival, spectacle: rehearsals toward a theory of cultural performance* (Philadelphia, 1984), pp. 208–40; Mervyn James, 'Ritual, drama, and social body in the late medieval English town' in *Past & Present*, no. 98 (February 1983), pp. 3–29; Charles Zika, 'Hosts, processions, and pilgrimages: controlling the sacred in fifteenth-century Germany' in *Past & Present*, no. 118 (February 1988), pp. 37–46; Darnton, 'A bourgeois', p. 120.

77 This pattern was apparent in virtually every procession, even those which took place in Dublin and which did not involve a cortège that marched out from a town to meet O'Connell. In May 1845 repeal leaders staged a grand 'levée' in the capital to mark the first anniversary of O'Connell's imprisonment. Three separate groups converged on the Rotunda for the formal ceremonies. Dublin trade bodies, bands, and citizenry marched there from the site of O'Connell's incarceration at Richmond prison. Meanwhile, a smaller contingent consisting of the mayor and corporation rode to the Rotunda in carriages from the Mansion House, preceded by fifty green-uniformed men carrying white wands. Finally, O'Connell and his fellow inmates, also in uniform, departed from the Liberator's house in Merrion Square. After the formal ceremonies everyone formed into a massive procession at the top of Sackville Street to escort O'Connell back to his house. Groups that had marched separately to the Rotunda now marched together. Significantly, O'Connell rode among a contingent of civic officials and Catholic

gentry who comprised the symbolic heart of the procession. Preceding them were local worthies and repeal activists, and behind them came the Dublin trades and thousands of citizens (*FJ*, 31 May 1845). It is significant that on occasions when repeal processions consisted of only one social group, O'Connell marched not at their symbolic centre but at their head. There was, in other words, no unifying gesture to be made. See, for example, the description of a procession at Tullamore when O'Connell led a few hundred gentry, clergy, businessmen, and professionals to the banquet that followed the monster meeting there (*FJ*, 18 May 1843).

78 Anthony Smith, *The ethnic origins of nations* (Oxford and New York, 1987), pp. 183–91, discusses the importance of landscape and sacred historic sites in modern nationalist movements.

79 Elias Canetti, *Crowds and power* (London, 1973), pp. 21–4, 32. See also Ozouf, *Festivals*, chap. 6; Harrison, *Crowds and history*, chap. 6; Brewer, *Party ideology*, pp. 188–9.

80 John Berger, 'The nature of mass demonstrations' in *New Society*, no. 295 (23 May 1968), p. 755.

81 *Dublin Evening Mail*, 31 May 1845.

82 Parades through this, the oldest, poorest, and most nationalist part of the capital, were a feature of separatist politics from the late eighteenth century onward. By the mid-nineteenth century it was *de rigueur* for almost every kind of nationalist procession to include the working-class area of south-west Dublin in its itinerary, especially a march past the site of Robert Emmet's execution on Thomas Street.

83 *Dublin Evening Mail*, 3 July 1843; *FJ*, 4 July 1843; *Times*, 5 July 1843.

84 It went from Richmond prison to Kilmainham jail to the Four Courts, the site of his trial, where his supporters held a mock burial of his original indictment. Organisers had hoped to take the parade past Dublin Castle, but 'influential gentlemen' persuaded them to change the route (*FJ*, 6–9 September 1844).

85 See the report of the Kells monster meeting, *FJ*, 25 April 1843. The five-mile procession that marched out from Tuam to meet O'Connell returned with him to the town square, where the magistrates and clergy delivered their formal greetings to him. The procession then made a circuit of the town before marching to the mass meeting at a nearby race-track (*FJ*, 26 July 1843).

86 Venedey, *Ireland during repeal year*, p. 27.

87 G.L. Mosse, 'Mass politics and the political liturgy of nationalism' in Eugene Kamenka (ed.), *Nationalism: the nature and evolution of an idea* (London, 1976), pp. 49–50; Pickering, 'Class without words', pp. 152–62, on the 'presentation' of Feargus O'Connor at Chartist demonstrations.

88 See *Limerick Reporter*, 18 April 1843; *CE*, 22 May 1843; *FJ*, 28 June, 26 July 1843.

89 *CE*, 22 May 1845.

90 To borrow a device from structural anthropology, a monster meeting might be depicted as follows:

	Procession	Meeting	Banquet
Structure	open/linear	restricted	closed
Class/Gender	inclusive	inclusive/segmented	exclusive/segmented
Space	public	semi-public	private
Movement	mobile	semi-stationary	stationary
Time	morning/mid-day	afternoon	night
Predominant Language	visual	verbal/visual	verbal

In this diagram processions and banquets represent what Claude Lévi-Strauss termed binary opposites. Whereas processions, for example, moved through public spaces and included members of almost every social stratum, banquets were stationary ceremonies that took place in private buildings and restricted participation to wealthier members of a community. In every category shown on the left, the open-air meetings represented a transitional phase between the two events.

91 Jacob Venedey spent the night at the home of a local shopkeeper and physician following the monster meeting in Athlone. His host's daughter attended the banquet, and the next morning, said Venedey, she seemed to recall every word of O'Connell's speech (*Ireland during repeal year*, p. 40).

92 *Times*, 19 July 1843; *FJ*, 12 September, 2 October 1843, 23 May 1845. At Mullaghmast, Co. Kildare—where scores of Irish had been lured to their deaths in Elizabeth's reign, and where a number of insurgents had been killed in 1798—a vivid painting hung over the speaker's chair during the banquet. It showed a group of Irish wolfhounds baying over the graves of those who had been killed, and beneath it the motto: 'No more shall Saxon butchery give blood-gouts for repast/ The dog is roused and treachery expels from Mullaghmast' (*FJ*, 2 October 1843).

93 CSORP.OR, 1843, Louth, 20/25/001. Sheil (*ca.*1800–60) was a printer or weaver from Drogheda. His verses, crudely printed in many volumes during the 1830s and 1840s, included *Sheil's shamrock, being a collection of patriotic and national songs on various subjects* (Dublin, 1840). Zimmermann analyses the assonantal rhyming structure of 'Sheil's nocturnal vision' (or 'The rights of man') in *Irish political street ballads*, pp. 106–7. Sheil apparently drew inspiration for his aisling poem from a section of the Rev. James Porter's *Billy Bluff and Squire Firebrand, or a sample of the times as it appeared periodically in five letters* (Belfast, 1840), pp. 16–18 (I owe this reference to Mary Helen Thuente).

94 See, for example, 'A new song on the repeal of the union' and 'A new song on the glorious repeal meeting at Cashel' (CSORP.OR, 1843, Tipperary, S.R., 27/12/117; 27/13/445; 27/15/205). This ballad was adapted and reprinted as 'Glorious repeal meeting held at Tara Hill' (Zimmermann, *Irish political street ballads*, pp. 224–5). See also a different song on the Tara meeting, U.C.D., I.F.C., MS S960, pp. 132–3, another version of which is printed in Robert Kee, *The green flag: a history of Irish nationalism* (London, 1972), p. 208. On the nature of political ballads and their use as instruments of communication, see Maura Murphy, 'The ballad-singer and the role of the seditious ballad in nineteenth-century Ireland: Dublin Castle's view' in *Ulster Folklife*, xxv (1979), pp. 79–102.

95 Victor Turner, *The ritual process: structure and anti-structure* (Chicago, 1969), p. 94.

96 Turner, 'Variations on a theme of liminality' in Moore and Myerhoff, *Secular ritual*, pp. 46–7; see also Turner's *Ritual process*, pp. 96–7; *Dramas, fields, and metaphors: symbolic action in human society* (Ithaca, 1975), *passim*; and *Celebration: studies in festival and ritual* (Washington, D.C., 1982). See also Brewer, *Party ideology*, pp. 310–11, n. 116.

97 In his later work Turner used the term 'liminoid' to describe such events in non-tribal societies. It is a term that best applies to nineteenth-century Ireland, but 'liminal' is used here for the sake of simplicity. See Turner, 'Variations on a theme of liminality' in Moore and Myerhoff, *Secular ritual*, pp. 36–52.

98 Ibid., p. 45. See also Brewer, *Party ideology*, p. 311, n. 116; Berger, 'Mass demonstrations', p. 755.

99 Because the term offered many things to many people, like other ambiguous catchwords and slogans, it was ideally suited to mass agitation. Similarly, John Brewer suggests that the Wilkite notion of 'liberty' and the concept of 'moral economy' formed the basis of *communitas* among crowds in eighteenth-century Britain (*Party ideology*, p. 311, n. 116). See also Oliver Mac-Donagh, 'Ambiguity in nationalism—the case of Ireland' in *Historical Studies* (Australia), xix, no. 76 (April 1981), pp. 337–52; D. George Boyce, *Nationalism in Ireland* (2nd ed., London and New York, 1991), p. 149; and Kertzer, *Ritual, politics, and power*, chap. 4, 'The virtues of ambiguity'. On the role of 'guiding metaphors' in ritual events, see Barbara G. Myerhoff, 'We don't wrap herring in a printed page: fusion, fictions, and continuity in secular rituals' in Moore and Myerhoff, *Secular ritual*, pp. 199–224.

Index